Military
Readiness

RICHARD K. BETTS

Military Readiness

Concepts, Choices, Consequences

The Brookings Institution
Washington, D.C.

Copyright © 1995
THE BROOKINGS INSTITUTION
1775 Massachusetts Avenue, N.W., Washington, D.C. 20036

Library of Congress Cataloging-in-Publication Data

Betts, Richard K., 1947-
    Military readiness : concepts, choices, consequences /
Richard K. Betts.
      p. cm.
    Includes bibliographical references and index.
    ISBN 0-8157-0906-4. — ISBN 0-8157-0905-6 (pbk.)
    1. Military readiness. I. Title.
UA10.B48 1995
355'.0332—dc20   94-44266
                                        CIP

9 8 7 6 5 4 3 2 1

The paper used in this publication meets the minimum requirements of the American National Standard for Information Sciences—Permanence of paper for Printed Library Materials, ANSI Z39.48-1984

Typeset in Palatino

Composition by Harlowe Typography, Inc.
Cottage City, Maryland

Printed by R.R. Donnelley and Sons Co.
Harrisonburg, Virginia

ⒷTHE BROOKINGS INSTITUTION

The Brookings Institution is an independent organization devoted to nonpartisan research, education, and publication in economics, government, foreign policy, and the social sciences generally. Its principal purposes are to aid in the development of sound public policies and to promote public understanding of issues of national importance.

The Institution was founded on December 8, 1927, to merge the activities of the Institute for Government Research, founded in 1916, the Institute of Economics, founded in 1922, and the Robert Brookings Graduate School of Economics and Government, founded in 1924.

The Board of Trustees is responsible for the general administration of the Institution, while the immediate direction of the policies, program, and staff is vested in the President, assisted by an advisory committee of the officers and staff. The by-laws of the Institution state: "It is the function of the Trustees to make possible the conduct of scientific research, and publication, under the most favorable conditions, and to safeguard the independence of the research staff in the pursuit of their studies and in the publication of the results of such studies. It is not a part of their function to determine, control, or influence the conduct of particular investigations or the conclusions reached."

The President bears final responsibility for the decision to publish a manuscript as a Brookings book. In reaching his judgment on the competence, accuracy, and objectivity of each study, the President is advised by the director of the appropriate research program and weighs the views of a panel of expert outside readers who report to him in confidence on the quality of the work. Publication of a work signifies that it is deemed a competent treatment worthy of public consideration but does not imply endorsement of conclusions or recommendations.

The Institution maintains its position of neutrality on issues of public policy in order to safeguard the intellectual freedom of the staff. Hence interpretations or conclusions in Brookings publications should be understood to be solely those of the authors and should not be attributed to the Institution, to its trustees, officers, or other staff members, or to the organizations that support its research.

For Elena Christine,
Michael Francis,
and Diego Fitzpatrick Betts

Foreword

MILITARY readiness is something that most Americans have valued in principle but misunderstood in practice. U.S. forces, throughout most of their history, have been woefully unready for the wars that were thrust upon them. During four decades of cold war this pattern changed. For the first time the United States maintained large standing forces in peacetime and attempted to keep them prepared for war on short notice. Since the end of the cold war, American strategy has been groping for a new equilibrium between the two historic norms of unpreparedness and high mobilization.

Clearly, America's post–cold war armed forces will be much smaller. But questions abound. Should readiness to fight tomorrow take precedence over readiness to fight next month or next year? Should the personnel strength, equipment, training, and provisioning of these forces remain at maximum levels so that our troops will be ready to fight at a moment's notice? Should we instead maintain a larger force in skeletal form that could provide a bigger capability but would need more time in a crisis to mobilize and get in shape? Should first priority go to maximizing military capability in the much longer term, when a major new adversary might emerge abroad, if doing so requires reducing current capability?

The answers to such questions—indeed, the very meanings of readiness—are surprisingly hard to pin down. In this book Richard K. Betts identifies and analyzes the complex factors, relationships, and trade-offs involved in the concept of military readiness and presents new ideas for understanding the policy choices that are posed by attempts to achieve or to maintain readiness. Betts began this project as a senior fellow in the Brookings Foreign Policy Studies program. He is now a professor of political science and a member of the Institute of

War and Peace Studies at Columbia University and director of the International Security Policy program in its School of International and Public Affairs.

For comments and criticism on earlier drafts or other helpful suggestions, the author thanks Asa Clark, Eliot Cohen, Joseph Collins, Joshua Epstein, Peter Feaver, Raymond Garthoff, Charles Groover, Michael Handel, Robert Jervis, Ethan Kapstein, Lawrence Korb, Jeffrey McKitrick, Thomas McNaugher, John Oseth, Barry Posen, Scott Sagan, Kevin Sheehan, and Jack Snyder. He attributes the completion of the book most of all to the support of his wife, Adela Maria Bolet. The project was developed under John D. Steinbruner, director of Foreign Policy Studies at Brookings. The manuscript was edited by Venka McIntyre, factual sources were verified by Michael Levin, the pages were proofread by Carlotta Ribar, and the index was prepared by Max Franke. Louise Skillings provided essential services at many stages in the production of the manuscript.

Brookings is grateful to the Ford Foundation and the John D. and Catherine T. MacArthur Foundation for financial suport that made the study possible.

An early version of chapter 4 appeared as "Measuring Military Readiness: Analytical Complexity and Policy Confusion," in the Spring 1992 issue of *Security Studies*. A few of the ideas behind the book germinated in "Conventional Forces: What Price Readiness?" in the January/February 1983 issue of *Survival*.

The views in this book are those of the author and should not be ascribed to the persons or foundations acknowledged above or to the trustees, officers, or other staff members of the Brookings Institution.

Bruce K. MacLaury
President

January 1995
Washington, D.C.

Contents

There is one controlling truth from all past wars which applies with equal weight to any war of tomorrow. No nation on earth possesses such limitless resources that it can maintain itself in a state of perfect readiness to engage in war immediately and decisively win a total victory soon after the outbreak without destroying its own economy, pauperizing its own people, and promoting interior disorder.

—S. L. A. Marshall, *Men Against Fire*

Amongst other objects of interest which Croesus, king of Lydia, showed to Solon of Athens, was his countless treasure; and to the question as to what he thought of his power, Solon replied, "that he did not consider him powerful on that account, because war was made with iron, and not with gold, and that some one might come who had more iron than he, and would take his gold from him." . . . I maintain, then, contrary to the general opinion, that the sinews of war are not gold, but good soldiers; for gold alone will not procure good soldiers, but good soldiers will always procure gold.

—Niccolò Machiavelli, *The Discourses*

The primary purpose of any theory is to clarify concepts and ideas that have become, as it were, confused and entangled. Not until terms and concepts have been defined can one hope to make any progress. . . . Anyone for whom all this is meaningless either will admit no theoretical analysis at all, or his intelligence has never been insulted by the confused welter of ideas that one so often hears and reads on the subject of the conduct of war. . . .

Theory will have fulfilled its main task when it is used to analyze the constituent elements of war, to distinguish precisely what at first seems fused. . . . Theory then becomes a guide to anyone who wants to learn about war from books. . . .

Theory cannot equip the mind with formulas for solving problems, nor can it mark the narrow path on which the sole solution is supposed to lie by planting a hedge of principles on either side. But it can give the mind insight into the great mass of phenomena and of their relationships, then leave it free to rise into the higher realms of action.

—Carl von Clausewitz, *On War*

Part I
Understanding Readiness

1

The Warrant for Readiness: Blood, Treasure, and Time

*D*URING the cold war, military readiness was a sacred cow. Thousands of Soviet tanks and nuclear warheads stood poised against the West, and the lesson of Pearl Harbor was branded on the brains of American strategists. In an atmosphere of titanic struggle, none but pacifists or radicals challenged the value of readiness, at least until they tried to figure out what it meant and how much of it was enough.

When the cold war ended, high readiness struck many citizens as unnecessary and wasteful. With Russia reduced from superpower to supplicant, how much was there to be ready for anymore? Countries threatening the United States by the mid-1990s were militarily weaker than any since the 1930s. Yet American leaders remained fixated on keeping readiness high, even as defense budgets plunged. They shuddered at the specter of "hollow" armed forces, the image first invoked with devastating political effect by General Edward Meyer in 1980 to describe the threadbare state of the army after post-Vietnam budget cuts. The Clinton administration even raised the priority of the issue by creating an unprecedented high-level overseer, a new under secretary of defense for personnel and readiness.[1] In early 1994, years after the crumbling of the Berlin Wall, the war against Iraq, and the crackup of the Soviet Union, U.S. military readiness was in some respects at a historic high. Yet many experts feared that readiness would soon plummet, while legislators confronted attempts by colleagues to fund other measures by diverting money from readiness accounts. By the end of 1994 the administration was scrambling to shore up falling readiness by allocating an extra $25 billion.[2]

What is going on here? If the end of the cold war did not justify cutting readiness, what would? If the government did not want to cut readiness, why did it reduce the defense budget so drastically? When the rhetoric of readiness persists through strategic circumstances as different as the cold war and the afterglow of victory, what does it really mean?

The simplest reason that the concern with readiness did not evaporate was that the highest hopes at the end of the cold war were dashed. The collapse of communism did not complete the end of history or make war obsolete.[3] Combat against Iraq, the return of prolonged war to the European continent for the first time since 1945, and the fragmentation and chaos in the arc from Dubrovnik to Dushanbe reminded Americans that in international relations bad things can come out of good, and stability can slip away with surprising speed.[4] Yet the fact remains that these problems are not in the same league with the old Soviet threat. Two other points justify a closer look at the issue of military readiness.

One is that readiness is vital, yet hardly anyone really knows what it is. As with general values like prosperity or justice, the consensus in favor of readiness in principle breaks down when policymakers try to put principle into practice. More than in controversies over how to achieve prosperity or justice, however, many of those engaged in disputes about readiness do not just disagree with each other about how to get it, but often are not sure themselves about what they are after. When the idea is conceived broadly, it includes technical and strategic objectives that conflict with each other. When the term is used narrowly, the technical issues become clearer, but the concept then provides no strategic guidance or criteria for resource allocation. Since this book is concerned with the strategic rather than the tactical significance of readiness, its purpose is to develop a definition that is both comprehensive and consistent. The second half of this chapter offers a definition that subsumes the interactions among technical concepts, political choices, and strategic consequences elaborated in the rest of the book.

First, however, it is useful to see why readiness became such a high priority in principle, and why the record of American military history justifies worrying about readiness even after the cold war. The United States has had two peacetime military traditions. The longest one was a tradition of rapid demobilization after each war and tardy remobilization for each new war. The second, dating from 1950, was the cold war tradition of peacetime mobilization: large forces in being, capable of immediate action. Both traditions have bearing on the future, but the lower level of threat that distinguishes today's situation from the cold war resembles the security situation that faced the United States for most of its history since the War of 1812. A glance at the rocky military record of earlier times shows that although we may not know what readiness is, we know it when we see it, or, more often, when we do not see it. In particular, the two hot wars that bracketed the cold war, those over Korea and Kuwait, are models of the opposite historic extremes of readiness.

Unreadiness: The First American Tradition

Throughout most of its history the United States proved unready for the wars that it wound up fighting. Until after 1950, American mistakes in preparation for war exhibited a typical pattern: a peacetime military establishment too small and understaffed to serve effectively as a base for rapid expansion, a late start in mobilization, deficient peacetime plans for economic conversion resulting in prolonged delays and bottlenecks in war production, and poor coordination of manpower recruitment and equipment manufacturing. The net result was an inadequate armed force—in terms of both quantity and quality—at the outbreak of war, which led either to initial failures in battle or lengthy delays between the declaration of war and engagement of the enemy.

In the glow of victory following those past wars, the consequences of unreadiness could be forgotten, but those consequences were often tragic. Of the engagements fought by the U.S. Army at the beginning of ten of its wars, by one accounting, half were defeats, and four were little more than pyrrhic victories. Only one, "the two-day battle of the Rio Grande in 1846 was relatively cheap, although even there losses approached 10 percent of the force engaged."[5] For a country as large and as rich as the United States, with resources and war potential far outclassing those of all its enemies since the War of 1812, this is a sorry record.

The First 150 Years

Two years before America's entry into the First World War, one observer's lengthy survey of the lessons of past conflicts led him to conclude that the country's regular army was never large enough to cope with war, and, more significantly, was never adequately organized for expansion upon recognition of the imminence of war. "No proper reserves have ever existed from which could be drawn the trained men necessary to raise the Regular Army to war strength," Frederic Huidekoper complained, and the nation invariably failed "to increase the Regular Army until the eve, and frequently after the beginning, of hostilities, with the result that it has rarely attained its full authorized strength during the war." Moreover, the nation suffered "the needless protraction of all our great wars . . . owing to the inefficiency of the troops employed."[6]

The most consistent inefficiency in American preparations for war was in the sequence of mobilizing military manpower and industrial production; the former always outstripped the latter. More men were mobilized than could be equipped in the War of 1812, the Mexican War, the beginning of the Civil War, the Spanish-American War, and both world wars. In 1898 *less than one-fifth* of the nearly 275,000 men mobilized by August "saw any kind of campaign service," and of those who did, many had to use obsolete rifles and wear winter uniforms to the tropics.[7]

Even if equipment and basic training could have caught up with mobilized manpower, the organizational strain of rapid expansion retarded advanced unit training or preparation for joint operations, or created other bottlenecks. When the Spanish-American War broke out, the army's ability to expand and coordinate was handicapped by its prewar size and structure. In the preceding quarter century, the entire army had averaged only 26,000 officers and enlisted men, and because these had been "scattered widely across the country in company- and battalion-size organizations, the Army never had an opportunity for training and experience in the operation of units larger than a regiment." The service had no mobilization plan or well-developed high-level staff, nor "experience in carrying on joint operations with the Navy."[8]

Similar coordination problems compounded delays in 1917. It took substantial time to induct manpower into the armed forces because the organizational apparatus for the draft had to be created. In just a few months the army expanded more than tenfold, to more than 2 million men, but there was no extensive training until five months after war was declared because of shortages of equipment and supplies. (There was one bright spot: barracks were constructed promptly. Recruits were well housed while they twiddled their thumbs.)[9]

World War I produced the most complete, integrated, and rapid mobilization of industry in American history, but logistical chaos from uncoordinated transportation plans thwarted the deployment of resources. War traffic overloaded the railroad system, and the shortage of shipping due to losses caused by submarines compounded the problem. Coastal ships were rerouted across the Atlantic, and their cargoes transferred to the railroads. Without enough ships to load supplies as they were delivered, shipments piled up, first in warehouses and sidings at East Coast ports, then in fields ten miles inland. At the same time, trains kept coming with supplies from the West. "Eventually congestion became so bad that traffic intended for eastern ports was blocked all the way to the west of Chicago," and then no railroad cars were left to load new cargoes.[10]

Despite this overload, war production was not developing quickly. Industries were not prepared to shift to munitions manufacturing. New tooling had to be done, new techniques and operations learned, and production lines organized from scratch. Production in the quantities estimated to match requirements did not begin until the year following the declaration of war. Maximum production of many items did not begin until the war ended. As a result, *only a fraction of U.S. potential power was made actual in time to weigh in combat.* Scarcely more than a tenth of the artillery pieces and tanks used by the American Expeditionary Force, and about a fifth of the planes, were produced in the United States. Fewer U.S. troops went into combat than did those on just the Union side of the Civil War, and the army's capacity would have been even less had the expedition into Mexico before entry to the European war not increased the readiness of the logistics system for deployments to Europe the following year.[11]

The base for the expansion of military personnel was also in poor shape. Upon entry to the war in 1917 the U.S. Regular Army had fewer than 122,000 enlisted men. It also had fewer than 6,000 officers, only two-thirds of whom had more than a year of service "and were available for general assignments." The National Guard stood at almost 175,000 officers and men, but that number was less than 40 percent of its authorized strength. The organization of the combat arms was unbalanced: there were almost four times as many men in the Coast Artillery Corps (available to repel improbable assaults on the American homeland) as in the field artillery (needed to fight the war in Europe). The army had only fifty-five airplanes, fifty-one of which were obsolete. The first squadron of American-produced planes did not appear over the front in France until August 1918, just three months before the war ended.[12]

In order to dispatch a single token division to France within a few months of the declaration of war in April 1917, the army had to take four infantry regiments from the Mexican border and fill them out with men from other units, new recruits, and reserve officers. Even then, only one American division entered the front line in France before 1918. No U.S. troops entered significant combat against the Germans until *a year after the declaration of war*, and there was no commitment of appreciable numbers until the last few months of the war.[13]

World War II

The situation was not quite so bad a generation later, but not all that better. The United States began preparing seriously for the Second World War more than a year before entry, though not soon enough to worry Hitler. When war broke out, he was unconcerned because the United States lacked a meaningful force in being that could intervene, and it would take two to three years beyond 1939 to develop one, by which time it would be too late.[14] Actually, Hitler was right about the time the United States would need; it was only his grand mistake—the invasion of the Soviet Union—that kept him from making the continent impregnable before the arrival of U.S. forces.

Between the German attack on Poland and the fall of France, American active-duty manpower increased by a third and thereafter grew rapidly, almost fivefold again by the time of Pearl Harbor.[15] As usual, the provision of military equipment lagged behind. The shock of the fall of France catalyzed serious mobilization, but little had come out of the pipeline by the end of 1940. Time was needed for the process of appropriations, awarding of contracts, construction of factories, and other prerequisites for large-scale production.[16] Men brought on active duty just before the United States entered into World War II "trained with sticks for guns when they might better have remained in shops and factories for another year or two to help produce the weapons and equipment they would need."[17] When France fell, the U.S. Army Air Corps had barely more than a tenth of the planes the German Luftwaffe was then estimated to have. The United States also had *no* heavy tanks at all to match the German Mark IV, and only 144 medium and 648 light tanks "on hand or on order."[18]

In mid-1940 the general staff planned to build an army of 4 million men by April 1942 but then had to cut that goal in half because a survey of industries showed that production could not be expanded fast enough to equip them. Even with that slash in the objective, *none* of the draftees and members of the National Guard who entered service in 1940 got into combat for two years, and "the bulk of the men brought into the Army in 1940, 1941, 1942, and 1943 did not see action before 1944." This was not because of the time needed for training but primarily because of the lack of equipment.[19] By mid-1941, after "a year of effort to create mobile striking forces for emergency action," only one division was close to being ready for deployment in combat.[20] Thirty-six divisions were in the process of formation. Even by December 7, 1941, "only a *single* division and one antiaircraft artillery regiment were on a full war footing. By February 1942, eight divisions were expected to be trained and equipped with essentials, but adequate ammunition for combat would be available for only two of them."[21] And in the navy, by the time of the attack on Pearl Harbor American carrier pilots had less than half the flight training time of their Japanese counterparts.[22]

Although recruitment was no problem, the lack of experienced cadres and developed command organization was. The shortage of officers diluted new units and delayed the growth of the force. The army planned a ninety-day training cycle to expand the structure rapidly, but this proved infeasible because the best-qualified regular officers and noncommissioned officers (NCOs) could not be concentrated in a few locations for a "methodically paced expansion of the existing units." Instead, the service was compelled "to scatter its invaluable trained personnel widely and rapidly through a too swiftly increasing flood of recruits." The problem was not brought under control until almost a year after Pearl Harbor.[23]

The lack of peacetime experience in fielding and sustaining large forces led to other imbalances that delayed commitment to combat. At the beginning of the war, divisional organization placed too much stress on combat elements and wound up with inadequate service and support elements. Trying too hard to field combat power, therefore, was counterproductive: "some combat units were idle for months after they were ready for combat."[24] Even apart from such problems, the "capacity to deploy and support forces overseas during the first half of 1942 lagged far behind the production of munitions and of trained and equipped forces ready for deployment."[25] When more ships were available and loaded efficiently at home, they nevertheless became idle when they arrived at congested ports where the construction of unloading facilities had not kept pace, because base development was not synchronized with transportation schedules.[26]

Synchronizing training schedules with equipment availability remained the problem affecting combat readiness most directly and for the longest time. As late as the spring of 1943, a year and a half after Pearl Harbor, troops in training had *half or less* of their tables of organization and equipment (TOE, the official measure of a unit's required equipment). Supplies were drained away from training to forces that were closer to combat in the theater of operations and that naturally had first call. This priority was sensible, of course, but it remained inefficient to mobilize personnel at faster rates than equipment.[27] The faulty phasing of recruitment, production, and training also caused some to be deployed with obsolescent equipment. In some cases when they did deploy with up-to-date weaponry, they got it only as they were loading for movement to the theater:

In November 1942 units of the 3d Infantry Division, en route to Africa as part of General Patton's Western Task Force found in the holds of their ships crates with instructions lettered on them forbidding their opening until the force was at sea. When opened, the crates were found to contain a kind of stovepipe device with ammunition apparently designed to fit it. No one aboard the transport had ever seen this equipment, which much later was identified as the 2.36 Rocket Launcher (subsequently commonly known as the "Bazooka"). Since it obviously was an ordnance weapon, one deck on the starboard side of the transport was cleared of personnel while two officer volunteers experimented with the new device. After some deductive study, one of the pipes was loaded, aimed at the Atlantic Ocean, and fired. The roar and backblast of the device was entirely unexpected and was followed by prolonged, enthusiastic cheers.[28]

This sort of bad timing in training might have been humorous if it did not imply lower effectiveness and higher casualties in combat. Indeed, the inadequate training of U.S. forces became all too clear when they were routed in their first encounter with German forces at Kasserine

Pass in Tunisia. The most tragic consequences of unreadiness in all its forms, however, were experienced in the first desperate battles against the Japanese. Washington did not have the option of postponing those battles, as it did in Europe.

Unreadiness and Defeat

Despite the time before the war in which defenses might have been prepared, the U.S. Army and Navy were unable to hold the Philippines in the spring of 1942. Serious efforts to improve military capacity in the area had not begun soon enough.[29] Nothing was done before the Commonwealth Government was established in 1935, and in the next six years the development of the Philippine Army and U.S. forces in the country proceeded at a slow pace because the highest priority was given to the buildup for the immediate defense of the Western Hemisphere. General George Marshall told President Franklin Roosevelt in 1939 that the Philippines could be reinforced only by sending the army's "few grains of seed corn." By the beginning of 1941 there was still tremendous tension between the objectives of expanding the armed forces and hedging against an emergency. The latter required keeping "the best-trained units in reserve as an expeditionary force rather than using them as an ideal training establishment."[30]

A major buildup in the Philippines did not begin until the end of July 1941, scarcely more than four months before the Japanese attack. Thus by the time war broke out American forces had fewer than 100 modern combat planes in commission in the islands. Shortly before Pearl Harbor, Secretary of War Henry Stimson asked Secretary of State Cordell Hull to prolong negotiations with Japan for several months, since the full U.S. bomber force planned for the Philippines would not be ready until February or March 1942. The buildup was rushed, poorly coordinated, and unbalanced. Personnel were sent without adequate preparation, and weapons were sent without supporting resources for their maintenance. As a result, the forces available were only partly serviceable. The story of fighter aircraft squadrons was particularly shocking. There were severe shortages of ammunition and oxygen, and without the latter, fighters had a limited ceiling. P-40 fighters had defective armament: gun mountings had to be adjusted, guns failed to fire even after adjustment, and guns rusted owing to the lack of proper maintenance after high-altitude flights. Trying to bolster capabilities in a hurry, Washington dispatched B-17 bombers to the islands before establishing adequate local defenses and warning systems. Only one airfield had a real antiaircraft defense, but even that was hobbled by obsolete ammunition. Some fighter pilots had no more than *fifteen hours* of flight training before they were thrown into combat.[31]

Despite the heroic mythology that grew out of the doomed defense of the Philippines, the U.S. 5th Interceptor Command performed poorly. It did not succeed in intercepting Japanese bombers during the five months before Corregidor fell. Its failure could hardly be attributed to being outnumbered, because Japan's two-to-one advantage was mainly in bombers, not fighters. The problem was simply that the U.S. pursuit force was untrained and ill equipped. Many of the pilots—and even their instructors—had just graduated from flight school and spent most of what little time they had in the islands before the war broke out flying obsolete and worn-out P-35s, since newer P-40s were just arriving (many were still in crates on the high seas when the Japanese struck). Some never even test-fired the guns of their P-40s before the first day of war.[32]

Half of the U.S. fighters dispatched to cover Clark Field on the day of the Japanese attack had to abort their missions because their inadequately prepared engines shot oil all over the windscreens, blinding the pilots. As for the bomber force on the scene, many of the B-17s lacked tail guns and armor; their crews had next to no gunnery training and had to learn on the job in combat. Of the planes that escaped destruction on December 8, many were soon taken out of service by mechanical problems. By Christmas, *barely more than two weeks into the war, there were only a half-dozen American heavy bombers in commission in the entire Southwest Pacific.*[33]

On the ground, raw manpower was not the immediate problem. Combined Filipino and American forces available within a week of Pearl Harbor numbered more than 130,000 men. The troops available to General Douglas MacArthur on Luzon *outnumbered the Japanese* force in the main landings in Lingayen Gulf by at least three to two. (Japan's General Masaharu Homma had only two divisions, two tank regiments, and another brigade to take the islands.) But the quality of U.S. and Filipino troops did not match their quantity. They lacked the training or discipline to contain the beachhead and prevent the Japanese advance. Of the infantry in General Jonathan Wainwright's North

Luzon Force, nine-tenths were untrained. Not one of the divisions under Wainwright had all of its authorized artillery, and what guns they did have were old. Bataan and Corregidor did hold out for several months, and U.S. war planners had anticipated that the Philippines would be lost, but this was in large part because of the failure to undertake preparations before the war. The official "orange" war plan (WPO-3) had estimated that the concentration of supplies on the U.S. west coast might make it possible to relieve the defenders within six months.[34] U.S. forces in the islands had "little time to build fortifications; communications were inadequate. . . . Food was scarce and there was a shortage of supplies of all types."[35]

U.S. military capability in the Philippines was obviously too low to prevent the Japanese conquest, but in another sense it was too high. If there had been *no* U.S. air or naval forces in the islands, Japanese war planners would not have had to decide to attack them as part of the move against British and Dutch possessions. As long as any American forces lay athwart the lines of communication between Southeast Asia and Japan, Tokyo could not take the chance of ignoring them. In undertaking the belated buildup of Philippine defenses, the United States confirmed this to the Japanese navy.[36]

As a result of these miscalculations and the ensuing military disasters, the Philippines were lost and nearly 10,000 U.S. troops were captured, of whom more than 6,000 died in captivity.[37] The attempt to defend the islands slowed the Japanese advance, but it also slowed American mobilization for war. The troops expended in the Philippines would otherwise have contributed to the "seed corn" for expanding the army and thus could have sped the ultimate day of reckoning against the Axis. As it was, counteroffensives did not get under way in the Pacific or North Africa until well into the year after Pearl Harbor.

Costs and Benefits: A Cold Calculation

Wait a minute. If things were so bad, how did they end up so good? The American military did *win* all these wars for which they were so unready. Why not just say that the United States was as ready as it needed to be? If coming out on top is all that matters, inefficiency in making war may be unimportant. That, however, would be like saying efficiency in economic performance is unimportant as long as the

United States has the world's largest GNP. It would also be no consolation to the troops who served as a finger in the dike, going into combat without the preparation or support that they could have had.

Nevertheless, the positive results of wars for which the United States was not ready suggests that readiness cannot be all-important. The military's depressing record in initial combat had two edges: a high price in war and a low price in peace. Throughout American history the lack of readiness for combat on preferred terms made for inefficiency, and sometimes made for the tragic waste of lives. But it also saved a lot of money. After all, wars are intense but infrequent events. For each year of high wartime expenditures, there were many more years of low peacetime defense budgets. The United States did not lose in either Korea or Kuwait. The difference was that it paid with a little extra blood after the outbreak of war in Korea, whereas it paid with a great many extra dollars before the outbreak of war over Kuwait. Total U.S. military expenditures in the course of the cold war were close to $12 *trillion* (in 1994 dollars).

In the two principal cases in this century—the world wars—unreadiness also reflected U.S. reluctance to intervene in the European balance of power or the war in China. Reluctance and delay increased the risk of allies' defeat, a risk obscured in today's memories by the successful outcomes of America's major wars. In World War I, however, the Russian withdrawal and German offensive in the West in the spring of 1918, before General John J. Pershing had completed the formation of the independent American First Army, brought the French and British close to defeat. In World War II, if Hitler had not obligingly attacked the Soviet Union, even a strenuous British and American effort to retake France would probably have failed. The Normandy invasion in 1944—which was a close-run thing in any case—was weakly opposed because Hitler had most of his forces, and most of those of highest quality, tied down on the eastern front.

As long as it was blessed by the luck that avoided allied defeat before the United States could bring its military potential to bear, the American delay in entering the epochal midcentury conflict provided a maximum strategic return on investment. The United States was able to reap many of the ultimate benefits of war while the Allies bore most of the costs of victory over the common enemy. The total casualties in World War II—especially the vast numbers of Russians and Chinese slaughtered in addition to British, French, Italian, German, Japanese,

American, Eastern European, and Southeast Asian fatalities—are un-known. A widely accepted estimate, however, is that *50 million* or more people may have died in the conflagration. That number was more than a third of the U.S. population at the time, but only 291,557 were American battle deaths; there were 113,842 other American deaths.[38] If one assumes the figure was close to 50 million, American fatalities altogether were *less than 1 percent* of the total. Moreover, hardly any U.S. civilians were killed (about two-thirds of the fatalities worldwide may have been civilians).[39]

At the same time, that war made the United States the most pow-erful country in the world, while Britain, the principal globe-spanning power of the previous era, bankrupted itself in the effort against Hitler and slid into steady international decline after its victory. From the point of view of cold calculation of national power over the long term, military unreadiness as the norm was not a bad bargain for Americans, except, of course, for those unlucky few who had to stand in the breach at places like Bataan and Corregidor. The bargain was possible only because international politics in the first half of the century operated under a multipolar rather than a bipolar balance of power. Epochal struggles could last for years without American participation. The system came to an end after 1945, when the United States emerged as the dominant global power and Communist might penetrated the cen-ter of Europe and the Asian mainland. Thereafter the traditional bar-gain was no longer an option for the United States.

Task Force Smith: Last Act in the Old Tradition

After 1945 the United States rapidly dismantled most of its huge war machine. Compared with the aftermaths of previous wars, how-ever, Washington was faced with much larger continuing military re-sponsibilities abroad. Germany and Japan had to be occupied and, after 1949, there was the historically unprecedented U.S. commitment to a major alliance in peacetime: the North Atlantic Treaty Organiza-tion (NATO). Initially NATO assumed the form of a classical alliance and simple guaranty pact: a U.S. declaration of intent to fight with its allies from the outset of the next war, rather than two or three years late, as in 1917 and 1941.[40] This did not involve a significant military presence on the ground in Europe (apart from occupation), or the expectation that a massive military establishment would be maintained from year to year in peacetime.

American demobilization was precipitous but did not proceed as far as it had after previous wars. Active manpower in uniform declined from about 12 million at the end of the war to about 1½ million five years later. This was a dramatic reduction, but one that left a peacetime military establishment six times the size of the one at a comparable time after World War I (total active strength was less than a quarter of a million men five years after the 1918 armistice). This difference reflected the emergence of the United States as the center of world power, but the full meaning of that new status did not become clear until the desperate days after June 25, 1950—the date that marks the watershed of postwar defense policy—when North Korea invaded South Korea.

As the defenses of the Republic of Korea crumbled, President Harry Truman sent American forces into the fray. Hopes that air support might suffice to shore up the South Korean defense were quickly dashed. When the decision was made to commit power on the ground, however, there was little to send. The only troops that could reach the scene quickly were occupation forces in Japan. A tiny group of infantry and artillerymen was hurriedly thrown together under the command of Lieutenant Colonel Charles B. Smith, who, ironically, had been on duty at Pearl Harbor on December 7, 1941; "Smith was leading the United States into war for the second time in ten years."[41]

Task Force Smith flew to Korea and deployed into a blocking position north of Osan on July 5. The unit comprised a mere 406 infantry and 134 artillerymen and lacked effective antiarmor capability. Newly developed 3.5-inch rocket launchers, which could penetrate the Communists' T-34 tank armor, and antitank mines, the most effective defense, were not available. Because special new high-explosive antitank (HEAT) ammunition was in short supply in the Far Eastern Command, Task Force Smith had only *six rounds* of it, and these were expended in the first minutes of battle. Two North Korean tanks were put out of action, but the regular artillery and most of the bazooka rounds available to the Americans thereafter bounced off the advancing T-34s. Fragmented and outflanked on both sides after six and a half hours of fighting, the U.S. unit withdrew under fire and had to abandon much of its equipment. When the battered elements of Task Force Smith pulled themselves together the following day, they found that about 150 men—more than a quarter of their strength—were dead, wounded, or missing.[42]

Other forces from the 24th division in Japan came into Korea on the heels of Smith's band but were badly mauled in encounters with the North Koreans. Additional reinforcements arrived but were unable to stabilize a line, and the Americans were pushed all the way south into the pocket around Pusan. The first ten weeks of the war, until MacArthur's stunning counterstroke at Inchon, were a disaster.

In part the problem was simply an inadequate number of men, heavy weapons, and supplies, and in part it was the poor quality and preparation of the units that did exist. In 1950 the U.S. Army had a nominal total of ten divisions in the active force, but these were almost all understrength and were kept on the books as combat units only by cutting the support elements vital for moving and sustaining them. Because the draft had expired briefly, "the Army was forced to rely on relatively short enlistment terms and increasingly lowered mental and physical standards. At the outset of the Korean War 43 percent of Army enlisted men in the Far East Command were rated in Class IV or V, the lowest ratings on the Army General Classification tests." Three of the four divisions in the Eighth Army in Japan were significantly below their authorized *peacetime* strength, and that level was only two-thirds of wartime strength anyway. Although some of the units in Japan increased in strength in 1949 and training for combat replaced occupation as their primary mission a year before the North Korean attack, there were not enough training ranges available in the country for practicing fire and maneuver. By the time they had to go into action few units "had reached a satisfactory level of battalion training, and combined training with air and naval support had just gotten under way. None of the four divisions had operated in the field as a division since World War II." When these units got to Korea, many of the men proved to be in poor physical condition for the rigors of combat. The units had no means of coordinating with South Korean forces, and command and control arrangements among themselves were completely inadequate. Air-ground operations, the one special advantage available to U.S. forces, were also poorly coordinated. In the first few days of U.S. intervention, for example, American and Australian aircraft mistakenly attacked friendly Korean forces, towns, and airfields numerous times, inflicting severe casualties (on just one of those occasions, they killed 200 South Korean soldiers).[43]

U.S. Eighth Army units were hampered by shortages of materiel, personnel, and training. Task Force Smith (with no armor at all) had to borrow equipment from other battalions, and units that followed were missing such basic items as mortar components and recoilless rifles. The short-range interceptors of the Far East Air Forces, organized for air defense and not designed for close support, proved less useful than piston planes that were in storage. The occupation army's deficiencies in training and discipline also came out when it went into combat. Although about a sixth of Task Force Smith's officers and NCOs had the advantage of combat experience from World War II, when tanks broke through the infantry at Osan and approached the artillery position to the rear, some of the younger howitzer crews bolted. Officers and NCOs had to haul ammunition, load, and fire the guns themselves until the panic subsided. Among the reinforcing units in subsequent days was the 34th regiment, which had suffered significant morale problems in Japan; not surprisingly, the 34th performed badly.[44]

These were not isolated or temporary problems. Medical readiness was so bad that half of the casualties in the first month of the war died, the highest ratio since the Civil War.[45] The story of U.S. attempts to deploy tanks in combat early in the war is almost unbelievable.[46] The rout of Task Force Smith showed the urgency of supporting American forces with armor, a fundamental element of any modern army, but the only readily available vehicles were war-weary M-24 Chaffee light tanks, which were no match for the North Koreans' T-34s. Depots in Japan "yielded *three* M-26 Pershing medium tanks with engine and electrical problems."[47] These were rebuilt, formed into a provisional platoon, and rushed to Korea. They still had "chronic problems with overheating engines" and defective fan belts, but went into action at Chinju at the end of July, more than a month after the war began. This desperately jerry-rigged group of three tanks and another provisional platoon of armored cars were knocked out within a few days.

Meanwhile a provisional tank battalion was being hastily organized in Tokyo, with M-4A3 Shermans that were being rebuilt. Personnel were dragged out of units all over the Eighth Army and from Fort Hood in Texas, yet many of those in the new unit were not armor specialists (some had even been working in the PX). At the same time, tank units were being formed in the United States, but one company had to equip itself by taking Pershing "monument" tanks off pedestals around Fort Knox. A battalion landed in Korea on August 7 "and went straight into combat—'a complete bunch of strangers with no training.'"[48]

The United States did recover in Korea, although as in past wars, the initial price of unreadiness was high. Unlike past wars, however, the Korean conflict had a lasting impact on military policy. In the new context of bipolarity, many officials in Washington feared that the North Korean attack signaled a Soviet plan to attack Western Europe, the arena of primary concern. Evacuating the continent and invading again after a buildup, as in 1944, was hardly a practical option for coping with the threat. Not only would such a course be far more costly than initial defense, it would probably be impossible, since the Russians would not have had to divert the bulk of their military power to an eastern front as the Germans did.

In the course of the following three years the U.S. defense budget tripled, and troops moved to Europe en masse. U.S. participation in NATO was no longer just in the form of the traditional guaranty pact; rather, the organization would develop into an integrated military structure with large forces in place in peacetime. No longer would the United States have a year or more after the outbreak of conflict to get its ducks in a row while allies held off the enemy alone. American forces would be expected not just to hit the ground running, but to be on the ground already, prepared to fight on the first day of war.

Cold War Mobilization: The Second Tradition

After 1950 the United States lived in an environment of permanent military mobilization. This state of affairs was utterly different from the rest of its history. Virtually everyone who supported the principal element of U.S. foreign policy, the commitment to containment of Communist power, was against returning to the tradition of military unreadiness. If anything, the legacies of Pearl Harbor and the retreat to Pusan turned readiness into an unquestioned virtue. In practice, however, the goal remained problematic. Whereas traditional unreadiness had been an economic bargain when other great powers could hold the line while the United States mobilized for war, the new commitment to readiness posed an economic burden. The United States came to bear military costs in peacetime several times higher than they had ever been in the past. The proportion of economic resources allocated to defense by the United States in the cold war was also consistently greater than that of allied nations. As if remembering that the British Empire's exertions against Hitler had helped precipitate its own decline, Americans came to worry periodically about whether constant peacetime military readiness was sapping the country's economic vitality.

Groping for a Peacetime Norm

The objective of cold war rearmament was to increase the size of standing forces and narrow the gap between actual and potential capability, but to a point midway between unreadiness and war footing. As General Marshall explained:

> This is a move to place us in a strong position from which we can go rapidly to the extent that may be developed as necessary. This is not full mobilization. This is . . . a raising up of the whole establishment to gain momentum from which we can open the throttle and go very quickly this way or that way. . . . The way to build up . . . to full mobilization, if that eventually is necessary, is first to get this [partial mobilization] program straightened out and put it on a very high level—you might say a high plateau.[49]

The most ambitious programs for maintaining high levels of military power proved insupportable. Army leaders planned for an unprecedented peacetime force even before World War II ended and promoted universal military training (UMT). In 1951 Congress approved UMT in principle, to replace the selective service draft. Under this system all young men were to serve at least six months of active duty and seven and a half years in the reserves. Congress rejected the implementing recommendations, however, and the system never went forward.[50]

For a brief time after the 1952 Lisbon Conference, NATO was also committed to developing and maintaining the conventional forces necessary to hold Western Europe against a Soviet invasion. The officially estimated requirements to meet this objective, however, were fatefully high: more than 90 divisions and 9,000 aircraft. By 1953 Eisenhower's "new look" defense policy moved to substitute nuclear firepower for these requirements, and for eight years the administration steadily cut the size of the army. The main mission of conventional forces was to hold off Soviet tanks just long enough for the Strategic Air Command (SAC) to lay waste to the Soviet Union; the principal commitment to readiness was invested in the nuclear striking arm.

The prospect of relying on nuclear escalation proved disturbing to the next administration when it confronted crises in Laos and Berlin in 1961. When John F. Kennedy sought to increase available nonnuclear forces by mobilizing reserve units and converting training divisions to combat status, it took "about seven months to raise the number of combat-ready Army divisions from 11 to 16."[51] The deficiencies in existing forces especially worried the president's main confidant, his brother Robert:

A survey was made of our conventional forces' readiness. I don't have the exact figures, but half the torpedoes for the submarines didn't have batteries; a third of the soldiers in Europe didn't have bullets for their guns; a fifth of the antiaircraft guns didn't work at all. It was the worst situation that you can possibly imagine. . . . If we were attacked, we didn't have forces that had armaments that could protect them for more than a few days.[52]

The Kennedy administration undertook a significant military buildup, which not only buttressed NATO capability but also laid the groundwork that later allowed interventions in Vietnam and the Dominican Republic that were much less disorderly than the one in Korea had been in the decade before. After the tragic experiment of gradual conventional escalation in Vietnam, the burgeoning of domestic spending programs, and the declaration of détente, defense budgets declined steadily for seven years into the mid-1970s, while a steady Soviet military buildup continued over the same period. When Iran and Afghanistan exploded at the end of the decade, a shock wave similar to that of 1950 provoked another round of worry about military readiness and brought on the largest peacetime defense buildup in U.S. history.

By the end of the first Reagan administration, however, with defense spending nearly 50 percent higher than in 1980, critics were charging not only that Americans had not gotten their money's worth but that readiness had not improved much at all and had even declined (see chapter 5). With the warming of East-West relations and Gorbachev's unilateral military pullbacks, Americans became less concerned with military readiness, but this change of heart had had a delayed impact on actual capability.

Desert Storm: Last Act in the Second Tradition?

The response of the United States to Iraq's invasion of Kuwait in 1990 seemed almost supernaturally crafted to contradict the historic pattern of American unreadiness for combat. Whatever one may think of the more important question of the political wisdom of the war against Iraq, in operational terms it was a stunning, indeed near-perfect, success. U.S. forces struck efficiently and decisively, defeated Iraq in just six weeks of air war and four days of blitzkrieg on the ground, and suffered negligible casualties.[53] (Total U.S. casualties in the war were barely more than those suffered by Task Force Smith in the first small battle in Korea.) When war came to America in 1941, the price for decades of saving on defense expenditures was the defeat, death, and torturous imprisonment of Americans in the western Pacific; fifty years later the payoff from decades of peacetime mobilization was a swift and comparatively cost-free victory.[54]

Within a few months of the invasion of Kuwait, the United States deployed a force of a half-million people in the region (the buildup to that level in Vietnam took more than three years). U.S. personnel proved to be superbly trained and practiced and were in all respects far superior to the Iraqis they encountered. Plans and tactics were coordinated and executed with hardly any apparent confusion. Iraqi defenses were quickly rendered helpless. The rate of U.S. aircraft attrition during the war was even lower than in *peacetime* operations.[55]

In contrast to the first year of the Korean War, when U.S. equipment and maintenance resources were in such poor condition that more than 60 percent of all tank losses were the result of mechanical breakdown, U.S. equipment in the Persian Gulf performed beyond the most optimistic expectations.[56] In nineteen days of long-range strikes by B-52 bombers (which dropped the bulk of explosive tonnage delivered by air), only one mission was canceled because of mechanical failure. In many instances, the combat availability of M-1 tanks, M 2/3 fighting vehicles, AH-64 attack helicopters, and AV-8B aircraft exceeded the 90 percent peacetime standard for fully ready units. In the case of the

M-1 Abrams tank, this was true even after 100 hours of offensive operations. On a 120-mile night move by the 3d Armored Division, *none* of its 300 tanks broke down.[57]

Although operations were surprisingly effective, problems lurked beneath the surface of success. Some parts of the air campaign, such as the attempts to destroy Iraqi SCUD missile launchers and to intercept SCUDs in flight with Patriot antitactical ballistic missiles, were not as spectacular as initially claimed.[58] These sorts of limitations of capability are not evidence of unreadiness, since it was apparently the inherent technical potential of the systems, not the lack of time to prepare them, that was responsible for disappointing results.

There are other reasons that the war against Iraq might not be seen as evidence of optimal readiness, as explained in chapter 7. The bottom line of Operation Desert Storm, however, remains that in contrast to most historical experience, American forces were fully as prepared as they needed to be for the war that they got. Yet this was in no small part because they got the war just before they climbed down from peak cold war levels of military preparedness. The success in the Persian Gulf did not resolve the question of how to assess readiness in the future. In light of the two American military traditions described in this book and the improbability that standing levels of military power similar to those in 1990 will be retained long after the cold war, the Gulf experience poses the question even more starkly.

Concepts: Pinning Down the Problems

Concern about three problems animates this book. First, military readiness is important: sometimes, as in 1950 and 1990, it is more important than any other public policy matter. The problem is that readiness is only called upon intermittently, indeed rarely, so paying for it over long periods of peacetime can be wasteful. But when it *is* called upon, time is usually short. Thus efficient coordination of proper changes in readiness with recognition of the specific times at which they are needed is terribly difficult. Peacetime choices, *whichever way* they tilt, pose risks. Lives and dollars ride on the decisions, but in different directions. Getting the answer wrong exacts a price in one currency or the other: either in blood in wartime or in treasure in peacetime.

The second problem is that the United States is moving through a secular change in its defense policy that makes choices about readiness easier in one sense but harder in another. They are easier because the threats to U.S. interests have shrunk so dramatically. Since the collapse of the only other global military power, the Soviet Union, it is obvious that far fewer resources need to be devoted to American military capability. Although political debate determines just how drastic the reduction will be, the end result is bound to be a standing force above the historic norm but below the cold war norm.

Decisions are harder, on the other hand, because the choices made are no longer marginal ones, as they were during the forty-odd years of the cold war. Decisions are not just about program adjustments up or down from year to year that can quickly rectify a mistaken set of priorities. The choices of the 1990s will establish limits on how well and how fast the United States will be able to rebuild the level of military capability to which it has been accustomed in recent times, should it prove necessary. This will not be a problem as long as the country does not need a big war machine again in short order. For most of U.S. history, however, when the norm was a small and rickety armed force in peacetime, the U.S. record in meeting military requirements in time was not very good. With the shakeout of the defense establishment in the aftermath of the cold war, the question for policymakers is which of the emblematic extremes, the debacle in Korea or the triumph in Kuwait, will prove to be the model for future military preparations?

These first two problems are the stuff of standard debates about defense policy, strategy, and budgets. The third problem, and the focus of the book, is that few people really know what military readiness is. Much of what follows is devoted to untangling the concept.

The historical cases discussed above have indicated that a wide range of problems are often cited as evidence of unreadiness: uncoordinated mobilization of manpower and industry, insufficient equipment and training, delays in organization and deployment. All these, however, are quite different in nature, as chapters 2, 3, and 8 explain. The conflicting notions in the past of what readiness is all about persisted, indeed increased, during the cold war. (If there is any doubt about how poorly the issue has been understood by either analysts or policymakers, look at chapters 4 and 5.) Contrary to popular belief, military readiness is not a practical and concrete issue. When policy debates are untangled, the essential problems turn out to be theoretical.

Deficient Definitions

The term "readiness" has often been used in two senses, one too broad and one too narrow. In common parlance the term is used in a vague and all-inclusive manner, merging the concept with that of military capability as a whole. Official attempts to define readiness more precisely, without excluding any possible meanings, have not proved much better. According to various official sources, readiness may be

—"the ability of forces, units, weapon systems, or equipments to deliver the outputs for which they were designed . . . to deploy and employ without unacceptable delays";

—"the capacity to perform one's mission when directed to do so. This is synonymous with preparedness";

—"a force's ability to fight with little or no warning";

—"balancing of manpower, investment and operations, and maintenance expenditures that produce the force structure capability of rapid sustained and ultimately full response to the threat";

—"a measure of the pre-D-day status of the force" in terms of "wartime requirements for operationally available materiel, and appropriately trained manpower";

—"the fraction of a force that can be committed to a fight without unacceptable delays and acquit itself well";

—"a function of force structure, materiel, doctrine, manning, and training."[59]

In 1994 the secretary of defense defined readiness of combat forces in terms of the "time it takes to mobilize, deploy to a theater of operations, and engage; military missions they should accomplish once engaged; and length of time they should remain engaged."[60]

It is hard to imagine what aspects of defense would *not* be covered by these descriptions. Indeed, in the first year of the Reagan administration, Major General William Campbell, the director of air force programs, testified, "Essentially every dollar we have in our budget ultimately supports our readiness and sustainability; part of the budget buys near-term combat capability, the other part buys tomorrow's combat capability."[61] Soviet definitions during the cold war were similarly broad: "Combat readiness is the capability of large units, ships, and subunits for organized commitment into combat with the enemy in the shortest possible time, under all conditions, and for their successful accomplishment of assigned missions."[62]

When experts discuss readiness among themselves, rather than with laymen whose interests lie in general policy implications, their usage of the term tends to be much more focused and technical. This professional usage refers not to capability in general, which includes the desired size and types of forces, but to the status of whatever forces do exist, that is, their immediate capacity for combat. Are they well-oiled, in fighting trim, and up to efficient employment in battle, or do they need time to be whipped into shape, supplied with essentials, repaired, or retrained? In this sense, the term used is "operational" readiness. It pertains to the "fill" of assigned manpower and equipment in existing military formations (how many personnel slots are empty, and how much of the mandated inventory of weapons, vehicles, communications gear, and other items are "on order" or unauthorized in peacetime, rather than in place); the extent of advanced training of individual personnel (for specific missions, as distinct from basic military training); the training of units in coordination with each other and with higher command echelons; the maintenance and repair of complex equipment; and the supplies of items that would be used up in initial combat, such as ammunition, fuel, and spare parts.

Some commonly used indicators of operational readiness reflect this technical flavor: "mission capable rates, mean times between failure of major components, average time to repair major components, cannibalization rates of aircraft . . . days of peacetime operating stocks on hand, days of war readiness, spare kits, days of other war reserve materiel on hand, number of major maintenance events required per sortie," percentages of equipment, personnel, and training in relation to requirements, maintenance backlogs, supply fill rates and back orders, flying hours, steaming days, battalion training days, exercises, reenlistment rates, mental categories of enlistees, matches of skills and grades to jobs, and personnel turbulence.[63]

For many purposes, especially meeting the tactical needs of commanders who could face battle in a short time, this more specific concept of operational readiness is the most appropriate one. And it was particularly proper that this narrower conception be the dominant one during the cold war, when the standing strategic assumption was that war on short notice was always a possibility. The narrower definition, however, *provides no guidance for defense policy*, especially in a time when the danger of major war seems remote.

What percentage of any defense budget should be allocated to training, maintenance, or spare parts as opposed to larger numbers of weapons systems and troop formations? The experts' narrow notion of readiness offers no answers to that question. Understanding how to get military forces up and running and in razor sharp condition says nothing about exactly at what points, over long periods in peacetime, those qualities of readiness should be brought to a peak, or what other elements of capability (such as sheer size of the force structure) should be limited in order to maximize operational readiness. The emphasis on immediate operational availability as the measure of readiness is an artifact of the cold war. In that period standing forces were very large; that is, the gap between potential and actual capability was much smaller than it was historically or will be in the future.

These general and narrow notions, although different, are both necessary. In the popular mind, readiness means how ready the military is *to win a war*; this notion focuses attention on the time it will take to amass a force large enough to defeat an enemy of some given strength. The professional usage focuses on how ready existing forces are to *perform efficiently* in combat; here the attention is on the time needed to gear up training, maintenance, stocks of spare parts, and other consumables for existing units, leaving aside the question of whether even peak performance of that number of units will be enough to win.[64] Both of these aspects of strength—the size of a force and its efficiency—determine the odds of success in combat, and the costs of success. A useful definition must incorporate both.

Comprehensive Definition: Capability in Time

The following three-part definition is broad enough to inform strategy, specific enough to be distinct from capability in general, and comprehensive enough to be compatible with the complexities and contradictions unraveled in the rest of this book:

—*Military readiness pertains to the relation between available time and needed capability*. The emphasis is on "relation." Readiness represents the variance of deployable capability with mobilization and alerting time.

—A country is militarily ready as long as the time needed to convert potential capability into the actual capability needed is not longer than the time between the decision to convert and the onset of war. This state is achieved when the government correctly estimates the amount of mobilization time it will have in a crisis before a war, or when it compensates for uncertainty by maintaining excess capability in peacetime. Readiness exists when there is a match between the military capability a nation *could* have, given enough time to pull up its socks, the capability it needs to *succeed* in combat, and the capability that it *does* have whenever it suddenly needs it.

—A country proves not to be ready when a gap between its actual and potential capability causes a gap between the supply of capability and the demand for it. The emphasis here is on "causes." In peacetime there is always some gap between potential and actual military power, which is closed in the process of mobilization. If enough of it is closed in time, supply meets demand. Unreadiness occurs when the country finds itself going to war with forces unequal to the task and unable to fight as quickly or effectively as they should, not because their potential is inadequate, but because the decisions necessary to *convert* war potential into available and effective forces were not made soon enough.[65]

Readiness thus depends on the impact of time on two ratios: one is the relation between the *supply* of combat capability and the *demand* for it, and the other between *actual* and *potential* capability. The first concerns requirements: the relative military power needed to fight successfully. The second concerns conversion: the difference between forces available to fight immediately and those that can be made available after preparation at full throttle. Neither ratio alone can determine readiness.

A gap between supply and demand does not in itself reflect unreadiness, because some countries are too weak to meet their requirements no matter how timely and strenuous their preparation. A Poland confronting a Germany would face the gap no matter how soon and how fully it marshaled its forces. A state's *first* task is to ensure that it has enough *potential* capability—either from its own internal resources, or from collaboration with allies—to be a match for its enemy. Unless that potential exists, readiness to exploit it is beside the point. A government that does not arrange its alliances or its economy so as to have sufficient military potential for defense should not plan to try to defend itself militarily and has no business worrying about readiness because war cannot serve its interests better than surrender.[66]

Nor is the ratio between actual and potential capability a meaningful measure in itself. It would be only if a country was expected to prevent a gap by keeping its potential military power fully available at all times. That is impossible in anything but a garrison state that is indifferent to civilian living standards and immune to popular resentment (as in North Korea). A garrison state that stayed permanently on a war footing in peacetime, moreover, would gradually reduce its military capability as well, because by starving civilian investment it would erode the economic base from which military power is drawn. The full-throttle supply of military power must await the moment of peril—which is what registers the measure of demand—or the power will be weaker than it could be when the moment comes.

There are penalties for exceeding optimal military readiness as well as for falling short of it. These problems are evident in two trade-offs. One is between the security of citizens and their comfort, or between "guns" and "butter." The other is between preventing war and being prepared to win it, or between deterrence and defense, on one hand, and provocation or crisis escalation, on the other.

In the first trade-off, if the government sacrifices internal welfare for externally deployable power, it runs the risk of turning means into ends. Military security is valuable to the extent that it enables citizens to pursue happiness; security at the price of impoverishment is a dubious blessing. In the second trade-off, too much readiness might increase the risks of conflict, rather than dampen them, by aggravating the "security dilemma."[67] That is, when states are suspicious of each other's intentions and feel vulnerable to each other's capabilities, having powerful forces poised for action on short notice could increase tension in a crisis and provoke preemptive attack. This was a central concern of nuclear deterrence theory, and in the latter part of the cold war scholars transposed these ideas about crisis stability to the world of conventional forces.[68] Even if it does not make war more likely, excess readiness could still encourage the adversary to react by arming more heavily. An arms race in which both sides keep up with each other leaves neither more secure and both poorer, although such results may be less common than advocates of arms control presume.[69]

These dangers, in principle, present significant reasons to avoid maximizing readiness (although it is hard to determine whether over-armament provokes enemies to attack more often than it deters them, or whether states make the mistake of overarming more often than the mistake of underarming). The assumption here is that excessive and insufficient readiness both have their share of costs, that both sorts of costs should be avoided, and that hawks as well as doves have good reason to avoid erring on the side of excess.

This book does not focus on the problems that excessive military readiness could pose for the civilian economy or the ability to avoid war. These vital questions are dealt with at length in public discussions and the academic literature. Instead, this study considers the obstacles to developing the right amount of readiness in light of the fact that overinsurance (maintaining an excess of ready military capability over time) can detract from readiness *itself* at a later date. The trade-off is not just between immediate military and economic risks—between vulnerability to attack or to insolvency—but also between immediate and long-term military risks. Even for hawks who want to err on the side of caution, it is not clear that this means erring on the side of excess readiness now, if that detracts from sufficient readiness later.

Arguments to Come

The rest of the book develops these simple arguments:

—Because a defensive national security policy requires the military to be ready over long stretches of time to fight successfully, a mean-ingful concept of readiness must cover not only the immediate situa-tion but the prospective situation some weeks, months, or years down the road.

—The optimum readiness at any given point in time will conflict with the optimum readiness at other points in time; maximizing the readiness of existing forces to perform immediately conflicts with max-imizing the size of the force that could be available to fight sometime later.

—Most notions of what readiness means, among both professionals and politicians, do not fully capture the distinctions outlined above, so policy debate about the costs and benefits of proposals to enhance readiness tends to be confused. When concern about the issue peaks, as it did in the late phase of the cold war, confusion also peaks.

Disagreement about various choices among ends and means is the essence of politics, but it is essential to know what the choices really are if the political rough-and-tumble is to be rational. Analytical confusion complicates policy. Many policy recommendations concerning military readiness are not only inconsistent with each other but turn out to be internally inconsistent.

In itself this is not an unusual problem. Confusion is a common feature of policy debate in a democracy, especially on matters that are highly technical and involve complex systems, such as economic or environmental policy. Unlike these other major issues, however, the readiness question evokes no regular interaction between theorists, on one hand, who think in terms of systems and multiple interactions, and practitioners, on the other hand, who establish agendas for policy debate and think in terms of a few variables. As a result, some underlying questions about cause and effect are never explicitly addressed. Except where it is lumped with the problem of surprise attack, the readiness question has not produced a developed body of theory or even a corps of policy analysts to disentangle the interactions and interdependencies involved in it. Analytical literature on the subject has appeared in technical journals on logistics and management, not publications concerned with security policy or strategy, and the technical analyses invariably focus on specific nuts-and-bolts problems of discrete units rather than readiness in some aggregate sense.

Because theoretical discussion of the questions has not advanced very far, most people's understanding of them proceeds from unstated assumptions that seem rooted in common sense, yet are misleading. One such assumption is that readiness consists of some ideal *level* that is to be attained and maintained. What the proper level should be is hotly debated, but the contenders tend to think in terms of finding and keeping some correct amount. People also tend to think of the process by which readiness is attained or lost as a *linear* and *cumulative* progression of choices about programs and resources. That is, the stronger and longer the effort that is made to increase readiness, the higher the level of readiness obtained. The task then should be straightforward: to identify the factors that increase readiness and allocate resources to them until the desired level, whatever it may be, is reached and maintained.

These assumptions are common sense, but they are only partly correct. They are appropriate for analyzing particular aspects of readiness in small segments of a modern military force over limited periods of time. They are not valid when it comes to understanding how the various elements of readiness in a large force relate to each other over extended periods of time. A conception of readiness that is relevant to total military capability and strategy over the long haul involves many factors, many of which *conflict with and damage each other*. For example, intense training exercises increase personnel readiness by testing and honing skills, but they degrade equipment readiness, because they put stress on weapon systems and wear them out. Does that mean that such training should be considered good for readiness, or bad?

The linear view obscures a fundamental problem: it turns out to be *impossible* to maximize readiness *in general*, to reach and keep one level of it indefinitely, because readiness is not all of a piece; the components move at different rates and in different directions. If readiness is to be conceived broadly enough to be a basis for strategic, budgetary, and organizational choices, it must be seen as a *complex system* composed of numerous variables, some operating in linear and cumulative fashion, and some in a *non*linear, self-negating, and cyclical way.[70] This suggestion, however, poses two problems.

First, it implies that policy choices involve trade-offs that are intricate rather than simple. To insist on this threatens to confuse the decision process further, rather than improve it. It is hard enough for the political system and large organizations to grapple with simple trade-offs. Second, the purpose of theory is to clarify, and complicating the formulation of a problem threatens that purpose. To clarify usually means to simplify, by exposing which elements of a complex reality are central in significance and which peripheral. In cases where reality is mistakenly believed to be simple, however, theory can clarify by illuminating the real complexity (although the theory should still generalize, outline patterns, and highlight the more important relationships among variables). The emphasis in this study is on the descriptive function of theory: to clarify patterns, relations, and trade-offs. The next several chapters survey the conflicting elements in the concepts and reformulate terms to produce an understanding of readiness that spans choices before, during, and after the cold war.

Before the right answers can be found, it is necessary to pose the right questions. The main question for policy and strategy should not be how to achieve readiness in any single sense. Rather, it is how to integrate or balance the answers to several questions over a long period of time:

—Readiness for *when*? What should be assumed about the time available for conversion? Should actual capability be brought up to the potential latent in an organized force (or in the civilian economy) immediately? Soon? Later? Much later? Should organized forces in peacetime emphasize active units or reserves? The proper size of the peacetime gap between actual and potential military power depends on these answers, which in turn depend on political estimates rather than technical calculations. The political judgments concern whether, when, and how an adversary will decide to go to war, and whether, when, and how decisionmakers will decide to authorize a surge of preparations in response.[71]

—Readiness for *what*? How much potential capability is needed to win? What kind of war determines the requirements against which readiness can be assessed? What adversary should forces be prepared to fight, under what conditions, and according to what strategy?

—Readiness *of* what? What are the time requirements for marshaling and deploying the various elements of net capability? Air, naval, and ground forces (and various elements within them) all have to deal with different problems in achieving or maintaining readiness. When boosting some aspects of readiness detracts from others, which should take precedence? How can the self-negating dynamics in the readiness equation be managed?

The decisions about military readiness that are most difficult are the ones that involve conflicts among the answers to these questions. Maximizing readiness in terms of time ("for when") implies increasing actual power, but as subsequent chapters of this volume demonstrate, this often comes at a cost to potential power. Yet facing a powerful enemy for an extended period implies maximizing potential power (readiness "for what"). Emphasizing equipment maintenance may be more important for certain forces, while training may take priority for others (readiness "of what"). How these questions affect each other is discussed throughout this book. The "when" question runs through all the analysis but is addressed most specifically in chapters 2 and 3. The "for what" question is emphasized in chapters 6 to 8, and "of what" is the focus of chapter 4. Chapter 5 considers how political decisionmakers grapple with technical uncertainties. Those interested in conceptual and theoretical issues should focus on chapters 2 and 3, while those interested in technical and political issues may find the other chapters more useful.

2

Readiness as a Stairway: The Linear Image

Readiness becomes an issue *when peace comes into doubt.* That is when the clock starts ticking in the military's transition from normal peacetime status to a war footing. Combat readiness matters even if conflict does not result in war, because it can affect deterrence, calculations of risk, political maneuvering, brinkmanship, and thereby the diplomatic outcome.

"When peace comes into doubt" covers a wide spectrum of tension, from a gradually developing political conflict to a crisis confrontation. A crisis, in turn, may be brief or prolonged. In any case, the amount of time available in which military capability can change from potential to actual capability is crucial. The most common view, or what is called here the linear image, is that capability increases with time during a crisis, as resources are pumped into the military, then absorbed and burned at faster rates than during normal peacetime. The less time available for the transition from peace to war, the less the capability that can be created, refined, and deployed during that time, and therefore the greater the capability that must exist before the transition begins. By the same token, the longer the transition time, the less valuable the capability maintained in peacetime. Readiness in this sense resembles a stairway: the longer the climb and the higher the step from which the climb begins, the higher the level reached (see figure A-1 in the appendix). Getting the right level of readiness requires balancing the constraints of time and capability: getting the right readiness for when without getting the wrong readiness for what.

The Main Dimensions

In peacetime, judging *how much* capability and what elements of it should be available *by what time* depends on predictions about the circumstances of future war. The problem this poses was evident in two choices the U.S. Army faced as it mobilized for World War II. One choice was about readiness for when. Creating a force that could deploy in battle early would strip away cadre from the training base, which could otherwise be used to expand the force available for action later. As mentioned in chapter 1, General Marshall had warned President Roosevelt in 1939 that reinforcing the Philippines would require sending the army's "few grains of seed corn."

The second choice was about readiness for what: which mission should come first. For a year and a half after war broke out in Europe, preparations for the defense of the Western Hemisphere took first priority. War plans revised in 1940 concerned an expedition to Brazil or other parts of Central and South America.[1] "South of the Border," not Southeast Asia, had first call on deployable power. Together, these decisions delayed the buildup in the Philippines, which began too late to prevent the disaster there in early 1942.

The first task in gauging readiness for what is to identify the enemy against whom military plans must be developed and forces deployed. Uncertainty in this regard affected readiness for the North Korean attack in June 1950 and the Iraqi attack in August 1990. Another problem is to balance the demands of different contingencies. Although the condition of the U.S. Army was astronomically better in the mid-1960s than it had been in 1940, for example, since it had far more resources, it still had difficulty balancing these demands. The advisory effort in Vietnam, even before the commitment of regular troop units in 1965, was straining the system elsewhere in the world.

> We had in Vietnam the equivalent of nearly five divisions' worth of captains and majors, about three and a half divisions' worth of lieutenants, and about three divisions' worth of master sergeants. . . . There was no provision in the Army's manning for these requirements; the people had to be taken out of existing units, leaving the leadership tasks there to be picked up by those who had been their followers.[2]

Once the contingency at issue can be specified, however, the question of readiness for what essentially boils down to how powerful is the enemy: what will be the "demand" that should determine the required "supply" of capability? Then the question of readiness for when will determine how big a gap between the actual and potential supply of capability can be afforded in peacetime. The limitations on resources, in turn, force a trade-off between optimizing readiness in terms of time or in terms of capability. The following discussion refines the definitions presented in chapter 1.

Speed and Effectiveness

The popular all-inclusive notion of readiness fails to distinguish readiness from capability in general. Official definitions avoided this problem during the cold war by breaking military capability down into four "pillars": force structure (jargon for the number and types of units); modernization (the replacement of obsolescent equipment with more advanced models); sustainability (the capacity to continue performing missions for long periods of combat); and readiness (immediate ability to execute a designated combat mission).

The last definition distinguishes readiness from capability as a whole but still fails to capture the interdependence of the questions for when? for what? and of what? Maximizing immediate capability for a small contingency now may detract from capability for a moderate contingency soon, or a big contingency later. The professional definition considers capability only in terms of how to optimize the performance of some *given* force within the *shortest* time, not how to get a force as powerful as is *needed* within a *sufficient* time. It focuses too much on speed (readiness for when) and not enough on effectiveness (for what). As long as effectiveness—which determines whether supply meets demand—is part of the equation, none of the four pillars of capability can be entirely separated from readiness.

Consider sustainability. In a few respects, it is useful to distinguish the immediate availability of a unit for combat from the amount of time that it can continue to fight once engaged. Some systems may be meant only to function briefly and at high intensity—as in the case of air defenses against bombers—so immediate responsiveness is the only important issue.[3] For the most part, however, immediate capacity tells little about results. Unless it can ensure that the battle is decided on the first day, a force that could fight spectacularly for one day but would collapse on the second is no more ready in any meaningful sense than is one that could not fight as well but could fight longer.

As one officer put it, "The largely academic distinction between readiness and sustainability is about the same as arguing that the family car with a quarter-tank of gas is 'ready' for a 500-mile trip."[4]

Speed alone, without reference to relative effectiveness against the enemy, cannot be a strategic imperative. A unit deployed into combat has to be ready to *accomplish* something, so the concept of readiness must combine both speed and effectiveness. Even nations with negligible mobilized military power have *some* standing forces in peacetime, and almost any military unit—however undermanned, poorly equipped, or untrained—has some measure of capability and can be physically thrown into combat on short notice. Units normally considered unready can be deployed if the need is great enough. During the crisis of January 1980, following the Soviet invasion of Afghanistan, the U.S. Navy upgraded its designation of some unready units because they were still able to perform some operational tasks.[5] And in 1988, when the newly deployed B-1B bomber was being raked with bad publicity about unreadiness because of malfunctioning components, the air force could state that "all but a few of the B-1s could be launched if a wartime crisis were to occur."[6]

There are minimum limits, of course. A unit could be so untrained or skimpily provisioned that it would not only be ineffective in battle but could actually be a liability to companion units on its flanks and thus might not be committed even in the most desperate circumstance.[7] In reality, however, there are few cases in which an existing unit could not be employed quickly. The question is whether it can accomplish much or would just be squandered if there is no time to bolster its effectiveness with additional equipment, supplies, and training before it has to fight.

If readiness were defined solely in terms of how fast a force could meet the enemy in battle, then the Light Brigade was ready for the charge at Sevastopol, the old men and children of the German *Volkssturm* were ready for the Russians in the spring of 1945, and the Argentinean garrison on the Falklands (Malvinas) was ready for the British counterinvasion in 1982. Readiness to be slaughtered, however, is hardly valuable. U.S. forces in the Philippines in 1941 were considered unready not because they were unable to fight immediately, but because they were unable to fight effectively. Task Force Smith was ready to intervene in Korea in terms of the time it took to move into battle, but not in terms of what it needed to succeed in battle. A unit that is available instantaneously is worth little if it is outnumbered ten to one, and hefty capability is useless if it becomes available only after the decisive moment has passed.

Readiness must therefore refer to the *mix* of speed and effectiveness that allows *satisfactory performance* in combat. If the requirement for speed is relaxed, resources can be released to meet a higher requirement for effectiveness, and vice versa. The mix may vary, depending on the circumstances and the opponent, as long as the force has the minimum amount of both characteristics. If time is needed to increase the effectiveness of the force before it can engage the enemy successfully, that amount of time must be less than the amount the enemy needs to achieve a fait accompli. If effectiveness must be compromised in order to engage the enemy sooner, the effectiveness must still be at least enough for the unit to avert defeat once engaged. In World War II, the initial American engagements were speedy but ineffective (against the Japanese in the Philippines), or effective but not speedy (against the Germans in North Africa). Forces thus proved unready for war in either theater.[8]

Combat effectiveness is a product of mass and efficiency. Mass is the basic organized capital stock, human and technical, of a military force; it is what professionals call the force structure pillar. Mass is measured in numbers of units: army divisions and battalions, air force wings and squadrons, naval ships and task forces. It establishes the limits of an *existing* force's combat *potential*. Efficiency is the degree to which units can *realize* their maximum potential performance. It depends on how well manned, equipped, trained, and maintained the units are. For reasons explained below, this study associates mass with "structural" readiness and efficiency with "operational" readiness.

Readiness in general can be conceived as *speed times effectiveness* (see table 2-1); if either one is zero, then the product is zero.[9] Effectiveness, in turn, can be thought of as *mass times efficiency*; for the product, a high amount of either factor can compensate to some extent for a low amount of the other. For example, if force A has twice as many units as force B, but B's are twice as efficient as A's, A is less than twice as effective as B. Since readiness lies in the relation between time and capability, it can be assessed in two ways: how soon a force can become fully effective for combat, or how effective a force can be if it is committed immediately.

TABLE 2-1. *Summary of Definitions*

Term	Definition
Net military readiness	Speed x effectiveness
Speed	Time in which unit is deployed into combat
Effectiveness	Mass x combat efficiency
Mass	Potential capability in existing force (number of organized units)
Efficiency	Degree of realized potential of existing force
Operational readiness	Speed x efficiency
Structural readiness	Speed x mass
Mobilization readiness	Civilian economic and demographic bases x military organizational base x conversion plans

Operational, Structural, and Mobilization Readiness

The critical combinations of speed and effectiveness are best understood by dividing readiness into three stages (see table 2-2). The two that involve actual capability are the "operational" and "structural" stages. As mentioned in chapter 1, operational readiness refers to specific aspects of a unit's status, such as personnel and equipment fills, levels of training, or maintenance backlogs. Operational readiness is about *efficiency* and is measured in terms of how soon an existing unit can reach peak capability for combat. Operational readiness is assessed according to inward-looking standards: the absolute potential inherent in the unit and the difference between its actual capability and that potential. This standard has nothing to do with how many units at that level of efficiency might be needed to beat the adversary, or what larger number of units at a lower level of efficiency might still

TABLE 2-2. *Summary of Stages of Readiness*

Stage	Time horizon	Potential capability	Actual capability
Unreadiness	> Decade	Latent	Negligible
Mobilization readiness	Years	Incipient	Embryonic/skeletal
Structural readiness	Months/weeks	Organized	< 100% of potential
Operational readiness	Days/hours	Realized	100% of potential

be able to fight successfully. It indicates how proficiently a unit may fight, but not whether it will win.

Structural readiness concerns *mass*; it is about how soon a force of the size necessary to deal with the enemy can be available. Structural readiness refers to the number of personnel under arms with at least basic training, the number of formations in which they are organized, the quantity and quality of their weapons, and the distribution of combat assets among land, sea, and air power. The standard for assessment is outward looking: the relative effectiveness needed to engage the enemy successfully. Structural readiness alone does not indicate who will win, since that may depend on whether the structure is up to snuff in operational efficiency. It does, however, establish the *limits of organized potential capability in existing forces* during the time span before mobilization from scratch could produce new units. Those are the bounds in which operational readiness becomes meaningful. The choice between emphasizing mass or efficiency is analogous to that between fielding a full football team of eleven players who are flabby, do not all have helmets, and have not studied playbooks or practiced together and fielding a team of eight who are in perfect physical condition, fully equipped, and have drilled to perfection. The former team is preferable if it has a month or so to get in shape, the latter if the game is to occur tomorrow.

When one considers operational readiness, the question is how effective can a unit be if it has no time to pull its socks up; when one assesses structural readiness, the question is whether a total force can become effective enough to win if it has enough time to pull its socks up. Just as readiness in general is defined as speed times effectiveness, operational readiness is defined as speed times efficiency, and structural readiness as speed times mass.

The difference between actual and potential capability that is stressed in the generic definition of readiness presented in chapter 1 is also a distinction in the separate categories of readiness here. Operational readiness depends on bringing the actual capability of an existing unit up to its potential, by making its available mass as efficient as possible—that is, by ensuring that the unit has all its designated personnel and equipment, that the personnel are fully trained in their specialties, and that the equipment is in working order. Structural readiness depends on bringing the requisite numbers and types of units into existence, converting the military potential inherent in the economy into actual military mass, that is, by recruiting personnel, producing equipment, and distributing them into coherent combat organizations during normal peacetime, before a crisis comes to call on power. Mass establishes the potential capability, and efficiency determines the match between the potential and the actual.

For the most part, it takes longer to develop structural readiness than operational readiness. With additional resources, existing units can usually spin up their operational readiness in hours, days, or weeks. To expand the size of the armed forces, however—that is, to recruit people from civilian life; manufacture new tanks, planes, and ships; and combine them in new organizations that can interact coherently—usually takes months or years. In many respects, therefore, some level of structural readiness is a prerequisite to operational readiness: a force cannot be any readier if it does not exist in the first place. For this reason operational readiness was not distinguished much from structural readiness as an issue in peacetime before 1950.

In earlier times the main issue for defense policy was the balance between economic vitality, which provided long-term war potential, and forces in being, which provided short-term capability. Thus before the cold war a third stage of readiness was more important; here it is called *mobilization* readiness. In principle, this would consist of the preparation of a small peacetime nucleus of military forces for structural expansion, and of the government administrative apparatus for coordinating the changeover of the civilian economy to war production. In practice, there was seldom any mobilization readiness until after World War I (see the discussions in chapters 1 and 8).

Operational readiness was also less important in earlier times because no matter how rusty the American units were, their enemies were either too weak to outclass them (as were the Barbary pirates, American Indians, or Filipino and Central American guerrillas) or too strong for existing U.S. forces to engage without a long period of structural expansion and reequipment (as were the Germans and Japanese in the world wars). Moreover, when all countries kept relatively small forces on active duty in peacetime and relied on mobilization; when state-of-the-art technology lacked sophisticated electronics, delicate mechanisms, and many varieties of complex machinery; and when troops required less training to perform their missions than they do in modern complex military establishments—the difference between long-term structural and short-term operational readiness was less clear. Technological complexity and the concomitant increases in support costs and the need for specialized maintenance personnel have sharpened the distinction.[10] In earlier eras there was much less difference between mass and efficiency. Before mechanization, weapons required little maintenance and men received brief training. Technology widened the gap between the potential and actual capability of organized forces. By the same token, economic and technical modernization continually lengthens the time required to create organized units. As a result, the balance between these types of readiness in peacetime has become progressively more important.

The purpose of readiness is to enable a military force to fight effectively on short notice. But what does short notice mean? By the standards of the first half of the twentieth century, when mobilization required years to produce large forces for combat, several months would be short notice. Structural readiness increases a government's ability to field forces within that time, and if maximized at the expense of resource allocations to operational readiness, increases effectiveness by producing a larger number of units. The only problem is if "short notice" means something much shorter—days or weeks instead of months—as it did for planners during the cold war.

The Big Trade-off

Constant operational readiness uses up huge portions of the resources available to the military and uses some resources in ways that are otherwise wasteful. Over extended periods of time, maintaining immediate military efficiency conflicts with economic efficiency. Since defense expenditures are fungible, structural and operational readiness are also in competition with each other: if money is spent on keeping existing units fully up to snuff, there is less available to spend on buying additional units to be kept in threadbare operational status. A given pot of defense dollars can be used to buy a large force that needs time to gear up for efficient combat or a smaller force that is able to fight well at a moment's notice.

Military Efficiency versus Economic Efficiency

Examples of various relationships among procurement, maintenance, logistics, and combat illustrate the competition between the goals of short-term military efficiency and long-term economic efficiency.

—Economies of scale in the production of weapons may be sacrificed if funds are diverted to operational readiness and the production of major systems is stretched out.[11]

—To reduce the vulnerability of aircraft in wartime, it would be desirable to disperse them as much as possible among a large number of bases, but doing so would conflict with efficient organization of logistics and maintenance systems. For example, in the late 1980s F-15s in Europe were concentrated on a few bases because the principal maintenance systems were located there.

—To maximize readiness and sustainability in terms of the availability of spare parts requires keeping more parts on hand than will be needed, because of uncertainty about which ones will be needed first, or how often. To be sure that there are enough of the ones needed, whenever they may happen to be needed, many others will have to stay on the shelf gathering dust.

—For dealing with depot maintenance backlogs, economy requires working with batch lots, which in turn requires waiting for a sizable backlog to accumulate. Maximizing availability of equipment, however, requires more speed in maintenance, and that means "having a lot of temporary people, which basically reduce[s] the productivity in those depots."[12]

—The army was criticized for selling workable construction equipment vehicles for rock-bottom prices, but this was done "after maintenance and spare parts problems on older vehicles began dramatically reducing readiness rates of units that would build roads, runways and front-line tank trenches during war."[13]

—If there is a premium on speed in supply, systems are more vulnerable to overpricing, which can help create fiascoes such as the $700-coffeepot scandals of the mid-1980s. In the navy in that period, officials admitted "that no independent check is made on the legitimacy of orders received by supply centers, saying that because of the priority given to a high level of readiness aboard aircraft carriers and at other facilities, 'maximum responsiveness to orders' is demanded of the supply system."[14] Procurement discipline is easier when there is no rush, and inspectors and accountants can evaluate contracts at leisure.

These sorts of trade-offs are not fully appreciated by policymakers at high levels. In misguided attempts to achieve maximal military readiness and economic efficiency at the same time, they can generate even more waste. Because of congressional pressure to keep inventories low during the defense buildup of the 1980s, the military junked "millions of dollars of valuable equipment," some of which was unloaded "at scrap prices while similar parts were being purchased new."[15] According to one observer, "aircraft mechanics frequently [threw] valuable parts in dumpsters before inspections because maintenance trucks [were] not supposed to have many parts on hand." Personnel were evaluated according to how quickly a plane could be "serviced and 'launched'" rather than by how much equipment was used.[16] Other anecdotes illustrate how the imperative to demonstrate efficiency by avoiding "excess" in inventories produces waste and confuses the criteria for commercial and combat efficiency.[17] If a unit is going to have everything it might need in combat, it will have to keep more than it normally needs on hand in peacetime.

These examples give some idea of the general nature of the problem, but they do not show the most difficult trade-offs, which involve the largest portions of the defense budget. The trade-off between investment in force structure or the purchase of constantly consumed operational readiness is another matter.

Readiness for What versus for When: Investment versus Consumption

As indicated in chapter 1, the historic trade-off was between wartime blood and peacetime treasure, between decades of enjoying the economic benefits of low military spending during peacetime and initial setbacks in infrequent wars. But suppose the burden of high military spending in peacetime is accepted. Even then the readiness question will not be resolved. A government may decide to allocate resources in ways that maximize immediate capability at the price of a higher capability that could be mobilized with a little more time. Is full efficiency for combat two days from now closer to genuine readiness than having a larger military mass that could be fully efficient with two months of fleshing out? The historic trade-off was between low military capability in the short term and high savings over the long term. During the cold war the trade-off was between keeping high military capability constant in the short term and higher military potential for the medium term.

Consider a hypothetical aircraft with a production cost, off the assembly line, of $20 million.[18] Assume that it can be manned and maintained at high operational readiness for $2 million a year, or at low operational readiness for $1 million, and that its life span is ten years.[19] If a total of $15 billion is available for the program, the choice is between a force of 500 planes at low operational readiness or a force of 375 at high operational readiness.[20] Investment in military hardware (structural readiness) is cumulative, but much of what makes for operational readiness (for example, fuel, flying time, or maintenance) is constantly consumed. A highly ready force has just as much actual capability at the end of the year as at the beginning, while a less ready force that absorbs the same resources but allocates them to purchasing additional units will have more combat *potential* at the end of the year than when it began—one-third more, in the hypothetical aircraft example. Under likely economies of scale in production, or diseconomies of high operating rates, the difference would be even greater if war came in the ninth year of the aircraft's life. A high operating rate puts greater strain on maintenance and repair facilities and stocks of spares, as the planes wear out. Over time, it may also reduce the inventory as crashes grow in number (although the crash *rate* may decline, since more practice in flying reduces the probability of accidents).[21]

The trade-off occurs at various levels of operational readiness among the units in an active force, but even more between the active and reserve forces. This indicates the importance of choosing the appropriate mix of active and reserve units in a total force. Reserve units cost much less: according to some estimates, ground force reservists can be maintained at 10 to 25 percent of the cost of active units.[22] Actives draw not only full-time salaries but also numerous fringe benefits (such as medical, family, and recreational services, and especially military retirement), all of which create high overhead costs. Operation and maintenance costs are also lower for reserves, who, because they train less, do not consume as much fuel, ammunition, food, spare parts, or other supplies. As a result, before the end of the cold war the National Guard and reserves spent only 10 to 15 percent of the army budget but provided a third of the divisions in the total army force.[23]

The price, of course, is that reserves are usually less effective and need much more time to prepare before deployment than do active units. There are well-demonstrated exceptions, such as the Air National Guard, although it offers a smaller cost advantage over its active counterparts than do the Army Guard or reserves. Moreover, when the army began assigning its reserve components more important responsibilities and quicker deployment times in the 1970s (and thus more equipment, supplies, and full-time cadre), their relative cost advantage declined. If structural readiness takes precedence, reserve forces are a better investment, whereas active forces are best justified by a requirement for rapid engagement.

As long as the manpower and capital available for the military are limited, plans must embody some mix of both structural and operational readiness. But which way should the emphasis tilt? The answer depends on assumptions about the time that will be available to ratchet up operational readiness before war begins and about the minimum effectiveness of the force necessary to win, once engaged. *Should we prefer a big force if it is too slow to fight as soon as might be necessary? Or should we prefer a faster force even if it may not be big enough to win?*[24] Net readiness requires some sort of balance. The proper mix depends on which risk seems higher: not having enough time to make existing forces fully efficient before combat, or not having enough forces. How to decide?

It is often hard to be sure, even in hindsight, especially when there are obvious deficiencies in both kinds of readiness. Task Force Smith suffered from inadequate tactical training. In the crucial first moments of battle, for example, the men firing one of the two available 75-millimeter recoilless rifles made the elementary mistake of siting it on a forward slope. When they let loose their first round, "the ferocious backblast slammed into the hill, provoking an eruption of mud which deluged the crew and jammed the gun." They had to strip and clean the weapon at the height of battle.[25] This was a problem of operational readiness. Task Force Smith's glaring weakness, however, was structural: it did not have enough men or advanced antiarmor weapons.

When the Iran hostage crisis and Soviet intervention in Afghanistan impelled U.S. power into the Persian Gulf, part of the strategic problem was that the military did not have the surplus forces to cover the new contingency. The administration had inherited and reaffirmed a commitment to field forces for a so-called one-and-a-half wars doctrine (to cover Europe and Korea), but in 1977 Jimmy Carter's Presidential Directive 18 called for the development of capabilities for rapid intervention in the Persian Gulf. The de facto shift to a "one-and-two-half" wars commitment, without any notable increase in the resources allocated for the new mission, left the military stretched thin when the hypothetical contingency loomed in 1980. The immediate strain, though, was operational: with five aircraft carriers in overhaul and out of action, the others were harder pressed to cover the larger slate of deployment requirements than would have been the case if only a couple were stuck in repair. At that time, moreover, the navy had only enough modern ammunition to fully load five out of thirteen carriers.[26]

Are there alternatives to the big trade-off? A few countries manage to have high force levels as well as high operational readiness. They maximize mass by including virtually the entire eligible population in the force and matching manpower with large amounts of equipment. Efficiency is heightened simply by applying even more resources, especially for training and communications to allow reserves to be deployed as soon as they are mobilized. North Korea has reduced the trade-off by having the most regimented society in the world, although much of its military equipment is old. The trade-off has been reduced even further in Israel, which should provide a more instructive model since it is a democratic country. The factors that facilitate the Israeli combination, however, do not apply to the United States.

First, Israeli commitment was traditionally spurred by a perceived threat that was far more intense and less ambiguous than the Soviet threat to the United States. For most of Israel's history, few of its citizens doubted that Arab countries would obliterate the state if they had the chance. The only comparable threat the United States ever faced in terms of capability came from Soviet nuclear forces, but there was never much to suggest any Soviet interest in launching an unprovoked attack on the U.S. homeland. Moreover, deterrence between the superpowers was much stronger than it was between the local contenders in the Middle East. The probability that the Warsaw Pact would launch an armored offensive against NATO was not even remotely close to the probability of military adventurism by Arabs or Israelis. NATO countries hedged against Warsaw Pact capabilities, but estimates of Soviet intent allowed them to avoid making huge peacetime sacrifices and turning themselves into garrison states on the Israeli model.

Second, for most of Israel's history its level of military effort has been staggering—at times taking close to a third of its gross national product (GNP)—but this burden has been eased by large external subsidies. Over the years private remittances from abroad, West German reparations, and massive foreign aid from the United States (equivalent to about a third of Israel's defense expenditure in many years, and close to half in some) have expanded the resource base. The vital importance of external subsidies is evident from Israel's government budget, which has sometimes been almost as large as its GNP. (Some years ago, the U.S. Central Intelligence Agency reported Israel's budget was *larger* than its GNP.)[27] The United States has no external sources of financial largesse.

Third, Israel relied on an offensive strategy (keeping combat away from its own territory, which often entailed preemption) to serve a defensive policy. Fourth, Israel (even more than the Soviet Union) relied on a short-war strategy, sacrificing sustainability to initial combat power. When Israel needed to prosecute a longer war in 1973, supplies had to be replenished by the United States: equipment and ordnance were stripped from units in Germany as well as stores at home and delivered by sea and airlift. The United States would not be able to sacrifice logistics for combat power even if it had an offensive strategy, because American forces must be moved and supported across vast oceans. Nor can the United States get logistical support from anyone else.

Although Israel receives huge subsidies, which are unavailable to others, and has been free of the logistical obstacles larger powers face, Israel has sometimes run into the tension between long- and short-term readiness. Manpower limitations put the system under strain in the War of Attrition:

> The conflicting demands of force-building on the one hand and daily operations on the other were all the more acute because of the new defensive tactics that were coming to the fore. The price of change is disruption. . . . Tank forces could not be trained in large formations if tanks (with many maintenance hours left over) were also to be ready to repel an invasion.[28]

If there is enough fanaticism like North Korea's or fear like Israel's to motivate the militarization of society, or if there is ample external support, it should be possible to soften the structural/operational trade-off. Countries like the United States, which see no threat severe enough to turn them into a garrison state and which have no benefactors to buy their military power for them, must choose between a premium on time and a premium on capability. If they most fear being surprised, they will tilt the mix of operational and structural readiness toward the former, and if they most fear being too weak to handle an adversary, they will lean the other way.

Benefits of Unreadiness

Choosing between operational and structural readiness means choosing between immediately available capability and capability available a bit later. The same is true of the choice between structural readiness and mobilization readiness, or no readiness at all. There the trade-off is between capability available in the near future, when the existing military structure can be fleshed out and warmed up, and capability available much later, after the economy's military potential is converted into actual forces and the military structure is built up from scratch. It is widely recognized that peacetime defense spending limits civilian consumption or investment. Less attention is usually paid to the fact that *current readiness may also limit future military capability*.

Consider a simplified example. Assume a span of peace that lasts fifty years. In the earlier example, a given expenditure of $15 billion would provide a force of 375–500 planes (depending on whether operational or structural readiness was emphasized) for ten years, after which it would have to be replaced. The cumulative cost of keeping such a fleet of aircraft in being over the course of fifty years would be $75 billion. What if, instead of choosing between the two dimensions of readiness during this period of peace, the government were to choose no readiness at all for the first forty years? It could "bank" the $60 billion that would have been spent on four generations of the aircraft and take the last decade of peace to begin the buildup for war. With the unspent $60 billion in the defense bank, as it were, and the $15 billion for the fifth-generation replacement, the government could then buy a force *five times* as large as the one it would have maintained all along. Or, if no more than the force of 375–500 were needed to deter or to fight the adversary at the end of fifty years, the country could simply allocate $60 billion to civilian purposes. (There are obviously important qualifications that limit the validity of this illustration.)[29] Although societies rarely optimize investment for military power in the long term when they economize on it in the short term, a large, expanding civilian economy still provides a larger margin than a garrison state has to reallocate resources to military purposes when a crisis develops.[30]

As far as the defense budget as a whole is concerned, unreadiness for decades could provide trillions of dollars for the civilian economy and the base for a much larger military at a later date. Consider another hypothetical illustration: garrison state A and civilian state B both start with GNPs of $1 trillion. For fifty years, state A spends $200 billion a year on defense, consuming all its potential surplus for civilian investment, and after half a century still supports a military establishment with an annual defense budget of $200 billion (20 percent of GNP) in constant dollars. For the first forty of those years state B, in contrast, spends $50 billion (initially 5 percent of GNP) on defense in order to preserve minimal mobilization readiness; it then accelerates to A's level of proportional effort for the last ten years, spending 20 percent of GNP annually. The forty years of low military spending, however, had released $150 billion annually for the civilian economy. B's fat and happy citizens consumed two-thirds of that amount, but the other one-third ($50 billion annually, $2 trillion cumulatively) went into investment and expansion of the economy. After the first forty years, therefore, B's economic base for potential military capability is vastly stronger than A's, so the same level of proportional effort in converting that potential for the past ten years would yield an actual capability much larger than that of country A. If A and B had gone to war during the first forty years, all else being equal, A's four-to-one advantage in military investment would have crushed B. But if the war came in the fiftieth year, the side that was militarily cautious from the beginning would be vastly outclassed by the one that wised up late. Thus what otherwise seems to be profligacy in regard to security is actually strategic wisdom as long as the country shifts its gears in time. The Soviet Union during the cold war may come close to the model of garrison state A, and Japan close to civilian state B.[31] The United States would fall between the two.[32]

If a country postpones converting potential capability from the economy into actual capability in the armed forces as long as possible, the capability useful for a crisis would not be wasted in peacetime. The problem, of course, is that countries seldom know how much notice they will have in advance of a crisis or how much time they will have for conversion. This problem does not necessarily mean that erring on the side of caution warrants high constant readiness, because minimizing risks in terms of time may raise them in terms of capability; taking no chances about readiness for when means taking more chances about readiness for what. If for what means a strong enemy who creates a high demand for capability to counter its power and constant readiness consumes resources otherwise available for future capability, then reducing vulnerability in the short term raises it for the long term.

To assume that the government will be able to pick the right time in a strategic competition to shift resources from structural to operational readiness is a gamble. To assume that it will pick the right time to begin the earlier and much longer transition away from complete unreadiness is not just a gamble but a foolhardy one. Investing in mobilization readiness is a hedge against the danger that the long process of amassing and organizing the basic structure will not be started soon enough, and it reduces the time basic conversion takes, as well as its inefficiency. If civilian state B invested more in mobilization readiness than the minimal $50 billion annual defense budget and did more groundwork to prepare for expansion in the form of economic conversion plans, military cadres and staffs, organizational skeletons, research and development teams, and standby production facilities, it could reduce the number of years needed to bring its actual military power up to its adversary's level.

These points show why readiness should be conceived in terms of qualitatively different stages as well as quantitative levels. More particularly, they show why structural readiness is a legitimate concept and not, as some experts would think, a confused mixture of two fundamentally different pillars of capability, force structure and readiness. Without much structural readiness, developing the capability for a crisis will take a long time; with it, the existing force will not be as operationally ready for an immediate crisis as it otherwise could be. Since the trade-off between time and capability suggests that either could be crucial, maintaining high operational readiness is not necessarily a more strategically cautious approach than emphasizing structural or mobilization readiness. The issue is reasonably simple in theory. How is it handled in practice? Korea and Kuwait have been presented as models of the extremes in initial wartime readiness. Consider now two models of the extremes in peacetime planning.

Readiness for When? Ten Years or Ten Minutes

The different dimensions of readiness are extremely difficult to balance because no one knows exactly when a crisis will erupt or when it will reach the turning point at which either the opponent will back down or confrontation will give way to combat. If plans underestimate the available conversion time, the government wastes money and reduces its potential military capability for the longer term. If plans overestimate conversion time, the government wastes lives at best and risks defeat at worst.

The British Ten-Year Rule: The Primacy of Potential

One extreme model is the legendary "ten-year rule" in British planning between the world wars. The stress is on legendary. The rule has been misunderstood in folklore, but the legend has influenced official thinking about readiness.

Those who see the whole interwar period as testimony to Britain's failure to get ready for World War II consider the ten-year rule the perfect symbol of the complacency that led to appeasement. Others, however, recognize that huge investments in military technologies that were subject to rapid obsolescence in the 1920s and early 1930s would have simply been wasted.[33] To them, the ten-year rule has redeeming virtues, for the reasons suggested earlier, namely, that current unreadiness can help future readiness. The real story lies between these extremes.

According to legend, the assumption that no war would occur for at least a decade guided British defense estimates and planning (the rule was renewed annually from 1919 to the early 1930s).[34] In hindsight, the ten-year rule seems arbitrary, and, since it allegedly retarded defense expenditures, foolish. (Ironically, the individual responsible for making it an automatically renewed standard, the least defensible form of the rule, was Winston Churchill. It was he who, as chancellor of the exchequer in 1928, recommended to the cabinet that the ten-year rule "should now be laid down as a standing assumption.")[35] History also proved mathematically that for the last several years that it was supposedly in operation, the assumption was plainly wrong; war came less than six years after the ten-year assumption was formally abandoned in 1933.[36]

The rule was not as irresponsible, however, as hindsight implies.

The Treaty of Versailles placed crippling constraints on Germany's armed forces (although covert programs and training in the Soviet Union evaded some of the strictures). Had Britain spent madly on defense in the 1920s, it would not have done much for its capabilities at the moments of reckoning in the following decade; and although the ten-year rule was certainly too arbitrary to begin with, it had been given up by the time Hitler accelerated German rearmament.

The rule was not repealed because of pressure from alarmed military leaders opposing economy-minded civilians. Following the example of France's Deuxième Bureau in 1933, the chief of Britain's Imperial General Staff agreed weakly that Germany might be able to go to war in five years. This estimate was supported energetically by civilian officials but was resisted by the military service chiefs. The Air Ministry and Admiralty opposed a rapid buildup. Sir Robert Vansittart of the Foreign Office and Sir Warren Fisher of the Treasury wanted to develop almost 50 percent more squadrons than did the air staff.[37]

Were the British chiefs naively pacific or gratuitously rejecting a gift horse? Hardly. They realized that attempts to purchase structural readiness too soon could interfere with long-term readiness. For the Royal Air Force (RAF) in particular it would have been folly to spend feverishly on aircraft in the 1920s or early 1930s. Aerial technology was changing rapidly and was still in its infancy. Why buy thousands of biplanes that would be immediately outmoded? In the interwar years the RAF assumed that "tactical aircraft became obsolete within two years."[38] If there is enough time before war to put factories into production, pile up large numbers of state-of-the-art weapons systems, and organize and train new formations within the military establishment, structural readiness is wasteful. Instead of structural readiness, then, the emphasis should be on mobilization readiness: production should be limited to prototypes, spending should be concentrated on research and development, few organized formations should be at normal strength (most should be skeletal), and personnel should be limited to a nucleus of professionals, cadres that form a base for expansion. In this sense, the ten-year rule was a boon for structural readiness because it helped justify the postponement of investments that would have been of no military value by the time of the Munich crisis.

The real story of the ten-year rule, as in most cases of bureaucratic and budgetary politics, is more prosaic than the legend. The term itself was not even in common usage until after the rule was revoked, and it developed a loaded meaning later. The rule was not really applied before 1924 and "was defined in different ways to suit the interests of the various elements in the government. Its meaning was always reinterpreted after the fact whenever that was convenient in order to justify changes in strategic policy which were desired for other reasons."[39]

In the early years after 1919 there was no firm application of a ten-year standard. In 1921 the Treasury claimed that the ten-year estimate permitted deferral of military spending, but from 1922 to 1925 naval and air force spending actually went *up* significantly. By 1923 the ten-year mark starting from 1919 was only six years away, so the rule was coming to encourage spending. Treasury recommended reinterpreting it to make it a rolling rule, but this step was not taken for another five years.[40]

Although many historians present the 1920s as a period of arms limitation and the 1930s as one of rearmament, British policy was fairly consistent throughout both decades:

> The period 1921–27 stands as a peak of British military preparations in peacetime, not as a trough. Its real military expenditure exceeded that of any other time except 1904–14 and 1935–39 and at least equalled that of any other state. . . . [Only in 1925 was it] finally presumed that the world had become stable. . . . *Nor was this assessment wrong.* It took the catastrophic breakdown of the international economic system in 1929–30 to destroy the possibility that a stable world might follow from the Washington Conference and the Locarno Pact. . . . [A]nalysis led British governments to take a strategic gamble, which they lost. . . . It was the actions of governments between 1929 and 1936 which created the deadly predicament of the later 1930s.[41]

What, then, was the real significance of the ten-year rule promulgated in 1919? During the first half of the dozen years that it was on the books it had either no discernible effect or it *increased* military spending. In hindsight it seems clear that structural readiness was not very valuable for British security in that period. From then until the rule was formally abandoned, military investment declined. This decline, however, did not cause the unreadiness for war in 1939. Adequate rearmament could have been undertaken in less than the six to seven years that turned out to be left after the rule was given up, but the decisions to accelerate rearmament were not made anytime soon after the abandonment.

In short, as a guide to policy *the rule did not succeed, but neither did it fail, because it was not really followed.* But how could it be? For realistic strategy, *there is no sort of evidence that could provide grounds for a long-term estimate* of when war is likely to occur. If an adversary manifests dangerous intentions and capabilities, the possibility of war in the short term cannot be dismissed. If the enemy manifests the threatening intentions but not the capabilities, the estimate of when war could come depends on how soon significant capabilities could be developed. That answer could be as much as several years, but hardly a full decade. Only when there is no intense conflict of interest, and no evidence of warlike intentions on the other side, is it tempting to assume that the possibility of war can only lie far in the future. Any long-term estimate, therefore, hinges on political warning. Political warning—unlike strategic or tactical warning, which depend on concrete indications of the status of capabilities—depend on subjective judgments about intentions and is therefore elastic, if not arbitrary.[42]

The assumption that war is possible in the near future obviates the risk of relying on long-term political warning, but at high cost. Reliance on a longer-range assumption permits more economy in military power over time. But how does one decide where in the long term to draw the line? If it is reasonable to bet that the level of political conflict with an adversary is too low to precipitate a war within a couple of years, why is it not just as reasonable to assume a period of several more years? If it is not safe to assume several years, why is it safe to assume one or two years? It is hard to indict the proponents of the ten-year rule unequivocally without endorsing the stringent short-range criterion, which most politicians and military leaders are loath to do.

Nevertheless, the British did err. In the years just after the ten-year rule was jettisoned, the RAF persisted in erroneously assuming that the Germans would plan a buildup as the British themselves did, by giving a high priority to measured efficiency. This led the British to underestimate German progress. In 1934 "the RAF looked at the Luftwaffe and saw itself a decade earlier, struggling to build an independent force and to lay secure foundations for the future. The only difference was that the Luftwaffe seemed to enjoy unlimited finances and enthusiastic political backing." Within five years, though, air intelligence was making precisely the opposite mistake, exaggerating German advantage: "Perceptions of a crushing German aerial superiority during the Czech crisis confirmed the government in the need to persist with appeasement." This was a serious mistake, since the extra year of time that Munich bought did not put Britain in a better position; the Germans increased their capabilities at a faster rate in that time.[43]

The ten-year rule in itself was not a catastrophic error because it did not deprive Britain of time to act; the country did not begin to make use of the available time until long after the rule was canceled. Since, in Churchill's view, about four years were needed to rearm, "it was not time that was lacking."[44] In these terms, however, the rule appears all the more divorced from meaningful calculation and judgment. If the ten-year estimate was not geared to the amount of time necessary to convert potential into actual power in the amount needed or bore no relation to the government's willingness to take such action, it had no point, other than to provide utterly arbitrary cover for decisions made on other grounds.[45] Strategically, the rule was an empty exercise; the grounds for assuming there would be no war within ten years were scarcely better than for assuming fifteen, twenty, or thirty years, or for maintaining no working assumption at all.

Moreover, the dilemma was not even resolved when political warning intensified in the late 1930s. Economic fragility, especially balance of payments problems, and the view that near-term military spending would weaken long-term military potential, continued to inhibit British rearmament despite Hitler's mounting depredations. Even after Munich, Chamberlain argued that " 'our financial resources would be one of our greatest assets in any long war,' and urged this as a reason for continuing to limit the rearmament programme." Not until February 1939 did the cabinet decide "to prepare an expeditionary force for service in Europe." In short, "the dilemma was that the more prepared Britain was to fend off Germany's initial attack, the less able Britain would be to finance a long war."[46]

The fact that the ten-year rule may have had benign or insignificant effects does little to redeem it. On the question of how much to invest in readiness, one mistaken judgment in the near term before a crisis or war can wipe out the worth of many years of saving. The British example suggests the range of risk involved in any approach that does not rest on constant readiness.

The Strategic Air Command's Ten-Minute Rule: The Apotheosis of Readiness

Does the British experience suggest that the other extreme is a safer norm? That seemed to be the assumption behind American strategy after World War II. With Pearl Harbor seared in their memories, American leaders became obsessed with the danger of surprise attack. Nuclear striking power also became the country's most important military instrument in their eyes. As a result, ensuring that the nuclear force could act quickly and decisively under any circumstances became the first priority of military planning. In the course of the cold war the Strategic Air Command's (SAC's) bombers and missiles (named Minuteman to reflect their response time) and the fleet ballistic missile force based in submarines became the model of the ultimate in readiness.

In the early part of the cold war, structural readiness was a prominent concern for the nuclear arm, as the new jet planes, the overseas bases and logistical infrastructure they needed, targeting data, and other fundamentals of a large force had to be developed, tested, and organized. Before the 1960s the day-to-day alert rates were lower than in subsequent years.[47] Nonetheless, the capacity to strike on short notice was a prime objective from the outset of the cold war, and few if any organizations in history put as much emphasis on peacetime operational readiness as SAC did.[48]

The organization was exempted from normal military personnel policies, which mandated rotation through different commands and staffs within the service. Personnel stayed in SAC for most of their careers (the same was later true of the navy's nuclear submarine service as well), and thus it did not have as many of the turnover problems that abound in most military organizations. In SAC's formative years, the exemption from normal peacetime personnel advancement standards boosted both morale and proficiency by allowing crews to compete in earning spot promotions.[49] The premium placed on high day-to-day alert rates, proficiency training, and exercises, however, took a serious toll on marriages and families. Nuclear submariners faced even more exacting demands. Because deployment required them to spend long months in claustrophobic conditions, the navy had to pour large amounts into incentive pay to retain them in service. Nuclear force commanders were also allowed no mistakes. SAC's most famous chief, General Curtis LeMay, was known to justify the peremptory relief of commanders whose units had problems by saying that he had no time to distinguish between the incompetent and the unlucky. Even long after the days of LeMay, SAC's commander in chief testified that for the various test inspections, "'perfect' is the lowest passing score."[50]

After the 1950s, when the basic structure of SAC had become well established and concern about airfield vulnerability had grown, there was seldom any debate about this priority. Although modernization programs provoked ample political controversy in later years, there was hardly any constituency for substantially trimming operational readiness in order to save money or pay for new weapons systems. The nominal rate in the latter part of the cold war was 33 percent ground alert for bombers and tankers, which, although not the highest ever (it was 50 percent for a time during the 1961 Berlin crisis), remained extraordinary considering the strain it imposed on a fleet of complex and aging aircraft. Moreover, the command retained the capacity to ratchet the rest of the bomber force up quickly to full "generated" alert, and the Minuteman intercontinental ballistic missile (ICBM) force was virtually *always* on *full* alert (the day-to-day rate was officially cited at more than 98 percent).[51] Airborne alerts for bombers were terminated in the late 1960s, but more because of safety concerns and bad publicity about nuclear accidents than for reasons of economy. By that time submarines made up a substantial portion of the U.S. nuclear force anyway. About 60 percent of the ballistic missile submarine force was kept at sea in normal times, with, by a common estimate, "half of them ready for launch in a few minutes, the others in a few hours."[52]

Nuclear hyperreadiness, prime emblem of the cold war, ended when the cold war did. Within a month after the Berlin Wall opened, the Pentagon proposed ending the program of keeping Looking Glass airborne command posts constantly aloft in order to save $18 million to $23 million annually. These aircraft, designed to preserve the capacity to control U.S. nuclear forces after commanders on the ground had been vaporized, had been in flight continuously since 1961, as a hedge against Soviet surprise attack. President George Bush initially rejected the recommendation to ground Looking Glass but put it into effect half a year later.[53] Then, after the abortive coup in Moscow that toppled the Communist party and destroyed the Soviet Union, the United States dramatically cut the operational readiness of the striking forces themselves, reducing alert rates for missiles and bombers. Structural readiness also fell by the wayside, as some systems were retired without replacement. The Strategic Air Command was abolished, and its aircraft transferred to the conventionally oriented Air Combat Command, with standby arrangements to be shifted to a new unified Strategic Command in a time of crisis. One of the most striking symbols of the change in nuclear readiness was the Clinton administration's plan to transfer B-52 and B-1 bombers, the mainstays of the old SAC, to Air National Guard and Reserve units.

Amity with Russia means that the United States no longer faces an enemy with tens of thousands of nuclear weapons, but the possibility of surprise attack of some sort by some adversary, at some time, will remain. Does the apotheosis of readiness represented by what may be thought of figuratively as SAC's ten-minute rule offer lessons for a future in which a major threat might reappear? The nuclear forces exemplified the ultimate in readiness, since they were prepared to fulfill their minimum missions upon tactical warning alone and could prepare for a maximum effort within days. They cannot, however, offer a very useful model for conventional forces.[54]

In contrast to conventional forces, nuclear weapons have the destructive power to permit a *small number* of units to fulfill a large mission. The minimal requirements for nuclear target coverage are also *absolute rather than relative*. In contrast to conventional forces, whose potential for successful action is usually measured in terms of the strength of the opposing forces they must engage, nuclear forces have a destructive capacity that is significant in its own right, irrespective of the size or quality of the enemy's nuclear capabilities. During the cold war there were intense debates over whether nuclear counterforce capability for "denial," which depends on relative numbers of weapons, was as important as "punishment" capability against population centers and economic assets. Even those who placed a high premium on counterforce and the relative size of nuclear striking capacity, however, would admit that the absolute capacity to inflict unacceptable damage or "assured destruction" was crucial in itself. The size of a conventional force, in contrast, means little apart from how it stacks up against the opposing force. Those who believed that marginal inequities in nuclear capability were important could still recognize that marginal differences in conventional capabilities are *more* likely to be important, because they could more easily spell a clear difference between victory and defeat in combat.

It is true that the very high unit cost of nuclear delivery systems made structural readiness a continuing concern and that greater controversy surrounded modernization programs such as the B-1 and B-2 bombers or MX missile than conventional weapon programs because each item had such a high price tag. The competition for resources between structural and operational readiness was still milder in nuclear forces. Moreover, compared with the effectiveness of armies and regular navies, the effectiveness of nuclear striking forces depends much less on prolonged operations in wartime, so sustainability is not as crucial for a nuclear force as it is for a conventional one. Finally, it is more feasible to subject a small number of personnel to extreme living conditions (or to provide compensating incentive pay) than it is to do so for the far larger numbers in conventional units.

It was not economical to apply the SAC standard of readiness across the board, but after 1950 it was recognized that the tradition of relying on a long mobilization time was too risky as well. Between those extremes lay several compromises. One, closer to the extreme of the British ten-year rule, relied on reacting to crisis or *intensified* political warning; its primary emphasis was on structural readiness, and it counted on a period of months in which operational readiness for the forces could be spun up. This alternative allows the largest overall wartime capability for a given amount of economic resources committed to defense over a long span of peacetime, but at greater risk of being caught short if the war begins sooner than anticipated. The other alternative, closer to the SAC extreme, would count only on *strategic* warning and would thereby accept less risk of surprise and put greater emphasis on operational readiness, but at the price of less *potential* capability for the first day of war than if more dollars had been invested in structure during peacetime. As chapter 6 shows, in the post–World War II period the two superpowers made different choices between the two compromises. The United States tilted toward the operational priority and the Soviet Union toward the structural.

The Conditional Value of Time

If readiness is seen as a stairway, a military force must pay a progressively higher charge to climb and loiter on each step in periods of political or strategic warning. The assumption, however, is that the higher the unit climbs, the more ready it becomes, until it reaches the top. If it does not reach the top before it enters combat, at least it is better off than if it had stayed on a lower step; if it reaches the top well before war starts, it wastes money waiting there, but at least it is in perfect shape to fight when the moment arrives. The trade-offs between long-term and near-term potential and between mass and efficiency may complicate the choices, but they do not alter the image of a continuum. Is it better to husband resources by putting few units on the staircase and counting on a long crisis to get more units and begin the climb (mobilization readiness)? Or is it preferable to spend some money on keeping a large number of units on the first step (structural readiness), planning to run them up as far as they can get during a crisis? Or should the same amount of money be spent to field a smaller number of units but to keep them poised on a high step where they can be sure to scoot to the top just before war breaks out (operational readiness)?

In any of these cases within the linear image, *time is an asset* because it allows the conversion of potential power to accelerate and makes actual power accumulate: the longer the conversion time, the greater the capability. If the peacetime balance between mobilization, structural, and operational readiness is not quite right, extra time will make it more right. For purposes of military readiness, at least, a prolonged crisis is better than a short one that ends in war too soon.

This assumption comports with American experience in the first two world wars of this century. In World War I the time for mobilization was too short to convert more than a fraction of American economic power into a deployed military force. In World War II, in contrast, the mobilization accelerated for two years before Pearl Harbor and peaked before the war ended. It is less clear, however, that readiness followed a linear pattern during the third world war of the century, the cold war. Prolonged partial mobilization, punctuated by crises at the brink of combat, revealed a more complex set of trade-offs for military readiness, in which time could be an adversary rather than an ally.

3

Readiness as a Wave:
The Cyclical Image

*T*HE LINEAR IMAGE of the relation between time and capability applies best when international events move in a linear sequence as well, from peacetime, to crisis, to war. For situations of prolonged and fluctuating crisis, or of episodic crises without war, some of the distinctions and categories outlined in chapter 2 break down. The linear image suggests a trade-off between structural and operational readiness during normal peacetime, because of opportunity cost: fungible funds can be channeled in either direction, so less of one type of readiness allows more of the other. With any given increment of funds, there is always a choice between buying an additional copy of a weapon system or buying extra fuel, ammunition, or training to boost the operation of already existing copies of the system. The trade-off does not apply when a crisis erupts. First, a crisis implies that war could be imminent and there is no time to increase structural readiness. Second, a crisis shears away budgetary constraints, allowing operational readiness to accelerate until the full potential in the existing structure is realized.

In terms of military risks, the only danger in the linear image is starting a buildup too late: by not developing enough structural readiness in peacetime or not starting the surge of operational readiness soon enough before a crisis gives way to combat. When normal peacetime is punctuated by periodic crises that do not usually end in war and when some of those crises turn into drawn-out alerts, starting the surge too late is not the only danger to military effectiveness. Once forces are revved up and running at very high levels of operational readiness, it is hard to keep them in that state for long. Like runners in a sprint, they soon tire and begin to slow down; if they cannot pass the baton, they eventually collapse. For forces in this position, readiness is more like a wave than a stairway and moves through crests and troughs as readiness rises, falls, and swells again. From this angle, more effort can produce *less* readiness, depending on the point in the cycle. Starting the mobilization clock ticking too soon may not just waste resources; it may actually reduce combat power. If peak levels of operation cannot be sustained without wearing down the structure, high operational readiness may be impossible to sustain without procuring more force structure too. The image of a stairway suggests the more time, the better; the image of a wave makes time an adversary as well as an asset.

Inconsistent Distinctions

Modern weaponry relies on complex and interdependent technologies and skilled personnel, which function at different rates, and wear out or require maintenance, resupply, replacement, rest, or training at times that do not automatically coincide. This view does not correspond with the image of a continuum in which structural readiness comes first and operational readiness second. Should purchases of spare parts, for example, be categorized as investment (for structural readiness) or consumption (for operational readiness)? Such uncertainty reflects a significant underlying problem in relating resources, readiness, and strategy. The problem is that some aspects of operational readiness cannot be provided on short notice or even with substantial lead times, but must be planned long in advance. For such cases the time-based distinction between structural and operational readiness—and even between mobilization and structural readiness—breaks down.

Investment or Consumption: Which Is Which?

The reason that purchases of spare parts blur the difference between operational and structural readiness is that the lead times for acquiring them are so long. Simple equipment like tires might be obtained in a matter of months, but things like avionics, radars, or engines take much longer to get. At some points during the 1980s the average time between the ordering and arrival of aircraft spares was *two years*. Some items took even longer: up to three and a half years for landing-gear components for the C-5 and C-141 transport planes. Air Force Logistics Command estimates of that period were that as much as four years might elapse before the industrial base could sustain engine production at a level required in wartime. Such delays were caused by lags between decisions and funding in the budget cycle; the increased complexity of weapons combined with shortages in the requisite raw materials, toolings and forgings, and in personnel trained for the given production line; competition with the contractors' nonmilitary orders (in peacetime the Pentagon has to stand in line and rarely bumps others from the queue); and increased competition on contractual bids resulting from the sensational publicity over the pricing of spare parts (there were several scandals in the mid-1980s over the purchasing of hammers and toilet seats costing hundreds of dollars apiece).[1]

For these and other reasons, the air force took almost four years to show clear results from a reallocation of resources toward operational readiness and sustainability. In the 1970s most of the service's budget had gone toward modernization, but in early 1979 Chief of Staff Lew Allen decided to shift course. By this time, however, he had to wait for the fiscal 1981 budget to implement the change, which in turn meant that the new funds for operational readiness would not be available before October 1980. Most of the mandated spare parts and munitions "did not begin trickling in until late 1982."[2] The navy had undertaken a similar initiative in 1974 to increase funding for aircraft repair. In that case, it took two years for the result to show up in higher "mission-capable" ratings.[3] The problem was compounded by the increased difficulty of projecting spare parts requirements for new complex weapons systems. In the past, estimates tended to be too low, and since the costs of high-tech spares are high, shortages of funding for them had a higher impact.[4]

Spare parts procurement is only one of the ambiguities in categorization of expenditures as operational or structural readiness. In another example, it could turn out to be impossible to exploit a period of intensified political warning to increase ammunition production dramatically, because of the need to hire labor and open new plants. Pilot training, which takes longer and costs more than any other military training program, is another example. "Training" in the generic sense is almost always categorized as operational readiness. Learning to fly military aircraft, however, takes well over a year, and the payoff is amortized over many years of duty. Initial flight training, as an investment in human capital, is therefore closer to structural than to operational readiness. On the other hand, advanced or intense tactical training designed to sharpen skills, such as that in the air force's Red Flag or the navy's Top Gun programs, can be considered operational readiness. The point is reinforced by the military's habit of rotating pilots out of flying assignments about the time that they are at peak form in developing their expertise. This practice constrains operational readiness because replacements are less experienced and adept than those who are moved out to desk jobs, but it expands structural readiness by providing a larger corps of trained pilots to draw on in the event of a mobilization for war.[5]

Compared with the lead times involved in procuring a whole new fleet of aircraft, lags of the sort just discussed are not so bad, but they still undercut the assumption that operational readiness is easy to gear up quickly in a period of heightened tension. Although shortcuts can be taken in emergencies, and contractors could be forced to push civilian customers aside, much of the reason for long delays lies in materials shortages and industrial preparedness problems, which usually cannot be overcome in a manageable time.[6] It might be reasonable to count on having a warning period of at least several months, or even possibly a year, but one cannot plausibly count on having a couple of years or more between a decision to open up the tap for operational readiness expenditures and the actual outbreak of war. Such an assumption for operational readiness planning would be akin to the British ten-year rule for structural readiness planning.

One way to deal with uncertainty about time available for surging readiness would be to load new weapons programs with large orders for spare parts at the outset, so as to provide the sustainability at the same time that the system is fielded. This strategy would be highly inefficient, however, because the extended period in which a new weapon is broken in after initial deployment leads to substantial modifications in the parts themselves or the quantities required. Another alternative is to set up a more elaborate mobilization base (which would probably have to be subsidized) with standby surge capacity for the production of spares. This would be far more responsive than the two-year average at the tail end of the cold war (an average that will probably get worse as defense spending declines). This, too, would be extremely inefficient, because it would require expensive but idle standby facilities. Some sort of intermediate versions of both these alternatives might be more feasible, although it would be difficult to find a realistic way to implement them. For example, program budgets and appropriations could, in theory, lock in commitments for the later purchase of ample stockpiles of spare parts for systems at the point they are deemed mature (fully shaken down, with a reasonable accumulation of experience to indicate failure rates). In any case, it is still impractical for general policy purposes to assume a simple match between levels of warning (political, strategic, and tactical) and levels of readiness (structural and operational).

Mass and Efficiency: Trade-off or Synergy?

The requirements of operational and structural readiness can be interdependent rather than competitive. For example, the money saved by limiting the equipment or training for reserve forces could, in principle, be used to buy a larger corps of reservists with less equipment and training. In practice, however, modern equipment and challenging training can also boost reservists' morale, which in turn induces reenlistment and thereby increases personnel end strength.[7]

Operational and structural readiness are easy to distinguish when the force in question is composed of a single type of weapon system that functions at the same level through most of its life span. The distinction blurs in the case of expensive advanced systems that must be retained long after their basic efficiency begins to decline and must be replaced by new systems in which it takes a long time to get rid of the bugs. Enhancing day-to-day readiness in this sort of situation may sometimes require spending more on structure (through modernization programs) rather than funneling extra resources to operating expenses.

Consider some relationships among operating costs, modernization cycles, and mission capable rates. When Senator Carl Levin asked the commander of SAC why projected mission capable rates for 1985 were lower than for 1981, General John Chain blamed not just the earlier underfunding of readiness accounts but also the declining reliability of the older hardware (B-52s and FB-111s). "In addition, the B-52 rates appear to have declined because of the retirement of the relatively more supportable, less complex, less capable B-52D [as opposed to G and H] aircraft."[8] Three years later, when operating costs for the remaining B-52s were up to $7,000 per hour, many Pentagon officials said the old planes should be retired because they were consuming too much of the money needed for operational readiness. The new

B-1, however, cost *three times more* per hour to fly.[9] The air force could explain that the B-1 costs were so high at the time because the plane was in the early phase of its entry to service. Since operating costs are usually highest at the beginning and end of a system's life span, modernization can throw a double whammy at readiness where very old and very new systems overlap in service.

Actually, it is a triple whammy, since successive modernizations produce progressively smaller forces. If the newer systems are less reliable or harder to maintain than the older ones, the shrunken size of the force may aggravate readiness problems rather than ameliorate them. Furthermore, modernization often adds to complexity, which reduces average reliability. As General James Mullins, commander of the Air Force Logistics Command, put it:

> The penalty for having an airplane down for parts is more severe than it used to be.
>
> In the days when we had 2,000 B-47s, the grounding of any one of these airplanes because of maintenance or supply shortfalls would have cost the country only five-hundredths of one percent of its strategic penetration capability. . . . [T]he grounding of just one B-1B for supply or maintenance will cost this country at least one full percent of its total bomber penetration capability.[10]

The navy maintains that high readiness (in terms of operations and training) requires a larger force. In peacetime about a third of ships are normally in overhaul, a third are involved in training and testing weapons, and only a third are deployed and "fully ready for war." Although having a large number of ships means less money is available for ammunition, spares, and sustainability, the part of the fleet in overhaul does not need to be armed or heavily supplied, so its "share" of supplies can be allocated to the immediately deployable elements.[11]

A high rate of naval deployment also increases the problems of matching manpower and hardware. The longer the sea tours, the more difficult it is to retain personnel in the service. If the total number of ships in the fleet is reduced while the desired number deployed stays the same or grows, sea tours will have to be longer; if the time crews spend at sea is reduced, the number of crews will have to be larger; or if both size of the fleet and sea tours are cut, readiness in terms of deployment will also have to be cut. Keeping up the number of ships by slowing the retirement of older ones, however, hampers operational readiness by raising maintenance costs.[12] The choices between mass and efficiency are not all consistent.

Another definitional problem is how to classify the refurbishment of expensive weapon systems. The service life extension program (SLEP) for aircraft carriers, for example, has been used to enhance operational readiness by overhauling existing platforms that are wearing down. This procedure takes a great deal of time, however, and while it is in progress the operational readiness rate for the carrier fleet as a whole goes down. At the same time, SLEP increases the total service life of a carrier (by about 50 percent), thus increasing structural readiness.[13]

In the near term, a trade-off between modernization and operational readiness can be handled by deferring modernization. In the longer term, however, this does not work. Bloc obsolescence will cause a precipitous drop in operational readiness. Earlier limits will avert this by allowing funds to be channeled to procurement. This was a choice the air force faced after the Vietnam War: whether to buy new planes or spare parts for the old ones. The service chose the former. As the F-15, F-16, A-10, and E-3A were phased in during the late 1970s, purchases of spares were deferred, and the operational readiness of F-4s and other older aircraft—as well as the newer ones, since limits on spares were spread across the force—was attenuated.[14]

Readiness against Itself: More Is Less

The difference between thinking of readiness as a stairway and as a wave has more than metaphorical significance. The rationale for high peacetime expenditures on operational readiness during the cold war was that war might erupt on short notice. But if maximizing the effort at one point actually weakens the forces shortly after, does the effort serve the purpose? No normal constant level of readiness can be as high as peak readiness. Unless the peak can be synchronized with the peaceful resolution of the crisis or the outbreak of combat, straining to reach the peak conflicts with the strategic rationale for high readiness because it creates periodic windows of weakness. Unless one starts the war at a time of one's own choosing, there is no sure way to make the degree of danger rise and fall in synchronization with the readiness wave, peaking at the crest rather than the trough. Policymakers can easily grasp the trade-offs along a continuum between less and more, but they find it harder to keep the choices straight when they have to juggle cycles.

Operations: The Best and Worst of Readiness

During peacetime military operations, units go into the field to practice their functions in the closest possible approximation of combat, or in a crisis they patrol a hostile area in anticipation of possible combat. Most military professionals consider such operations to be the best form of training. The more intense the pace of operations, the better the training is; some skills improve exponentially with only moderate increases in the tempo of operations. According to one analysis of army unit status reports, when units operated their vehicles at high rates, a difference of less than 15 percent in operating mileage was associated with changes in readiness ratings of as much as two full categories (between marginally, substantially, and fully combat-ready).[15] Forces operating at a high tempo abroad, particularly naval forces, are also better prepared to respond instantly to fast-breaking events in their region.

The price of achieving peak readiness through such operations is its evanescence and self-destruction. For a time, field deployment sharpens a unit to its maximum potential and helps establish the reliability of equipment. But what the one hand giveth to training readiness and immediate availability of weapon systems for combat the other taketh away from ongoing equipment readiness and sustainability. Operations overheat the system: they consume human energy, run down machinery and supply stocks, and exhaust the units involved. Long flying hours make pilots more skillful but more tired and wear out their planes and ground crews. As exercises run on, maintenance loads and backlogs increase. Later, when the deferred maintenance is finally performed in order to regain material readiness, equipment may have to be removed to a repair depot. Even if it can be serviced within the unit, training time suffers, so personnel readiness falls. According to one study, army unit readiness drops about 20 percent after field exercises.[16]

Highly paced operations can also compromise safety. The more systems move at a high pace, the greater the risk of accidents. The 1989 turret explosion on the U.S.S. *Iowa* occurred during a readiness exercise. Later that year a rash of accidents at sea led the navy to suspend all operations for two days in order to review procedures for keeping safety under control. In 1992 a readiness drill with sleepy sailors in the middle of the night on the carrier *Saratoga* led to the accidental firing of two missiles that hit a Turkish destroyer and killed five Turkish sailors. And although peacetime operations improve morale among ground forces, where they last only a brief time, prolonged deployments in the navy mean boredom and isolation from families, which reduce personnel retention rates. In maximizing readiness today, highly paced operations erode readiness tomorrow.[17]

Consider some cases. In the 1958 Taiwan Straits crisis, U.S. naval forces escorted convoys resupplying Nationalist Chinese garrisons on the offshore islands of Quemoy and Matsu and flew combat air patrols over the straits. The commander of the Seventh Fleet noted the price to his carriers of operating on the edge: "My CVA group commanders were a little too enthusiastic, and we had 4 bad crashes and lost 3 pilots before I got them slowed down. I have to get some of these carriers off the line pretty soon or we'll have breakdowns in more ways than one."[18]

Operations in the Middle East and Indian Ocean during the Iran crisis of 1979–80 were a prime example of the strains imposed by prolonged readiness. As the commander of the Pacific Fleet pointed out, ships deploying to the area could get only 70 percent of desired maintenance time. The high tempo improved personnel experience but hurt the material readiness of ships and planes. Climatic stress also took a toll: "The monsoon season in the Northern Arabian Sea produces dust storms far out to sea. Sophisticated electronics, weapons, and ventilation systems fall prey to the dust, heat, and high humidity."[19] A decade later when forces deployed to the Persian Gulf in Operation Desert Shield, accidents mounted as they geared up for combat. Helicopters practicing night operations in the disorienting desert terrain flew into the ground, and other training accidents took place. Within two months there had been twenty-two American deaths, and restrictions on night operations had to be imposed in the interest of safety. Nevertheless, the number of deaths rose to more than a hundred *before* the war began in mid-January 1991.[20] This was close to half the number of fatalities from enemy fire during the war itself.

Ironically, even the training benefits from such operations may be less than expected. Operations in a potential area of combat may be the closest forces can come to "the real thing," but they may actually limit the attention given to the honing of combat skills. The Iran crisis deployment during the Carter administration increased naval flight experience because of the constant combat air patrols, but this was "offset by the reduction in formal missile firing exercises for both aircraft and surface combatants . . . in the Indian Ocean where there are almost no missile range facilities."[21]

Later, when the navy deployed off Lebanon, the carrier air wings involved were rated C-1 (the highest readiness rating) at the outset. Because the criteria required bombing practice runs every month (which was impractical without ranges), the official ratings dropped to C-3 (marginally ready) after a month deployed. Authorities up the line decided that this was ridiculous and changed the criteria so that the wings could qualify as C-1.[22] Yet the fact remained that the units in question, though razor sharp in flying, were not practicing their strike missions as much as units in a more relaxed environment with the time for the full program of training. Similarly, the marines ashore in Lebanon were highly ready but at some cost to the broader readiness of the corps. As one general testified at the time, in Lebanon the marines were

> exercising, doing Marine things; as opposed to being aboard ship. . . . But the Navy-Marine team readiness to make amphibious landings is getting rusty . . . due to our inability to conduct amphibious exercise and training drills. . . . So in one sense, in a microsense, our readiness has improved but we are concerned about the duration of our deployment there because the other capability atrophies.[23]

Peak readiness of the particular operating force may be attained directly from cuts in the readiness of other forces. To come up with $20 million per month more than had been budgeted for operations for the unanticipated costs of the Persian Gulf escort mission operation in 1987, the ordinary solution would have been a supplemental appropriation. Secretary of Defense Caspar Weinberger forbade such a request, however, lest it subject the administration's regional policy to a vote in Congress. Instead the navy found the money by trimming flight training, maintenance, and exercises elsewhere, especially in the Pacific Fleet.[24]

Another point to note is that crisis operations do not always bring a force closer to executing its wartime mission. A unit deployed for a crisis contingency may have to be removed from its position for a wartime assignment somewhere else, as was the case in the 1980s when naval forces were deployed in a confrontation with Libya, instead of staying poised for their assignment in a major war with the Soviet Union.[25] The spate of post–cold war "peace operations" has posed yet another problem. When forces are deployed for humanitarian missions (as in Somalia or the Kurdish area of northern Iraq), their combat training may suffer at the same time that the operations have to be funded by diverting money from maintenance (O&M) accounts, the principal pool of funds used to support operational readiness. When Secretary of Defense William Perry begged Congress for additional appropriations to cover emergency action in Rwanda, in order to avoid funding the operation from cuts in maintenance and purchases of spare parts, he complained, "We're an army, not a Salvation Army."[26]

Alert Fatigue and Readiness Decay

Contradictory dynamics in operational readiness threaten security in peacetime. The frictions are more dangerous in crises. Since 1962 the main crises faced by the United States have involved enemies who posed only a modest threat (such as Iran in the 1980 hostage crisis or the 1987–88 escort operations), rather than the Soviet Union. Moreover, in one of those cases (the hostage crisis) U.S. conventional forces would have had the tactical initiative and were not at serious risk of preemptive attack by Iran.

The problem is more serious in a situation that could precede a major war and in which the force in readiness is in a defensive and reactive position. Here the dilemma is agonizing: whether to move the force to a taut and temporary peak of readiness (in case the enemy might strike at the next moment) or to keep it in a slacker but more enduring state of readiness (in case the confrontation drags on and the enemy could strike at any point throughout an extended period). The problem is illustrated by the Martin-Bellinger report of March 1941, which explained how to avoid what ultimately happened at Pearl Harbor on December 7 and why it was not done:

Run daily patrols as far as possible to seaward through 360 degrees to reduce the probabilities of surface or air surprise. This would be desirable but can only be effectively maintained with present personnel and material for a very short period and as a practicable measure cannot, therefore, be undertaken unless other intelligence indicates that a surface raid is probable within rather narrow time limits.

An attempt to protect against surprise attack without relying on strategic warning, or maintaining a completely reactive stance, can increase vulnerability at certain points in operational cycles rather than reduce it. Relying on warning to prompt a surge in reconnaissance or energize the proper level of alert, on the other hand, can be equally disastrous. Admiral Husband E. Kimmel in Hawaii received an explicit war warning from Washington on November 27, 1941, eleven days after U.S. intelligence lost track of the location of Japanese aircraft carriers, but this did not prevent the disaster of December 7.[27]

The problem in 1941 carried over into the first day of war. After U.S. forces in the Philippines received word of the strike against Hawaii, commanders disagreed about what to do with the B-17 bombers at Clark Field. One plan called for them to launch a strike against Japanese bases on Formosa, but General Lewis Brereton reportedly opposed attacking before they were fired on. And although they were aware of the danger of leaving B-17s on the field, the planes "couldn't be taken off for every alarm, they had to be serviced, and the crews had to eat."[28] The bombers took off, in anticipation of Japanese attack, came back down, and were caught on the ground and slaughtered nine hours after Pearl Harbor had been hit.

The U.S. military experienced the conflict between attaining maximum readiness immediately and doing so a while later only once in a confrontation with the Soviet Union. In October 1962, for the only time in history, the Strategic Air Command went to Defense Condition (DEFCON)-2 status—the readiness level just short of wartime—and was kept at that level for a month as the Cuban missile crisis unfolded. The alert was maintained after the Soviet Union agreed to remove the missiles and until it agreed to remove IL-28 bombers. Maintaining that level proved difficult, and SAC's readiness began to fray by November 12 (more than a week before the alert ended), when the secretary of defense and chairman of the Joint Chiefs of Staff reported that "SAC should stand down as soon as possible because the present alert involves burning out large amounts of spare parts."[29]

In subsequent years the danger remained that forces could exhaust themselves just before the moment of truth. In the early 1980s, for example, an investigation reported that "current shortages in all six sonobuoy systems are so critical it is likely the Navy Anti-Submarine Warfare (ASW) forces *will deplete all existing stocks in an alert period prior to commencement of actual hostilities*."[30] Such difficulties in sustaining high alert add to the problem of "crisis stability," for once readiness crests, the force must "use it or lose it."

The use-it-or-lose-it problem was a factor in the decision to go to war against Iraq. When President Bush decided in the fall of 1990 to reinforce the initial Desert Shield force deployed in the first phase of the crisis and not to rotate units home, the stage was set for an early choice between war or withdrawal. The rigors of desert duty precluded keeping a huge portion of the U.S. military there indefinitely. The use-it-or-lose-it problem developed in another form after the war started. By late February, ground forces were close to being overtrained; commanders worried that their readiness would decline if they did not move into combat soon. " 'The politicians have to realize that you cannot keep soldiers at a fever pitch indefinitely,' said the commander of a British armored brigade. 'We've finished our practice. The guns are loaded. The troops are on a knife-edge of anticipation. It is time for a quick, positive decision.' "[31] They got it within days.

Alternatives

One way to avoid getting caught in the trough of an operating force's readiness cycle is to duplicate the force required for the fulfillment of missions and have the two forces rotate in operation and rehabilitation: as the readiness of one set of units wanes, the other's rises and takes over. This was the solution chosen for the fleet ballistic missile force, which fielded two crews for each submarine and kept more than half of the total number of submarines deployed at all times. SAC did the same thing, although with a much smaller portion of the total bomber force, during the years 1957–68 when it maintained a day-to-day airborne alert, and in subsequent years it maintained a normal runway alert of between a quarter and a third of the force. The expense involved was acceptable because of the high priority of the nuclear deterrence mission, the modest number of boats or bombers needed to duplicate a force large enough to cover the critical targets, and the American obsession with not repeating what had happened at Pearl Harbor and Clark Field.[32]

Duplication and rotation are more problematic for conventional forces because of the greater expense. This solution is feasible in some cases, especially in those that involve prolonged operations and alert and require only small forces. It has been suggested, for example, that the U.S.S. *Stark*, which was struck "accidentally" by Iraqi aircraft in 1987, or the U.S. Marines in Beirut before the barracks bombing of 1983, might have been less vulnerable if they could have maintained higher states of alert. To do so, however, would have required "more frequent rotation of units into and out of high-threat areas. . . . This of course would require additional funding" and more units.[33]

The army's version of the duplication solution for the mission of the North Atlantic Treaty Organization was the program of "pre-positioned overseas materiel configured in unit sets" (known by its acronym, POMCUS), which stored equipment, ready to go, in depots in Germany. In an emergency, troops could be flown quickly to the scene, fall in on the equipment, and go into action several weeks sooner than if the entire units had to be transported from home. The price was high. The plan to position equipment sets for six divisions, while the divisions remained in the United States in peacetime, amounted to a dual equipping of one-third of army divisions, and an even higher proportion of total divisional firepower.[34] The program had conflicting effects on readiness. POMCUS increased unit availability by reducing the time needed to deploy active divisions into combat and by keeping in mint condition the equipment many of those divisions would use; it reduced operational readiness to the extent that the equipment was pre-positioned at the expense of what could be used for training back in the United States.

Both aspects of this problem have cropped up in the past. In 1978 decisions to increase POMCUS stocks led to diversion of equipment from the reserves, and by 1980 the Army reserves and National Guard were down to about 40 and 70 percent, respectively, of wartime equipment requirements. In contrast, in 1984 Congress restricted the rate of pre-positioning for fear that it "could deprive some active and reserve units of modern equipment needed for training." The army was directed to defer filling POMCUS until active units had at least

70 percent of assigned equipment and reserve units had at least 50 percent.[35]

POMCUS had different effects on structural readiness, depending on the time covered. It increased structural readiness in the short term because it raised the number of divisions that could be put in the field on short notice. It reduced structural readiness in the medium term—the time after which units moving by sea could arrive in the battle area—because the duplication of equipment sets reduced the number of active units that could be fielded if every tank had a crew, rather than if each crew had two tanks (one at home, one in Germany). In the longer term, however, POMCUS duplication boosted structural readiness again because the equipment left behind in the continental United States could be used by late-deploying reservists, or, in a long war, by new units. If it is assumed that the size of the force to be deployed by a given time must be the same whether equipment is pre-positioned or not, then POMCUS can help structural readiness by reducing the transportation assets required for rapid "lift" and thus allow more resources to be allocated to combat formations.

Duplication is also the solution applied to the navy's aircraft carrier force. This strategy is more controversial, however, because it is such an expensive way (although sometimes the only way) to keep a relatively small number of attack aircraft within striking distance of trouble spots. In this case, too, keeping constant operational readiness requires more structural readiness, instead of being traded off against it. According to official norms, three carriers are needed for every one kept constantly on station, the other two being in transit, training, refitting, or extended refurbishment at home. (In practice, surge operations have often managed to keep a much larger portion of the carrier force deployed forward for extended periods, though at the price of worse "downtime" later.) A smaller carrier force could cover force projection commitments, but only at the price of slower response time, since the smaller force would have to deploy, operate, and refit less often and spend more time waiting in ports.

The smaller-and-slower-force solution does not reject operational readiness altogether but compromises between its conflicting demands. It substitutes longer-lasting moderate readiness to deploy for more intense but fast-disappearing readiness at the scene. The compromise can reduce expense and flatten the wave for some types of forces, making the crests lower but the troughs higher. It reduces the pace of operations but keeps the force poised for deployment. This could mean just ready to take off, on the ground, instead of already in the air, or poised in port rather than steaming near a potential target area. This stance does not allow the force to strike as fast as if it was deployed, but it is less wearing and still leaves the force able to respond fast enough to avoid being struck. This is what SAC did when airborne alert was abandoned, and reliance on strip alert was substituted.

For conventional forces, the comparable posture would be to keep units sitting at their bases loaded with supplies and with equipment repaired, tuned, and ready to move, instead of having the units in the field building higher readiness for a while but burning it up quickly. In the naval area, this is what the posture of Soviet forces used to be, in marked contrast to the American practice. The U.S. Navy often kept "25 to 30 percent of its ships forward deployed at a high state of readiness," while the Soviet figure was about 15 percent by one reckoning some years ago, and less than 10 percent according to later editions of the Pentagon assessment *Soviet Military Power*. (The difference in deployment rates for ballistic missile submarines was even more striking. The Soviet Union kept a smaller percentage of its missile submarines at sea, but if the boats on alert *in port* were counted, it kept a higher percentage of its submarine missile force on alert than the United States did. The Soviet system also needed only one crew per boat, in contrast to the U.S. system.) Soviet naval exercises were usually brief and close to home. By keeping less than a tenth deployed far away, the Soviet Union kept the capacity to deploy up to *half* of its major naval combatants on short notice. The more ships kept at anchor, the quicker the total force could make a transition from peace to war.[36] In short, the Soviet Union considered it "more important to be ready to go to sea than to be at sea."[37] The cost of the Soviet practice, compared with the American, was that personnel had a lower level of training and were less versatile; the benefit was that the maintenance load was lighter and equipment more readily available.

These differences indicate there are two forms of high operational readiness. One is dynamic, the type that comes with high-paced operations on the verge of combat, with vehicles under way, units tracking adversary units, and fingers close to triggers. This can be thought of as "running" readiness. The other type is static and is associated with waiting in port, in barracks, or on runways at home, with equipment shined and tuned, operations being simulated on computers, and personnel sitting around prepared to move out. This might be considered "standing" readiness. Both the benefits and costs of running readiness are more extreme than those of standing readiness. For naval power, running readiness permits the quickest application of force, but it cannot last long enough to keep the option open indefinitely. For land-based air forces, in contrast, standing readiness allows a faster response; unlike ships steaming in a potential combat zone, planes cannot fly for long without coming down. Standing readiness is not quite as close to combat operation, but is longer lasting. The problem with running readiness is friction, overheating, and burnout; the problem with standing readiness is that joints become creaky, skills grow dull, and the whole system slackens as the wait is prolonged.

Which of the two is the more logical choice for coping with a crisis depends on technology and doctrine. When the intercontinental bomber force relied on standing ground alert during the cold war, the response time sacrificed was negligible as long as the alert force could be confident that tactical warning would allow its planes to start and take off before incoming missiles arrived, as long as it could cover the necessary minimum of the target list, and as long as U.S. bombers would not be called upon to strike first. At most, this posture added a few hours to the bombers' time to target, in comparison with airborne alert. Aircraft carriers, in contrast, have long transit times between U.S. ports and trouble spots in Asia, the Indian Ocean, Persian Gulf, or eastern Mediterranean. Unless they are deployed near the scene, the gap between a decision to commit them to combat and the execution of the decision could be quite long. It is the mandate for high-speed action (as well as a professional interest in developing proficiency for its own sake) that has kept naval forces attached to running readiness. A strategy that seeks to exploit naval forces for offensive surprise also makes an operating condition preferable, since it keeps forces close to the prospective scene of action.

Otherwise, standing readiness is usually preferable for an offensive strategy. A force can move quickly from standing to running readiness, but not the reverse. It is easier to prepare and execute an attack when units are not constantly coming and going.[38] Purely reactive forces have more reason to stay running in a crisis owing to their specific functions: in air defense units, for example, "the grace period for non-operational equipment is a scant 10 minutes."[39]

In normal peacetime, the logical choice of emphasis between running and standing readiness depends on whether the priority is personnel and training or equipment and maintenance. One way to reduce that trade-off is to invest more in training simulators. For some weapons, modern simulators can come close to experience with the real system. For others, however, the gap between simulated and real experience is substantial. Nevertheless, simulators do help to make up for the reduction in the honing of skills in a lower operating tempo, and they also improve efficiency and safety in actual operations. Major aircraft accidents in the 1950s "ran at about 20 per 100,000 flying hours" but went down to 3.76 in 1980 and 2.76 in 1983 as simulators came into greater use. Data from some studies also showed that simulators kept reservists' training on a par with that for active forces.[40]

Choices in Practice

In 1987 the deputy commander of the U.S. Atlantic Command reported, "The Navy is operating at a tempo higher than during the Vietnam War."[41] This was stated as a point of pride rather than a problem. But why should a service be doing more with its forces in peacetime than in wartime? Why did the U.S. Navy reject the mix of running readiness deployment and standing readiness in port that the Soviet Union had chosen? Even pundit Edward Luttwak, never pusillanimous when military resources were involved, criticized the American services for hyperactivity and too much "mindless operation."[42]

Leaving aside nonroutine deployments such as those prompted by crises in the Near East, the penchant for high operating tempos appeared to be driven by the priority accorded to personnel proficiency. More broadly, it reflected a greater concern for efficiency than for mass and for training over equipment availability or sustainability. Sometimes the devotion to operations made the air force reluctant to report unit readiness in terms of immediate availability for combat. The practice of the U.S. Air Forces in Europe (USAFE) was to report a rate based on an estimate of the number of aircraft that could be available for action given a certain number of hours of preparation (the number was classified but apparently was greater than twelve). The General Accounting Office (GAO) criticized that practice because it led forces to report numbers of ready aircraft "significantly higher than the readiness posture indicated by statistics on actual daily aircraft operational condition."[43]

The air force countered that its practice was realistic, presumably because of strategic warning time that could be assumed, and also because the "actual daily status of aircraft is lower than that achievable and not a good measure of readiness because it reflects the results of using a standard peacetime workweek for maintenance personnel rather than an expanded wartime workweek." Keeping a larger number of planes instantaneously available "would result in less training for aircrews and reduced morale for maintenance personnel." The GAO nevertheless insisted that this practice compromised deterrence and improperly subordinated readiness estimates to "peacetime training needs rather than crisis requirements."[44]

The more relaxed standard could help near-term equipment readiness, as opposed to immediate availability. General David Jones, chairman of the Joint Chiefs of Staff in 1980, testified that it could be preferable to "have a non-ready aircraft that can be ready in 48 hours. . . . I don't want all my airplanes in commission. I want people doing preventive maintenance."[45] Emphasis on training as a justification for high operating tempo, however, became more questionable when taken to the lengths of sacrificing wartime sustainability. Despite increased funding for air force spare parts in the mid-1980s, supplies went down because of the increase in flying hours as well as aircraft numbers. To keep up the pace of flying the air force had to dip into war reserve stocks and cannibalize planes.[46] It insisted that training had to take precedence and that the cost to sustainability was trivial.[47]

Yet this issue arose not long after a congressional staff report had noted that war reserves were in short supply and that "production lead times for most critical items exceed the point where war reserves will be depleted by several months or years prior to the required production buildup."[48] Anyone familiar with dubious reporting practices (such as those discussed in chapter 4) would also be skeptical of the service's claim that the damage to stocks was negligible.[49] If war could occur in the near future, spares for sustainability would be needed more than a marginal increment of training; a weapons system manned by a less than fully competent crew is inefficient, but the reverse combination is worthless: no matter how sharp the pilots, their skill is of little value if they have nothing with which to shoot. If the warrant for drawing on war reserves was that war would *not* occur in the near future, on the other hand, it is not clear why war reserves should be stocked.

If combat can be assumed to lie beyond a horizon of several years, neither the costs of structural readiness nor of standing operational readiness are warranted. Reliance on a long warning does provide some justification for operating activity, however, to the extent that high tempos maximize the proficiency of crews, maintenance training, and experience in managing support functions, which contribute to *mobilization* readiness by honing the quality of the professional cadre that would constitute the base for expansion (see chapter 8). Therefore the greater emphasis given to operational "running" readiness by American services makes more sense if the probability of war is highest either in the immediate present or in the very long term than if it is higher in the intermediate term. This difference further limits the usefulness of the linear image of readiness.

Readiness Waves and Coordinated Mobilization

The linear image of readiness suggests that the more time a country has in which to *get* ready, the better. The cyclical image suggests that the longer a force must *stay* ready, the worse. Together, the two points reinforce the conclusion that erring in favor of high levels of effort at all times is not necessarily the prudent response to uncertainty about how near or how far away war might be.

The image of a wave, in which readiness rises and falls, applies most to operational readiness because it is harder to keep organizations running at a fever pitch than at a more moderate pace. The margins of tolerance in time are compressed, there are too many moving parts to coordinate perfectly, and the whole system has less slack with which to adjust to friction. The wave image can also apply to structural readiness, but more for political reasons than technical ones. In the case of operational readiness, a prolonged crisis without war wears down the components in the military system; in the case of structural readiness, a prolonged peace without crisis wears down the military policy consensus in the political system.

A buildup in structural readiness puts increasing strain on civilian programs that are in competition with the military budget, so the strategic consensus for the buildup must be sustained in the face of growing economic costs. If the strategic consensus was weak to begin with, it may not withstand the economic and political counterpressure indefinitely. Or if the consensus was strong, but peace endures for a long time after the buildup, the need for high levels of forces in being may come to seem less and less apparent. The first problem almost arose during the mobilization for World War II before Pearl Harbor, and the second arose periodically during the cold war.

After the fall of France in 1940, the United States was expanding its forces rapidly even though domestic political opposition to involvement in the war remained high. For the first time in U.S. history, conscription was undertaken while the country was still at peace. With a large and well-developed training base and organizational infrastructure, conscripts can be cycled steadily, with new ones entering the force as old ones leave. In this way the military is able to maintain a force of large size through a long period of peacetime (as occurred after World War II). In 1940, however, the base for expansion in the peacetime army was very small. A rapid increase depended heavily on the mobilization of reserve and National Guard personnel. But such forces could not legally be called up for more than a year. The Selective Service Act at that time also provided for only one year of active service for conscripts.

By mid-1941, the end of the year-long National Guard mobilization was in sight and the peacetime draft was unpopular with large segments of the public who were not anxious to enter the war. The buildup of the army, which was accelerating with much difficulty, could come crashing down if Congress refused to extend the terms of service for the guard, reservists, and draftees. That summer, with the Germans advancing in Russia, Congress did come up with the necessary legislation, but barely. On the day the Wehrmacht reached the Black Sea, thereby threatening to outflank the British in the Middle East, the House of Representatives passed the extension of service terms by the hairbreadth margin of 203 to 202.[50]

During the cold war the level of standing military forces went through several cycles of rise and decline that coincided roughly with shifts in perception of the Soviet threat and competing claims on economic resources. The tripling of the defense budget after the North Korean attack established a new plateau from which military spending varied incrementally over the next four decades: downward under Eisenhower, upward under Kennedy and Johnson, down under Nixon, more or less flat in the Ford and early Carter terms, up at the end of the Carter presidency and through the first Reagan administration, down again in the second Reagan and Bush administrations. These shifts were surrounded by considerable political controversy: in the elections of 1960 and 1980, for example, challengers made the "missile gap" and "decade of neglect" leading campaign issues.

Compared with the problems of national mobilization before 1950, however, fixing alleged shortfalls in structural readiness was not as big a problem at any juncture in the cold war. This was because the baseline of forces in being during the cold war was so high. A well-developed force structure provided a secure base on which to add or subtract units. Even large absolute increases in mass were small in relative terms, so disruptions were manageable. Management was a bigger problem in the area of operational readiness, not only in preventing precipitous drops during prolonged crisis deployments but also in measuring where operational readiness stood.

Part II
The Cold War

4

Muddled Measurement: Lies, Damn Lies, and Readiness Statistics

WHEN EVERYONE agrees that something is vital in principle, but they are not sure what that something is in practice, the stage is set for controversy. Analytical confusion and political gamesmanship compound each other. The preceding chapters explained why it is difficult to forge a consensus on concepts of readiness. Actual policy, however, is not made in terms of such abstractions but in terms of day-to-day details and traditional bureaucratic categories. This chapter and the next consider how the latent conceptual confusion discussed earlier ramifies in actual administrative and political attempts to promote readiness.

The political debate and maneuvers surrounding the issue of readiness are taken up in chapter 5. This chapter is concerned with the technical ambiguities that make it possible for the political process to avoid facing important aspects of the issue. Underlying the political confusion is the failure of professionals and technicians to establish clear terms of reference or standards for success. Even when politicians or bureaucrats want to make honest choices about readiness, they find it hard to do so without descending from the heights of policy into a morass of technical details. High-level officials, and even their personal staffs, seldom have the time to master the morass. They often wind up being buffeted by selective compilations of data purveyed by competing interest groups within the bureaucracy. The focus here is on operational readiness, which is harder to pin down than the structural variety. The examples that follow of political maneuvering on the readiness issue are drawn primarily from the 1980s, when controversy about this question reached its peak. Three main analytical problems have limited progress in policy debate.

First, although numerous efforts have been made to devise models of readiness, few of these models are comprehensive or are known beyond a small professional circle of logisticians. Not until the 1980s did complex models of the military balance in Europe begin to creep out of the proprietary confines of consulting firms and Pentagon staffs and into wider arenas of debate, and even then there was tremendous controversy over their validity and utility. Readiness modeling remained far behind in the evolutionary process of interaction between analysis and politics.[1]

Second, good models of operational readiness are difficult to formulate because their subject is in large part an ecological phenomenon, a jumble of vectors whose interdependencies are hard to trace or isolate.[2] This makes it hard to determine the relationship between inputs (resources allocated to readiness) and outputs (performance in combat). Reporting systems reflect the former, but definitions are based on the latter.[3]

Third, even if the conceptual problems could be straightened out and good models were available and policymakers could grasp them, other problems remain. Good models are useful only as long as the data fed into them are reliable. Data on operational readiness, however, are more dubious than other information on military capability. The difficulty associated with aggregating measurements in general, as well as the career incentives that those who gather data have to fabricate or distort, should make people skeptical about what ostensible information about readiness really shows.

Shifty Standards

Readiness lends itself to political controversy because critics and apologists alike can find ample evidence to support their positions if they use the relevant indicators selectively. A deeper problem, which abets politicization even if such slick selectivity in the presentation of data can be policed, lies in the complex interdependence of conflicting indicators and the different meanings that any given indicator can impart in different contexts.

Levels of Analysis and Problems of Composition

Modern military forces are composed of specialized units, which in turn are composed of individual weapons and soldiers. The questions about how to assess readiness differ in each of these three categories.

Readiness is easiest to assess at the lowest level: that of individual soldiers, sailors, or airmen. They can be deemed ready for combat if they have the prescribed training and the equipment they are supposed to carry into battle. For an individual weapon system, such as an aircraft, the questions are a bit more complex, but still easy to grasp. Are its components in working order? Does it have fuel and ordnance? Is the crew trained for combat? These points can be summarized in a "materiel condition" or "mission capable" (MC) rating. "Full mission capable" (FMC) status applies if the systems "are safe and have all mission-essential subsystems installed and operating as designated." If the equipment is "safely usable and can perform one or more but not all assigned missions" because of missing or inoperative subsystems, the weapon is "partial mission capable" (PMC). The mission capable rating for a collection of individual systems—a unit, such as a squadron—"is the sum of FMC and PMC."[4]

At the next level of complexity—the unit—shorthand assessment is trickier. If a unit's status is designated solely in terms of MC ratings for equipment, combining minimally and maximally capable systems, it is hard to know how far from marginal the unit's overall capability is. If attention focuses on how many systems are fully prepared for all missions, overall capability will be understated because the technological sophistication and multimission versatility of many modern weapon systems mean that very few are ever likely to be *fully* mission capable.[5] Just as easily, if attention focuses on how many are *partly* mission capable, capability is likely to be overstated since nearly all but the unflyable could be included. "With regard to the term 'Mission Capable' it was noted by one high-ranking officer, 'If you can get the wheels up and clear the fence you are mission capable.'"[6] A third alternative, between the FMC and PMC measures requiring maximal or minimal capability, was the practice of the U.S. Air Forces in Europe (USAFE) of counting aircraft capable of performing their *primary* missions. This practice was still biased toward overstatement of immediate availability (USAFE included unready aircraft that could be made ready within some amount of time in the official count).[7] It compensated, however, for what otherwise would have been an understatement of near-term availability.

One convention used in the 1980s for aggregating different measures into a bottom line was the unit status and identification report (UNITREP, or USR) and its C-rating system (C stands for condition).

Under this system, a unit's condition was broken down into several basic indices. In the army, the main indices were personnel, equipment on hand, equipment status (subsuming MC ratings), and training (see table 4-1).[8] The report assigned a rating from one to four in each category: C-1 (fully combat ready); C-2 (substantially ready, meaning minor deficiencies); C-3 (marginally ready, meaning major deficiencies); or C-4 (not ready for combat, meaning unable to perform wartime functions). There is also a C-5 rating, meaning not ready owing to removal from service for scheduled overhaul. "The difference between C-4 and C-5 is that a unit in the latter group is undergoing routine or planned maintenance, while the C-4 unit breaks down at a time when it is supposed to be in a state of good repair."[9]

The separate category ratings were translated into a composite unit rating. Since normally the rule was that the composite rating must equal the lowest of all the separate ratings, rather than an average, the system tended to understate status (in contrast to simple MC ratings), and the understatement increased with the level of the organization. Consider the extreme hypothetical case: there are 15 divisions, consisting of 15 battalions each, for a total of 225 battalions; 210 of the battalions are C-1, and 15 are C-4. If the C-4 battalions were distributed evenly throughout the force, *all* of the divisions would be listed as unready for combat. If all of the C-4 battalions were clustered in a single division instead, the picture would be entirely reversed: only one division—less than 7 percent of the total—would be considered unready, while 14 would be C-1, or perfectly ready. Thus with *no* change whatever in the readiness of the components, the overall rating of the force could alter drastically, from no readiness at all to nearly complete readiness.

That reductio ad absurdum illustrates the problem.[10] In practice, of course, it does not crop up in such extreme ways, but it does occur. In 1984, for example, although 25 percent of all army divisions dropped in their C-ratings, the number of battalions within divisions that were rated ready increased.[11] Some rating standards pose the reverse problem. In armored units in Europe in the 1970s, ratings for vehicles such as tanks, which are necessary for combat, and support vehicles, which might not be, were averaged to give an overall equipment readiness rating. "Thus a situation could occur where many of the critical vehicles in a unit are not combat ready; and yet because of an abundance of other types of vehicles which are combat ready, the

TABLE 4-1. *Condition Rating Criteria*

Condition	C-1	C-2	C-3
Personnel strength	Available strength not less than 90% of full MTOE	Available strength not less than 80% of full MTOE	Available strength not less than 70% of full MTOE
MOS	Not less than 85% of full MTOE required strength are personnel in the available strength who are qualified to perform duties of the position to which assigned	Not less than 75% of full MTOE required strength are personnel in the available strength who are qualified to perform duties of the position to which assigned	Not less than 65% of full MTOE required strength are personnel in the available strength who are qualified to perform duties of the position to which assigned
Senior grade	85% or more of required E5 and above assigned and available	75% or more of required E5 and above assigned and available	65% or more required E5 and above assigned and available
Equipment on hand	Not less than 90% of full MTOE reportable lines at or above 90% fill, and pacing item at or above 90% fill (same for aircraft)	Not less than 90% of full MTOE reportable lines at or above 80% fill, and pacing item at or above 80% fill (same for aircraft)	Not less than 90% of full MTOE reportable lines at or above 65% (60% for aircraft) fill, and pacing item at or above 65% fill (60% for aircraft)
Personnel strength	Available strength not less than 90% of full MTOE	Available strength not less than 80% of full MTOE	Available strength not less than 70% of full MTOE
Equipment readiness	Average MC rate equals or exceeds 90% (75% FMC for aircraft)	Average MC rate equals or exceeds 70% (60% FMC for aircraft)	Average MC rate equals or exceeds 60% (50% FMC for aircraft)
	Pacing item MC rate must be 90% or greater (75% for aircraft)	Pacing item MC rate between 70% and 89% (60% and 74% FMC for aircraft)	Pacing item rate between 60% and 69% (50% and 59% for aircraft)
Training	Two weeks or less (0–2) required to attain fully trained status	More than 2, but less than 5 (3–4) weeks required to attain fully trained status	More than 4, but less than 7 (5–6) weeks required to attain fully trained status

Source: Army Regulation 220-1, June 1981.

MTOE = military table of organization and equipment; MOS = military occupational specialty; MC = mission capable; FMC = full mission capable.

unit is classified as ready."[12] At the same time, as the next point suggests, there may sometimes be a good reason to rate according to the lowest common denominator of components.

The third level, above individuals and units, is that of large theater forces combining different types of units. The unified and specified commands covered this to some extent with SITREPs, assessments of capability fed into the annual JCS capability report to the secretary of defense. The SITREP included sustainability ratings (S-ratings), comparable to C-ratings (S-1 means fully sustainable in combat, S-2 substantially sustainable, S-3 marginally sustainable, and S-4 not sustainable).[13] In general, however, the Department of Defense recognizes continuing problems in assessing the readiness of joint forces, that is, large commands with components from two or more of the separate armed forces.[14]

The status of a large force is not necessarily the sum of its parts: "Force readiness is not merely a composite of unit readiness. Unless a force has achieved proficiency in the command and control of maneuver, fire support, and combat support units, the fact that each unit may be ready does not imply that the force is ready."[15] This problem can feed back into uncertainties about how to estimate the situation at the lower unit level. A battalion commander, for example, "is required to report on the readiness of his unit without knowing how much and what kinds of support he will receive from brigade and corps level organizations."[16] C-ratings measure only the status of the unit itself and the self-contained resources it is supposed to have. According to those criteria, a battalion could be rated C-1 yet be utterly unable to perform its mission if not provided with the means to deploy to the scene of action.

Reporting systems thus have deficiencies in their own terms—that is, problems in establishing norms for data on particular units at particular times. The next layer of problems has to do with aggregating data across units and services, and over time. As a result of these problems, some information may be understandable, or accurate, or meaningful, but seldom will it be all three at once.

Hypersensitive and Insensitive Criteria

One set of problems flows from simple deficiencies in the definition of indices. In the mid-1980s, for example, S-ratings counted war reserves pre-positioned abroad, but not all the stocks in the continental United States, even though overseas commands might draw on them in the event of war.[17] The army provides other examples. In 1984 General John Vessey, the chairman of the Joint Chiefs of Staff, was stung by press reports that 25 percent fewer army units were certified combat ready than in 1980. Part of the reason for the statistical decline was that modernization programs had been converting units to newer equipment, replacing old M-60 tanks, for example, with M-1s. Changes in authorization for the new models triggered an immediate change in the requirement against which unit status was to be measured, even though many units did not receive the equipment immediately. Thus artificial equipment shortages were automatically created by the rating convention. In the words of investigators for the House Appropriations Committee, "The requirements change so far in advance of equipment availability that readiness rating validity is made absurd."[18]

Some specific yardsticks may be quite valid in themselves yet have a disproportionate impact on overall unit ratings, creating misleading impressions. Within half a year after bad publicity in 1980 about the number of army divisions rated unready, the ratings improved significantly. Critics suspected sleight of hand, but army leaders cited the quirks of the rating system. Marginal differences in personnel fill accounted for the overall change. In 1980, overseas units had priority for manpower, so shortfalls in the total pool were absorbed by units based in the continental United States. The total number of divisions rated C-4 went down when noncommissioned officer (NCO) strength in Europe, which had been at 106 percent, was reduced and reallocated to stateside divisions. The major statistical improvement brought about by marginal change reflected the reality that, as General Shoemaker testified, "There is a very fine line between the lowest C-3 and the highest C-4 rating."[19]

The preceding example suggests how a specific index may make a more general composite rating excessively sensitive to minor variations and lead observers to infer greater differences in capacity for combat than really exist. The reverse sort of problem is an index that is less sensitive than it might be and therefore may lead the observer to note less difference than might really exist. A past case in point was the army, the only service which does not fully measure required skill levels . . . in UNITREP ratings. The Army uses a five-digit code representing the career field, skill level, and special qualifications of each soldier's occupational specialty. The fourth digit indicates the soldier's skill level. For UNITREP purposes, however, the Army measures only against the first three digits. This means the Army is measuring only whether it has personnel in the required career field but not whether they have the required skill level.[20]

Similarly, one of the most frequently cited indices for air force readiness is flying hours, but that is not automatically a good indicator of training. A crew can go up, put the plane on autopilot, or do essentially nothing new (a practice not entirely unknown in previous years when additional monthly flight pay required at least token time in the air). If the crew cannot practice coordinated maneuvers with other aircraft or test the weapons—and the astronomical price tags on many modern munitions preclude much live-fire practice—the flight may not do much to improve effectiveness.

Consistency and Comparability

The problems just described are compounded by confused standards for the aggregation of data across space and time. Distortions or inconsistencies are hard to avoid, given the uneven and unpredictable interactions among evolving changes in technology and organization (which alter the categories of evaluation); in enemy capabilities (which should drive American requirements); in the economic environment, as a result of factors such as oil prices or exchange rates (which create major differences in output from similar inputs); and in political attention or controversy (which encourage revision—justified as refinement—of standards for assessment). Aggregation can be impeded by the simplest of obstacles, as the following examples demonstrate.

First, because of differences in U.S. and NATO standards, as well as in norms among the American services, the C- and S-ratings have not provided accurate comparisons of readiness across those various forces.[21] Differences among the American services alone have been numerous.

—At a time when navy and air force C-ratings included the status of war reserve stocks, the army's did not.

—Most S-ratings for army components were based on the weight of stocks, whereas in the navy they were based on the dollar value of inventories.

—The services calculated the backlog of maintenance and repair in three different ways.

—Despite the fact that the Joint Chiefs of Staff asked all services to measure aircrew training according to the levels required for wartime, the navy went its own way (as usual) and used peacetime authorized levels as the benchmark.

—Out of five general questions for implementing the UNITREP surveyed by the General Accounting Office in 1986, *there was not a single one on which the army, navy, air force, and marines all shared the same standard for measurement.*[22]

Second, even *within* the same services, standards shift rapidly. Thus although policymakers should logically be interested in charting trends over time, the data may not correspond from year to year. The army's standards for desired equipment levels in units, for example, changed *every year* for a quarter century after 1961.[23] Or, in regard to sustainability, Defense Department guidance and the services often define requirements in terms of the number of days' worth of action afforded by stocks of consumable items, such as munitions, and base five-year plans on estimates of such requirements, but the bases for estimates vary more frequently than every five years:

> The estimated consumption for a given number of days of high explosive (HE) ammunition for the 155mm howitzer may change from one year to the next because of the introduction of a new target acquisition device, an updated estimate of the threat, more (or fewer) 155mm howitzers in the force, the introduction of a new round for the 8-inch howitzer, or any number of other factors. . . . [T]he estimated consumption of a particular item can (and is likely to) vary significantly even when the objective number of days remains constant.[24]

When confronted by criticism of the declines in C-ratings, JCS Chairman Vessey argued that those ratings were nearly useless for year-to-year comparisons because of the constant change in standards for measuring progress: "It is sort of like painting a moving train."[25] Comparisons or estimates for large commands that cut across separate services can also be confounded by differences in the basic method of calculation. The level-of-effort method, which calculates requirements in terms of usage over a given period of time, was used for most army munitions in the 1980s, whereas the threat-oriented method, which calculates requirements in terms of the number of enemy targets, was used for many air force and navy munitions.[26]

Third, even when standards within services are consistent, ratings that are specific enough to capture many relevant details may fluctuate too frequently to be useful. Aircraft carrier C-ratings were known to change quickly owing to the multitude of elements involved (such as personnel, arrival of weapons, maintenance backlogs) and their constant turnover. In just the first quarter of the year, carriers were rated C-1 for 6 percent of the time, C-2 for 40 percent, C-3 for 7 percent, C-4 for 15 percent, and C-5 for the remainder.[27]

Dubious Data

Complexity undermines assessment for a variety of reasons: multiplicitous indices point in different directions; no coherent judgment can take into account all possibly relevant indices; the indices selected for evidence can determine judgment of whether readiness is up or down; even the same index or datum may demonstrate reduced readiness in one respect at the same time that it shows greater readiness in others; and there are often few clear grounds on which to approve one selection over another. Therefore, the same body of data can usually be mined to demonstrate that readiness has improved or that it has declined.

Context, Presentation, and Manipulation

Aircraft cannibalization is a practice normally regarded as evidence of impaired readiness: a whole expensive integrated system must be taken out of service in order to keep other planes operating, the time and labor required to remove parts (and later to reinstall them in the cannibalized plane) makes the job more complicated than if the parts are simply available in stocks, and the cannibalized parts get more wear than is normal, thus increasing the breakdown rate. The need to cannibalize reflects shortages of spare parts. Thus a GAO report criticized the B-1 bomber program at length both for parts shortages and cannibalization rates higher than the average for other planes.[28]

Premature purchases of large amounts of spares for new weapon systems, however, rather than boosting readiness over the long term, can be quite wasteful, since the shakedown process often reveals needed modifications. Indeed, later in its report the GAO noted, "The Air Force has ordered millions of dollars of B-1B parts based on assumptions that may no longer be valid."[29] In some circumstances, therefore, citing increased cannibalization as a net loss for readiness could be mistaken.

It is almost as easy, however, to present data that mask the bottom line. Under the backup aircraft inventory (BAI) program, aircraft at one time were assigned to units for the explicit purpose of being cannibalized, in order to keep the other planes in the unit flying. Yet the squadron's performance was judged only in terms of the aircraft specifically assigned for combat. Since that number was lower, the reported rate of availability would be higher.[30] Thus operational readiness was rated high at the expense of structural readiness (since the backup aircraft could otherwise be formed in additional units). In the context of the preceding B-1 example, the BAI program might be considered alternately good and bad: good for the early phase of a weapon's deployment, bad for when it has passed through shakedown and into maturity.

Sometimes data point in opposite directions, and either side in a debate may legitimately cite support for its concerns. This state of affairs naturally throws a lay observer into complete confusion. When Senator Carl Levin complained in 1984 about a 37 percent growth in cannibalization of F-15s, the air force admitted a 29 percent increase in terms of raw numbers of incidents but argued that "a much more meaningful comparison normalized to account for inventory and flying hour changes—cannibalization per 100 flying hours—actually decreased by 20 percent." And to answer the senator's concern that half of spare parts requisitions for combat aircraft were coming out of cannibalization and withdrawals from war reserves (the stocks that were to be husbanded for wartime sustainability), the service provided data that, although perhaps perfectly accurate, could hardly be intelligible to a busy politician (or even most high-level civilian officials in the Pentagon):

While it is true that in fiscal year 1983 62% of NMCS conditions for the primary TAF forces . . . were satisfied by cannibalizations or WRM withdrawals you must also view that in context. For example, for fiscal year 1982 for all USAF aircraft 75.4% of all requisitions were filled from stock. Of those items back-ordered only 16.9% resulted in a NMCS condition. Of those that resulted in NMCS condition 57% were satisfied by cann or WRM withdrawal. That's 57% of the 17% of all back-orders, not requisitions.[31]

Phew! Now, *there* is a way to keep Congress from micromanaging! Any effort to improve the intelligibility of data, however, risks oversimplification, as illustrated by numerous charts prepared for Senate briefings showing ship and aircraft readiness for 1981–86: the trends moved in perfectly straight upward lines. Such a rendering could only have been done by crudely massaging away the details in year-to-year changes.[32]

Meaning can be distorted by focusing on changes without referring to the baseline from which they proceed, by citing absolute numbers without referring to percentages (or vice versa), or by treating one change in isolation from others. A $79 million reduction that cut 20,000 flying hours for the air force in 1984 seemed alarming to some legislators, but those hours came out of a total of 2.4 million and still left the service with 31,000 hours more than the previous year.[33] On the other hand, data for 1980–86 indicated that Tactical Air Command (TAC) flying hours went up 70 percent, but it was a mistake to infer that this dramatically improved combat proficiency because, owing to "increases in aircraft inventory, changes in pilot-to-aircraft ratios, and staff flying, the average flying time of line pilots only increased 13 percent."[34]

Air force spokesmen also dismissed figures showing a 15 percent increase in units rated C-3 and C-4 after 1980, noting that the number of C-1 and C-2 units *also* grew in the same period because the total number of combat units increased.[35] They also cited data indicating that squadrons could "perform 62% more combat sorties on short notice than they could in 1980."[36] In similar fashion, when Senator Levin complained that the army had fewer units with the highest level of authorized strength (ALO-1) in 1983 than at the end of the Carter administration, the service countered by pointing out that more than 100 reporting units had been added to the active force, and more than 150 to the reserve component.[37] Conversely, a decline in total battalion training days was put in perspective by pointing out that the number of army battalions had gone down, so training days per battalion were really remaining constant.[38]

The point underlying these data and the political wrangles about them (see chapter 5) is that for some time during the Reagan administration the *number* of operationally ready units increased, but the *proportion* of the total force that was operationally ready decreased. Structural readiness improved more than operational readiness.[39] Politicians and bureaucrats, however, seldom cite conflicting data or emphasize ambiguity in readiness trends. More often they cite only the data that point in one direction. Selectivity can be legitimate, since some form of simplification is always necessary, but it easily lends itself to distortion. Although such distortion can be innocent—since the data are complex and can be approached from different perspectives—at times it is purposeful: those in authority have a strong incentive to supply positive results, while those out of power are motivated to discredit the performance of the "ins."

Manipulating information is standard behavior in politics, especially when officials are justifying policy rather than making it. In internal memos to the services in 1980, Secretary of Defense Harold Brown cited data that indicated that little more than 60 percent of air force and navy tactical aircraft were ready, whereas in external discussion that aimed to contain bad publicity, Assistant Secretary for Public Affairs Thomas Ross referred to less stringent standards, which enabled him to say that 70–80 percent were mission capable.[40] Four years later, Secretary of Defense Weinberger reported to Congress that, in comparison with 1980, 39 percent of major military units were rated fully or substantially ready. That statistic masked *declines* of 25 percent and 15 percent in army and air force units by averaging those embarrassing figures with the navy's alleged 100 percent increase.[41] (As noted earlier, the navy's rating system allowed fewer negative measurements than did those of the other services.)

Skewed presentation of information might be less of a problem if the administrators who marshal the data could be made more competent or scrupulous. Even then there would be no guarantee of better results, however, because not all of the basic data are accurate.

Sloppy and Deceptive Reporting

However careful the highest officials may be, they can do no better than the facts they are given to use. Facts bubble up in dizzying profusion through the chain of command. The volume of confusing information is so large because tremendous resources and time go into amassing it. (The volume and redundancy of the reporting requirements have sometimes been so great that they overburden commanders and reduce productivity. Although the dollar cost of reporting is very high, it is not appreciated because budgetary accounting does not attribute it to reporting per se. This leads some critics to argue, in effect, that an obsession with readiness can detract from readiness.)[42] Another reason that the high demand for information can be counterproductive is that personnel who collect the data at the working level have little reason to take the job seriously, especially when they discover that much of what they strain to compile is never used properly.

One system that ran into such problems was the maintenance data collection (MDC) system used by the air force for more than a quarter century. Numerous studies and reports concluded that the MDC suffered from frequent and gross errors in recording. Some aspects of maintenance were either over- or underreported by a factor of two. Mechanics had no incentive to record the information carefully because they did not know how it was used, received no feedback from the consumers, and developed the attitude that the work was "merely an exercise." As a result, the tendency to transcribe information incorrectly was all the greater when it involved "long strings of alphanumeric data." Base-level managers, in turn, had little incentive to demand accurate data because they could not use it for local purposes. A 1983 report concluded, *"inaccurate and incomplete data . . . pervades the Air Force maintenance system."* But like the drunkard who looks for his house key under a street lamp not because he lost it there, but because the light is better, officials who recognized the deficiencies of the data continued to use the system because it was the "only available source of reliability and maintainability information" in the service.[43]

Commanders and their staffs who are held accountable for the status of their forces are faced with a more insidious problem. They have to put themselves under the gun because in estimating the readiness of their units, they are implicitly grading their own performance as managers. So "self-reporting is not necessarily accurate reporting."[44] Republican critics of the Carter administration cited such problems in the 1st Tactical Air Wing at Langley Air Force Base during the Near East crisis of 1980:

This unit, the most prestigious fighter unit in the air force and one of the first U.S.-based units slated to go to Europe or the Middle

East in an emergency, was reporting that it was operationally ready. Nonetheless, a surprise inspection found that only 35 percent of its aircraft were actually mission-capable; that is, the unit was fifteen percentage points below the C-3 standard.[45]

Attempts to quantify readiness can produce artificial or misleading results if the categories used fail to capture the whole picture. Realizing this, the services (except the navy) have allowed commanders to change the rating up or down by one notch if their on-scene grasp of the situation suggests that the data do not reflect reality. In theory, their self-interest could bias the results in either direction: newly arrived commanders would have an interest in a poor rating, as a baseline from which they could later claim improvement, and as grounds for obtaining additional resources; commanders nearing the end of their tours would have an interest in a high rating, to demonstrate their managerial success.[46]

In practice, the dominant tendency seems to be to inflate ratings. Army and marine officials interviewed by GAO analysts said that commanders' subjective changes were usually upgrades, and in 1983 congressional investigators surveying reports for active army units for more than a year revealed that *"not one unit shows an increase in USR rating without a commander's subjective upgrade."*[47] Although the navy at this time did not allow subjective judgments, GAO investigators maintained that reported readiness of that service's tactical air forces also tended to be inflated.[48]

Most pointedly, major discrepancies emerged between the USR C-ratings reported for some Army National Guard units and their actual status when called up after Iraq invaded Kuwait. As leading members of the House Armed Services committee discovered:

One guard hospital unit arrived at the mobilization station rated C-2 and, therefore, supposedly deployable. It had more than 80 percent of its authorized personnel. The problem was that it had none of the 12 *doctors* required by the unit.

One brigade reported itself to be C-2 overall despite being short 179 mechanics.

Each unit assessed its own ratings under pressure to inflate ratings to make unit performance look better. Several of the officers interviewed . . . said higher headquarters inflated their ratings before sending them on to Washington.[49]

According to folklore among field grade officers, practices that inflate readiness have been around a long time, and they do not seem to have changed. Examples abound in professional journals. In the late 1980s a navy captain charged, "The surface force is notorious for loading a ship undergoing inspection with supplies and operational equipment stripped from sister ships, suggesting a willingness to substitute inspection scores for real readiness."[50] A retired army colonel complained at the end of the 1970s that his service focused too much on insignificant short-term statistical indicators, and he recounted testimony from other officers about dishonest reporting.[51] Earlier in the 1970s an air force officer complained of rampant dishonesty in the rating system, noting numerous examples of falsified reports or devices found by maintenance and supply officers to circumvent norms. The latter observer described the typical fate of subordinates who provide commanders with unwelcome news about readiness.

[They are] grilled unmercifully, berated, coerced, and finally tossed out with the admonishment to come back . . . next week or next month with the problem cured. Guess what? The staff officer dutifully returns at the appointed time and the problem is better. The senior officer looks over the "good" reports and congratulates himself on his management ability.[52]

This phenomenon may reflect excessive standards for readiness imposed by superiors as much as self-serving corruption among those reporting. Because management information systems establish goals in terms of fixed percentages of training accomplished or aircraft available, which may not necessarily have much to do with mission accomplishment, "it becomes a game to beat the system."[53] The problems are akin to those faced by managers who struggled to meet production quotas in a planned economy.[54]

There are potential solutions to these problems, but they, too, have their limitations. Self-serving reporting can be avoided by relying on disinterested inspections (such as the one that caught the 1st Tactical Air Wing up short in 1980), as long as practices that defeat inspection purposes, such as the borrowing from sister ships noted above, are forbidden. Substituting inspections for *all* self-reporting, however, would require either a vast reduction in the data compiled or a vast new horde of inspectors. In any case, routinized inspections may not eliminate all self-serving subjectivity; they may even turn it in the opposite direction. Inspection regimens create an incentive to gear efforts to passing tests, which are not always consistent with rounded training.[55] Inspectors, by virtue of their mission, also have an incentive to find fault, thus deflating readiness in their reports.[56]

The conflict between individual self-interest and accuracy could be reduced by delinking individual performance evaluations from unit management systems, that is, not judging the commander or staff officer by the quantitative readiness data for the units in their charge. But how else should success in handling a unit be judged? Such a change could also entail a different cost: there would be less incentive for commanders to achieve inventive efficiency and to get more readiness out of a given amount of resources.

Another alternative is to rely more heavily on major exercises: to test unit status, but also to test the utility of models and indices used to estimate it. Some exercises reveal glaring and unanticipated deficiencies (as Nifty Nugget did in 1978), and others show the system to be in better shape than expected (as Coronet Warrior did a decade later).[57] Major exercises are very expensive, however, and cannot be held frequently. They also drain readiness while testing it. Exercises are vital for periodic investigation, but not as a day-to-day monitoring device. In the post–cold war era of lower defense spending and increased emphasis on mobilization readiness over structural readiness, other priorities will constrain this option even more.

Blurry Boundaries

However difficult it may be to aggregate readiness data, political decisions must be made. The trouble is that those who must make them do not have many sources to draw on for thorough and disinterested analysis of readiness. Since the relevant data are by and large classified, nongovernmental analysts cannot undertake comprehensive assessments; at the same time, most research contractors or governmental analysts like those in the General Accounting Office are usually asked to deal with limited aspects of the problem on an ad hoc basis. The annual force readiness report (FRR) to Congress, for example, listed indicators but did not usually put them together in a composite judgment or draw direct conclusions about how resource inputs yield readiness outputs. The FRR developed into a multivolume exercise, which was more than anyone in Congress or all but the most intrepid staffers could digest.[58]

Political decisions must be based on broad pictures or limited collections of data. The higher the political level, the simpler the yardsticks used to reach the decision. One simple set of yardsticks comes from the division of general appropriations into categories for procurement or investment, which relate primarily to structural readiness, or for operations and maintenance (O&M) or operations and support (O&S), which relate primarily to operational readiness. Most procurement expenditures have long lead times; for some weapons, many years elapse between the initial funding and final fielding of the completed system. O&M funds—for things like depot repairs, modifications, operations, and training—are usually expended within six months of allocation.[59] On balance, focusing on O&M or O&S as the general measures may be the least unsatisfactory basis for shorthand judgment of resources devoted to operational readiness. Several distortions, however, are latent in the breakdown.

One problem is that although the breakdown of totals in O&M and procurement should offer the best basis for charting trends over a period of years, the allocation of data between the categories is not consistent from year to year. That is, the data points connected by lines on a graph may represent collections of apples and oranges. Published budget figures in 1988, for example, suggested that O&M funding had grown 35 percent since 1980, but that figure included numerous programs—costing $4.3 billion in fiscal 1987—that had "migrated" to the O&M account from elsewhere (for example, funds for the evaluation of nuclear propulsion systems went from R&D to O&M in the navy's accounts). These migratory funds apparently accounted for a fifth of the advertised percentage growth of O&M.[60] In a more recent example, the Clinton administration's initial defense budget requested a 1 percent real increase in O&M. This involved funding for new initiatives that had little to do with readiness, however, such as $888 million in aid to the former USSR, and funds from other accounts were transferred to O&M. The air force claimed that the shift in accounting masked an actual cut of 2.6 percent in its O&M budget.[61]

In principle, this problem could be rectified by more consistent categorization, but in practice it would be difficult to enforce the standards. Since military technology, organization, and the number and types of activities do not stand still, budget categories cannot be frozen. The norms themselves would be difficult to establish since terms of reference change over the same periods of time that administration policies or constraints also change. The best hope is that whatever inconsistencies prove irremediable for these reasons, they will turn out to be a marginal proportion of the total figure and thus an insignificant distortion.

A second problem is that funds properly categorized as expenditures for operational readiness in the appropriations process may wind up being spent for purposes that should really be counted as investment. Sometimes the purposes are fairly innocent, as in a case from the mid-1980s of local commanders who used O&M funds to buy automatic data processing equipment.[62] More suspect was the use of O&M funds for the construction of military sites in Honduras, also in the mid-1980s. In theory, U.S. troops who deployed periodically to that country in those years were engaged only in exercises, not based permanently, and money for exercises could not legally be spent for permanent installations unless specifically appropriated for that purpose.[63] This sort of activity may be questionable as a matter of policy or law, but the total funds involved are also probably a minor part of the total funds involved in comparisons of resources allocated to readiness and investment. When such nickel-and-dime distortions are added to others, however, their cumulative impact on the reliability of general data can be significant.

Additional distortions arise from the fact that the O&M appropriations category includes items that at first glance seem to belong more in the procurement account, while procurement in turn includes items whose main function seems to be to support operational readiness or sustainability. This would not be a problem if common sense could be applied and the categories revised to reassign the apparently misplaced items to the correct overall account. The functions of some of the items in question, however, are too broad or ambiguous to permit a consensus about which category they belong in; indeed, they contribute to both structural and operational readiness in ways that are hard to disentangle.[64]

Is the construction of a maintenance hangar, or aircraft shelters, or hardened support and command and control facilities a matter of investment (where these programs usually show up in the accounts) or combat readiness (which is what the programs produce)? How should legislators count statistics that lump backlogs in depot maintenance (the repair of vehicles with combat or direct support functions) and real property maintenance (the removal of asbestos, fixing roofs, painting barracks)? The decay of buildings seems to have little to do with near-term combat potential, yet spokesmen like NATO Supreme Commander General Bernard Rogers and Deputy Secretary of Defense William H. Taft argued strongly that the morale and combat capabilities of forces are affected by the quality of facilities in which they work and live.[65] Army sociological studies have also found that policies that promote family stability correlate closely with the combat readiness of units.[66]

Rationales of this kind tend to stretch the point and cloak it in the flag of current readiness in order to legitimize unglamorous elements of long-term investment. At the same time, some major procurement programs with big price tags are seldom cited as readiness expenditures but should be. Airlift and fast sealift assets, for example, offer little in the way of long-term combat potential. They may even detract from it, since the funds could be spent on larger numbers of weapons or troops that could be moved at a leisurely pace in multiple trips by smaller fleets of ships and transport planes. The only justification for spending a great deal on fast lift is to increase the immediate availability of combat forces at the scene of action. This logic could be extended to an extreme, counting the cost of foreign base networks as readiness expenditures. They allow the United States to project forces at long ranges quickly, rather than waiting for months or years to obtain access abroad and build and consolidate logistical infrastructures before moving into large-scale combat, as occurred in the Pacific in World War II.

So where should policymakers draw the line in allocating different categories of expenditure to different dimensions of readiness? Any arbitrary line might suffice as long as it was widely understood and consistently used over many years so that trends in the data could be tracked clearly. But the obstacles to such analytical consistency cannot be legislated away.

Trends at the End of the Cold War

Even if policymakers cannot have confidence in the data, they must still make judgments. The best they can do is rely on the least misleading compilations. If doubts about data can be put aside, which compilations are most relevant? This chapter concludes by illustrating how different general categories of data can foster different impressions of the overall state of military readiness. Such impressions, more than the judgments of specialists with green eyeshades, are what inspired the political debate about readiness in the last decade of the cold war.

Basic Measures

It is easier to evaluate changes in the structural readiness of forces than in their operational readiness because personnel and pieces of equipment can be counted with less ambiguity than their respective level of training or working order or their functional interdependence can be assessed. By the latter part of the Reagan administration there was clearly more structural readiness than under Carter, as the intense modernization and modest expansion of forces was being completed. The growth in costs of obtaining manpower without conscription and of obtaining weaponry of ever increased sophistication can easily be seen by comparing two bird's-eye views of the military in the late 1960s and at the end of the cold war. The military budget for fiscal 1989 was about the same in real terms as it had been twenty years earlier, at the height of the Vietnam War. The size of the 1989 force in terms of men and weapons, however, was far smaller than in 1969: the army had only about half of the manpower (772,000 versus 1.5 million); the navy had 580 ships, including 14 carriers, compared with 890 ships and 22 carriers; the air force had 22,000 pilots and 9,300 planes versus 41,000 and 14,000. Combat aircraft cost 59 percent more in 1989, and naval combat ships cost 46 percent more.[67]

Broad comparisons of this kind do not indicate the extent to which the higher quality of modern weapons or changes in uncounted dimensions such as logistics compensate for the reduced quantity of hardware and personnel. Yet there is no simple, generally accepted alternative to such crude "bean counts" to provide an overall impression of change. Analysts offer more complex units of account, or models for simulating combat capacity. Such methods of calculation are opaque to policymaking generalists, who may not even notice them. Moreover, among analysts there is no consensus about which of the more sophisticated approaches is the most valid.

When experts cannot agree about the accuracy of analytical conventions, the terms of reference for high-level decisionmaking will most likely be those about which there is least doubt. As inadequate as simple bean counts may be, there is little debate about the data; numbers of personnel and weapons can be counted objectively, while their quality or effectiveness must be estimated in a more subjective manner. Thus if any characterizations of change in force structure are likely to inform decisions at a high level, they will probably be broad ones such as those outlined above.

The problems are much bigger when it comes to assessing general changes in operational readiness. First, although there is a broad consensus on what basic factors should be used to measure structural readiness (namely, totals of manpower, weapons, and units), there is no such agreement on what indices provide the best measure of operational readiness. Second, even when indices of operational readiness are identified, the basis for counting is unclear. Structural bean counts deal with a few variables (the number of personnel or weapon platforms in a force). Measures of operational readiness (for example, unit ratings, equipment and personnel fills, training, and sustainability) each comprise numerous components whose status varies widely from day to day as individuals enter and leave service or rotate between positions; as equipment is delivered, repaired, or discarded; and as units exercise or stand down. Third, even when one can measure status within the various categories, it is hard to estimate their net effect. For example, if training is up but maintenance down, is readiness up or down? What if company-level training is up 30 percent while battalion-level training is down 20 percent? *Disaggregated data are less likely to be distorted, but they provide a weaker basis for conclusions. Aggregated data are more relevant in principle but less reliable in practice.* Since relevance is the test for policy, and hope in analytical progress springs eternal, policymakers will almost always focus their attention on aggregated data.

The alternative to trying to pin down fluid and conflicting outputs is to look at trends in aggregated measures over time. The simplest of these, and the closest equivalent to bean counts in terms of accepted reliability of the data, are the budgetary categories of O&M or O&S. The pitfalls of accepting trends in these accounts as an index of operational readiness were explored above and are comparable to the dangers of taking bean counts as measures of capability. But, as with bean counts, there may be no other presentations of the data that are simple enough to command a consensus on facts and serve as the currency of political debate. It can be useful to compare O&M accounts over time, but these accounts are at best measures of *effort*, not results. Impressions of results can only be gotten from specific ratings of unit or weapon system status.

Snapshots of Results

Readiness statistics are impossible to compare systematically in an open publication because the data are usually declassified only in sporadic clumps. Some selected snapshots of five general categories, however, can show how both good and bad data about operational readiness could be cited within short spans of time in the closing phase of the cold war.

ON UNITS. Air force spokesmen in the mid-1980s could report a steady decline in both the number and percentage of units rated C-4 (not ready for combat) and an increase in the number of C-1 and C-2 units, while critics could report an increase in the number and percentage of C-3 (marginally ready) units, all because the total number of units grew. The army could boast that the number of units meeting or exceeding their authorized level of organization (ALO) had increased, while critics could fasten on the other fact that the overall ALO requirements had been reduced, with a trend toward more ALO-2 and fewer ALO-1 units mandated in the structure.[68]

ON EQUIPMENT. In 1988 the services reported that mission capable rates for all sorts of aircraft had increased markedly since the beginning of the decade, but that there were only slight improvements or even slight declines for ground force equipment. In the navy, three quarters of surface ships were materially ready at the end of the 1980s, up from half at the beginning of the decade. After 1987, however, ships awaiting overhaul gradually increased because of funding shortages.[69]

ON PERSONNEL. For most of the 1980s good recruitment results and the concentration of army improvements in equipment modernization rather than expansion of the size of the force kept manpower from being a problem. Administration witnesses regularly bragged about great success in enlisting personnel of high quality and retaining more of them than in previous years. The trade-off between the growth in force structure and operational readiness, however, was still to be seen. In 1984 administration figures showed that "programmed struc-

ture" for the military services (the number of personnel slots necessary to fill all military units and organizations) had outstripped "programmed manning" (the number of those billets actually slated to be
filled). Assistant Secretary of Defense Lawrence Korb testified that the
difference created "about a 1% reduction in the percent of the structure that will be manned in FY 85 relative to FY 83," but the 1 percent
change in the total meant an absolute increase of more than 25,000
unfilled billets. On the other hand, Korb cited an improvement in the
balancing of qualifications with billets, as overstaffed occupations were
reduced. Over- and understaffed occupations combined went down
from 7.7 percent in fiscal 1983 to 5.5 percent in fiscal 1985.[70]

By later in the decade the situation had changed more clearly, in
part because the cumulative increase in manning requirements as a
result of the structural expansion in earlier years coincided with a
reduction of the defense budget total. The reduction led the Defense
Department and Congress to target manpower as the simplest source
of savings. Over the first six years of the Reagan administration, when
aggregate funding was going up, Congress had provided 58,000 additional personnel for the navy, about two-thirds of the increments
requested. By 1987 the service claimed it would require another 33,000
over the next four years, a period of prospective stasis or decline in
the size of the financial pie. By 1988 the administration budget called
for military manpower cuts of 34,000 in one year, including almost
9,000 in the army, the service that had benefited least during the
Reagan buildup. Looking for offsetting evidence in favor of operational
readiness in all this, however, one could cite plans to increase armor
training in the army at the same time strength was declining, or plans
to cut equipment purchases and demobilize formations in order to
keep active ones at full strength. The commandant of the Marine Corps
proclaimed the latter alternative as his preference, and navy officials
broached the possibility of mothballing ships as the prospective response to the manpower crunch.[71]

ON TRAINING. Critics could point to specific indices by which training was slighted—for example, declines in the absolute number of
flying hours or training days at some points in the mid-1980s—and
these were indeed cited, even by presidential candidate Michael
Dukakis. For the most part, however, training was one area in which
it was easiest to make the case that the military was serious about

operational readiness, especially in the army. That service presented data showing consistent increases after 1980 in battalion training days, flying hours, money for reserve component training, overseas deployment training for the National Guard and Reserve, and the number of battalions cycled through the National Training Center at Fort Irwin (which provides the ultimate in realistic tactical and operational instruction and exercises for select units). Some indices declined. For example, operating tempo for tanks was reduced by 15 percent and then 20 percent between fiscal 1984 and 1990, but such reductions were partly offset by the increased use of high-tech battle-training simulators, which was reported in all of the services. The air force also increased "Red Flag" activity (the program code name for exercises simulating combat with Soviet pilots) by a third after 1980. In 1989 the army absorbed its budget cut by trimming modernization and military construction in order to keep giving high priority to training.[72]

ON SUSTAINABILITY. The good news in the mid-1980s was that most of the trends were in the upward direction; the bad news was that actual levels of stocks remained lower than officially estimated requirements even after a cumulative increase of more than 50 percent in the total defense budget, and there was no prospect of meeting requirements in out-years, *even if the total budget continued to increase.* The uncertain news was what these two facts really meant, since stipulated requirements kept changing.

On the first point, exemplary data included the Reagan administration's rough doubling of the share of the defense budget going to sustainability and increases of 50 percent and 250 percent, respectively, in air force and navy munitions stockpiles by 1986. Ground force munitions stockpiles also increased, but by smaller amounts (about 20 percent for the army, a bit less than 50 percent for the marines).[73] On the second point, a Joint Chiefs of Staff logistical game indicated that stocks were sufficient only "to fight one war, in Korea, and this for only a limited time."[74] The 1983 House Appropriations Committee staff study painted the situation pessimistically, even for that limited situation:

To overcome the shortage problem, U.S. and ROK forces are expected to conserve ammunition by exercising a controlled rate of fire. . . . This conservation measure is to be employed against an enemy whose tactics rely on mass formation and continuous attacking waves of troops. One artillery commander commenting on his presently authorized basic ammunition load (3 days) said that he fired that amount in less than one day in Vietnam.[75]

Defense Department figures near the end of the first Reagan administration placed the services' munitions sustainability in terms of proportion of procurement objectives at around three-fourths for the army, just over a fifth for the navy, a little under a third for the air force, and just under half for the marines. At that time even the *projections*, which assumed uninterrupted real growth in the military budget, estimated that by 1990—more than a decade after defense spending began rising—none of the services but the Marine Corps would reach its complete objective for munitions sustainability, and both the navy and air force would still be close to a third short.[76]

By 1987 data were, as usual, mixed. On the positive side, all the services had improved their percentage of requirements objectives in munitions sustainability; annual funding in that category had begun to decline (since the defense budget as a whole declined after 1985), but at less than the annual rate at which it had risen during the expansionary phase; and cross-decking of naval ordnance had declined substantially. On the negative side, there were still serious gaps between official objectives and actual inventories. The Central Command, which is generally considered to be the collection of conventional forces that should be the most ready of all (recall its origins as the Rapid Deployment Force), did not even have as much as half of its stipulated requirement in *any* of four categories of sustainability (supplies and equipment, POL, and two categories of munitions). And Chief of Staff John Wickham said that the army in general had supplies for three months of combat, but that after that there would be a nine-month gap until U.S. industries could begin delivering weapons to replace losses.[77]

But wait a minute. Once again one must ask how much can such figures really mean? Are "requirements" really requirements? They are slippery, not solid, estimates, and the frequent changes in them are cause for skepticism. In extreme cases such as the army's multiple launch rocket system, estimated requirements have *doubled* in a single year. From 1982 to 1989 "the requirements for half of the munitions items varied by more than 23 percent of their average level."[78] Moreover, Chief of Staff Wickham's uneasiness about having only three months of combat stocks brings up the larger question of readiness for what? U.S. allies in Europe in that period had stocks much *lower* than those of U.S. forces, in part because they preferred a strategic doctrine relying on the threat of nuclear escalation rather than prolonged conventional war. What good would it have done for the United States to raise its own stocks to meet objectives that the allies did not believe in?

Trends in Overall Effort

With regard to the aggregated measures of effort, there are various ways to characterize salient trends. During Ronald Reagan's years in office, O&S accounts grew at an average annual rate of about 2 percent, as compared with about 7 percent for investment. Over this course, O&S's share of the total defense budget declined from 63 to 55 percent. (Within these O&S totals, the decrease in personnel's budget share was about double the decrease in O&M's share.)[79] In the Reagan budget plan for the 1980s the average ratio of O&S to investment costs (1.19) was more than a third lower than it had been in the 1970s (1.87).[80]

A different compilation (see table 4-2) that includes procurement related to operational readiness—spare parts, munitions, and some support equipment—suggests only slightly less disparity in relative effort: closer to a 3 percent average annual increase for the readiness budget, and a 6 percent increase for modernization and investment. In the expansionary phase of fiscal 1980–85, the Defense Department budget authority increased by more than half and modernization and investment by more than nine-tenths, but operational readiness spending by only a third. In the fiscal 1985–89 phase of decline, on the other hand, the pattern was reversed: budget authority fell at more than twice the rate of operational readiness spending, and modernization and investment decreased at more than three times the rate. (In two of those years, fiscal 1987 and 1989, operational readiness funding went up, whereas the budget total and procurement funds went down.) By fiscal 1989, after four years of gradual decline following the big expansion, total defense budget authority stood at a third more than the fiscal 1980 amount, expenditures for modernization were up somewhat less than two-thirds, and the readiness funding level was just over a fourth more than at the beginning of the decade. Cumulatively, therefore, structural readiness outstripped operational readiness by these measures.

It was at this time, however, as Gorbachev's reforms in the USSR

TABLE 4-2. *Department of Defense Budget Trends and Priorities, 1980–89*[a]
Percentage change

Budget category	Period		
	1980–85	1985–89	1980–89
DOD budget authority	+52.9	−10.8	+36.4
	(+8.9)	(−2.8)	(+3.7)
Investment[b]	+92.0	−15.8	+61.6
	(+14.1)	(−4.2)	(+6.0)
Readiness[c]	+33.3	−5.1	+26.5
	(+5.9)	(−1.2)	(+2.7)

Source: Calculated from data in Lawrence J. Korb and Stephen Daggett, "The Defense Budget and Strategic Planning on a New Plateau," in Stephen Daggett and others, *The Military Budget on a New Plateau: Strategic Choices for the 1990s* (Committee for National Security, 1988), pp. 13–14. This table shows the changes from the last cold war buildup, beginning late in the Carter administration, to the end of the cold war. From the buildup's peak in 1985 until fiscal 1993, the defense budget fell about 30 percent in real terms and "the portion devoted to military procurement fell more than 50 percent." Les Aspin, *Report of the Secretary of Defense to the President and the Congress: January 1994* (Department of Defense, January 1994), p. 93.

a. Figures in parentheses are annual averages.

b. Includes modernization, R&D, and military construction.

c. Includes O&M, personnel, family housing, and readiness-related procurement (spares, munitions, selected support equipment).

were gathering momentum, that the probability of a secular change in U.S. defense policy began to sink in. What became clear within the next few years was that these trends in marginal emphasis on investment or operational readiness would not be fixed in the normal manner of incremental shifts in funding, but that a basic shakeup in planning assumptions and the budgeting base was under way.

These sorts of problems were never of much interest to anyone but gnomes in green eyeshades. The end of the cold war and reversal of the consensus in favor of military readiness makes them seem even more arcane. They make it easier to understand the political controversies discussed in chapter 5, however, because of the simple point they illustrate. By the end of the cold war, sensitivity to the importance of readiness had peaked and compilations of relevant data had proliferated. Yet, after years of dealing with the question, experts were no closer to a consensus on what was being achieved. If the experts could not clear up what was going on, it would be no surprise if politicians muddied the issue even more.

5

Readiness as a Political Football: Proclaiming Priorities and Evading Choices

*P*OLITICAL LEADERS have always genuflected to military readiness, but it was rarely a major issue in peacetime. By the latter part of the cold war, however, it became the subject of a high-profile controversy. Nearly everyone in the executive and Congress agreed that readiness was a high priority in principle and then proceeded to attack each other for not doing the right things to provide it in practice.

These controversies were imbued with both confusion and dissimulation, as is common in politics. In contrast to the analytical problems surveyed in chapter 4, the political problem was due not so much to the complexity of measuring readiness as it was to the confusion about concepts. The controversies in the Carter and Reagan administrations demonstrated the reluctance of soldiers, bureaucrats, and politicians to face trade-offs and to admit that readiness could rarely be boosted in one respect without limiting it in another. The mistake was in arguing about readiness in general, rather than about readiness for when, for what, or of what. In particular, confusion resulted from the reluctance of conservatives to admit that improving structural readiness posed a cost to operational readiness and the reluctance of liberals to admit that readiness consisted of more than operational efficiency.

The Politicization of Readiness

When the term "readiness" was used by critics on the right, it often embraced all aspects of military capability, structural and operational. This was consistent with the blanket indictment of the Nixon, Ford, and Carter administrations for the alleged "decade of neglect" in the 1970s.[1] The choice between emphasizing consumption (operational readiness) or investment (structural readiness) could be ignored because the large projected budget increases in the Reagan administration obscured the trade-off; choices never seem as exacting when the pie is growing. Critics on the left more often used the term in the narrow professional sense of operational readiness, contrasting it with modernization and force structure. This usage allowed them to be *for* military readiness without promoting huge defense budget increases, since spare parts or other day-to-day elements of operational readiness had lower price tags than the big-ticket weapons procurement programs. Critics on that side could question appropriating funds for some of these items by demanding "first things first," namely, that already existing forces be brought up to par before new ones were added.

Partisan Criticism

Readiness problems drew a certain amount of publicity throughout the postwar period, even when domestic support for high levels of military effort had waned. General Accounting Office investigations of army units in 1972 and 1977, for example, received some attention, the latter of which led Senator John Culver to speak of "the readiness crisis."[2] In that year Congress passed Public Law 95-79, which required the Defense Department to provide an annual force readiness report (FRR). It was the intensification of the U.S.-Soviet conflict after the events of 1979 in the Near East, however, that made readiness an ongoing issue rather than a fleeting story. The invasion of Afghanistan—following closely on the Iranian revolution, the occupation of the U.S. embassy in Tehran, and the sacking of embassies in Tripoli and Islamabad—had a galvanizing effect similar to that of the North Korean attack in 1950. The general crisis heightened debate about the aggregate size of military forces, or structural readiness. Particular events such as the disaster of the Desert One hostage rescue attempt crystallized anxiety about operational readiness.

Jimmy Carter's opponents fastened on both issues, but without differentiating them or recognizing that the two forms of readiness were in competition with each other. In contrast to the situation three decades earlier, when the North Korean attack revolutionized defense policy, the United States now had a large military establishment. Although critics pushed for increases in the size of forces, there was no thought of tripling the overall effort, as was done between 1950 and

1953. Because of the high existing baseline of structural readiness, the sharpest criticism focused on gaps in the operational readiness of the existing forces.

As the presidential campaigns accelerated in the summer and fall of 1980, a chorus of horror stories about readiness shortfalls resounded throughout the press around the country. The *New York Times* reported Army Chief of Staff Edward C. Meyer's concern about the "hollow army" and the anxiety of others that only six of the navy's 13 aircraft carriers and 94 of its 155 air squadrons were rated ready for combat; the *Baltimore Sun* reported the complaints of numerous officers about program cuts, including planned reductions of ammunition stocks from ninety to thirty days, and war reserve stocks from thirty to fifteen days; the *Washington Post* said that half of all combat aircraft were unready because funds were being used to procure the planes themselves; the *Pittsburgh Press* reported that F-15s had "only a day-and-a-half supply of air-to-air missiles"; the *Norfolk Virginian-Pilot* told of a spot check on an F-14 unit that showed less than half the planes were mission capable; and the *Daily Oklahoman* described readiness deficiencies of all sorts.[3] A former Republican secretary of defense together with a soon-to-be assistant secretary published a study with a litany of shortages and deficiencies, reporting among other things that a third of all combat units in the military were not ready to fight, almost another third were officially rated only marginally ready, and half of all aircraft carriers were unready, while only one lacked major deficiencies.[4]

The administration responded by explaining that the rating system exaggerated unreadiness, but it was soon buffeted by charges of keeping embarrassing data from Congress and attempting to corrupt the rating system.[5] Congress had already picked up the ball, holding hearings on the subject. Defensive administration testimony on the subject pointed to the 1976 baseline of operational readiness, the situation just before Carter took office, which made the data look favorable by comparison. Such statistics for the Carter period included a reduction in the number of ships awaiting overhaul, from sixty-eight in 1976 to fewer than twenty; the approaching elimination of navy and air force repair backlogs; investment in new training centers; increased exercises and flying hours for air force and navy pilots; steaming increases of 10–40 percent for navy fleets; higher capacity for rapid reinforcement of NATO; increases in ammunition storage; and plans for more pre-positioned equipment in Europe.[6] The administration also directed the services to emphasize the readiness of existing weapons over the procurement of new ones in the 1982 budget.[7] By this time, however, it was impossible to prevent the political inflammation of the issue. In a special set of hearings in September, for example, Republican representative Marjorie Holt browbeat a hapless witness about it.

> Mrs. HOLT: Have we closed that gap here, that readiness gap, have we? Yes or no?
> General CAMPBELL: There are mission areas—
> Mrs. HOLT: Yes or no?
> General CAMPBELL: We know how ready we are.
> Mrs. HOLT: Yes or no. Are we ready?
> General CAMPBELL: We are ready in some of our plans and some of our missions.
> Mrs. HOLT: We are not ready and you know you are not and everybody else knows we are not.[8]

After Reagan accelerated the military buildup that Carter had begun, the ousted Democrats gave the new "ins" some of their own medicine. During the 1982 elections, for example, the sourcebook produced by a Democratic party group advised congressional candidates to mention the Reagan program's penchant for "hardware over readiness," and the Republican majority's rejection of amendments offered by Democratic senators to fund more ammunition procurement and naval steaming time.[9] The question of a readiness crunch due to competing investment priorities drew some comment in the press, but did not attract much attention until the next presidential campaign year.[10]

Caspar Weinberger began 1984 with a report to Congress ticking off the old list of readiness problems under Carter and claiming great successes in remedying them. His assistant secretary for manpower, installations, and logistics, however, had to send him a seven-page memo warning of "serious" army equipment shortages that would "not get fixed very quickly with the level of funding now projected," air force consumption of war reserves for training and prospective readiness below air force objectives for the coming four years, unfinanced maintenance backlogs, and underfunding of spare parts procurement across the services. "We must recognize that all of our readiness-related programs are not fully funded," Lawrence Korb told

FIGURE 5-1

Weinberger, "despite our pronouncements about the high priority we accord to readiness."[11] The voluminous 1983 House Appropriations Committee staff report and other information on readiness problems were publicized in long press stories in mid-1984 and resurrected by Democratic critics in the election season.[12] At the height of the campaign, Senator Carl Levin publicized embarrassing points such as the statement by Admiral William Crowe, then commander in chief, Pacific, that after almost four years of Reagan defense budgets, "We currently have critical shortages" of support items and spares.[13]

The Democrats linked the holes in operational readiness directly to the magnitude of the Reagan defense buildup, making the case that the money was being spent inefficiently and was producing a flabby military rather than an agile one (see the cartoon in figure 5-1). The administration counterattacked with a report detailing improvements in readiness (emphasizing overall capability more than operational readiness per se)[14] and speeches by Secretary of Defense Weinberger charging that critics' claims about readiness would weaken deterrence by encouraging enemies to underestimate American capability.[15]

Democrats in Congress, still feeling the sting of 1980, gave administration witnesses a hard time, especially when they raised the possibility of revising data in ways that the officials argued would be more accurate but that skeptical legislators charged would be self-serving. Senator Sam Nunn reminded the army chief of staff that "a lot of the 1980 campaign was fought on the readiness of our forces," and shortly later warned him, "if you change your whole readiness ratings right in the middle of this [1984] election . . . you'd better have a good press conference." When the chief argued that the current rating method was wrong, Senator Levin shot back, "What you're telling the American people is 4 years too late."[16] The issue became so highly charged that political sensitivity permeated the chain of command. In March General Richard Cavazos, head of Forces Command, complained in a message to the army chief of staff: "Seemingly boundless consumption of flying hours and other aviation resources in support of unprogrammed training exercises in Central America is a significant and growing concern. . . . The political ramifications of a further 'readiness' drop prior to the elections are self-evident."[17]

The political fisticuffs over readiness became a dispute over data as legislators and executives argued about what the facts were and how they should be handled. Levin and Korb sparred over data on army training days, air force flying hours, Marine Corps exercises, and over which statistical nuggets told the real story. Senator Nunn, however, was particularly miffed by the administration's fast-and-loose standards for which data should be released to the public, and in what form. He excoriated the administration's witness for complaining that figures indicating readiness slides in the army and air force had been improperly leaked, while the administration had handed the press more dubious figures that cast a better light on the situation.[18]

Readiness remained a political issue after 1984, and more and more a matter of statistical gamesmanship. Administration representatives presented rafts of data showing upward changes in readiness.[19] Yet in the 1988 presidential campaign Governor Michael Dukakis still argued against procuring so many new weapon systems "when we haven't got fuel for our tanks in Europe, when the air force is now complaining that they can't get spare parts and maintenance, when they haven't got enough flight time for their pilots."[20] The 1992 election was the first in sixteen years in which military readiness was not raised as a campaign issue. After Bill Clinton came into office, however, Republicans began to take up the issue again. In 1993 Senator John McCain asked for detailed data on readiness from all of the services.[21]

Institutional Conflict

For more than half of the cold war a divided government made it difficult to distinguish between partisan and institutional grounds of conflict. With opposite parties controlling the presidency and Congress, the grounds overlapped. The differences between the executive function of formulating and submitting the budget and the congressional function of ruling on it, or between the evaluations of authorization committees in Congress and the allocation of specific funds by appropriations committees, nevertheless complicate the controversy over who really promoted or blocked the emphasis on operational readiness.

Since the principle of readiness was a sacred cow, no one wanted to accept responsibility for hurting it. The services and the administration tended to blame Congress for not funding the readiness that its members then complained was missing. Just before the 1984 election year flare-up, for example, Congress cut administration requests for naval manpower, causing fill levels to fall from 87 to 83 percent. Shortly after the controversy of 1984 the navy asked for an increase of 15,000 personnel to man new ships but Congress provided only a third of that number; for the following year, fiscal 1987, the navy asked for 11,400, and got half.[22] When Senators Nunn and Levin complained about a decline in army spares and depot maintenance, Assistant Secretary Korb countered by pointing to the similar problem in the ammunition account. He cited previous cuts by Congress and said that the service was "reluctant to risk the moneys in this year's budget because if they put in for it and didn't get it, they would lose it. . . . This year they were saying let us put in what we will probably get."[23] In 1986, however, the administration's fiscal 1987 budget cut its own previous year's budget plan for 1987 purchases of spare parts by 32 percent for the army, 22 percent for the navy, and 39 percent for the air force.[24] And the following year Senator Alan J. Dixon berated the administration for sharp reductions in requested funding levels for readiness and sustainability programs "in the context of a defense budget that is projected to grow—to grow—by 3 percent in real terms each year for the next 5. This tells us something about the priority of readiness and sustainability programs . . . in the Department today."[25] Yet again a year later, in early 1988, Secretary of Defense Frank Carlucci complained, "Despite all the rhetoric on the Hill in support of readiness . . . look at the account in 1988 that was savaged the most. It was O and M [operations and maintenance]."[26]

Which side of the separation of powers had the real grounds for recrimination? *Both.* First, until the crises in the Near East just before the Reagan administration, Congress was not united in pushing more operational readiness expenditures; the appropriations committees tended to go harder on those accounts than complaints in the armed services committees would have led an observer to expect. By fiscal 1981 the House and Senate authorization committees had moved to bring O&M budgets under their review, and they established special subcommittees to examine readiness issues.[27]

The main point, however, is that *both the executive and legislative charges against each other were valid,* because the two sides were focusing on different things. The administration could criticize Congress for cutting funding requests for operational readiness because the administration budget request as a whole (including procurement, as well as readiness and sustainability) was for more across the board than Congress was granting. Congress could cut the *absolute* amount in administration readiness requests without making the cuts disproportionate to cuts in the budget as a whole. Congress could criticize the executive, however, for failing to give high enough relative priority to readiness accounts (compared with other parts of the budget). In short, the executive complained about insufficient *amounts* for readiness in the appropriations, and Congress complained about insufficient proportional *emphasis* for it in the budget.

This dispute over relative priorities is mirrored to some extent in the views on the executive side—among the military services, military commands, and civilian and military leadership in the Pentagon. In general, it is the civilians in the Defense Department, the chairman of the Joint Chiefs of Staff (JCS), and the commanders in chief (CINCs) of the unified and specified commands who are most concerned with operational readiness for war. The CINCs in particular have the responsibility for fighting a war should it occur. It is the services, on the other hand, that are most concerned with procurement and with longer-term, structural readiness. The services, however, had more influence on the formation of the defense budget, so it is not surprising that modernization and force structure usually wound up taking precedence, especially when the administration favored decentralized decisionmaking. In the early Reagan years, despite claims by administration leaders that readiness had *higher* priority than procurement, funds for modernization almost doubled, whereas those for readiness and sustainability went up only a third.[28]

Within a service, the constituency for operational readiness can be weakened by reorganization and by the patterns of interaction with outside bodies. Moreover, paradoxically, efforts to centralize control of some functions can weaken them. One account illustrates how these problems occurred in the army, and why a shift from "tail" to "teeth" eroded the support elements necessary for sustainability. With reorganizations in the 1950s and 1960s technical service functions previously handled by army organs themselves were absorbed by new separate bureaucracies (such as the Defense Supply Agency or Defense Communications Agency) that focused on "management of hardware rather than on integration of hardware with personnel, training and doctrine." The new agencies were primarily staffed by civilians who were unfamiliar with tactical support units in the old technical service organs.[29]

The changeover in 1962 led to the disappearance of mission focus, ironically, the reverse of Robert McNamara's general management objective. His planning, programming, and budgeting system (PPBS) led to three independent Defense Department systems for planning strategy, operations in war, and budget allocations. "In theory the systems mesh. In practice, however," argues John M. Vann, "they are nearly mutually exclusive." The JCS used the joint strategic planning system based "on a Panglossian vision of the future unconstrained by reality . . . with full knowledge that the forces [were] unaffordable," and they ignored logistics, concentrating instead on combat units. War planners used the joint operations planning system, which works within the confines of what is really available. "One might expect that their knowledge of today's shortfalls would then become the foundation for what DOD buys in the future. . . . Instead, because of a fear of compromise of war plan details, this information lies fallow in the Joint Staff . . . to avoid divulging to OSD what needs to be fixed."[30]

Staffers in the Office of the Secretary of Defense (OSD) were supposed to allocate resources through PPBS, but their information on strategy and plans came from the first, unrealistic JCS process, rather than scenarios geared more specifically to theaters, which the war planners use. Thus in this case McNamara's centralization led to less integration rather than more:

> The principal effect of using an unachievable scenario and set of assumptions in both strategic and resource planning is that it gives the services latitude to plan and fund any programs they choose and still remain within broad OSD planning and programming guidelines regardless of the real effect on individual CINC theater war plans. Thus, the Army can add more divisions instead of support forces and claim that it is getting closer to an unachievable goal, and who could argue against that?[31]

Beyond these organizational forces, larger political pressures worked in the same direction to "improve" the teeth-to-tail ratio, which led the Defense Department to place more and more support forces in the reserves.

To overcome obstacles to an emphasis on operational readiness, various proposals for the reform of defense organization in the mid-1980s recommended giving the CINCs a voice in budgeting. Others recommended upgrading the position of assistant secretary for reserve affairs, and still others promoted the more radical step of establishing a separate under secretary of defense for readiness, to give readiness partisans bureaucratic clout. The rationale for the new position was to remedy the dispersion of oversight of readiness concerns among several assistant secretaries, whose advice could only be integrated by the secretary or deputy secretary of defense, neither of whom has time to give the questions adequate review.[32] The position was ultimately instituted at the beginning of the Clinton administration.

A different reorganization, which had beneficial side effects for readiness, was the formation of the U.S. Transportation Command (TRANSCOM), to integrate air and sealift and ground transport. This enhanced coordination and planning of mass movements.[33] While coordination was a problem, the principal readiness problem in regard to lift capability for major war was that there was not enough of it. For TRANSCOM to help much in dealing with that aspect, other reforms providing more budgetary influence to CINCs would have had to proceed further.

Budget Trends and the Bias for Structure

When policymakers prefer to avoid hard choices, operational readiness can suffer coming or going. Whether the defense budget grew or shrank during the cold war, powerful incentives and illusions reinforced the priority accorded to investing in force structure and weapon modernization irrespective of rhetorical genuflections to the import of immediate combat readiness. This choice may have been sensible in bad budgetary times, since declining appropriations usually coincide with declining estimates of the danger of war. It is ironic, though, that in periods of budgetary expansion—which reflected a consensus about a heightened Soviet threat—immediate readiness for war did not receive greater emphasis.

Cycles and Squeezes

The primary incentive working against operational readiness is the desire to avoid losing hardware. In bad budgetary times that means hardware already in the inventory that might have to be junked or mothballed if funds are diverted to keep other systems more ready, or in good budgetary times it means hardware available for procurement that can expand the inventory. "When organizations experience budgetary feast," as Franklin Spinney has written, "they tend to add long-standing desires ('the wish list') to the items already being procured."[34]

This tendency to shortchange operational readiness, however, should not be overestimated; the pressures can sometimes work the other way. Unless radical measures are undertaken, such as grounding aircraft or mothballing ships, "operating costs are relatively uncontrollable in the short term because existing forces demand a certain level of support." In the second half of the 1970s, this combined with declining or level budgets and regular underestimates of operations and support (O&S) costs on the order of 2 percent to cause reductions in investment funding below what had been planned.[35] By many measures naval operational readiness in particular *increased* in the late 1970s.[36]

Overall, however, the squeeze is more likely to operate in the reverse direction. The principal excuse for favoring investment is that deficiencies in operational readiness will get fixed just a bit later. This would not be an illusion if defense budgets, once on the way up, kept going up, or leveled off for a long period without reversing course. This never happened in the cold war era. After the Korean War military spending declined in about as many years as it increased. Between fiscal years 1951 and 1989 budget authority grew in nineteen years and declined in nineteen, while outlays grew in twenty-one years and declined in seventeen. When wartime years (1951–53, 1965–73) are excluded, budget authority grew in fourteen of the peacetime years and shrank in thirteen, outlays grew in fifteen and went down in twelve. From 1951 to 1968 neither the phases of expansion nor those of shrinkage ever lasted more than three years. The phases were more extended in the 1970s and 1980s: seven years of decline after 1968, seven of growth after 1978, and finally a phase of decline lasting from 1985 until the end of the cold war. (The decline continued, of course, in the post–cold war era.)[37] For planners paying any attention to budgetary history during the cold war, one point should have stood out. Growth and decline in the defense budget were cyclical variations around a plateau established in the early 1950s. Over time, expansions and contractions balanced each other in a zig-zag pattern.

When the Reagan administration plotted defense procurement in the early 1980s, however, the five-year defense plans did not assume a zag in the out-years following the zig at the time they were locking in numerous contracts for the production of new weapon systems. By assuming indefinite growth in the budget, they could assume the availability of ample funds in the out-years to provide operating support for the hardware that would be stacking up. As a result, the emphasis in spending shifted more markedly toward investment, as opposed to accounts associated with operational readiness, than in previous peacetime. Before Reagan, variations in emphasis balanced out over time. Budget authority for operating accounts changed favorably compared with that for investment (meaning it grew more or declined less) in nine of the peacetime budget years and changed unfavorably in nine. From fiscal 1981 to 1989, however, the change in relative emphasis was favorable to operational readiness in only two years (1987 and 1989).

In the first Reagan administration the expansion of the pie of resources obscured the trade-off between structural and operational readiness in the near term: as long as more money could be allocated to *both* investment and O&M, the difference in emphasis could seem less important. Wishful thinking offered a way out of facing up to how the eventual budget downturn could make the initial emphasis on procurement damaging to operational readiness in the long term. Statements by some military leaders were quite striking in this respect. They did not evince ignorance of the past pattern of fluctuation. They seemed to think, however, that lectures to legislators on the importance of consistency might fend off the cyclical reduction in resources. The commander of the Atlantic Fleet, Admiral Frank Kelso, admitted that he would be willing to sacrifice a bit of operational readiness to get a larger fleet but said, "I must have reasonable readiness if you want us to carry out the missions. . . . It would be better, though, to have a smooth growth in funding. What we need is a long-term plan for defense spending that we can stick with rather than more cyclical funding."[38] Reflecting an implicit hope that the political process could be frozen, that sort of stance represented naïveté at best and irresponsibility at worst. The one way in which the administration's and military leadership's stance might seem less naive is if it was cynical—if they realized and accepted the priority of structural over operational readiness, even while denying to congressional critics or the media that they were making such a choice.

At first glance the error might seem negligible, if all the expensive bills for new hardware and force structure expansion could have been paid before the phase of budget expansion ended. Then, without major outlays for procurement, a level or even gracefully declining budget would have afforded appreciable funds for keeping the newly acquired equipment ready. To some extent this was indeed the logic in the plan, especially since there had to be some lag between acquisition costs and operating bills. Even this view of Reagan administration planning does not hold up well. As of early 1985, when the budgetary expansion was being capped, Defense Department projections envisioned a continuing steady growth in the percentage of defense spending for procurement, research, and development (from about a third in 1980 to nearly half in 1990) and a continuing decline in the proportion for O&M (from about a third in 1980 to barely more than a quarter in 1990). In absolute dollar amounts, the data showed modest but steady increases for O&M through the early 1980s, but these were dwarfed by the rate of increase for procurement.[39]

Even if planning for out-years had been more balanced, some problems would remain. That is because not all of the bills for procurement come due soon after appropriation. It may take many years to complete the construction of ships and aircraft, and the outlays to pay for the construction are made gradually throughout those years, long after Congress provides the budget authority for them. Authorizing numerous lengthy procurement projects in one year's budget creates a large backlog of obligations that must be paid out later. In the early 1980s this was great enough to constitute a "bow wave," such that by the middle of the decade outlays were bound to grow even if budget authority did not.[40]

If bills come due after the consensus for continuing increases in military spending collapses and previously authorized programs are allowed to run their course, actual annual expenditures (outlays) can be reduced only by draconian cuts in current authorizations:

> Deficits, of course, are a function of outlays, not budget authority. Congress, however, appropriates the latter, not the former. . . . The fast-money accounts (associated most closely with the readiness of forces) should be the most vulnerable when deficit reduction becomes a congressional imperative. A dollar cut from procurement budget authority reduces outlays (and the deficit, other things being equal) a mere 15 cents in the first fiscal year, while a dollar cut in operation-and-maintenance budget authority saves fully 73 cents in outlays.[41]

Since close to 40 percent of mid-1980s outlays were determined by the backlog and about 29 percent were accounted for by personnel, housing, and management, "only about a third of the defense budget [was] open to manipulation without cutting pay, people, or retirement."[42]

As it turned out, the winding down of the cold war at the end of the 1980s made it possible to plan cuts in personnel and the overall size of the armed forces. This meant that despite declining budgets there was less of a bind in keeping force structure operationally ready in the early 1990s than there had been in the early phase of the Reagan buildup, or than there would have been if significant investment in force structure had continued. Nevertheless a bit of the problem remained even by the time of the Clinton administration. After six months in office, Secretary of Defense Aspin found outlays running from $5 billion to $6 billion over budget, a gap that could be closed only by cuts of $8 billion to $20 billion in budget authority. Underfunding of the administration's five-year defense plan, combined with political pressures to keep a large force structure (see chapter 7), is also likely to produce a crunch in operational readiness in coming years.[43]

For coping with the "bow wave" problem, an alternative to cutting nonprocurement accounts such as those for operational readiness or slashing authority for future procurement and personnel to the bone would be to cancel projects already under way, leaving half-built ships or planes to rust. Cancellation is extremely inefficient, not just because it sacrifices sunk costs but because it requires the payment of cancellation penalty fees as well. One way to avoid a wrenching blow to structural readiness if defense outlays have to be cut in order to rein in the deficit is to let operational readiness erode.

Budget Planning Problems

The barriers to achieving a budgetary balance between structural and operational readiness during the cold war were not easily resolvable, even with wiser administrative attitudes. A large part of the problem—the cyclical ups and downs of the defense budget as a whole—was a reflection of the tendency of the political system to react or overreact to tidal trends in the popular perception of external threat rather than to experts' views of long-term efficiency in the allocation of resources toward a constant goal. Even if this had not been an obstacle, other uncertainties could have frustrated the balance.

First, costs can vary considerably, especially since much of operational readiness involves consumable commodities or expenditures abroad and changes in the larger economic conditions surrounding those expenditures are beyond the control of planners. In 1987, for example, fuel accounted for about half the estimated cost per flying hour for a mature B-1B;[44] volatility in energy prices would shift judgments about readiness costs for that weapon significantly. Or, changes in foreign exchange rates can erase resources appropriated for operations abroad. In 1988 the army saw nearly half a billion dollars evaporate because of the fall of the dollar against the deutsche mark. Currency exchange rate changes caused the air force to divert money from funds allocated for fuel.[45]

A different example of the result of unanticipated changes in the economic environment was the effect of U.S. airline deregulation on the structure of the Civil Reserve Air Fleet (CRAF). Tighter competition between the civilian companies, entailing hub-and-spoke reorganization and shorter flight segments, led them to move toward smaller two-engine aircraft. As they stopped ordering wide-body aircraft appropriate for long hauls, their inventories began to diverge from those that would be most needed for CRAF mobilization.[46] Thus domestic economic change inadvertently undermined the type of airlift needed for readiness to transport large numbers of ground forces.

Irrespective of these problems, there is no clear, accepted method for arriving at across-the-board estimates of what ratio in expenditures between investment or procurement and O&M or O&S (which includes military personnel and part of the costs for family housing along with O&M) yields a proper level of overall readiness. Nor is there a consensus on how to relate resource inputs to readiness outputs as overall levels of spending change and forces are modernized. William Kaufmann estimated that "annual operating and support costs will, on the average, constitute about 11 percent of the value of the capital goods inventory when high force readiness is being maintained and that these costs will vary directly with changes in the inventory."[47] Franklin Spinney assumed that operating budgets must rise in the same proportion as procurement budgets to maintain the same level of readiness. As chairman of the House Armed Services Committee, however, Les Aspin charged that these approaches overlooked two facts. First, acquisition costs rise more than operating costs; for example, the F-15 costs three times more to produce than the F-4, but less than three times as much to operate. Second, there is a gap in time between production and the later costs of operation, which separates the budgetary allocations for the two.[48] Sometimes the lag is quite extended. Six years into the Reagan buildup, the head of the General Accounting Office estimated that the addition of new ships to the fleet would almost double O&S costs between fiscal 1986 and 2000.[49] Moreover, there are significant ambiguities in how O&M or O&S accounts reflect operational readiness expenditures and inconsistencies in what data are included in those accounts from year to year (see chapter 4).

There is a further reason not to assume that operational readiness costs should be in constant ratio to procurement spending. Operation, maintenance, and support requirements vary significantly over the life of a system, in a tub-shaped curve: high in the beginning shakedown phase, as kinks are worked out and the organization learns how to live with the weapon most efficiently; low and stable as the system matures and functions normally; and high at the end, as it wears out. It is hard to account for this pattern in highly aggregated data because at any given time the military organization has numerous systems in various stages of life, between breaking in and breaking down.[50]

These sorts of uncertainties make it difficult to establish a tight link between changes in operational readiness budgets and in readiness ratings for units. (It is infeasible to do a systematic comparison of the funding and ratings because most ratings are classified, and only fragments of this information make their way into open sources.) It is particularly difficult to estimate the point of diminishing returns from increases in operational readiness funding. The effects of increments of proficiency training can only be judged subjectively. As of the mid-1980s, for example, the Strategic and Tactical Air Commands lacked "studies or empirical data to support either the number of sorties/flying hours required for a fully combat-ready status or the number of additional . . . hours required for enhanced proficiency."[51]

In this context, it is not surprising if budget cutters facing a choice of trashing a tangible, clearly countable bomber or trimming the time that a fleet of bombers flies see the latter choice as the path of least resistance. More dispiriting is the fact that it is sometimes impossible to discern any significant direct relationship between increases in resources and operational readiness. In 1987 the director of plans and policy for the European Command (EUCOM) testified that readiness condition ratings (C-ratings) had stayed constant for the previous five years even though O&S funding had gone up markedly.[52] Yet it is not the budgetary inputs or peacetime measures of effort that fight the enemy and determine who wins or loses the war. That depends on combat units whose status is evaluated by the ratings—armored divisions, tactical air wings, naval task forces—not training days, depot maintenance backlogs, or peacetime flying hours. Not surprisingly, administration and military leaders came to blame the unit rating system for apparent anomalies.

Explaining Away Problems

When the cold war was in full swing, none in political or executive authority wanted to admit that they were deliberately compromising operational readiness. In view of all the obstacles in the way of a confident measurement of readiness, it should not be surprising that administrations and services always had an excuse when they were criticized for allowing readiness to decline, or that critics adopted the same excuses when they moved into positions of authority themselves. The typical techniques for deflecting criticism were to deny the validity of criteria cited by critics, to conflate conflicting criteria, or to change the criteria by revising the official rating system.

Criticizing the Criteria

One common answer to criticism was to point out how peacetime accounting standards understate real wartime capability. Secretary of Defense Harold Brown decried the misleading focus on C-ratings (which he characterized as a peacetime management device) as indicators of overall readiness.[53] Other Carter administration spokesmen in 1980 deemphasized poor mission capable ratings by noting that in an actual emergency there would probably be enough warning to allow time for reaction: limitations on the use of war reserves and cannibalization would be lifted, maintenance shifts could be extended, unnecessary scheduled maintenance or inspections could be deferred, and personnel could be recalled from leave. The rating of a number of units as not ready, moreover, obscured the fact that elements from several squadrons rated C-4 (not ready for combat) could be combined to get a couple of ready ones, or that a C-4 squadron might be able to perform a mission other than the one that was the basis for the rating, or that if the unready rating was due to undermanning, rapid infusion of personnel could raise it quickly to C-1 or C-2. "For all of these reasons, mission-capable rates for most aircraft types and missions will generally underestimate our ability to fly sorties in the early stages of a conflict."[54] (Indeed, at the height of the Near East crisis that year an aircraft carrier rated C-4 was sent to the Indian Ocean, and it did function operationally.)[55]

These arguments did not mollify Republican critics, who hooted them down. Four years later, nevertheless, speaking for the Reagan administration, Secretary of the Navy John Lehman offered arguments quite similar to those the Carter administration representatives had given to indicate why statistics on naval air readiness erred on the side of caution. In 1988 General William R. Ward made the point most graphically: "In my year-and-a-half *in combat I never was even for an hour with a unit that was other than C-4.*"[56]

Another recurrent defense was that apparent changes were illusory and that poorer ratings were the result of applying more demanding criteria of measurement. The answer to congressional questioning about problems in the Army National Guard in the spring of 1979 was, "The Army instituted new readiness reporting criteria in October 1978, which are more stringent than previous criteria."[57] A year and a half later, the House Budget Committee was told that readiness reporting had been standardized and made more rigorous during the year: "When the new, standard criteria were installed, the ratings went down—not the readiness, the ratings." Harold Brown also declared in a speech that in the preceding four years, "We have made the standards tougher."[58] In 1984, the administration was confronted by congressional complaints that the number of army divisions and brigades slated to maintain highest readiness (ALO-1) had been reduced and responded that the reason was a tightening of the criteria. Officials also accounted for reduced air force C-ratings as "more indicative of improved measurement standards and increased requirements [than] an actual decline in military capability."[59] Around the same time Air Force Chief of Staff Charles Gabriel said, "We have changed the yardstick for measuring readiness. We had a 6-foot bar to jump over [in] 1980. We subsequently raised it to 8 or 10 feet and we're not doing so good jumping over it now."[60] Assistant Secretary of Defense Lawrence Korb provided an example: "In 1980, all that most Air Force squadrons needed was to have 15 days worth of supplies to get a ready-to-go-to-combat rating. Now they need to have 30 days . . . but because the criteria have doubled, one might say we are not as ready as we were, when in fact we are more ready."[61] Official spokesmen often refer to toughening of rating standards; seldom do they claim that standards have been relaxed. Critics, though, sometimes make that charge.[62]

It is not surprising that Reagan administration spokesmen would deflect criticism about operational readiness with some of the same arguments that Carter's people used, but it is surprising that they would have to do so. Considering the large growth in military budgets, most would expect ratings to go up even if the standards were toughened. The bulk of the largesse that descended on the military at that time, however, went to buying new weapon systems. Thus the fact that burgeoning defense budgets did not boost C-ratings across the board—indeed, that they coincided with some appreciable declines— reflected the difference between structural and operational readiness.

The fact that officials had to confront criticism of poor readiness as late as four years into the Reagan buildup led them to confuse that difference.

That difference, as outlined in chapter 2, was never made explicit in the vocabulary of defense policymakers, who usually assumed that "readiness" referred to *immediate* readiness. Giving priority to structural over operational readiness might be justifiable, given that mass as well as speed and efficiency determines effectiveness, but the preference for modernization was seldom rationalized in those terms. The legitimate defense would be to argue the necessity of compromising readiness now in the interest of readiness later, but few would ever admit to deliberately diminishing readiness in any sense.

Conflating the Criteria

When called on the congressional mat in 1984, Army Chief of Staff John Wickham admitted, "one could argue, how come, with all this modernization you don't get readier." His explanation was "a deficiency in our reporting mechanism," which failed to register the increase in capability created by distributing M-1 tanks, Bradley infantry fighting vehicles (IFVs), Apache helicopters, and other new systems to army units.[63] In a speech the general complained about media reports of lower unit readiness because only one out of four categories in the C-ratings—equipment on hand—was the source of the declines.

> This is not because we have worse or less equipment than before but because we have changed our tables of organization and equipment to reflect requirements for newer equipment. Our reporting system pinpoints those units which still require issue of the new equipment. . . . This status report, then, is a static indicator; a management tool that provides a snapshot of a unit's status at a specific point in time. Readiness and capability are dynamic.[64]

When the army subsequently published its supporting document for the 1987 budget, it declared readiness to be the "top priority," then noted the addition of modernized equipment as the main evidence.[65]

These statements mixed definitions in the manner so common among laymen, merging operational and structural readiness. Rather than differentiate and admit the trade-off between readiness now and readiness later, apologists muddied the difference between readiness (capability in variance with time) and static capability. This conflation was common even among experts, who feared that differentiating between the two dimensions of readiness would provide congressmen an excuse to cut procurement.

An egregious example was when Senator James Exon asked General Harold Stone, chief of staff of the European Command, whether, if the budget had to be reduced, the cut should come from modernization or readiness. The general deflected the question by saying that readiness included basic hardware—"tanks, air defense weapons, artillery, aircraft." When Senator John Tower followed up this surprising statement by asking, "Modernization is a part of readiness? Is that correct?" Stone answered, "Yes, sir."[66]

Officials scrambled in the 1980s to avoid the hard choices and cover up the actual secondary priority of operational readiness. They simply could not afford to admit that building capability for the long term entailed some sacrifice of immediate readiness for combat. The assimilation of new weapons, especially in the quantities that the army faced in the 1980s, undermined near-term readiness because it upset "the balance among component parts of the organization"[67] and required retraining and familiarization by operators and maintainers. Nor was it reasonable to dismiss the trade-off as trivially temporary. The switchover from the F-4 to F-15 and F-16 led to some long drops in tactical air readiness. One squadron went from C-2 to C-5 and took *two years* to climb back to C-2 owing to shortages in war reserves, spare parts, and supporting logistics.[68]

Nevertheless, it had been difficult throughout the decade—and especially at the beginning, when the bow wave of modernization was gathering force—to shake most of the military free from the combination of rhetorical devotion to operational readiness and actual devotion to force structure. In 1982, for example, the commander of the Tactical Air Command reported that shortages of spare parts continued "to be the biggest limitations to sustain sortie rates," that average lead times for correcting the problems were two years, and that for some components the anticipated "get well dates" were a decade away. Yet the same report cited increases in force structure from thirty-five to forty wings as "our number one priority."[69] But to pursue this real priority of structural modernization, it had to ride on the popularity of "readiness." An air force briefing for the Senate Armed Services Committee cited budget requests for pay and allowances, aircraft and missile procurement, technology research and development, and military construction as "readiness" items. When pressed by Senator Levin about where the prime emphasis for funding of the Strategic, Tactical, and Military Airlift Commands should be placed—on modernization or readiness—the air force leaders refused to answer. General Richard Ellis would say only that it was necessary to "place major emphasis on both modernization and readiness. They are inseparable."[70]

Changing the Criteria

Since those who favored force structure did not dare to challenge the sacred cow of operational readiness, they had to try to discredit evidence indicating that operational readiness was slipping while defense spending was burgeoning. Faced by a controversy over lower C-ratings, despite a tremendous growth in resources, the response was the old one of discrediting the formal rating system, first, by denigrating the standard unit status report (UNITREP); second, by shifting attention away from narrow mission capable measures of immediate availability for combat and toward other models and measures that emphasized broader concepts of capability; and third, by reforming the rating system.

Numerous military spokesmen testified to the inadequacy of the UNITREP. Many argued, as did Admiral Staser Holcomb, that "we turn out to be much readier than the UNITREP reporting system leads us to believe." Others did not contest the accuracy of UNITREP ratings but downplayed their significance because they did not depict overall capability. Senator Gordon Humphrey grumbled at one point, "Everybody keeps telling us what C-ratings are not good for. I am beginning to wonder what they are good for."[71] That comment suggests the success of official apologists in obscuring the trade-off between near-term and long-term readiness. The apologists were really complaining that C-ratings did not depict improvements in structural readiness, yet that was as it should be as long as operational readiness is of any interest in itself.

The discovery of failings in the readiness rating system in the mid-1980s was scarcely new. Indeed, *the UNITREP system itself had been instituted as a reform to deal with problems in the preceding system*, the Force Status Identity Report (FORSTAT), against which the same objections had been leveled. In regard to bad readiness reports in 1978, the

Defense Department had said, "FORSTAT measures things and numbers of people but does not measure unit capability," which was the criticism echoed by apologists years later about the UNITREP.[72]

The justification for shifting from FORSTAT to UNITREP at the end of the 1970s, however, was presented primarily in terms of how to improve the gauge for *operational* readiness, and it sounded like quite a laudable effort to make the system more accurate. One major change in 1980 was to shift the standard by which readiness shortfalls were measured from the level of resources authorized in peacetime to the level required for wartime.[73] Army Chief of Staff Bernard Rogers testified in 1979 that the change would "improve credibility at unit level" by eliminating computations that could mask problems; revising the designation of reportable equipment to bring it closer into line with "relative importance to the unit mission"; preventing "peaking" that could artificially boost readiness on dates when reports were due; and disallowing the "masking of shortfalls in one category by excess assets in others."[74]

If one really wanted to improve the *operational* readiness reporting system, the switch from FORSTAT to UNITREP should have been an excellent reform. Indeed, *UNITREP did the job too well*, highlighting deficiencies in operational readiness in *both* the Carter and Reagan administrations. Anti-Carter critics publicized such ratings with alacrity but were later chagrined when the credit for Reagan's buildup was compromised by persisting deficiencies of the same sort. Less than a decade after the reform of FORSTAT by UNITREP, the latter system was replaced by another: Status of Resources and Training System (SORTS). The replacement helped contain concern about readiness deficiencies by blurring the extent to which the new system was to measure immediate capacity for combat.

Under SORTS, "combat ratings" were changed to "category levels," while "equipment readiness" switched to "equipment condition." The official explanation of SORTS for army reserve components stated that "category levels do not project a unit's combat capability once mobilized," yet defined the new C-1 to C-5 categories in ways quite similar to the old UNITREP (see table 5-1). The exception was that, in contrast to the UNITREP standard, a C-4 unit could "if the situation dictate[d] . . . undertake portions of its wartime mission with resources on hand."[75]

Officials also sought to develop new indices that would incorporate

TABLE 5-1. *Criteria for SORTS Resource Category C Levels*
Thresholds are percentages of prescribed wartime requirements

Category C level[a]	Personnel	Threshold	Equipment and supplies[b]	Threshold	Equipment condition[c]	Threshold	Training[d]	Threshold
C-1	Total	90	Combat	90	Combat	90	Completed	90
	MOS[e]	85	Aircraft	90	Aircraft	75	Operational crews	85
	Grade	85	Other	90	End-items	90	Number of days required	14
C-2	Total	80	Combat	80	Combat	70	Completed	70
	MOS	75	Aircraft	80	Aircraft	60	Operational crews	70
	Grade	75	Other	80	End-items	70	Number of days required	28
C-3	Total	70	Combat	65	Combat	60	Completed	55
	MOS	65	Aircraft	60	Aircraft	50	Operational crews	55
	Grade	65	Other	65	End-items	60	Number of days required	42
C-4	Lower		Lower		Lower		Lower or longer	

Source: S. Craig Moore and others, *Measuring Military Readiness and Sustainability*, R-3842-DAG (Rand Corporation, 1991), p. 12, based on a 1986 Joint Chiefs of Staff document.

C-5: "Unit not prepared, undergoing service-directed resource action."

a. The percentage fill by pay grade may be used optionally.

b. The services provide supplemental methods for measuring the status of unique equipment (such as air force mobile communications equipment and navigation aids) that is unsuited for measurement by percentages.

c. Equipment must be fully operational within the mission or alert response time or seventy-two hours, whichever is shorter.

d. Each service designates *one* method of reporting training status for each type of unit.

e. MOS = military occupational specialty.

the value of modernization and other improvements, and they channeled discussion toward other measures besides those narrowly focused on immediate mission capability. The army, for example, touted other sources of data or analytical models such as OMNIBUS, Total Army Analysis, exercises, and especially the new "measuring improved capabilities of army forces" (MICAF) model.[76] Chief of Staff Carl E. Vuono presented MICAF explicitly to focus on modernization and capability beyond what UNITREP could represent. Two years after the 1984 controversies, the MICAF presentation cited active force capability as nearly 50 percent better than in 1980, reserve components 24 percent better, and the total force 39 percent better. The explicit contrast with the UNITREP picture, as seen in figures 5-2 and 5-3, was marked—but this was because the MICAF data depicted "combat unit *potential*" (mass, or structural readiness in the terms used in this book) rather than *actual* capability immediately available (the normal meaning attached to the term "readiness" in professional circles).[77]

Within one decade, three different systems for readiness reporting (FORSTAT, UNITREP, SORTS) were used. The second was more rigorous than the first, and the third less rigorous than the second. This cycle reflected the two-edged quality of greater attention to operational readiness, the way in which such attention could threaten emphasis on investment and modernization.

Analytical and Political Clarity

Readiness was more politicized as an issue in the 1980s than the analytical traffic could bear. As chapter 4 showed, even professional experts have been hard-pressed to provide reliable measures of operational readiness. It is probably a mistake even to seek exact estimates of operational readiness *at a high level of aggregation*, because that goal may be impossible to achieve. Solid analytical tools for providing such measures, in ways that would obviate the ambiguities and contradictions surveyed in this chapter and the previous one, have not been developed. This is not simply because efforts were slipshod. The proper techniques may not exist to be found, since the complexity of modern military forces imbues readiness with many facets that combine in different ways. If one aspect detracts from another (such as the trade-off between personnel training and equipment maintenance), it is impossible to argue about the overall level of operational readiness with any quantitative precision.

FIGURE 5-2. *Unit Status Reporting System (USR)*

EOH Rating[a]

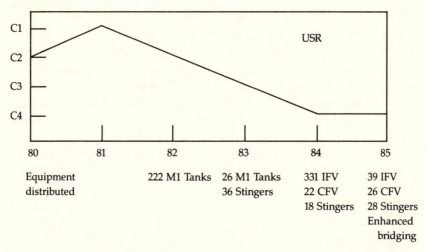

		222 M1 Tanks	26 M1 Tanks	331 IFV	39 IFV
Equipment distributed			36 Stingers	22 CFV	26 CFV
				18 Stingers	28 Stingers
					Enhanced bridging

Source: *Defense Department Authorization and Oversight Hearings on H.R. 4428, Department of Defense Authorization of Appropriations for Fiscal Year 1987 and Oversight of Previously Authorized Programs,* Hearings before the House Armed Services Committee, 99 Cong. 2 sess. (GPO, 1986), title III, p. 852.

a. Equipment on hand.

FIGURE 5-3. *Measuring Improved Capabilities of Army Forces (MICAF)*

Relative combat unit potential (1980 base)

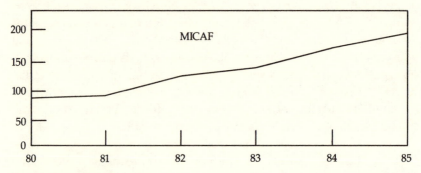

Total change, 1980–85, +113%.

Source: See figure 5-2.

This may not be a terrible problem, especially after the cold war. Part of the reason for the controversy in previous years was that administrative and political leaders put too high a premium on operational readiness and pushed the military system from top to bottom into contorted efforts to show that it was being achieved. Too much was expected from the data and from commanders, and bureaucrats tried to wring from the system better evidence than the techniques of compilation or assessment were capable of producing. Since the cold war has ended, civilian policymakers have been less fixated on combat readiness. The pressures on the military to corrupt the reporting of readiness or the selling of it to Congress may ease as a result.

As should be clear by now, much of the political combat over the issue was not due to the problem of measurement but to confusion over the differentiation of operational and structural readiness. Chapters 2 and 3 made the case for including more criteria than immediate availability for combat in the definition, because the size and modernity of forces may determine their effectiveness as much as their efficiency does. If the objective is to be ready to handle a bigger threat a bit later, additional force structure is a better investment for readiness than is immediate operational perfection.

Yet the distinction between structural and operational readiness was never articulated or consciously adopted in the professional or political lexicon. Military leaders defending the Reagan buildup implicitly embraced it in their attempts to justify the administration's emphasis on the procurement of new weaponry, but they did not want to admit that boosting future effectiveness required compromising immediate efficiency. That would not have accorded well with all the rhetoric of alarm and assertions about the immediacy of the Soviet threat. Congressional critics could thus legitimately show that in some respects budget buildup coincided with readiness reduction, because the only official definition of readiness in play was the one that reflected immediate capability.

It was reasonable to focus on operational readiness during the cold war, when a high level of constant mobilization was taken for granted, and planning was dominated by the prospect of a "come-as-you-are war." Now it will be less feasible to ignore the tension between maintaining actual capability and nurturing potential capability. Both of these problems—the confusions during the cold war and the prospect of harder choices after it—suggest how important it is that politicians, administrators, and commanders stop thinking of readiness as all of a piece, or in terms of an aggregate level, and that they not look for or trust any single index of it. They should either take the time to dig in and disaggregate the data or accept that they can get along without precise estimates. They should face the fact that some aspects of readiness necessarily entail degradations in others, and decide deliberately which ones they want to boost and which they can afford to let slide. If they want to make coherent judgments about readiness, they need to become far more accustomed to working beyond the one-dimensional terms of reference that produce the kind of befuddlement all too typically revealed in congressional exchanges such as the following one from the height of the Iran hostage crisis in early 1980:

Senator NUNN. I am puzzled by your statement . . . that individual combat readiness has generally improved over the past 5 years. . . . It was my impression that it was the other way around. . . .

Admiral LONG. . . . I am talking about the individual unit readiness . . . as opposed to the readiness of the entire command where we are talking primarily [about] sustainability. . . .

Senator NUNN. When you say units, you mean ships, you don't mean people?

Admiral LONG. I mean ships, including the material conditions, the manning of a ship insofar as the trained personnel and the state of training. . . .

Senator NUNN. You mean we are about to get to the stage that we are going to tie up ships that we thought could fight better than they could 5 years ago? Something is wrong. . . .

Admiral LONG. . . . 5 years ago we had some very severe materiel and maintenance problems in the fleet . . . investment has now paid off with ships in better materiel condition. . . . What I am also saying is that we have a personnel trend that is going the wrong way, and that it is numbers of supervisory people we are losing. That trend could have a serious effect on readiness. . . .

Chairman STENNIS. Admiral Long, it is not clear to me just where you draw the line. You talk about the individual readiness of a ship and the individual readiness of people. . . .

Admiral LONG. I am not intentionally trying to confuse you, Mr. Chairman. . . .

Senator NUNN. Admiral, could we summarize that subject by

saying that the materiel readiness has improved but the personnel readiness has gone down?

Admiral LONG. I think that is a fair statement.[78]

Those who criticize an administration for spending on new hardware and force structure rather than maximizing maintenance or training of already existing forces—as congressional Democrats did in the 1980s—cannot claim the mantle of readiness in general. Rather, they implicitly argue that the time element in readiness (for when) should have priority over the capability element (for what). The logic in this view is that the possible imminence of war is a greater danger than the amount of enemy capability that U.S. forces would face in such a war. Those who argue in contrast that modernization and force structure should be given higher priority assume the reverse, that the strength the United States needs to be ready to exert is a greater concern than how quickly it might have to do it.

The main political problem in the later years of the cold war was that all these priorities were seldom recognized by those engaged in the debate, and the trade-offs were virtually never acknowledged by those who did fully understand them. Evading conscious choices may seem less costly after the cold war, since readiness is considered less important. It could turn out to be more costly in the future, however, because there will be much less slack in the system, less slush in the pool of defense resources, and much less room for the leaner forces that remain to absorb the consequences of muddled decisions.

6

U.S. and Soviet Readiness: A Comparison

*T*HE IMPLOSION of the Soviet Union removed the challenging standard against which the United States measured military readiness during the cold war. Conflict with a second-tier power such as Iraq, or Iran, or North Korea is now the more probable threat. But it always was. It was not the probability of war with the USSR (which was almost always low) that made the Soviet military the preoccupation of U.S. defense planners. Rather, it was the capability of the Soviet military, which was the only power that left open the question of whether the United States could avoid defeat in the event of an all-out effort in war. An adversary like Iraq could raise questions about American readiness in terms of speed or efficiency but not in terms of potential to prevail in combat. The Soviet Army raised *both* questions for more than four decades. Reviewing the problem as it existed in the cold war is useful historically and also serves one main purpose for the future. It illustrates choices and trade-offs that the United States might have to confront if it ever again contends with another superpower or coalition of comparable capacity.

Net Assessment

What was most striking *at first glance* in the comparison of U.S. and Soviet military capabilities during the cold war was the gross disparity in their size: the numbers of men under arms, major weapon platforms, and combat formations. This was true even earlier. During World War II, despite losses of 7.5 million military personnel, the USSR created 686 rifle divisions as well as numerous other formations and kept more than 500 divisions on active service at a single time.[1] The United States, in contrast, initially planned to mobilize 213 army di-

144

visions, but never managed to create more than 91.[2] The contrasts most often cited in the cold war were the ratios of total manpower (more than two to one in favor of the Soviet Union in active forces and four or five to one in reserves, depending on ambiguities in counting), ground force divisions (five or six to one in Soviet favor), and main battle tanks (more than three to one in Soviet favor).[3] Part of the overall structural disparity was accounted for by gross differences in effort: higher Soviet military spending throughout the 1970s and 1980s; Soviet investment in quantity of weapons versus U.S. emphasis on quality; disproportionate American allocations to sea and airpower; and differences in the units of account (Soviet divisions were smaller than American ones).

A less frequently noted point was that part of the difference was due to the disproportionate emphasis on operational readiness in the U.S. forces. Had the Soviet Union spent as much per unit on training, logistics, and maintenance, it would have had fewer units. Hawkish assessments of the balance of power too often ignored the difference in operational readiness. The discussion below deals with this aspect of the superpowers' forces at the apex of their cold war maturity, emphasizing examples from armor and airpower.[4]

Absolute and Relative Standards

Much of the confusion and controversy about the cold war balance of military power was due to the fact that structural readiness was judged by comparing U.S. and Soviet forces to each other, whereas operational readiness was not. Official U.S. readiness assessments tended to gauge U.S. forces in terms that were *tactical* in scope and *absolute* in character. That is, assessments were about how close specific units or weapons were in peacetime to their maximum potential efficiency in battle, according to their own tables of organization and equipment, without reference to whom they would be fighting. Maximum potential for a given unit means 100 percent personnel strength with perfect training, full equipment with up-to-the-minute maintenance, and sufficient supplies to fight until new supplies arrive.

In practice, prime ratings like C-1 or FMC (see chapter 4) did not require a unit's capability to be at 100 percent of its potential, because *perfect* operational readiness in peacetime was recognized to be unnecessarily costly and harmful to other military objectives. The criteria used to arrive at that judgment were *strategic* in scope and *relative* in character. Therefore the issue was not the speed and efficiency of any particular unit for an unspecified contingency, but the net effectiveness of all forces combined for a given war against a specific opposition. That meant looking beyond American forces and how far short of perfect running order or proficiency their tanks and gunners or planes and pilots were, and toward their adversaries and how much they could throw at the U.S. military, how fast, and with what proficiency of their own. The measure then was not the runner's performance against the clock but against an opponent.

But relative readiness is harder to estimate. First, it depends on two sets of capabilities (the enemy's as well as one's own), and the difficulties in measuring one's own are compounded because of the secrecy and deception practiced by the adversary. Second, the question hinges on the big trade-off between structural and operational readiness. Which constraint is likely to be greater in a crisis: the lack of time to gear up and realize the potential of the existing force structure, or insufficient potential in the existing force, whether it is realized or not? These two sides of the issue are well illustrated by the different postures of the U.S. and Soviet forces in Europe during the cold war. For the United States, operational readiness was bound to look worse when viewed in terms of what it could be at best than it did when matched against the Soviet Union. In a large and complex military establishment it is never feasible to meet criteria of perfection, except for a few showcase units. The Cold War balance is best understood by pursuing two other questions, which were seldom asked at the time. First, how did U.S. operational readiness stack up against that of the Soviet military?[5] Second, how were those differences linked to choices about structural readiness in the two systems?

Analytical Issues

The information available for estimating Soviet operational readiness was always sparse. What American analysts could glean from Soviet sources or the intelligence the U.S. government collected was less detailed or systematic than the data compiled on NATO forces. Even less information was available for unclassified analysis. Data in open publications were seldom documented, often contradictory, and less reliable than the data on U.S. forces. From its formal structure, descriptions of plans, and stated goals, Soviet readiness appeared heroically high. But the stories of former enlisted men and junior officers or the minimum time requirements for deployment inferred from the amount of time that was used to prepare for attack in some past cases made Soviet readiness seem pitiful. As in the American case, some of the information may have been fabricated. Herbert Gold-hamer, citing Soviet sources, reported:

> The need to bend training and operational routines to the exigencies of socialist competition leads to wholesale falsification of results in the military units. . . . Getting "good marks" is more important than having a good unit. . . . Questioned as to why he used an ineffective procedure, a platoon leader replies, "That is how they will question them at inspection and that is how we train them." A young flying officer complains that the young officers acquire certain skills but forget them in a month without practice. "The [flying] schedule is not set up for us but for inspection purposes." In many units in order to safeguard performance ratings, an inexperienced small-unit commander "is replaced by a more knowledgeable comrade. . . . Thus . . . the individual with the greatest experience is able to improve . . . while the individual lacking experience becomes merely an observer."[6]

Even if accurate, available data could easily be misused by applying double standards. For example, official U.S. figures often claimed very high readiness rates for Soviet tactical aircraft that were hard to square with other known information. In 1980 the Defense Department cited Warsaw Pact frontal aviation as 85 percent ready within twelve hours, 90 percent within eight days, and 95 percent in thirty days.[7] The following year the Defense Intelligence Agency testified, "Soviet tactical aircraft are maintained at nearly total readiness, and flight-time is sufficient to allow total readiness within hours, rather than days."[8] In 1988 the Pentagon reported 90–95 percent operational availability "at all times" for fighter-bombers and 75–80 percent for bombers.[9] These characterizations appeared to count all deployable aircraft without reference to whether they could execute missions or be sustained in action. Figures attributed to American aircraft, on the other hand, were often lower because they were based on more demanding mission capable standards. Even a figure of 70 percent availability cited for the MiG-23 and Su-19 in one prominent study implied the need for a grain of salt since the rate publicized for the American F-111D was only half that high (34 percent fully mission capable).[10]

Double standards could work the opposite way, too. Sometimes asymmetries in the organization of military functions meant that apples and oranges *should* be compared if the bottom line was to make sense. For example, more than four-fifths of the personnel in U.S. Air Force Central Supply and Maintenance were civilians, but comparisons of Soviet and American manpower usually excluded those U.S. civilians while including their uniformed equivalents on the Soviet side.[11] Conversely, some optimistic analyses that denigrated the Soviet logistics system focused on assets organic to the military that were comparable to the militarily self-contained system of the United States, although the Soviet system relied heavily on elaborate arrangements for transferring assets from the civilian sector. Also, critics of American "threat inflation" often dwelt on the gap between Soviet theory and practice, citing anecdotal evidence about how Soviet practices at the unit level bore little resemblance to what would be inferred from formal norms or official reports. A similar concern in interpreting U.S. data, however, made the comparison less unfavorable to the Soviet Union. Stark accounts of such gaps between reports and reality on the American side can be found in muckraking memoirs.[12]

Training and Performance

On average, Soviet military manpower was less proficiently trained than American soldiers were. That difference did not necessarily indicate lower effectiveness where the Soviet force was much bigger than the American one with the higher average skill. Nor did lower skill in certain categories necessarily represent a deficiency if the category in question had a different role in the integrated structures and strategies of the two sides. When one considers the margin of advantage conferred by U.S. qualitative superiority over the Soviet-model Iraqi forces in 1991, however, it is likely that the Soviet pattern represented a significant weakness seldom indicated in cold war U.S. assessments of the military balance.

Bounding Conditions

The effectiveness of personnel must be considered at two levels: leadership and command (the officer corps and career noncommissioned officers, NCOs), and the troops. The record of operations against the Germans in World War II made Soviet leadership and command seem artless, rigid, slow, and cautious to some analysts in the West. That stereotype, however, was fostered by German reports, and by the Soviet performance in the first two years of the war. Soviet competence improved notably after the early phase.[13] The Russians themselves conceded the gross deficiencies in the early years of the war. Citing Soviet official history, Earl Ziemke writes:

> The great and persistent Soviet weakness was lack of initiative at all levels, which resulted in dogmatism, slavish dependence on orders from the top, and preference for the fixed and approved formula even when it was contradicted by reason or experience. That weakness had been made much worse by the great purges of the 1930's, which . . . had made conformity a near absolute prerequisite for survival.[14]

Reports of the same problems abounded in more recent times and were cited as evidence that Soviet adaptability in combat was too sluggish for the execution of successful breakthrough operations.[15] Critics saw this as a cultural and theoretical problem: the Soviet model of command emphasized formulaic solutions and precisely planned operations rather than the inventive individualism encouraged by the German model. The historical record of the United States was not entirely stellar either, at least until the magnificent performance against Iraq. In language that echoes critiques of Soviet command style, John Shy summarizes the U.S. Army's traditional problem:

> At least through the First World War: the professional response to the chronic American weakness in command-and-control was to plan more thoroughly, leaving as little to chance as possible. But thorough planning, with its natural deemphasis of unexpected situations . . . led to rigidity and, often, heavy losses. In other words, the command-and-control weakness and its chosen professional remedy were but two aspects of a single larger problem: inadequate preparation of commanders and staffs . . . the result too often seems to be that the troops, even when inadequately trained and armed, are readier for war than the men who lead them.[16]

At the troop level, the quality of training varies according to whether the military in question is a professional volunteer force or a mass conscript organization. Training is usually more intense and cost-effective in the former, since long-service personnel can develop and hone a wider variety of skills and will remain in the force to practice them for a longer time. Training is more rudimentary and costly in the second type of force since conscripts serve for a shorter time, and the training must be repeated for each new batch. The United States lived with both systems during the cold war: conscription in the first half, voluntary enlistment in the second.

In practice the difference was not always as clear as proponents of the U.S. All Volunteer Force (AVF) hoped. For much of the period after the draft was terminated in the early 1970s, personnel turnover rates continued to be very high. This hampered training above company level and led to more frequent repetition of the training cycle. Even in the 1980s, as the House Appropriations Committee staff reported, turbulence remained "one of the most frequently cited reasons for readiness and training degradation." According to some commanders, the composition of their units changed so rapidly that they had virtually new ones every three months. Part of the problem was the forward deployment of a large portion of the American military, which made external turbulence—frequent rotation of personnel between units in the United States and abroad—inherent in the system. This aggravated internal turbulence, that is, transfers within a unit due to promotion or other requirements determined by the commander.[17]

Another difference between professionalized and mass military establishments that is less clear in practice than in theory is the average quality of their personnel. With a smaller force and more selectivity, the education and aptitude levels of American recruits might be expected to exceed those of the huge herd that the conscript-based Soviet force accommodated. This depends entirely, however, on the popularity of military service. If service is attractive in all strata of the population and more individuals wish to enlist than can be taken, the AVF can select all its entrants from above-average candidates. If not, the conscript system has the advantage since compulsion can guarantee that the average quality of inductees at least equals that of the population at large.

For the better part of the 1970s the quality of American recruits lagged behind desired levels, and by 1980 well *over half* of army volunteers (57 percent) were category 4 (the lowest acceptable mental category). With pay raises, high civilian unemployment, and a resurgence of nationalism in the early 1980s, recruiting flourished, and the services could turn marginally qualified applicants away. But in the late 1980s the old problems resurfaced, as the number of people in the relevant age group declined. At the end of 1988 the army was accepting nearly three times as many of its recruits from category 4 as in the preceding three years.[18] Conscription, however, does not preclude such problems if it is selective rather than universal and thereby allows educated elites to escape. This happened in the United States in the 1960s as the size of the eligible youth cohort (the baby-boom generation) outstripped the additional manpower requirements imposed by the Vietnam War.[19] It also happened to some extent in the USSR. Despite conscription, the Soviet Union did not fare better in the educational level of recruits, simply because its overall educational levels were lower. The Soviet system began to move tentatively toward the American model before the union collapsed. Reform proposals of the late 1980s cited the limitation on effective training forced by the conscript system as a reason for abandoning it.[20]

Quantity of Training

U.S. forces trained more than Soviet troops did. The latter were often diverted by civilian functions such as construction or harvesting or were constrained by severe winter weather.[21] Depending on what is counted, however, the difference in training time was not consistent. Some Soviet junior officers, especially reservists, were reported to be minimally trained.[22] This was not uniformly true, however, especially for careerists. In the past the Soviet curriculum for armor officers, for example, was far longer than the American one. The Soviet tankers took either a three- or five-year training course (including two to four six-week periods in line or maintenance units), compared with a twelve-week basic course for American officers. For noncommissioned officers the situation was reversed: U.S. NCOs had four professional development courses as against one for Soviet *praporshchiks*.[23]

By some measures, armor crews in the USSR spent more total time training. According to a U.S. Army study, Soviet tank companies had a 50 percent longer training week, underwent gunnery training and crew qualification twice as frequently as American counterparts in the 1970s, and did not face the competing activities that distracted U.S.

crews (administration, fatigue details, range guards, and so forth).[24] By other measures, the Americans came out ahead. Although Soviet crews may have spent more time in study or instruction, they spent less time actually maneuvering, firing, and using their vehicles. According to U.S. estimates, Soviet gunners fired only a tenth as many live rounds as American tankers, and according to Soviet Defense Minister Dmitry Yazov even less, while Soviet pilots flew only 30–60 percent as many hours as American and other NATO aviators in the 1970s and 1980s, and they had higher accident rates.[25]

The larger Soviet force structure had lower average operational readiness not only because of such practices but also because most *basic* training was carried on within line units. This problem was mitigated by the program of pre-draft training through the initial military training (NVP) program in schools and the All-Union Voluntary Society for Assistance to the Army, Air Force, and Navy (DOSAAF). After 1967 such programs became compulsory, in part to compensate for a reduction in the term of conscription. The programs evolved slowly because of the massive organizational and material resources required. The core consisted of 140 hours over the course of a year or two and included instruction in regulations, small arms, drill, tactics, military law, and technical specialties. Limits on qualified instructors, visual aids, some types of weaponry, ranges, adequate maintenance of equipment, and other forms of support left the program unsatisfactory, but it improved somewhat with time. By 1971, more than half of a sample of servicemen had received such preinduction instruction, and within a few years more than 70–80 percent of draftees were estimated to have gotten it. By the mid-1970s a third of draftees were estimated to already have military *specialties* beyond basic training, and the DOSAAF program continued to expand. By the late 1970s almost all seniors in high school had been through the NVP program. Komsomol camps also stressed military training.[26]

Although few believe the DOSAAF to have been very effective, the question should be, compared to what? Folklore suggests that weekend training for the U.S. Army National Guard is no more impressive. Seen against high expectations, DOSAAF training was a joke, but compared with the alternative—no military skills at all upon entry— it was more significant. For example, a Soviet airborne officer in 1971 complained that half of his newly inducted troops had never jumped before, "but to most military forces in the world it would seem extraordinary for a paratroop unit to receive inductees of whom half had already made jumps."[27]

Poor training, nevertheless, was recognized as a problem by the late 1980s, especially given the cumulative strains of assimilating complex technologies. Some soldiers in the first units sent to Afghanistan had only marginal combat instruction, but training units apart from field units "were introduced for those going to Afghanistan and training improved accordingly." By the mid-1980s specialized mountain warfare training was quite advanced.[28]

Quality of Training

Soviet training emphasized specialization, simplicity, and primary unit stability, whereas the U.S. system tended to emphasize the opposite qualities. In the Soviet army, instruction was not oriented to complex tasks, and "although there are frequent references to cross-training, on-the-job training in one skill appear[ed] to be the rule."[29] Soviet conscripts normally *repeated* the training cycle *four* times, learning the same job over again. Training constraints also limited Warsaw Pact aircrews to single roles, in contrast to the flexibility that characterizes NATO flyers. American soldiers got more cross-training. For example, U.S. tankers shifted among the several positions in a crew and all got gunnery training. In contrast, Soviet crew members sometimes remained in the same position for their entire tour. This made it more likely that an American unit could continue to perform in battle or be rapidly reconstituted after taking casualties. Although on balance, cross-training did give the U.S. troops an advantage, because of the flexibility it provided, it could also dilute skill in a particular specialty. And although Soviet crews were less versatile, they were more stable. They stayed together for eighteen months, about triple or more the average time for American crews.[30]

The Soviet trade-off between the factors conducive to proficiency fitted with the USSR's larger system of relying on draftees for active forces and on the mobilization of reserves for war. Specialization and repetitive practice retarded the decay of skills and meant that reservists recalled within a few years of discharge could still function:

A Soviet tank driver/mechanic will do no other job for 2 years as a conscript. Certainly, he will not be versatile, but he will never forget how to drive a tank and, once having learned on a T-62, he will be perfectly capable of driving a T-64 if required to do so. Will a tank driver in a regular NATO army, who has just done a two-year tour as a company clerk, be any better at driving a tank . . . ? Yet the cost of the regular soldier is very much greater than that of the conscript.[31]

The Soviet approach also compensated for the reliance on conscripts by emphasizing massed fires more than first-round hits and individual crew performance. By some accounts, however, the combat training regimens were unchallenging. As one emigré officer reported, "We knew that firing range in our sleep": where all the targets were, exactly when they would pop up, the angles at which to fire. By comparable accounts, however, the U.S. system had such problems too.[32]

Similar differences could be seen in aviation. The initiative of Soviet pilots was confined. Their maneuvers and tactics were restricted by ground controllers, training emphasized a rigid repetition of flight paths and profiles, and the limits on flying time allowed pilots to do little more than maintain proficiency in takeoff and landing. The flying time compared poorly with that for pilots in the U.S. Air Force and Navy, although not quite so poorly with the latter: because of the difficulty of carrier flight operations, navy pilots also spend most of their training time on takeoff and landing skills.[33] Because rigidity and stability remain sides of the same coin, however, the net assessment is ambiguous:

It is often agreed that the quality of the U.S. and NATO aircrews is higher. . . . There is little quantitative analysis to support this argument, but people often point out the differences in U.S. aircrew screening, general intelligence and aptitude . . . U.S./NATO generalist training for many aircraft types versus single aircraft training of Soviet and Pact crews, and the highly pervasive Soviet emphasis on strict . . . command and control versus the Western emphasis on individual initiative and aggressiveness. The Soviets, however, keep aircrew members in a single aircraft, thus increasing their aggregate experience, and they have higher retention of aircrew members, while U.S. retention rate problems place more inexperienced members fresh from flight school into Europe.[34]

The Soviet system may have succeeded in inculcating technical basics, but the American system, especially in recent times, emphasized more intensity in tactical training. The U.S. Army's National Training Center at Fort Irwin was developed to present opportunities for select units to engage in challenging maneuvers against staff trained in Soviet doctrine and equipment. The navy's Top Gun and air force's Red Flag programs provided pilots with similarly intense approximations of combat.[35] Soviet flight training was narrow, and the single role given to Warsaw Pact aircrews reduced their flexibility in comparison with that of American and NATO flying personnel.[36] The U.S. system was less stable but more supple.

Soviet forces were also at a disadvantage in the scale of unit training. About a fourth of the personnel in the Group of Soviet Forces in Germany (GSFG) rotated every six months, and much basic training went on within deployed units. Furthermore, the use of equipment was kept to a minimum in order to preserve running order. As a result, most Soviet forces did not exercise frequently at battalion level or higher. NATO servicemen may have spent twice as much time in exercises. About a third of each Soviet Frontal Aviation regiment may have been allocated to training, and many regiments included new pilots with little experience.[37]

Morale and Care of Troops

If troops are miserable, ill-fed, abused by their superiors, and lacking in unit esprit, they will not fight effectively. Information about low morale comes from subjective assessments and is hard to weigh against the benefits of structural readiness that flow from the diversion of resources from the care of troops. As Goldhamer reported, coercion to use free time to acquire skills, as well as low pay and spartan living conditions, brought per capita training costs for Soviet forces far below those in the West.[38]

Anecdotal evidence painted a depressing picture of Soviet military life: housing, nutrition, and discipline were reported to be poor, recruits were brutally hazed and frequently beaten, and other degrading and abusive conditions had to be endured. In reviewing novels about life in the armed forces, an emigré who served as a Soviet political officer said these accounts portrayed an army that was "still an integral part of Soviet society," which was "in the midst of a profound economic, social, and moral crisis." This picture "sharply contrasts with what is presented in Western studies. There the Soviet military is described as a very special 'island of efficiency, discipline, and hi-tech,' quite different from the rest of the corrupt society."[39]

Support and Sustainability

Compared with the USSR, the United States and its NATO allies placed more emphasis on "tail" (logistics and support functions) than on "teeth" (combat units). This implied that Western forces could fight better and longer, unit for unit, but that the East could have more forces with which to replace ones that were worn down.

Maintenance

U.S. and other NATO forces dedicated more personnel to equipment maintenance than did the Soviet Union (40 percent more per plane in theater air forces), they trained the maintenance personnel twice as much, and they provided mechanics with better equipment and more spare parts. Soviet forces relied on officers not just for directing maintenance activities but also for performing many of the functions directly, whereas the system in the West vested almost all of these responsibilities in enlisted specialists.[40] The time required to repair equipment was often longer in the East, where the system seemed in some respects to have the worst combination of centralization and decentralization. For combat aircraft, the Soviet military used a two-tiered system, in which any plane that could not be fixed on the flight line within the unit had to go to a remote depot. The American system uses three tiers, with an intermediate level that facilitates quicker turnaround for cases not serious enough to need the depot. In other ways, the Soviet system was less centralized, but not for the better. Aircraft grew more complex but the official structure failed to provide sufficient diagnostic and repair technology, with the result that individual units came to devise their own maintenance equipment. But because the units were in competition for evaluations, they had little incentive to spread their innovations to other units.[41]

Similarly, Soviet armored battalions had a negligible organic maintenance capacity, which amounted to a headquarters and service platoon that could send out no more than a couple of vans with four mechanics apiece. Even many routine repairs like replacing tires were done at regiment or division level. Battalions themselves were virtually limited to preventive maintenance. This would probably prevent tanks evacuated after breakdown in combat from returning before the operation was over. Since experience from World War II onward indicates that many armored vehicles incapacitated in combat are repairable with a few hours of work, the Soviet practice was likely to produce more net attrition in a battle area and reduce capacity to exploit breakthroughs. The system also required more planning and coordination of maintenance activities by higher levels of command.[42]

In the U.S. Army system, battalions have several support platoons and the organization "is far more conducive to the rapid-paced, unpredictable situations on the battlefield." The battalion commander can establish priorities for repair on the basis of his own tactical requirements and "he can sustain his force should situations arise where lines of communication are severed." The Soviet counterpart depends on an array of higher managers to allocate resources to fixing his vehicles, which increases the burden of communication, coordination, and speedy action in combat.[43]

Two aspects of the Soviet pattern mitigated the inefficiency of maintenance organization. One was that the Russians believed that their basic equipment—such as tanks, artillery, and trucks—was simpler and more reliable. Repair problems were supposed to be minimized by the standardization of parts (for example, the same chassis was used for numerous armored vehicles and missile carriers). Because old equipment was stockpiled rather than discarded, standardization also facilitated cannibalization.[44] In designing new models, Soviet planners also tended to use existing components and redundant circuits. "This duplication could either be regarded as a backup method for sustaining combat ability after damaging hits, or as mute testimony to the unreliability of Soviet systems due to frequent failures." As modernization made equipment more complex, these solutions became less practical. Technical simplicity became less of an offset for the system's reliance on conscripts, and less and less fixing could be accomplished near the front line. Nonstandardization of maintenance equipment also negated some of the relative advantage in standardization of parts.[45]

The second mitigating factor was that most Soviet weapon systems were parked and seldom used in order to minimize wear and tear on them in peacetime. Most American weapons, in contrast, are constantly run by troops in training.

The Soviet concept of material readiness stresses conservation of resources by limiting the use of military equipment in peacetime. They apparently believe that limited use is the best way to ensure that equipment will be ready on short notice during a crisis. That is one reason the Soviets normally keep a smaller percentage of their forces deployed than we do, and . . . generally maintain lower operational tempos.[46]

This practice of keeping weapons "packed away like a family's best china" except for special exercises once or twice a year coincided with a program of more frequent maintenance per hours of usage than is common with weapons in the West.[47] The MiG-21 fighter aircraft, for example, got regular overhauls after every 200 flight hours, triple the rate for many Western aircraft. This represented exceptional and perhaps even extravagant preventive maintenance, which meant replacing some parts early, whereas the U.S. Air Force left them in until they failed.[48] Some Soviet weapon systems required such frequent maintenance because of their lower durability. T-62 tank engines reportedly wore out completely after 500 hours or less of use, whereas those in American M-60s lasted much longer. Most Soviet tanks in the 1970s were driven less than 400 miles a year, in contrast to 500–600 miles for U.S. counterparts, and the annual mileage put on American tanks went up significantly in the 1980s. Similarly, Soviet tanks were estimated to have only about two-thirds the mean time between breakdowns of NATO vehicles. However, some Soviet weapons in inventories of other nations such as Egypt proved able to function without overhauls for far longer times than was the Soviet practice.[49]

The advantage of the Soviet system was that it could be expected to maximize the rate of weapons availability at the outset of war. In a long war, the disadvantage would have been that the availability would degrade faster than in the American force. If the average life span of a weapon in combat was less than the expected running time for the simpler and less durable Soviet systems, however, the Soviet choice in the trade-off between quantity and quality and immediate readiness and sustainability may have been the right one.[50] If, however, the American edge in quality translates into an exponential advantage in attrition ratios, a notion that some believe was confirmed in the war against Iraq, the Russians made the wrong choice. Soviet maintenance practice maximized equipment readiness for wartime at the expense of training readiness in peacetime, or of skill and endurance in wartime.[51]

Logistics

NATO forces had a much lower teeth-to-tail ratio than those of the old Warsaw Pact. This is reflected in the fact that NATO regularly outspent the Warsaw Pact nations in its military budgets but regularly fielded much smaller numbers of men, combat formations, and weapons. The difference in emphasis on combat and support elements translated into an overall advantage in combat sustainability for the West. The size and importance of that advantage were debatable.[52] Nonetheless, differences were significant. In the 1970s the U.S. Air Forces in Europe had almost twice as many people per combat aircraft as the Soviet air army in East Germany, and the West German Luftwaffe had almost four times as many.[53] The Soviet Army had more trucks than the U.S. military, but their loading arrangements were poor and they had insufficient fuel or drivers. (These problems contributed to the extreme Soviet dependence on rail transport, which increased the potential vulnerability of Warsaw Pact forces to NATO air attacks.) In the early 1970s motorized rifle divisions were optimized for combat but were sustainable for only five days. The high levels of ammunition consumption in the 1973 Middle East War, however, prompted a change.[54]

Some of the Soviet shortages of the early 1970s were rectified in subsequent years. Additional storage depots were constructed and existing ones expanded. Ammunition and fuel stocks positioned in Eastern Europe and the western theater of military action grew to more than 3 million and 9 million metric tons, respectively, which, by Defense Department estimates, provided sustainability for two to three months of combat. When East German secrets and sites were uncovered after German unification, it turned out that ammunition stockpiles were at the high end of or beyond U.S. estimates. These stocks could also be supplemented by strategic reserves located in the USSR. Stocks of bridging equipment and material to repair roads, railways, and airfields were also pre-positioned. The increases in stocks exacerbated the problem of tactical transport, but military motor transport grew by 30 percent and reduced dependence on the mobilization of civilian vehicles.[55] The Soviet Army also reorganized its logistical system, consolidating previously fragmented supply and service functions under single materiel support commanders at all levels from front to regiment. This change appeared designed to simplify coordination and quicken responsiveness in unanticipated circumstances of combat.[56]

Transition to War

This section is a survey of estimates of comparative U.S. and Soviet readiness to wage World War III, an issue that dominated strategic debates but happily remained hypothetical throughout more than forty years of competition between the superpowers. (Even with high-level alerts in the worst crises over Berlin, Cuba, and the Middle East, Washington and Moscow never undertook full-scale mobilization and reinforcement of conventional forces in Europe.) Two questions were crucial: how effective could Soviet reserve forces be without months of retraining, and to what extent could the higher operational readiness of U.S. forces compensate for their smaller size?

Ground Forces

The difference between operational and structural readiness is clearer in the American system than in the Soviet one. To begin with, active and reserve units are distinctly separate in the U.S. Army, but on the other side a spectrum of categories melded the two in varying proportions. In the United States, a large proportion of the active army and Marine Corps are kept at high levels of operational readiness in peacetime. In the dark days of 1980 much publicity was given to leaked information indicating six divisions were rated not combat ready. That figure, however, still meant that 60 percent of the total, or ten divisions—including all six of the ones stationed abroad—*were* ready (and within a year the number not ready was reduced to one). For much of the time during the late 1980s *all* of the army's organized divisions were rated combat ready. The number of ready U.S. divisions was low, but the proportion was very high, even with the low 1980 figures. As Harold Brown said at the time, "Critics fail to point out that roughly two-thirds of all the divisions of the Soviet Army would be rated, by these same [U.S.] standards, as being in our lowest readiness category."[57]

When compared with the standards for active American divisions, the proportion of divisions that the Soviet Union kept at high levels of readiness may have been even smaller than the one-third suggested by Brown.[58] At that time, and throughout most of the 1980s, the top U.S. rating (C-1) required a unit to have at least 90 percent of its mandated personnel and equipment, while the *lowest* rating that still qualified as ready (C-3) required strength still higher than the Soviet divisions of intermediate readiness (so-called category II divisions). The low C-3 rating also left a U.S. division almost competitive with the Soviet divisions that qualified marginally for category I status. The American C-3 standard was at least 70 percent of personnel and 60–65 percent fill in 90 percent of reportable equipment items, while the Soviet category I standard was between three-quarters and full strength in personnel, though with full equipment.[59]

Soviet category II divisions were normally at about half strength in manpower. They were nearly fully equipped, though usually a bit less so than category I formations, and many of their fighting vehicles were kept in storage. These category II divisions would rank in the American C-4 category ("not ready") or close to the worst active or best reserve divisions in the American force. Because the U.S. rating system relegates an entire unit to the lowest category of any rated item (meaning that a unit rated C-1 in most departments but C-3 in one counts as C-3 overall), the real comparison with the Soviet Army during the cold war was even more favorable. Non-Soviet Warsaw Pact divisions were also less ready than those of NATO. Even the category I divisions of East Germany, Czechoslovakia, and Poland ranked far below U.S. standards of high readiness.[60]

Soviet category III divisions were cadre formations, which in peacetime had between a tenth and a half of personnel strength and from one-third to "most" of the equipment for wartime deployment, although it was generally older.[61] These were more comparable to average American reserve or National Guard units, although the latter did not have as many full-time cadres. The USSR also maintained a number of mobilization base divisions. After the late 1970s most of these became low-strength cadre units with 5–20 percent of personnel and expanded equipment and garrison facilities, thus merging into what the U.S. designations would count as category III status. By the late 1980s only five thoroughly inactive mobilization base divisions remained in the Soviet structure.[62] Moscow also reportedly planned to build "invisible" or second-generation divisions from duplicate command cadres and old equipment maintained with standing divisions.[63] The proportion of Soviet ground forces that was in each of these categories is hard to pin down. Earlier figures tended to allocate roughly a third of divisions to each of the categories I, II, and III. Posen estimated that slightly more than 20 percent of divisions were in category I, slightly less than 20 percent were in category II, about 45 percent category III, and about 15 percent mobilization base. Referring to more recent Soviet designations, the Defense Department lumped categories I and II under "ready units," and category III and mobilization base divisions under "not ready," and said that about 40 percent of forces were in the "ready" portion (including all those in East Germany).[64]

What gradations of readiness meant for the time required to deploy into combat was long debated, and official estimates varied over time. Two decades ago one Pentagon estimate—which revised earlier estimates for category III divisions upward, from two weeks necessary for deployment to at least twelve—suggested the Soviet Union would need a month of preparation to attack just with category I forces.[65] Near the end of the cold war the "ready" forces were alleged to be deployable in combat after a "brief" period of preparation.[66] For substantial portions of each year, however, even category I divisions suffered from bloc turnover because of induction periods, when masses of conscripts, many of whom were basic trainees, entered and departed the units. A category I division at 80 percent strength, therefore, may have had "only about 65 percent trained manpower."[67] The U.S. Army sometimes claimed that even category II divisions could deploy within "a few days," but other sources said a month.[68] Estimates of the time that category III divisions would need after mobilization before they could deploy ranged from two weeks to just over three months.[69]

The softness of these estimates suggests that there was little firm evidence about what the Soviet Union itself viewed as the times necessary for mobilization and deployment to combat. The Voroshilov lectures discussed three levels of combat readiness—constant or routine (postoiannaia), increased (vysshaia), and full (polnaia)—but did not indicate how long the execution of measures between the low and high end was supposed to take; they did indicate, though, how the process could be telescoped if time were pressing. Reservists and equipment were supposed to assemble within 24 hours of alert, according to that document, and when the "increased" level of readiness was reached, units were supposed to be able to clear their installations within 20 minutes (this figure was reached by calculating the flight time for U.S. intercontinental ballistic missiles).[70] There is no indication whether these norms were usually met in exercises, and the time for refresher training between those ends of the process was not discussed.

The estimating problem was not simply the lack of sources. There was no single "real" answer waiting to be discovered, because the amount of time required for refresher training depends on the degree of effectiveness required.[71] On occasions in the past Moscow did it both ways, quickly and slowly, according to the exigencies of the situation. It committed forces on short notice (against Hungary in 1956) and after prolonged preparation (against Czechoslovakia in 1968 and Afghanistan in 1979).[72] Except for airborne units, *the forces that actually attacked in these cases were generally category II and III.* "In many cases their intended first-category reservists had already discharged their legal obligation in the pre-invasion call-ups carried out in order to exert diplomatic pressure, and had to be replaced by lower categories, further complicating the process."[73] Remember as well that the Soviet-style Egyptian and Syrian armies had only fifteen days' notice of the decision for war before they attacked in October 1973.[74]

Operational Readiness, Structural Readiness, and Strategy

Which approach was better? In most dimensions Soviet operational readiness was inferior to that of American forces. That disadvantage was seldom appreciated in U.S. assessments. But U.S. forces were more flexible because they had to be—smaller forces need more versatility, while bigger forces can substitute specialized units for versatile ones. The Soviet system compensated for a lower overall level of competence by having a larger but highly differentiated force. The emphasis in the Soviet forces made most sense in conjunction with offensive strategy. (This does not presume that Soviet objectives were offensive, only that their military strategy aimed to have as much of a war as possible take place on their enemies' territory rather than their own, no matter who might be responsible for starting it.) Moreover, practices that gave rise to inflexibility at the tactical level may have increased flexibility at the operational and strategic levels.

This was particularly true in regard to maintenance and sustainability. Soviet divisional logistics looked spartan in part because divisions in combat were to rely for support on higher formations than their U.S. counterparts would. This dependence limited the Soviet divisions' potential to exploit *opportunities* on the battlefield but was less *dangerous* for a force operating on the offensive than it would have been for a reactive one. In contrast to the defending side, the attacker has less need to keep all of its units along the line well supplied and prepared for engagement at any time; the attacker knows which sectors will witness the heaviest efforts and can concentrate transport, ammunition, and fuel in them. By husbanding larger proportions of resources at army and front levels, the Soviet logistics system allowed commanders to channel them to the main axes of attack and thereby increase offensive efficiency. The units that would be starved would be those that did not need to be fed. In this sense, less was more: less flexibility at the tactical level, compared with NATO units, was the logical price of attempting to maximize "flexibility at the decisive operational level of command."[75]

By the same token, less organic maintenance capability in subordinate units made it possible to centralize repair assets that could move to damaged vehicles in the wake of an advancing unit. Although this practice did not solve the problem of the scarcity of trained maintenance personnel, it avoided dispersing them to areas where they were not needed or to forward echelons that would not have had time to stop and patch themselves up.[76] In contrast, the extra capacity for combat support built into U.S. units allows them to maximize their operational capability in the face of gradual attrition but is wasted in the units that do not happen to be engaged.

In this light, the limits on Soviet sustainability appear to have been less of a deficiency than some have suggested, especially in view of the fact that American analysts have often overestimated enemy logistical requirements in past wars.[77] However, the extent to which mass, specialization, and centralization can be more desirable than smaller, adaptable, multipurpose forces should not be exaggerated. Some such Soviet peacetime practices were not conducive to wartime effectiveness, as was clear in the system of aircraft maintenance:

> The flow-line method—its rigid sequences of operations, exact positioning of personnel and equipment, and its narrow time norms—may . . . be practicable under conditions of certainty, [but] "much of maintenance is characterized by randomness of defects." . . . It is very hard to see how, even in peacetime, one goes about "pre-

determining" the sequence of repair operations that will be required *after* a sortie during which unforeseen breakdowns may occur. . . . Moreover, the familiar "fixed positions" of the flow-line may not be available in war. . . . Where, however, do Soviet ground support personnel receive training in other, more flexible methods?[78]

A trade-off between tactical and operational flexibility may also be hard to manage. A shortage of organic maintenance capacity in an advancing force may have a modest impact if the main elements of the force are not technologically complex or extremely sensitive to friction. This is progressively less true of modern armored and air forces as they develop. Even in World War II it could be said that "more than any other motor vehicle, the tank is subject to defects. Some part is always in need of attention." If campaigns are not quick, moreover, the reliance on centralization and planning can more easily break down. This happened to the Germans, who are often thought to have been more efficient than the Russians. In the early phases of World War II, the Germans had no serious problems with the supply of spare parts. After they invaded the USSR, however, the centralized system of repair broke down, and the coordination of new tank production with that of spare parts collapsed for some time.[79]

Modifying the Trade-off between Speed and Mass

The United States could have maintained larger ground forces if it had mimicked the Soviet Union and emphasized reserves and graduated readiness. One reason that Americans kept a much larger proportion of the total force in active units and put more emphasis on operational readiness in general was the fear of a surprise attack. As long as NATO was not interested in taking the strategic initiative— choosing the time, place, and circumstances in which to begin the war—this concern was a sensible basis for planning. Virtually all wars of the past half century have begun with some measure of surprise.

The probability of a surprise attack by the Soviet Union at any time during the cold war was never high, but that is because the probability of *any* Soviet attack was low. Those who pooh-poohed the danger of surprise often confused the two issues: the probability that war would occur and the probability that *if* war occurred, authorities on the re-active side would have done everything that they had planned to do to prepare their forces for it. Precisely because deterrence was so strong and initiating World War III would be so risky and hard to rationalize, leaders would have been likely to see enemy preparations in a crisis as defensive (a more rational explanation). If war between the United States and Soviet Union had ever occurred, the apparent insanity of the risk made it almost certain that it would have come as a surprise. The political and strategic reasons for this are overwhelming.[80]

A reactive strategy and sensitivity to the possibility of surprise, therefore, naturally encouraged higher levels of actual capability for short-term readiness and less potential capability for the long term than if reserves or low-readiness active forces were emphasized. The choice was reflected in the U.S. POMCUS program, which heightened the deployability of active forces for the defense of Western Europe (see chapter 3). Shortages in both POMCUS sets and existing airlift, however, left the capacity for rapid reinforcement of NATO below the officially stipulated goal—ten divisions in ten days—even under the flush defense budgets of the 1980s. Funding for additional transport aircraft reduced the gap, but airlift capacity just before the end of the cold war was still more than a quarter below the requirement established in a congressionally mandated mobility study, and less than half of what some analysts estimated would be necessary to meet the schedule. Sealift was similarly short.[81]

Reserves and Readiness

Reserve forces were crucial to estimates of the amount of power that NATO and the Warsaw Pact could bring to bear in early battles because the same amount of money can purchase more part-time units than full-time ones. Readiness is harder to gauge in reserve units than in active units. This difference increases the tension between structural and operational readiness. It is no accident that American dependence on reserves grew over the same period that anxiety about operational readiness increased. The desire to reduce the Soviet quantitative advantage in forces made U.S. investment in reserves attractive, yet the desire to maximize readiness against surprise attack pushed in the other direction.

The New Importance of American Reserves

The integration of active and reserve personnel in Soviet units reflected the long-standing importance of reserves in that system. In the

United States, reserves played a less vital role in military strategy for much of the postwar era, in part because of the policy of rapid nuclear escalation and in part because of the large amount of manpower that conscription provided for active forces. The stronger interest in a prolonged conventional defense that came with the shift to the flexible response doctrine in the 1960s also stimulated the growth of active ground forces. By the beginning of 1965, just before the large-scale intervention in Vietnam, the active army had over 10 percent more men than at the end of the Eisenhower administration. By the early 1970s, however, with the Nixon doctrine and U.S. withdrawal from Vietnam, active army manpower fell to about 20 percent below the 1965 level of the flexible response buildup and stayed there for the rest of the cold war. Even after the Reagan buildup, active ground force manpower remained 5–10 percent below what it had been at the nadir of Eisenhower's cuts at the end of 1960.[82]

In the early 1970s the rapprochement with China and detente with the USSR provided rationales for the reductions. When detente soured later in the 1970s, however, the option of reconstituting active ground forces on the earlier scale no longer existed. The draft had been abolished and the All Volunteer Force had increased the cost of active army manpower even at the lower number. Strategic incentives and economic constraints had converged on a more significant role for reserve forces in military planning, and the army moved to the so-called total force concept, which intermingled reserve and active forces in mobilization and deployment planning to an unprecedented degree.

Two sorts of domestic political pressures conditioned the significance of this shift. One was the complex of organizational proclivities and suspicions that led the professional military to purposely constrain the capacity of active forces for independent action. The other was the set of political links between Congress and local interests in the National Guard. These political considerations meant that the total force concept was an improvement as long as one could assume that in a crisis the machine would work the way it was designed to work but was of dubious usefulness if it was likely to experience a normal amount of friction. Past cases offered ample grounds to doubt that mobilization in practice would conform to the assumptions of planners divorced from politics.

The military's bitterness over the Vietnam experience provided the motive for the total force concept. Against the consistent recommendations of the military leadership, that war had been prosecuted without any reserve mobilization at all until the *Pueblo* and Tet crises of 1968, and a tiny one even at that point. The president's refusal to mobilize was associated with the strategy of gradualism in applying force in Southeast Asia, a strategy that most military professionals believe prolonged the war, cost needless casualties, crippled military effectiveness, and provoked public antipathy. The total force plan established an active-reserve force mix that would make it impossible to deploy active divisions alone on a large scale. Army leadership believed it would then be impossible for civilian leadership to make a cavalier commitment to war; in a future crisis political leaders would have to make a more conscious decision to put up or shut up. The integration of reserves also made it possible to increase structural readiness in the active force, by adding three divisions without increasing manpower.[83]

The professional military's urge for an all-or-nothing commitment, however, has been linked with a preference for formulaic planning that depends on prompt political decisions for mobilization but takes little account of the odds that such decisions will be so prompt. If unit A can be ready in ten days after mobilization and unit B in twenty days, and at least twenty days of strategic warning will be available before units are needed for battle, units of type B are the better investment (since they do not need the extra resources to be ten days readier all the time) *unless* authorization to mobilize is delayed after the receipt of warning.

Executive hesitancy about mobilization is not the only reason to beware of a gap between plans and practice. For reasons rooted in the Constitution and militia tradition, the reserve system in the United States is entangled with state and local politics. This was exemplified in the mid-1980s when several governors refused to permit National Guard personnel to be deployed to Central America for training exercises or announced that they would not authorize such deployments if asked. If they could stop training scheduled by the federal government, some observers wondered, "could they also interpose state authority at some time in the future to block deployment in a controversial military venture?"[84]

In the past Congress has also imposed organizational arrangements and funding levels for the reserve system that the executive has considered inefficient. For example, Secretary of Defense Robert McNamara sought to merge the National Guard and reserves and put them all under federal control, on the grounds that state governors did not need their own armies; Congress rejected the change. Or in 1988, when Congress was cutting the administration's overall defense budget request, members of the House Armed Services committee sought nearly $1 billion more for the guard and reserves than Secretary of Defense Frank Carlucci had requested. And as the political system adapted to the end of the cold war, Congress and the executive clashed again over how cuts in force levels would be distributed, with the secretary of defense seeking heavier reductions in the reserves than Congress wanted.[85] Political considerations favor the reserves when it comes to dividing up the defense budget pie, but they do not always promote efficient military utilization. In the 1968 mobilization,

> Readiness considerations gave way to concerns that recalled units should be geographically representative (seventy-six units represented thirty-four states), that the contributions by the Army National Guard and Reserve components would be proportional, and that every state would be left with enough capability to handle civil disturbances. By these criteria, some units selected for call-up were manned and equipped at levels lower than similar reserve units that were not mobilized. . . . [T]his mobilization took place under what should have been "ideal" conditions.[86]

Issues in Reserve Readiness

The performance of most U.S. reserve units mobilized for the Persian Gulf crisis in 1990 was reassuring. That case followed a decade of investments in reserves that were atypical in American history. As post–cold war defense budgets slide downward, it will become unclear whether the record in the Gulf or the historic pattern is closer to current reality.

U.S. reliance on the reserves grew substantially after the mid-1970s. Additional resources raised their readiness over historic levels, but that was not saying much. Estimates of reserve readiness were also more dubious than estimates for the active forces. It was always easier to have confidence in the readiness of active forces because they usually had higher percentages of the personnel and equipment required for combat, they engaged full-time in developing their capability from day to day, and the skills they acquired in training were less likely to have atrophied.

The difficulty of evaluating reserve forces is evident from the prevalence of both underestimates and overestimates of readiness in past cases. In 1914, the Allies paid a high price for making the mistake of believing that the Germans would not be able to use reserves in the initial attack.[87] In the United States, in contrast, until the 1990 Persian Gulf crisis, reserve ground forces usually proved less ready than anticipated and not qualified enough to be committed to combat quickly or as separate units. In World War II the army had to replace all National Guard officers over the rank of lieutenant colonel, and many of those in lower ranks, with regulars. Most reservists wound up being used as fillers. During the cold war there were four call-ups. In the first three, units needed about *seven months* of training before they were deemed ready to deploy. (For the enlisted men, that was as much time as was needed to induct, train, and deploy draftees from scratch!) Some divisions called up for Korea needed about fourteen months before they could deploy. Contingency plans for Berlin had assumed that reserves could be ready within three to five months after mobilization, but many units actually needed as much as three times that amount of training. In the May 1968 call-up after the *Pueblo* capture, army assumptions that the units activated would be ready for combat were dashed; not a single one of the seventy-six units mobilized met the standard, and all were rated C-4 in equipment. Thirty-five U.S. Army Reserve units did go to Vietnam, but not until they had trained for another six to seven months.[88]

The situation has not always been that bad. The record in the war against Iraq was much better, although there were significant problems in that case, too, as chapter 7 shows. Over time, the U.S. Air Force Reserves and National Guard, in particular, have improved since the embarrassing mobilization for Korea. Almost a year after the outbreak of the war, the commander of the Air Defense Command said that most of the units "are not in a position to do what is expected." Neither of the two air guard wings in the Strategic Air Command "*ever* achieved fully combat-ready status prior to its return to state control." Air units mobilized for the 1961 Berlin crisis "had extremely limited operational capabilities." But those mobilized in 1968, after the program had received more emphasis, performed very well in Vietnam.[89] In recent years air reserve units have generally been considered highly proficient—in many cases more so than *active* units—because they get to fly more and have large numbers of full-time administrative and maintenance personnel. By the early 1980s these units demonstrated that they could deploy within three days, and by the late 1980s they were required to be ready within two days of notification. This impressive level of operational readiness, however, vitiates a good part of the cost advantage that is the prime attraction of reserve forces. Their operating costs have been about two-thirds of the cost for counterpart active units.[90]

Tactical airpower is likely to be effective as an independent instrument only in limited engagements or against a small and much weaker enemy, and those sorts of contingencies are the ones least likely to require mobilization. For a real war, the ground force reserves remain central. Throughout the cold war, the actual readiness of these units almost never matched the levels stipulated in plans. When the army tested the mobilization system with an extensive exercise in 1976, soon after the shift to the total force concept, serious problems were found that suggested units would not meet their planned deployment times or integrate effectively with other forces in Europe.[91]

Readiness improved with subsequent infusions of resources, and by the end of the 1980s reserve forces accounted for almost half of the U.S. force structure and just over half of the army's manpower.[92] Under the total force concept, reserves became integral to large-scale operations of any sort. In a marked change from the situation that prevailed between the end of the Korean War and the end of the Vietnam War, *active* units came to depend on augmentation by reserves. This was reflected in the combined increase in units and decrease in manpower. At the beginning of the last Berlin crisis, for example, the active army had eleven regular divisions (and three training divisions) and 870,000 men. Three decades later, the army had over 60 percent more regular divisions but 10 percent less active manpower. Half of the eighteen active divisions in the service at the close of the 1980s were incomplete in peacetime; they included the so-called roundout brigades or battalions from the reserves. Reserves were scheduled to provide "*more than 40 percent* of the Army forces deployed during the *first thirty days* of a European war," about half of the tactical logistics for the force available at the outset of mobilization, "and more than 75 percent of the support required by the six-division augmentation force." The army could not even commit more than five and a half of its *active* divisions to combat without mobilizing reserves for tactical support.[93]

This dependence was not reflected in readiness assessments. Army divisions have not always considered the status of their roundout units when determining their own C-ratings.[94] (In peacetime the active army has no control of such reserve units.) As for reserve units themselves, 90 percent of the National Guard but only 50 percent of army reserve units were required to report C-ratings in the late 1980s. Most of those that reported did so only twice a year, reducing the odds that such ratings reflected their average condition: "The October reports are usually made shortly after the summer training period, when unit readiness is at a peak."[95] As for reserve units themselves, 20 percent were supposed to deploy within a month of mobilization as of the mid-1980s, but only half of those early-moving units met deployment criteria. On average, the readiness of reserves improved more than that of active forces during the first Reagan administration, yet reserve units (usually rated C-3 or C-4) remained much less ready than active ones (most rated C-2 or C-3). By 1987 three-quarters of reporting units were rated C-3 or better, but this coincided with the switchover from the UNITREP to SORTS reporting system (see chapter 5). By the end of the 1980s, with new or reorganizing units excluded, 82 percent of Army National Guard units were reported C-3 or better.[96]

Personnel Strength

After the Vietnam War the size of the army guard and reserve looked like a tub-shaped curve. Once the draft-induced hordes of the Dan Quayle generation ended their six-year obligations in the mid-1970s, numbers plummeted. Unit end-strength fell by about a quarter between 1974 and 1977, and in the latter year about half of units (43 percent of the National Guard and 54 percent of the U.S. Army Reserve) were rated not ready. The strength of the selected reserve (formed units) increased steadily after 1978, although not quite as fast as it had fallen. Then from fiscal 1980 to 1989, the strength of all the selected reserve components together (the bulk being army) grew by a whopping 135 percent.[97]

Attrition and turbulence also declined after the 1970s, at which time some units had an annual turnover of more than 50 percent. This record had been particularly crippling to readiness because reserve units have little time to train together.[98] Of the National Guard and army reserve entrants in 1980, 30–40 percent, respectively, "failed to complete even two years of a six-year obligation"; by 1986 the combined turnover rate, though still high, had been cut by roughly a third.[99] Concern that more than 20 percent of a unit's members might be hard to find and assemble in an emergency was allayed in 1987 when a no-notice exercise located more than 90 percent of those called.[100] In the 1980s the full-time cadre in reserve units grew, to become one of the principal sources of increased effectiveness. In the late 1970s army National Guard and reserve battalions only had about 2 percent full-time manning. This figure compared with about 20 percent (30 percent by 1986) for the far readier air force reserve and guard, and approximately 20 percent for Soviet category III divisions. By the late 1980s U.S. Army Reserve full-time personnel grew to 9–12 percent of total strength, with a goal of 15 percent.[101]

The situation of the individual ready reserve (IRR)—those personnel not assigned to units—has usually been less clear than that of the selected reserve. The IRR is supposed to supply fillers and replacements for casualties in the early days of combat, but very few receive any annual training. During the 1970s, IRR strength fell even more precipitously than that of the selected reserve, and its recovery was weaker. It went from more than a million men in 1972 to less than 150,000 five years later, then climbed gradually. In the first year of the Reagan administration, the IRR was about 200,000 (40 percent) short of the official requirement, and by 1987 it was still 45,000 short of the number estimated to be needed for the first ninety days of mobilization.[102]

Even after the Reagan buildup, the IRR was needed to fill out *active* combat battalions, since only 7 percent of them were at the highest authorized level of organization (ALO-1, which mandates full manning in peacetime). Almost a fifth of active army battalions and about a third of active combat service support (CSS) companies were normally at or below 80 percent manning (ALO-3).[103] Service planners estimated that 70 percent of enlisted men in the IRR would respond in a call-up. Some members, however, had wound up in the IRR through the transfer in lieu of discharge program, because they failed to complete their original active or reserve duty obligations. A National Guard general raised the question, "if we couldn't find them for a weekend drill, how are we going to find them for war?"[104] In the Persian Gulf War, nevertheless, 75 percent of the 20,000 called from the IRR appeared.[105]

Equipment Strength

Although the personnel strength of the reserves was gradually rebuilt, the shortage of equipment remained a weakness. Even by 1986 the U.S. Army Reserve and National Guard had barely more than two-thirds of their *authorized* equipment. Shortages were more striking than the numbers implied, since the authorized peacetime levels are lower than official wartime requirements. Despite increased appropriations, the situation was no better by 1989.[106]

In earlier years the reserves suffered because their weapons were diverted to supply other nations or to fill POMCUS stocks. Congress restrained this practice. The result, however, was not fully consistent with strategic plans, because local political interests promoted egalitarian distribution of equipment to units in various places. Except for discrimination in favor of roundout units for active forces, which must deploy immediately, early-deploying reserve units did not receive a clear priority over others for equipment.[107]

Despite heavier investments in the 1980s, the peacetime personnel and equipment strength of U.S. Army Reserve and National Guard units were at best comparable to Soviet category III forces and by most estimates were below that standard. Given the huge disparity in numbers of NATO and Soviet divisions, the question was whether other qualitative advantages mitigated the net assessment of manpower and weaponry. On the Soviet side, questions about the numbers of personnel available did not apply. Unlike the United States, the USSR did not maintain reserve units as distinct entities, except for specialist units. Millions of discharged conscripts remained subject to recall to fill out existing divisions. For a hypothetical prolonged war, the disparity was less significant since the United States could reinstitute conscription. In that situation, however, a disparity in available equipment would have favored the Soviet Union. The United States did not match the Soviet practice of mothballing most obsolete weapons, and U.S. defense production capacity and shortages of strategic materials made it unlikely that new units could be outfitted and trained for combat as soon as they could be inducted and organized.[108] This was the main U.S. problem throughout its earlier history, when military technology and manufacturing were much simpler.

The particularly interesting question for net assessment that should have been raised in this context concerned the intermediate phase of

a hypothetical war, after U.S reserves and Soviet category III formations had been called up and were preparing for deployment. How
would they compare in speed and effectiveness? The principal issues
here were about training.

Training

The recovery of personnel strength in U.S. ground force reserves
after the 1970s was a mixed blessing. Numbers went up, but average
experience went down, and the proficiency of active forces benefited
at the expense of the reserves. The All Volunteer Force emphasized
retention in the active forces, thereby creating a "low-flow" force that
in turn reduced the number of personnel entering the reserves with
extensive active duty service behind them. In the lower-strength reserves of the late 1970s, up to 70 percent had prior active service. In
contrast, the Soviet conscription-based "high-flow" force provided a
steady stream of large numbers of reservists with a couple years of
active duty experience.[109]

The improved American reserves of the 1980s had to rely much
more on the reserve training program. It was not uncommon, however, for new recruits to be on unit rolls for two years before finishing
their initial entry training. Subsequent training for army guard and
reserves (about thirty-eight days a year of weekend drills and summer
camp) is notoriously poor. Only about half of training time is effective
time, owing to subtractions for maintenance, travel time, personnel
administration, medical checks, and "Mickey Mouse" activities such
as preparation for inspection. Many units lack weapon ranges and
facilities within reasonable travel distance from their headquarters. At
the least, active units train more than three times as much as reserves,
and by some estimates active army forces train *seven times* as often as
reserves. The time problem is compounded for National Guard units
by the fact that, until they are federalized, they are controlled by state
governors and have state missions for which they must train—such as
riot control or disaster relief—at a cost to training for war. Yet under
the total force plan, many reserve units were supposed to be as well
prepared for war as their active counterparts.[110]

One aspect of this general problem is the difficulty of providing
sufficient training in a specific military occupational specialty (MOS)
and maintaining a match between the special skills of individuals and
the positions in the unit to which they are assigned. Even when en-

trants to the reserves do have prior service, they often have to be retrained to fill their new billets. (Active forces emphasize combat units, and reserve forces concentrate more on support, so the transferability of skills from active to reserve service is limited.)[111] In 1983 only 55 percent of naval reserves and 64 percent of personnel in National Guard divisions were qualified in their assigned MOS. By 1987, after years of the Reagan defense buildup, the army reserve, guard, and Marine Corps reserve were still citing the MOS mismatch problem as a crucial handicap to readiness, and according to the most recent Defense Department annual report, the problem remains. In any case, MOS data are not too reliable because testing requirements are often not fulfilled. In fiscal 1987 and 1988, 40 percent of army reservists who were supposed to take the skill qualification test did not do so; among the reservists who did take it, the passing rate was 25 percent below that of soldiers on active duty.[112] Demographic and organizational problems make it difficult to deal with the mismatch. Because of the mobility of American society, reservists frequently move their domiciles and transfer from one unit to another. The odds are not high that the old MOS a soldier holds will correspond to an available billet in a new unit. Civilian employers and the geographic dispersion of reserve units are serious obstacles for programs designed to send reservists to advanced military schools and also make it difficult to coordinate equipment, training, and wartime assignments. "On the average, a reserve battalion is dispersed over a 150-mile radius, and some extend to over 300 miles. Active component counterparts are typically clustered within a mile or less of each other."[113]

To deal with the dispersion problem, plans were developed for regional sites where maintenance training could be concentrated with the most recent equipment available. To improve the readiness of special skills, it was also proposed that individuals be assigned to pools. These personnel would be exempted from weekend drill and would not have to fit into local units, where open billets for their specialties would be rare. Rather, they could be available for assignment nationwide. The army developed a plan for such a system, a hybrid between the selected reserve and IRR, calling it the individual selected reserve (ISR).[114]

This sort of initiative toward more intensive technical training and nationalizing some of the reserves would be more helpful if annual training could be concentrated instead of diffused in widely separated weekends and two-week summer camps that do little to consolidate learning or keep up its momentum. When the navy tried experimenting with a three-week training cycle, however, it found high resistance among reservists' employers and families. The army addressed these problems with reforms designed "to allow reserve component units to train on fewer tasks than a like active component unit."[115] This may be the best way to handle the inevitable contradiction between available training time and equipment, on one hand, and expected levels of performance, on the other, but it moves in the direction of the Soviet pattern, which substituted mass and differentiation for efficiency and versatility.

Even after the big effort to boost defense in the 1980s, U.S. ground force reserve units still faced obstacles to efficiency. One was that the army often changed their missions faster than training programs for those missions could be completed. The regular sequence of individual, small-unit, and battalion or brigade-level training takes several years to complete under the best of circumstances for reserve units working part-time. (Higher-level tactical coordination was often not achieved because units were broken up and trained at different locations during annual summer camps.) Missions were changed and thus the training schedule revamped as often as every three to five years.[116] Another problem was the organizational barrier to developing competence among reserve officers. First, many officers are commissioned through state officer candidate schools, which provide their training on weekends and during two-week summer stints and therefore cannot come close to duplicating the amount and intensity of training officers receive in the active forces. Second, the unit-vacancy system of promotion, which fills open slots from within units rather than by bringing in the best qualified personnel from somewhere else, often puts officers into specialized positions for which they have not had training.[117]

Although all of these problems suggested that U.S. reserve forces would not have been as ready for World War III in practice as war plans called for them to be, the problems did not seem horrible when matched against those of the USSR.[118] The formal Soviet system involved a highly detailed set of reserve training obligations, under which the susceptibility of individuals to periodic recall was geared to age and rank. In practice, however, training for reserves was less frequent and less comprehensive than the maximum formal obligation.

Some reservists were never called at all for refresher training.[119] Most of them did "not know what unit they will be assigned to during wartime mobilization and have never trained with that unit."[120] Stories about confusion and delays in Soviet mobilization due to lack of proficiency resemble the record of past U.S. reserve call-ups. The United States also exercised for mobilization and the reinforcement of Europe each year, but the Soviet Union seldom exercised its deployment system on a similar scale.[121]

The lack of regular refresher training was often cited as the prime weakness of Soviet reserves, which meant that they would have had to engage in extensive retraining after mobilization if they were to be used as more than cannon fodder. If Moscow had filled its divisions with a random sample of the tens of millions of men in the reserves, or even the several million discharged from active service within five years, decaying skills or a mismatch with new equipment would certainly have been significant problems. Given the available numbers, however, a little selectivity could have reduced the problem substantially. The Soviet military needed 2.1 million reservists to bring its formations to full wartime strength. At least three-quarters of that number were being regularly discharged from conscript service *each year* in the 1980s. Like the United States, moreover, Moscow invested in reserve force improvements in the 1980s, including higher numbers of recently trained reservists.[122]

Where did all these varying comparisons leave net assessment for the contingency that was the dominant concern for more than four decades after World War II? By the end of the cold war, U.S. and Soviet choices about operational and structural readiness had begun to converge. Even before the USSR unraveled, Gorbachev's cuts in forces reduced the structural readiness that had so characterized the Soviet military system. After the crack-up of the union, Russian strategists planned more reductions in the size of their forces and increases in their mobility and readiness.[123] Meanwhile the American system had given higher priority to structural readiness, as could be seen not only in weapon modernization programs but also in the increased number of ground force divisions (while active manpower was kept constant), the partial integration of the reserves and active forces via roundout units, and the greater dependence of war plans on prompt utilization of reserve forces.

On balance, U.S. active divisions appeared substantially more ready than most Soviet category I divisions, Soviet category II divisions seemed substantially more ready than most U.S. reserve units, and U.S. reserves and Soviet category III divisions should have been roughly equivalent. U.S. reservists were better trained from year to year, but Soviet cadre divisions had many more full-time personnel and could draw on a larger number of reservists with a recently completed regular tour of active duty behind them. Furthermore, the historical record gave no reason to assume that U.S. ground force reserves—at least the combat units—could deploy as fast as category III formations. U.S. reserves took close to seven months after mobilization to deploy in most of their postwar call-ups (though less in 1990–91), but Soviet units deployed within a few months even in the prolonged pre-attack mobilizations against Czechoslovakia in 1968 and Afghanistan in 1979. Giving U.S. reserve units more resources, equipment, and full-time cadre in the 1980s also brought them close to the status of Soviet category III divisions. The fact that U.S. reserve units have some annual training also gave them an edge, if one assumes that Soviet call-ups would not discriminate according to discharge dates. Training, however, is the least malleable factor in U.S. reserve readiness as long as the two-week limit cannot be breached.

Past experience never provided a worst-case test. The time for reorganization, refurbishment, or retraining that either the Americans or Russians took in their cold war mobilizations for peripheral conflicts was not driven by the imperative to commit forces at the soonest possible moment, as it would have been if they were going to war with each other. Although there was never a worst-case test, the reformed U.S. reserve system—and the entire military establishment—was called to a test of sorts in 1990, just as the epochal struggle with the Soviet Union ended.

Part III
After the Cold War

7

Readiness and Strategy after the Cold War

*T*HE INSTITUTIONALIZED CONFRONTATION of the cold war was a good laboratory for exploring the linear and cyclical qualities of readiness and the interdependent choices about military mass, speed, and efficiency. How much does all of this have to do with a world in which there is no other superpower to challenge the United States? Some of the cold war readiness issues will continue to be a concern on a smaller scale, while different issues that were dormant during the cold war—ones more reminiscent of the U.S. military tradition antedating the era of peacetime mobilization—will arise.

Unless the United States disengages from strategic involvement in other regions of the world, it will continue to need a force capable of combat on short notice. That force will be one with less structural readiness than was necessary for war with a Soviet Union positioned in Germany, a few hundred kilometers from the English Channel. Some observers decided that after the cold war, the necessary standing force should be something slightly larger than the Desert Storm force, that is, one that could fight a war against a power like Iraq. Others, including the Clinton administration in 1994, claim that twice that size a force is needed, so that the United States could engage and defeat two such medium-sized powers at once.

The second view is discussed later in this chapter. The first, in favor of keeping a Desert Storm equivalent, is both sensible and misguided. It is sensible inasmuch as Iraq or Iran represents the more powerful of the post–cold war threats that can now be identified, and it would be wasteful to maintain more actual capability than necessary to deal with actual threats. If potential threats on a larger scale (hostile powers more comparable in strength to the old Soviet Union) begin to emerge, they should be dealt with by converting U.S. potential into actual capability, that is, by remobilization. The problem of mobilization readiness is discussed in greater depth in chapter 8. The idea that a Desert Storm equivalent is needed for the post–cold war era is also misguided, however, because to keep that sort of capability will require more than a force of the size and configuration that actually deployed to the Persian Gulf and fought there.

For all these reasons, it is appropriate to review the conflict that bridges the cold war era and the current one: the war against Iraq. Operation Desert Storm represents a model of operational military success to emulate (leaving aside the more important policy and strategy questions about whether the war was necessary or the political results worth the price). The reaction to the invasion of Kuwait contradicted the historic record of unreadiness and disaster in cases like Bataan, Kasserine, and Osan. If the result of combat is what counts, one could never ask for better readiness than that exhibited by U.S. forces in 1991. To what extent Desert Storm actually tested the peacetime readiness of U.S. forces, however, and to what extent it can serve as a model for the future, is less clear.

The Lessons of Desert Storm

The nearly perfect performance of U.S. forces in operations against Iraq was due in large part to three factors.

—*Readiness for what: the choice of enemy.* Iraq's military power was high in quantity but low in quality. Baghdad had bought a modern military machine but grafted it onto a social and technological infrastructure that, while modernizing, remained primitive in several important respects. Training was especially deficient, because of political inhibitions as well as limited resources and education.[1] The integration of combat and communication systems and the professionalism of Iraq's military command lagged far behind the country's levels of manpower and weapons.[2] Because Iraqi might turned out to be more fragile than most estimates had indicated, U.S. vulnerabilities were not exploited.

—*Readiness for when: time to prepare for combat.* The full potential of existing structural readiness was realized, as time and rapidly infused resources were exploited to achieve maximum operational readiness. Between the invasion of Kuwait in August 1990 and the beginning of the air war in January 1991, the American military mobilized, filled out, and deployed units to Saudi Arabia; set up bases, headquarters, logistical networks, communications systems, and supply stockpiles; and trained over, and over, and over again for the attack. The preparation time amounted to more than five months for the air war and almost *seven months* for the ground war. Not all of this time was necessary for ultimate success (for example, VII Corps did not move out of Germany until November), but it certainly helped. Given this time for crisis mobilization, peacetime structural readiness was tested, but operational readiness was not. Had Iraq attacked Saudi Arabia early in the Desert Shield period, before the buildup of U.S. air and armor units to reinforce the light elements of the 82d Airborne division, the ultimate outcome of the war might have been the same, but the initial phase might have looked more like the historic American norm.[3]

—*Readiness of what: capitalization on the cold war.* The United States fought Iraq with forces developed over the course of four decades of mobilization for war with a superpower, the Soviet Union. The Reagan buildup, which had boosted the regular baseline of cold war capabilities, had also crested not long before Saddam Hussein struck. Since the cold war had ended months before the invasion of Kuwait, this meant that *available structural readiness was higher than needed* to fight Iraq. As a result, active and reserve units could be cobbled together in ways that would be impossible in a mobilization where available forces did not exceed the number planned for the most demanding contingency. If the U.S. military establishment in August 1990 had been one designed with an Iraq-sized threat in mind, rather than the much larger Soviet threat, it would have had much less slack and flexibility.[4]

In its next war the United States faces reasonable odds of enjoying the first of these advantages, less probability that it will have the second, and little chance of the third. A review of the war against Iraq thus serves two purposes. First, it reveals the limitations of readiness in a situation in which it should have been as close to perfect as could ever be expected. Second, it brings to light questions about how readiness and strategic choices can affect each other: specifically, how levels of structural readiness could encourage an offensive strategy rather than a defensive one. Such questions are important to consider in the post–cold war world because the threats to the United States are now lower than they used to be, but U.S. capabilities are lower as well.

Time and Capability

The length of Operation Desert Shield—the buildup phase from August 1990 to January 1991—was the key to Desert Storm's smooth success. This in turn was linked to the fact that Washington and its allies held the strategic option, since Iraq settled into a defensive position after swallowing Kuwait. The coalition opposing Baghdad could choose whether or not to go to war, so it could also choose when combat would begin. It had the luxury of going to "war by appointment."[5]

The long buildup period was utilized in numerous ways to field a large force and pump up its operational readiness. Soldiers were given time to become acclimated to the desert, and complex weapon systems were modified and adapted ad hoc in order to operate well in desert conditions. For example, when wind and sand were found to be eroding Apache helicopter blades, a soldier came up with the idea of protecting them with epoxy tape. As units encountered various aspects of the new environment, in the words of the commander of army forces in the Gulf, "We'd find a problem and we'd fix the problem."[6]

In economics, time is money. In strategy—as long as one has the option of exploiting the initiative—time is capability. The U.S. decision to mount a counteroffensive and eject Iraq from Kuwait allowed readiness to develop in the linear fashion, by climbing the stairway steadily until it reached its peak around the chosen H-hour. A deterrent strategy focusing on the defense of Saudi Arabia, though, would have had to deal with the cyclical qualities of readiness, as the buildup wave eventually crested and fell.

In particular, time was used to move equipment from the United States and Europe, and then to prepare and maintain it in optimal operating condition. Huge stockpiles of spare parts and consumables were built up. Repeated training exercises were also undertaken, simulating battle conditions in the Kuwaiti theater of operations (KTO), practicing assault and the breaching of fortifications, and planning air strikes according to every conceivable wartime requirement. For example, every single one of the mission profiles flown by one Marine F/A-18 squadron in the first week of the war had been rehearsed in the Desert Shield period.[7]

Some of the time during Desert Shield was needed to make up for slippages in planned timetables. A shortage in fast ship transport put deployment of heavy armor behind schedule. Only 24 percent of the ready reserve force ships in the Military Sealift Command activated in the August 1990 surge were on time; 30 percent (14 out of 46) were between one and five days late; 22 percent were six to ten days late; and 24 percent were at least eleven days behind the timetable.[8] "Ships with breakout schedules of five and 10 days took, on the average, 11 and 16 days to break out." Nor did the airlift system work at full capacity at the beginning.[9] The discovery of inadequacies in computer and telecommunications systems meant that "the Air Force supply system envisioned for the theater had to be completely abandoned," mistakes in priority codings led to backlogs, and "the supply system began to resemble a water pipe crimped at both ends."[10] Although the readiest of army reserve units were called to service first, 15 percent of those mobilized in the first three months of Desert Shield were rated not deployable (that is, below C-3); during the following two months, more than one-third of army units that were called up were rated not deployable.[11] In late December 1990 Norman Schwarzkopf's deputy, Lieutenant General Calvin A. H. Waller, caused a public flap when he warned that U.S. forces would not be ready for war by the January 15 deadline that the Bush administration had set for Iraq to withdraw from Kuwait.[12]

Some readiness problems were eased by violating earlier cold war plans that allocated the bulk of capabilities to deterring Soviet attack in Europe. Large numbers of precision-guided munitions and missiles (as well as troop units of VII Corps) were drawn out of U.S. units in Germany. The air force also "stripped many fighter planes based in the United States of spare parts to make combat-ready those sent to the gulf," making those left in the states less able to go to war elsewhere.[13] Had the invasion of Kuwait occurred during the cold war and had Washington chosen to respond as forcefully as it did in 1990, underwriting capability to face Iraq would have undercut normal readiness for the main standing threat. (This is what happened in the course of the Vietnam War.)

Other problems were obviated by a combination of good luck and skill that kept the war shorter and less bloody than has been anticipated in most early estimates. For example, capabilities for surge production did not come to a test, because there were war reserve stockpiles of so many items. "There were some valuable insights, however, from surging in the production of those items which were (or potentially were) in short supply." According to the official report on the war:

> The greatest demand for increased production was for secondary items such as engines, transmissions, spare parts, and troop support items, rather than major end items. . . . The need was for quick surge capability to overcome deficiencies in war reserves of those secondary items. . . . [I]n some cases, industry's ability to meet surge demands was marginal and could have had serious consequences had the offensive begun sooner, lasted longer, or been more demanding. For many items, the time required for industry to surge to maximum production capacity was six to nine months, even for relatively inexpensive, low-technology items, such as clothing, sandbags, and barbed wire.[14]

Medical readiness was also not put to a test, since American and allied casualties turned out to be so low, and Iraq elected not to use its chemical warfare capabilities. After four months of the Desert Shield buildup, however, there were still significant shortfalls being reported in desired medical preparedness. These included missing modern equipment such as suction machines to clear respiratory systems, advanced surgical sutures, electronic monitors, and pumps for intravenous drips. Ten days before the air war began, one navy surgeon was quoted as saying, "We'll end up practicing medicine as it was practiced in the 50's or 60's."[15]

Protective arrangements for countering Iraqi chemical or biological attacks were inadequate in the early stage of Desert Shield and were never brought all the way up to desired levels, even during the war. There were problems with the supply of drugs, detection and decontamination equipment, and collective protection systems. Only two producers were available to provide nerve agent antidotes and chemical protective gloves, and they almost got out of the business before the invasion of Kuwait; then they were unable to provide sufficient quantities when needed. Less atropine was supplied to the theater than necessary to meet the target total of two doses for everyone.[16] It takes little imagination to think of the scandal that would have ensued had a shortfall been revealed after an Iraqi chemical attack on U.S. forces.

Reserve Readiness for the Gulf

The Persian Gulf War was a major test of the reliance on reserve units embodied in the total force concept, and the results were mixed. For the most part, mobilization was a success story. In the largest call-up since the Korean War, individuals reported without incident; there were hardly any "no-shows." By the peak of mobilization at the end of the war, 231,000 reservists had been called to duty, and more than 105,000 of them were serving in the theater of operations. Most reserve units performed effectively, providing combat support and service functions that active forces could not fully supply. At the height of the U.S. deployment, more than 70 percent of the 22d Support Command's personnel were reservists. In most cases, the integration of active and reserve units proceeded smoothly. A majority of the reserves called to duty had high enough readiness levels to perform their missions with little postmobilization training.[17]

The Gulf War experience calls attention to the impact that reserve readiness can have on choices in strategy. Despite its good showing in general, reliance on the reserve system posed big problems for either of the two main functions expected of any military commitment: maintenance of the *threat* of force, in order to support a defensive or deterrence-by-denial strategy, or the actual *use* of force in combat. In contrast to the reassuring performance of reservists in air combat or ground combat support and service roles, the record of reserve units assigned to ground combat was not reassuring.

The system did not make it practical to use reserves in general for a deterrent strategy, which would have required prolonged deployment, or to use ground combat reserves in the offensive that eventually took place. The two alternatives required both too much and too little time for the system as designed, once it had to operate under natural political conditions. Prolonged deployment would have strained the capacity of the total force to rotate and replace reservists in specialized support roles. Once the decision was made to move from deterrence to active use of force, however, there was not enough time to get ground combat reservists ready for action. The former problem helped push political leadership toward choosing an offensive strategy; the latter prevented combat reserves from playing the role for which they had been designed.

The problem should not be exaggerated. The Bush administration might well have chosen to start the war when it did anyway, for other reasons, and it would not have been physically impossible to maintain a long-term defensive deployment along the Saudi Arabian border, especially if the force was smaller than the one deployed by the end of 1990. Nevertheless, the limitations imposed by mobilization and readiness timelines made nonoffensive alternatives less feasible. This experience is a leaden lining in the silver cloud of Operation Desert Storm because it suggests the discomfiting prospect that after post–cold war demobilization is complete, when structural readiness is much lower than it was in 1990, heavy reliance on reserves may push strategic choices further away from defensive options at the same time that some essential elements of reserve forces are ill adapted to implementing the alternatives.

How does what happened point in this direction? Despite official commitment to the total force principle for nearly two decades, it was not implemented immediately upon the decision to contest the Iraqi invasion. President Bush did not issue the first authorization for a reserve call until three weeks after Kuwait had been occupied. Then it was only for 48,000 personnel and excluded ground combat units. At that time, August 22, 1990, the law limited reserve component activation to ninety days, with one ninety-day extension. In the face of uncertainty about how and when the Iraqis would be countered, this discouraged early reserve mobilization in general and made employment of roundout combat brigades impractical because of the necessary training time and transportation costs. Early in the fall Secretary of Defense Dick Cheney testified before the Senate Armed Services Committee, "We're concerned that once we get them in, get them trained up and ready to go, we'd only have them in Saudi Arabia for 60 to 90 days, and that's not long enough to justify the expense that would be involved."[18] Cheney also told the House Armed Services Committee in September that the roundout brigades were not called because of the desire to limit the size of reserve mobilization.[19]

Since active duty forces had to deploy without their roundout brigades, replacement brigades had to be transferred from the regular army. As long as a surplus of active combat units existed, that was not a problem. Indeed, it would have made little sense to deploy reserve combat units in place of active ones.

That surplus existed, however, only because the cold war had just ended at the most perfectly convenient time imaginable. Had the cold war still been on, Washington would not have been able to redeploy as many forces as it did (most obviously, the corps of armored units from the Seventh Army in Germany) without contradicting the prime commitment for which U.S. forces were designed (war in Europe against the Soviet Union). Had the cold war ended earlier, on the other hand, demobilization would have been further along, and the cushion of forces to draw on for the Gulf would have been much smaller. Even so, with the redundant amount of structural readiness that existed in 1990, there was still not enough slack to avoid difficult choices.

Had President Bush wished to sustain a long-term defensive presence in Saudi Arabia, it would have had to be smaller than the multi-division, multiwing force that was in fact deployed during Operation Desert Shield. Otherwise, it would have been necessary to use reservists in the rotation in order to sustain the flow of personnel replacement in the region. Over time, such rotation might have destroyed the reserve system, since few civilians would voluntarily remain in units called periodically for tours in austere, sweltering bases in the desert.

In the fall of 1990 the Joint Chiefs of Staff were finishing a plan for rotation in the Gulf. Bush and the Arab allies at the time decided that they did not want a long-term presence of American forces in the theater. Even if they had, it would have been difficult because *non*combat reservists integral to the deployments (for example, linguists, water purifiers, and chemical decontamination specialists) were not all easily replaceable by other reservists to be called later.[20]

Early in November Congress doubled the limit on combat reservists' active duty to 360 days, and the Bush administration announced an additional buildup of forces in the Gulf, and mobilization of reserves totaling 188,000. This time combat reserve units were included. The administration then announced that troops in the theater would not be rotated until the crisis was over. The navy also dispatched six of its fourteen aircraft carriers to the Gulf, a deployment that could be sustained only by straining the carrier force and its personnel to the limit.[21]

Together these decisions made war virtually inevitable if Iraq did not withdraw from Kuwait, an inevitability later made explicit when the January 15 deadline was announced. That deadline, however, did not mesh well with the delay in the decision to mobilize reserve units for ground combat. The decision to mobilize the combat roundout brigades came more than three months after Baghdad had struck, and the combat units were those who needed the most time of any of the reservists for refresher training before they would be ready to accomplish their missions.

There were some bright spots in the performance of combat reserves. For example, one Marine Corps tank company, which had trained in peacetime on M-60s, managed to retrain for eighteen days after mobilization on very different M-1s, arrive in Saudi Arabia on February 19, 1991, go into battle a mere five days later, and perform successfully.[22] But for the most part the story of these units was a sad entry in the record of Desert Storm. Not a single army reserve armor or mechanized infantry unit saw action, although three roundout brigades were activated. Post-mobilization training in the United States revealed many of the deficiencies that critics had worried about: in general proficiency, various functions such as vehicle maintenance, and especially in leadership. Less than a tenth of the officers in one brigade had extended active duty experience. Staff procedures proved to be a problem, inhibiting roundout units' ability to coordinate in combat with other headquarters. More than one of the top commanders in the units were reassigned. By the end of February the three brigades "either had been certified or were about to be certified by the Army as ready for combat, if needed," but by that time the four-day ground war in Kuwait and Iraq had ended.[23]

Everything could have worked perfectly if the whole plan had been known and implemented at the outset, but that sort of fine-tuned coordination of technical and decisional factors virtually never occurs. If the roundout brigades had been called up immediately in the first phase of mobilization, they would have been ready to fight by the time the counteroffensive against Iraq was mounted. For this to have happened, the government would have had to decide earlier than it did to extend the duration of the call-up, or to choose an offensive strategy for the near future. The leaders of the regular army would also have had to welcome the implementation of the total force concept rather than resist it, as some apparently did, preferring to handle the mission with active forces that they considered more reliable.

There is one way in which the actual sequence and results of mobilization could be judged to make sense. That would be if the combat reserves were really only a hedge against a prolonged war and higher attrition, and if they were expected to be available in the theater only a month or more after the counteroffensive was initiated. That notion is completely inconsistent with the rationale for the roundout brigades, rooted as it was in cold war plans for the NATO central front, which linked the units directly to active divisions. Since the cold war surplus of active forces was available for the Gulf War, however, it was reasonable to change the concept ad hoc in order to let active forces do the job. (It appears that in reality pressure from members of Congress to employ reserves as planned was more responsible for the decision to mobilize the roundout brigades than was the administration's strategic calculation.)[24]

Although the importance of this question should not be exaggerated, the reason that it was of only limited significance in the war against Iraq is the same as the reason that it could be a bigger issue in the future: the cushion of surplus forces from the cold war. The point is put in perspective by noting that, given the availability of numerous combat units in the active forces at the time, the roundout brigades "accounted for less than 7% of the total number of Reservists who were called to active duty."[25] In the next war, the option provided by the cold war surplus will not be available, and a larger portion of structural readiness could come to reside in the reserves than at any time since before the Korean War.

To solve these problems, policymakers could improve the training and operational readiness of guard and reserve units, so that they come closer to the active units they are supposed to join; continue planning to use reserve units in combat early, but accept inferior levels of operational readiness and performance in those units; institute a more staggered and variegated system of unit readiness, and organize combat reserves in units of smaller size than divisions;[26] or reduce reliance on reserve units altogether.

The Clinton administration's strategy review settled on variations of all of these but the second.[27] Reserve forces were scheduled to be cut by a larger percentage than active forces; more resources were targeted for reserve equipment, training, and full-time support; and plans called for reorganizing army National Guard units into thirty-seven brigades (instead of divisions), including fifteen "enhanced readiness brigades" that were to be made capable of deployment within ninety days.[28] These initiatives will help—just as reforms in the decade before the war against Iraq improved reserve readiness substantially—and they will help in direct proportion to the willingness to sacrifice the cost advantage of reserves by diverting resources to them from the actives. The aim of bringing *combat* reserve units close to their active counterparts in proficiency, however, is a perennial will-o'-the-wisp. There is simply no way to train reserve ground forces close to the standards of active units in the limited time available each year.[29] If reserve forces are to be more effective, bigger departures from tradition should be considered.[30]

Experiments for Future Reserve Readiness

After cold war demobilization is complete, reserve forces will retain a major role and will still be faced with social and political constraints on training time. Many proposals for fixing reserves have already foundered on these constraints in the past. In an epochal transition from a half century of high mobilization to a smaller military establishment, however, the case for experimenting more boldly with innovations can be made more easily.

If all thirty-eight days of American reserve training could be concentrated in a single annual stint—or even if the total number of days was reduced but concentrated—operational readiness could be improved in two ways. First, the training time would be more effective. Second, it would be more feasible to delocalize unit organization, which would ease the problems noted in chapter 6 of mismatches between MOSes, billets, and the equipment available for training. That is, if personnel could assemble for three or four weeks at a time, it would be economical to man units with individuals from widely dispersed areas and fly them to the unit training site. This would not be practical for the National Guard, given its state functions and local political significance, but such obstacles would be less significant for the rest of the selected reserve.

Although officials appear convinced that exceeding two straight weeks of annual training would drive large numbers out of membership in the reserves, compromises are worth testing. One possibility would be to establish a half-dozen or so *national* army reserve battalions or brigades (associated with active divisions) to be manned by individuals who agree to train for 20–30 straight days each year. While a majority of reservists would reject such a commitment, the plan would only require that a limited percentage of them, nationwide, participate. Without attempting the experiment it would be wrong to assume that there are not a sufficient number of individuals who could handle the family and job problems imposed, which in turn might be softened by some program of bonuses.[31] Another variation would be to keep the two-week limit for training periods, but have two or three such periods each year rather than one, and dispense altogether with weekend drills, which many consider useless.

That small a number of units would not make a crucial difference, but it could help to stagger the readiness of U.S. forces according to deployment schedules and lift availability. There is no reason that all reserve units (or active ones) should strive for the same level of effectiveness in peacetime if the speed of their deployment in wartime would differ. Yet careful staggering has not always been the rule. Although authorized levels of organization in the army National Guard were geared somewhat to deployment schedules (roundout units having somewhat higher authorized levels), there were "virtually no differences" among army reserve units. The attempt to give adequate training resources to all units apparently took precedence over movement schedules.[32]

For some time after post–cold war demobilization is complete, the reserves' traditional lack of equipment should cease to be a problem; with fewer personnel and units in the Total Force, equipment produced in the 1980s can be redistributed. When that equipment becomes obsolete, the problem will reemerge. Until then, training time will remain the biggest obstacle to reserve readiness, and it will always be the hardest to resolve. Apart from constraints posed by reservists' primary family and job obligations, some of the main obstacles to reform lie in the deeply rooted traditions of localized organization of reserve units and state political control of the National Guard and its command structure. Federal authorities have tried citing grounds of functional efficiency to challenge those traditions and structures in the past and failed. There is little reason to expect much more success in radical organizational reform in the future. Indeed, the country's intractable deficit and budgetary constraints mean that it will be hard to avoid backsliding:

Reserve forces may also become the great pork barrel in American politics during the 1990s. Congressional dispositions are always to promote local concerns. As Congress struggles with fewer resources and less opportunity to dispense particularistic benefits to their districts in the years ahead, reserve forces may become the only

game left in town. With fewer categorical grants to dispense, reserve units become a much more attractive commodity.[33]

The conflict between the militia tradition and the efficacy of a modern military, with its dependence on high levels of professional skill,
was evident over a half century ago, when reserves were mobilized
for World War II. The conflict only grows as military complexity grows.
Technocratic reformers like Secretary of Defense Robert McNamara
did not overcome it when they tried, not only because of the political
strength of the National Guard, but also because in the context of high
cold war defense spending, this was not an issue worth a huge political
struggle.

The strategic costs of local influence over reserve forces, however,
have become more extreme. A case could be made that the executive
should now mount a major campaign to assert more federal control
over the organization of the reserve system, arguing for it on national
security grounds and emphasizing the smaller margin for error in the
compact post–cold war total force. Military leaders of the active forces
could be trotted out to campaign against parochial interests that
threaten the contribution of guard and reserve units to real national
security.[34]

Evaluating all these options in a vacuum is difficult. They depend
on larger assumptions about how much post–cold war military readiness of any sort the United States needs to maintain, and what proportions of it should be structural or operational. These questions in
turn hinge on yet larger premises of policy and strategy, which should
not necessarily bear much resemblance to those underlying the status
of U.S. forces that went to war with Iraq. Those forces fought the first
American war of the post–cold war era, but they had been developed
for the much more demanding requirements of the era that had just
closed.

Strategy and Plans

The kinds and amounts of readiness the United States needs after
the cold war depend on who it might have to fight, how much time it
will have to convert potential into actual power (that is, economic
potential into structural readiness, and structural into operational
readiness), and how it intends to fight. These questions have to be

answered, at least provisionally, or there is no basis for military policy and strategic choice. But no one can have much confidence in the answers as long as no impressive adversary to American power has yet been identified. The first step in establishing a basis for plans is to recognize the obstacles to planning.

Can Strategy Determine Structure?

Strategic rationalism assumes a logical sequence in relating ends to means in which strategy is the independent variable and force structure the dependent variable. First, it is presumed, policy objectives are chosen; second, the most efficient military strategy for achieving those objectives is determined; third, the forces best suited for implementing the strategy are designed and their costs figured; and fourth, the resources necessary to acquire such forces are diverted from the civilian economy to the military, and the forces are procured and fielded. Any other sequence appears irrational because means become disconnected from ends.

For many good reasons, as well as bad, the proper sequence in principle is rarely followed in practice. Occasionally decisionmakers or implementing bureaucracies are just irrational or incompetent, or let secrecy undermine coordinated planning.[35] The problem that is less easy to remedy lies in the obstacles to coordinating economic, technical, and organizational lead times with political changes. Policy objectives, threat assessments, or marginal willingness to pay economic costs to reduce strategic risks can shift instantly and often—because of either external or domestic changes—but complex military forces cannot. Moreover, the resemblance between contingencies envisioned for planning purposes and those encountered when war comes is usually loose at best. Forces available for use at any given time are those bought according to decisions made years before, when aims and assessments were often different. Strategy, therefore, often has to change to accommodate the means that happen to be available, rather than the other way around.

These uncertainties are less of a problem at some times than at others. During the cold war, policy objectives and defense budgets were both fairly constant for long periods. The main strategic decisions (apart from wars in Korea and Vietnam) revolved around how much to rely on nuclear deterrence or conventional defense. For forty years after 1950, changes in the size and readiness of forces were incremental variations around a high baseline. Defense debates were by no means trivial: they just focused on specific adjustments rather than basic shifts in the relation of variables.

Prospective enemies envisioned in the planning process were consistent: the Soviet Union throughout the cold war, China through the first half of it. Equally constant were the highest-priority theater of prospective combat (Europe) and the secondary theaters (Korea, and in the last decade of the cold war, the Persian Gulf). War in Vietnam did not fit conventional planning assumptions very well, and the strategy pursued there turned out to be wrong, but structural readiness to pursue a strategy based on conventional forces was no problem because it fell out of the large force developed according to plans for the main contingency. And for Operation Desert Storm, it could not have been an onerous challenge for Central Command to adapt itself to facing Iraq when not long before it had been planning against a scenario of Soviet invasion. The routine assumption of a superpower-sized adversary in threat assessments matched with a commitment to high peacetime military mobilization kept the strategic planning problem manageable. The routinization of cold war strategic planning, however, did not spring full blown; it took several years of groping during the late 1940s and the Korean War before the bounds came into focus.

Since the end of the cold war the United States has been facing more of a strategic tabula rasa, something closer to its first peacetime military tradition. Much of the past record suggests that it would be foolhardy to bank on peacetime strategic planning to tailor military capabilities for the correct contingencies, at least until the emergence of threat, and the incipient mobilization that follows, clarify the bounds. (At the end of World War II, for example, air force planning for the coming era focused not on the Soviet Union, but on the prospect of a resurgent Germany and Japan!)[36]

Even when mobilization against an identified threat is under way, strategy cannot drive structure. Rather, they evolve in reciprocal interaction. To get a sense of the problem, consider the World War II experience. If there were powerful inhibitions against deriving forces and supplies from strategic decisions even in wartime, when objectives are necessarily clearer than in prewar planning, they show why it should be unrealistic to expect better in peacetime planning.

Even after war broke out in 1939, U.S. military planning focused for some time on organizing for defense of the Western Hemisphere, at the expense of preparations in the Philippines, or for fighting in Europe. As Klaus Knorr reminds us, "In 1939 the United States did not foresee—and hardly could have foreseen—the proportion of its forces which would be committed to fighting in the tropics or in desert country or in Western Europe or in Italy; or the most effective balance of army, air force, and navy in the war to come; or the weapons and types of equipment that would be of greatest importance."[37]

War planners wanted a logical approach, a strategic grand design or master plan to govern production, logistics preparations, and the allocation of resources to various types of forces. The army designed a victory program in 1941, but it did not work. Organization for co-ordinating the war effort "was still in a state of flux, the art of require-ments determination quite imperfect," and calculations of available manpower, production capacity, and merchant shipping—which de-termined the scale and rate of overseas deployment—"could not be predicted very far into the future."[38] Industrial lead times (which were shorter for the military equipment of a half century ago than they will be in the future) meant that if strategy was to drive structure, strategic projections would have to stipulate what kinds of battles there would be, and where they would be, between six months and three years ahead. The war proved too unpredictable for that. Careful plans in 1942 fell by the wayside as "emergencies dictated deployments" to North Africa and limited offensives in the Pacific.[39]

Feedback from experience in battle also altered assumptions about strategy, organization, and equipment—particularly in regard to mechanization and aviation—as combat progressed.[40] In World War II it proved possible to change course quickly, giving strategic judgment some room for maneuver. After the battles of the Coral Sea and Mid-way, for example, plans to build five big battleships were postponed and cruiser construction was cut back "to release facilities, materials, and manpower for the construction of additional aircraft carriers." Within a year and a half, fifty attack and escort carriers joined the fleet.[41] In the future, technical complexity and lead times will make this sort of rapid adjustment within a war in progress unlikely, which further highlights the barriers to putting strategy before structure.

In World War II, "a satisfactory strategical foundation upon which to base a scale of military priorities never became available."[42] What happened instead? First, some important decisions about manpower, materiel, and supply simply took shape independently from strategy.

The Joint U.S. Strategic Committee was charged with providing guidance for mobilization priorities but was not in charge of formulating strategy; strategy evolved gradually out of discussions at higher levels and adjustment to the results of campaigns. The president himself refused to link production objectives with specific strategic decisions, preferring to keep options open.[43] As a result, in some critical cases structural decisions drove strategic ones. The most significant case was the set of decisions on the production of landing craft—curtailed in the middle of the war—which delayed the invasion of France. Winston Churchill "was to wonder in mid-1944 how history would ever understand why the 'plans of two great empires like Britain and the United States should be so hamstrung and limited' by an 'absurd shortage of . . . L.S.T.s.'"[44]

Second, planners moved away from trying to conform to a strategic grand design. They shifted to developing a *pool* of multipurpose forces and support elements "that could be drawn on flexibly for whatever courses of action the strategists should decide upon." In doing this, they came to identify the concept of "balanced" effort with shares of resources to be allocated to the separate services, the merchant marine, and supply of allies.[45] Flexibility for adjustment, rather than optimization for specific campaigns planned well in advance, was the solution to the inability to hew to a strategic line.

When the world's largest economy moves into an all-out war effort, it can produce a pool of resources that is so big and so flexible that it can cover most contingencies. Thus once production has been maximized, the pool may provide the best of both worlds. The structural readiness achieved does not depend on prior strategic guidance, nor does strategy depend on the structure. Once the pools are filled and the transportation system well greased, the forces can be put to the service of whatever strategic choices are made along the way. In the time that the buildup is accelerating and catching up with wartime demands, however, the forces available may drive strategy more than the reverse.

Attack or Defend?

In the cold war and its epilogue, the war against Iraq, the limitations of structural readiness did constrain strategic choice in one important way. They made it difficult to maintain a strong defensive posture over long periods of time in areas outside those in which U.S. forces were permanently stationed (Europe and Korea). The discussion in chapter 3 of readiness "waves" and alert fatigue in crisis deployments illustrated how maintaining wartime levels of operational readiness in peacetime for long periods requires a redundant structural readiness, so that units can be rotated to the scene of crisis to replace those that wear out from high operating tempos. This is primarily a problem for naval and air forces, which depend more on sophisticated technologies that require constant maintenance, although it is also a problem for ground forces attempting to stay at peak levels of training in austere environments. The discussion earlier in this chapter showed how the Bush decision to carry out reinforcement without rotation made it virtually unavoidable that the defensive Operation Desert Shield would be abandoned for an offensive solution to the confrontation with Iraq.

This is not to say that the November 1990 decision caused the United States to choose to go to war; indeed, the reverse is more likely. Nor is it to say that defensive strategy generally requires larger forces than offensive strategy. That notion contradicts conventional wisdom (although when the focus of attention shifts from the tactical level of analysis to the strategic, prevalent assumptions about the lower force ratios required for defense are simplistic and not borne out in a majority of relevant cases since 1939).[46] It does appear, however, that difficult problems are likely to emerge where there is a *combination* of defensive posture, an operation at the end of a long supply line in areas remote from well established bases, and a prolonged crisis with a constant prospect of combat.

Such a combination is probable for post–cold war crises. The U.S. base structure around the world had been shrinking before the cold war ended and is not likely to expand much in the future. It is also likely that U.S. military reaction to challenges will be handled by naval forces and airpower more often than by ground forces. Keeping substantial offshore forces on station for long periods in the Indian Ocean after the Iranian revolution, or in the Persian Gulf, was not easy during the cold war and could become harder as active forces are cut. Should this make the United States more willing to consider the first use of force in future confrontations, to avoid the use-it-or-lose-it problem of cyclically enervated forces? Or should cuts in forces be limited in order to reduce the odds that such choices will be faced?

New Missions?

After the cold war, United Nations "peacekeeping" and "peace enforcement" operations proliferated, and the United States was expected to share the load. Whether domestic political support for contributing to such peace operations will survive controversies over Somalia, Haiti, and Bosnia is quite doubtful in 1994—the Clinton administration backed off from early enthusiasm and issued official guidelines that make it hard for crises to qualify for American participation in multilateral intervention. If such involvements do occur on any appreciable scale, however, they raise questions about the costs to regular operational readiness.[47]

For many elements of U.S. forces supporting peacekeeping or enforcement, participation does not compromise readiness for conventional missions and may even enhance it. Logistics and transport units in these cases do more or less the same sorts of things they would do in war, so participation in peace operations may provide useful training. For those U.S. troops engaged in policing on the ground, however, or flying endless patrols over no-fly zones, activities do threaten to compromise readiness for conventional combat. The costs to regular combat readiness have led some in the military to resist making significant commitments to peace operations. Others in the military establishment deny that such costs are significant because they assume that peace operations can be accomplished by forces organized for regular operations.[48] That denial is wishful thinking.

Traditional peacekeeping is defined in terms of interposing military forces between local belligerents who have decided to accept a truce. Peacekeeping personnel are expected to monitor the truce but not to enforce it and may use force only in self-defense. The number of units involved in such cases will usually be small, but in most cases they will not be able to train much for regular combat. The longer they are deployed for observer functions (or for humanitarian functions such as delivering food or medical aid), the rustier they will get, and the more extensive will be the necessary reorientation and retraining when they return to a conventional role.

Commitment to "peace enforcement"—a vaguer concept that implies more forceful action to establish order—poses different and bigger problems. The ill-fated intervention in Somalia illustrates them. First, such operations are likely to require large forces, which must necessarily be diverted from those available for other contingencies. Commitment in a peace enforcement operation may not damage structural readiness, but it limits operational readiness, since reorganization or redeployment would inevitably take time similar to that needed to pump up stateside units rated C-3 or C-4 to higher readiness.

Second, using force to impose civil order in a manner that is not counterproductive requires different training from the sort best suited to normal combat. The rules of engagement, in particular, often need to be different. In areas densely populated by civilians—an urban market, for example—it is not desirable for troops to return fire automatically when attacked by snipers, to engage in reconnaissance by fire, to rely on fire support from artillery or tactical airpower, or to use other standard tactics that are normally safest and most effective for units in conventional combat. Learning, unlearning, and relearning sharply different operating norms of this sort—in effect, different battle drills—is not at all a quick or easy task for personnel and units that must become accustomed to rapid coordinated action.

Third, any commitment to peacekeeping or enforcement on a large scale could limit structural readiness for conventional missions by skewing the distribution of types of units. Forces most suited to peace operations are likely to be manpower-intensive, light infantry rather than high-firepower forces. Emphasis on such units would contradict the trend toward greater reliance on high-technology, capital-intensive forces. Finally, many United Nations peacekeeping operations tend to be of long duration (some missions in Cyprus, Lebanon, and elsewhere have lasted for decades). If the United States had to maintain a constant level of forces in some location like Bosnia for several years, normal rotation would require the cycling of large proportions of the force (for some categories like infantry units, potentially *all* of them) through such operations.[49] The British army had this problem for many years in Northern Ireland.

The only way to evade trade-offs like these would be to procure and maintain separate and additional units for peace operations alone. This would mean not counting them as part of the regular military establishment available for standard missions, charging them in effect to the State Department rather to national defense. This is no practical solution, and the Clinton plan rejected it.[50] Even if the public and legislators wished in principle to boost spending for this purpose, the incidence of peace operations would be episodic, and their scale highly variable, so the earmarked units would not be constantly engaged. In the face of typical budget pressures, the notion that such forces could not be counted as available for regular missions would become politically untenable.

The only alternatives, however, are to minimize U.S. commitments to peace operations or to accept the higher risk that other missions may come up short. As the secretary of defense reported at the end of the Clinton administration's first year:

> In the Cold War, a large force to counter the Warsaw Pact gave decision-makers a huge reserve to draw upon for regional conflicts. Now DOD plans for situations where almost all U.S. forces might be engaged in two nearly simultaneous MRCs [major regional conflicts]. With virtually no slack in the force structure, U.S. readiness posture must be rebalanced across the force every time some element of the force engages in even the least demanding tasks (for example, relatively modest but complex missions for humanitarian assistance or disaster relief). . . . Service Operations and Maintenance (O&M) accounts may eventually require more funds for reimbursement of funds diverted to support unprogrammed U.N. peace operations or to cover depot and base maintenance.[51]

The Next Big War

The opposite of having a breaking readiness wave encourage leaders to resort to force would be to develop a pattern of readiness that supports deterrence and reduces the odds of war. It is easy to do this where one's adversaries are weak, although deterrence does not flow automatically from capability. (U.S. deterrence did not fail against North Korea in 1950 or against Iraq in 1990, because it was not attempted.)[52] Deterrence will be harder to implement against some future adversary that seems as powerful as the USSR was once believed to be. The most vital strategic question is how to anticipate circumstances that would require the United States to renew its military capability for major war.

If it proved impractical to calibrate force development to contingencies during World War II, when there was no question of wasting resources in peacetime readiness that would never be used and there was no unsettled political question about whether the American strategic objective should be to attack or defend, it could hardly be more practical during the cold war. Then, readiness for when could never be known in regard to the main contingency, namely, war with the Soviet Union. That is why the proper balance between structural and operational readiness was the subject of constant controversy. Now that the cold war is over, the problem of estimation is compounded, for the same reason that people have to be so happy about the end of that epochal conflict: there is no known great power adversary to serve as the target and guiding force for U.S. strategy.

Both the Bush and Clinton administrations recognized the indeterminacy of when, why, or how conflict on the scale of the cold war standard could develop again. When officials in the Bush administration began to grapple speculatively with the question, they got into hot water. Draft defense planning guidance developed in early 1992 reportedly included among its scenarios one involving an attack by Russia and Belarus on Lithuania and Poland and also discussed the general objective of preventing the rise of any competing superpower. The negative reaction when news of this scenario leaked out led the administration to eliminate any detailed discussion of these points in the final version of the guidance.[53] The main planning debate evolved into the question of whether the United States should be ready to fight two medium-sized wars at once (for example, in the Middle East and against North Korea) or one at a time.[54]

When the Clinton administration initially considered planning to handle two contingencies sequentially rather than simultaneously—in what was dubbed the "win-hold-win" option—critics charged the new team with defeatism, and Asian allies shuddered. The administration backed off and then showcased plans for forces that would allegedly handle two major regional conflicts (MRCs)—the notional wars in the Persian Gulf and Korea—at nearly the same time.[55] To do this, however, it would be necessary to keep high force levels, despite large budget cuts. Critics then pointed out that this logically implied that the difference would have to come out of operational readiness or modernization.[56]

Thus the political process whipsawed defense planning for the post–cold war era. Where Clinton was faulted from the right for not taking prospective threats seriously enough, the Bush alternative had been blasted from the left for old thinking and alarmism. In response to the leaks about the contingencies used for planning purposes in the Cheney Pentagon, Senator Carl Levin complained, "Some of these scenarios are incredibly unlikely."[57] (The senator did not indicate how many of America's wars had not been "incredibly unlikely" before they occurred.) With no consensus on the nature or extent of military threats to U.S. interests in the new world, how should strategists deal with the trade-off between time and capability?

The decision to stipulate a requirement for simultaneous offensive operations in two MRCs was not simply overinsurance; indeed, it was not harmless. If maintained, it would in all probability reverse the proper priorities of the three dimensions of readiness in the post–cold war world by bolstering structural readiness at the expense of operational and mobilization readiness. (Why operational readiness is more helpful to mobilization readiness than is structural readiness is explained in chapter 8.)

The two-MRC standard represents a refusal to choose between strategic pressures from the right and budgetary pressures from the left. In itself this is not unprecedented. In the past, official requirements stipulated in Defense Department guidance often exceeded what was actually achieved. In the judgment of most seasoned observers, even the large military buildup of the Kennedy administration failed to achieve the ambitious "two-and-a-half-war" standard developed in the McNamara Pentagon—the criterion that U.S. forces should be able to fight major conventional wars against both the Soviet Union and China, as well as a small war somewhere else, such as Cuba.

Indeed, just prosecuting the war in Vietnam (which must count as something like two-thirds of a war, in the Pentagon lingo of the time) led the Defense Department to hollow out U.S. forces in NATO (especially noncommissioned officers, signal equipment, and other supporting infrastructure) and strip the central reserve of troop units in the continental United States. The Persian Gulf War of 1991 also stripped enough from U.S. capabilities elsewhere in the world that it was unrealistic to imagine fighting another midsized war somewhere else at the same time. Both the wars in Vietnam and the Gulf were undertaken by the hefty cold war military establishment. To pretend that the United States could do better in coordinating simultaneous wars with the shrunken military of the post–cold war era would be a charade.

A more reasonable solution is to embrace the plan for sequential rather than simultaneous operations—the win-hold-win option—and to point out that critics who painted this as defeatist were simply wrong. A plan to fight a defensive holding action for a prolonged period in a secondary theater is not at all the same as surrender. It also comports with the principle of economy of force, reducing the risk of defeat in detail in the event that splitting forces would mean fighting two losing battles at once.[58] The U.S. plan for World War II was, in effect, to hold in the Pacific while winning in Europe.[59]

A serious effort to maintain the two-MRC charade, however, would put a premium on keeping up the number of major combat formations (divisions, wings, carrier task forces), since these are the main index by which readiness for what is represented. Unless defense budgets grew, it would ultimately prove hard to maintain the necessary force levels without skimping on training or cutting overhead in ways that would eventually undermine operational or mobilization readiness.

One official justification for the two-MRC standard was that it provided a hedge against the emergence of a greater-than-expected single threat. According to the report on the bottom-up review, "It is difficult to predict precisely what threats we will confront ten to twenty years from now."[60] As chapter 2 in this book should have demonstrated, however, expensive investments in structural readiness are not a sensible way to maximize capability for the long term; rather, strenuous current efforts sustained for long periods may limit the economic base for later expansion. Structural readiness should be geared to the strength of currently plausible adversaries. The post–cold war environment is not one in which current structural readiness should be kept up at the risk of eroding the underpinnings for later remobilization if the world becomes more dangerous again.

In regard to *major* war—that is, one involving a great power as opposed to a middle power like Iraq, Iran, or North Korea—there is now no better standard by which to answer the readiness for when question than the British had when they articulated the ten-year rule in the 1920s, because there is no answer to the prior question of readiness for what. Facing the main contingency of concern during the cold war, defense policy debates about how much time should be assumed would be available to rev up readiness for war with the Soviet Union ranged between several months and a few days.[61] This focused debate on the balance of structural and operational readiness. Between the crackup of the Warsaw Pact in 1989 and the crackup of the Soviet Union in 1991, official estimates changed quickly to assuming much longer times; by August 1990 the Pentagon figured that after Soviet withdrawal from Eastern Europe, Moscow would need close to two years to mobilize for invasion.[62] After the toppling of Communist rule and the end of the union, which detached half of the USSR's old population from Russia, this question became almost beside the point. *For great power threats, the United States has come back to the traditional question of how much actual readiness at all is necessary, rather than the cold war question of what is the ideal balance between structural and operational readiness.*

Speculating on which great powers could or could not become military threats to the United States in the post–cold war future is beyond the scope of this book. Such prediction involves basic articles of faith in international relations theory about the causes of war and peace. Whether great powers like Japan and Germany could turn from allies to adversaries, or whether successful economic development will make Russia or China into superpowers more daunting than the Soviet Union used to be, are ultimately the crucial questions in this regard.[63]

Unless and until some threat on that scale emerges, issues of structural and operational readiness will revolve around potential conflicts with middle powers such as Iran or Iraq. The overall readiness question, however, will be more like the one that faced the United States before 1938 or that faced Britain when the ten-year rule was cooked up. Deciding when a rising threat warrants large-scale rearmament— as Washington had to do in 1917, 1939–40, and 1950—is a matter of high policy. To judge by past experience, it would be reckless to assume that such a decision will be made neatly or expeditiously in the future. All this strategic uncertainty leaves two main challenges for planning.

The first is to maintain a balanced set of nuclei, or clusters of "seed corn," for as many different types of military capability as possible, so that an exploitable base exists from which to expand structural readiness of whichever elements of capability seem most needed when the time comes. In a sense, this is the miniature version of the World War II "pool" solution described above. Otherwise, whole sets of skills may have to be haltingly rediscovered and reinvented. With the available military resources in decline, however, diversification competes with the aim of retaining standing structural readiness for the middle-sized threats that are already apparent.

The second challenge is to prepare the groundwork for remobilizing to cold war levels of readiness. Whenever it proves necessary to face the prospect of another major conflict, it would be better not to have to start from scratch. How should the United States organize itself to shift from military unreadiness for a major conflict to sufficient structural and operational readiness to dissuade a powerful new adversary from attacking, or to be prepared for initial combat when a major war occurs? That is, how should the United States *be ready to get ready*? That is the subject of the next chapter.

8

Between Two Traditions:
Mobilization Readiness

A s Americans celebrated the end of the cold war, U.S.
military and economic policies grappled with measured
demobilization. This chapter is about the opposite problem, one that
the United States does not yet face but could have to confront in the
future. That problem is *re*mobilization, which means changing course
again sometime after the current conversion of the military and economy back toward pre–cold war levels of effort is complete.

Standing down from the cold war will not re-create as much military
unreadiness as was typical historically. Inertia, and the unprecedented
legacy of a full half century in which the United States became accustomed to maintaining large amounts of military capability, work
against that possibility. But the better things go in the world, the
further back toward the historic norm readiness will go.[1] Then, if things
go bad again, it will pay to know how to re-create a large effective force
more quickly and efficiently than in previous emergencies.

There is nothing to be gained by trying to repeal the post–cold war
demobilization, arguing that military readiness should be kept at the
cold war heights to which Americans became accustomed. That is a
losing game not only politically, but also strategically. Machiavelli was
correct in pointing out that iron can trump gold, which is why the
nation can never dispense entirely with military readiness; but although "gold alone will not procure good soldiers," no modern military machine can be built or nurtured without it.[2] Over time, the more
gold a state accumulates, the more iron it can buy. Constant strength
pays only against constant danger. *Over the long term, potential military
strength is inherent in actual military weakness*, because an expanding
civilian economy is the font of future military power.

In the absence of a big immediate threat, the hardheaded strategist

210

who worries about having to deal with powerful enemies will postpone the conversion of potential to actual power until such a threat develops. Recognizing and deciding to react to that development is the main problem, a political issue of the highest importance. Cases surveyed earlier suggest that premature decisions for conversion are less likely to occur than tardy ones. Therefore it pays to be ready to catch up fast.

The problem is, it is not obvious how to accomplish conversion in a way that maximizes both speed and efficiency. As Klaus Knorr noted, there are three determinants of military power: military potential inherent in economic power; the value a nation places on military power, which decides how much of that potential is "actually transformed into military strength"; and skill in the conversion of resources.[3] The third of these factors is the subject of this chapter, since, as is commonly noted by critics, *the United States has never adequately and fully planned for a mobilization before it occurred.*[4] Great inefficiencies, delays, and failures occurred because of uncoordinated initiatives that worked at cross-purposes. These problems did not prevent ultimate success in war, but they raised its price.

If the United States has to mobilize large standing forces again from a low peacetime baseline, will it be able to do better than in the past? That depends in part on the kinds of structural and operational readiness that are preserved in military forces in peacetime, but also on the capacity to coordinate conversion efficiently. That capacity to convert is the third dimension of readiness, the readiness to get ready, or *mobilization readiness.*

Obstacles, Plans, and Politics

The meaning of mobilization here contrasts with the meaning it sometimes carried in the cold war, when it referred to calling reserve forces to duty or surging weapons production.[5] In the present context, it is closer to "mobilization base" and "reconstitution," but these terms are not used here because they have specific technical connotations to specialists.[6] The discussion that follows is about prospective mobilization in the broadest sense: the reconversion of industrial and manpower resources into military forces on a grand scale comparable to past mobilizations for major war. Because of that, the lessons of such past mobilizations are considered in detail.

What Is the Problem?

In an emergency mobilization, the government intervenes in the economy to redirect the allocation of labor and capital, rapidly and massively, to the production of large amounts of new technology, manpower trained in military skills, complex organizations, and a military-industrial infrastructure. All these activities in turn have to be integrated and coordinated. In effect, a different economy has to be created overnight: one in which the products of military power and organization, rather than the commodities normally demanded by citizens, have highest priority. With a single customer (the government) for the new products, and with the increase in demand for them precipitous rather than gradual, the market is ill-equipped to handle the conversion. The price system cannot accomplish the needed shifts in production because it is "too indirect, too slow, too erratic."[7]

The alternative to the normal market process, however, introduces many of the economic inefficiencies associated with command economies. Although necessary to some extent, the loss of market efficiency is a drag in the race with the adversary, since it limits the quantity or quality of forces produced in a given time. Waste is inherent in precipitous conversion; it is "unavoidable . . . unless mobilization has taken place gradually prior to war. An industrial economy is a complex and delicate mechanism, and the shift from one control arrangement to another can hardly proceed without confusion and faulty decisions."[8] Readiness for mobilization, therefore, involves whatever measures can anticipate and mitigate the inefficiencies of rapid conversion. The purpose of this mobilization readiness is not just to increase efficiency, but to save lives (improving the odds that troops will not have to be committed to combat before being optimally equipped and trained) and to avoid absolute waste in production (reducing the odds that the bulk of military production will bear fruit only after the war is over).[9]

What sorts of inefficiencies are at issue? As Klaus Knorr wrote early in the cold war, after studying the experience of mobilization for World War II,

> A state of war generates changes that tend to diminish the employment of resources as well as their productivity. . . . Workers and other resources may be unemployed temporarily as production is

converted from peacetime to wartime goods or, subsequently as supply bottlenecks condemn resources to temporary idleness . . . inventories of raw materials and reserves of foreign exchange may be depleted. . . . Too many workers, and especially too much skilled personnel, may be drafted into the armed forces. . . . Higher taxes and diminishing supplies of consumers' goods may impair the incentive of labor and management to work hard and long hours. . . . Factor productivity will also tend to fall as war-induced scarcities and clumsy government regulations interfere with the smoothly synchronized flow of materials, fuel, labor, tools, and parts that is characteristic of peacetime production; and unfamiliarity with new products and the changing specifications of munitions will interfere as well.[10]

These problems do not work themselves out quickly, and they create imbalances among the various crash programs, imbalances that increase the time and cost of conversion. Answers to the questions of military readiness for when and of what become ensnarled with each other. The interdependencies among various components are not obvious or easily controlled.

Maximizing the speed at which certain components in the process reach fruition may slow down the rate at which the composite force achieves readiness. When a decision is made to mobilize, the urge is to do everything as fast as possible, so things that are doable quickly often get done first, whether or not they are the things that are needed first, or are even at all useful in the absence of things that take longer to do. *Coordination and phasing* become the biggest problems, as bottlenecks tie up manpower and materiel unproductively at various stages. Speed and efficiency in some aspects of mobilization wind up being utterly wasted because of slippages in some other aspect on which their contribution depends; ultimate combat outputs become hostage to the weakest link in the various intersecting chains of production. The stumbling mobilization experiences surveyed in chapter 1 illustrate the following pathologies:

—Integrated weapon systems are not produced because some components pile up in excessive numbers while others are not manufactured at all, or are produced out of the sequence in which they are needed.

—Troops are recruited in huge numbers but sit around and wait or waste time in "Mickey Mouse" activities because they lack the equipment with which to train, while equipment orders are slowed because of labor shortages in factories due to military conscription.

—Individual soldiers and small units (companies, battalions) are trained in basic military skills, but cannot be molded into complex units (divisions, corps) and trained for large-scale operations because experienced cadres or organizational structures have not been developed.

—Large units are formed and accomplish advanced training but then wait at home or at intermediate bases because transportation and logistical networks are lacking to deploy and support them in theaters of combat.

—Crash programs aggravate imbalances, creating "logistics snowballs" in which activities grow out of control, until "a huge accumulation of slush obscures the hard core of essential combat support and the mass becomes unmanageable." This not only causes waste but endangers combat effectiveness as "unnecessary supplies and personnel block the flow of the necessary resources."[11]

—Political and administrative leaders attempt to rationalize the rapid conversion by centralizing authority and stipulating priorities, but bureaucratic parochialism and confusion lead to inconsistency and an inflation of priority ratings and thereby derange the rational solutions. Because priority ratings are often determined "without consideration of the supplies available, they are, at best, mere 'hunting licenses.'"[12]

Many of these problems can be subsumed under the general rubric of organizational and systemic unreadiness for conversion. Peacetime and wartime economies are both very different and very complex, each dependent on different combinations of experience and skill. Complex systems can never be transformed quickly without breakage or breakdown.[13] Or as Klaus Knorr put it, "War is, for most societies, not a frequent enough experience to result in a ready stock of relevant skills."[14]

Can these imbalances and inefficiencies that plagued past mobilizations be prevented or mitigated in the next one? Readiness for mobilization minimizes the proportion of conversion time that is waiting time and the waste of resources in the transition. Mobilization readiness requires the government to maintain knowledge, plans, organizations, cadres, a base of standing forces, and standby mechanisms and facilities at a level that will enable it to coordinate the conversion of resources into military capabilities in proper sequences and at efficient rates, or at least with less waste and delay than would occur if the process were started from scratch.

Two sets of obstacles stand in the way of accomplishing this objective. One is technical and economic: it is enormously difficult to manage complexity and anticipate specific crucial interdependencies, especially as the terms of reference constantly evolve with technological innovation, industrial and demographic development, and perceived changes in external threats. The second is political: the logic of planning frequently conflicts with the logic of politics. The former implies coherence, control, and careful integration in advance; the latter promotes competition, compromise, ad hoc and incremental adjustment, and delay.

Planning for Coordination: Theory

The main problem for planning is to anticipate the various bottlenecks that can stall the conversion of resource inputs to combat outputs. Some of the most important obstacles are those related to synchronizing the mobilization and training of personnel with the development and production of equipment (see table 8-1). In principle, this implies careful phasing of technological development, personnel recruitment, equipment production, training at various levels of expertise and organizational complexity, transportation of units to theaters of operation, deployment for combat, and the resupply of engaged forces. Preparedness for conversion would avoid letting the excessive allocation of resources to one phase stall progress in another.

Since it is vital to coordinate sequences of qualitative development and quantitative expansion in both technology and manpower, the processes with longest lead times need the biggest investment in peacetime. Such processes include, in particular, technical research, design, development, and testing (for readiness to produce state-of-the-art equipment), and military education in the development and integration of structures, networks, staffs, and procedures for fielding and coordinating combat and logistical capabilities (for readiness to produce trained units able to operate together). Mediating all this activity are military organizations, which must also be elaborated at various stages.

Understanding the proper phasing in principle, in the sense of the simple illustration in table 8-1, is only a small part of the problem. As

TABLE 8-1. *Synchronizing Readiness*

Manpower	Organization	Industry
Peacetime (mobilization readiness)		
Leadership nucleus	*Skeletal/embryonic*	*Development*
Staff colleges	High overhead	Research
OJT/rotation	Experimental units	Design
Advanced schooling	Standby facilities	Testing
Sandtable exercises	Cadres/staffs	Engineering
Mobilization simulations	Multiple plans	Prototypes
Mobilization (conversion begins)		
Force expansion	*Unit development*	*Production*
Recruitment	Training base	Basic equipment
Basic training	Logistical units	Support equipment
AIT	Large-unit HQs	Transport assets
Small-unit training CP exercises	Battalion ships/squadrons	Advanced combat equipment
Structural readiness (mass/quantity)		
Force integration	*Unit coordination*	*Supply*
Large-unit combat training	Divisions wings	Ammunition spare parts
Joint exercises	Naval task forces	Consumables
Operational readiness (efficiency/quality)		
Deployed forces	*Independent combat*	*Force sustainment*
Transport to TO	Corps/armies/fleets/air forces	Replacement equipment/ consumables for resupply
Movement to battle area	Joint task forces	
Battle		

times change, so do the technical variables, and they usually change a great deal between major wars. These changes (for example, in the relative importance of battleships and aircraft carriers in World War II) are often not clarified until the test of war itself. Moreover, to keep the overall increase in readiness linear, particular elements may have to be organized in ways that appear inefficient in their own terms, isolated from other aspects of the process. For instance, to maximize the speed and efficiency of combat units it may be necessary to accept apparent inefficiency in logistics, as demonstrated by experience with shipping and resupply in World War II:

> Whereas efficient transportation . . . emphasized the movement of freight and personnel in the mass, efficient supply demanded the delivery of specific items to specific destinations at specific times. A shipload of war material delivered safely overseas was half wasted if half the cargo consisted of filler items not needed immediately, while urgently needed tanks and signal equipment (bulky in relation to weight) had been loaded, in the interests of saving cargo space, on a later vessel [smaller items were used as filler]. . . . [E]fficiency in transportation was not an end in itself, but had to be measured in terms of effective supply.[15]

Mobilization readiness would contrast with the normal historic pattern, in which "mobilization takes effect through a vast and accelerated learning process: learning not only in the narrow sense of acquiring new information, but also, and more profoundly, in the sense that individuals must acquire new patterns of orientation and behavior."[16] Mobilization readiness would keep this sort of learning on ice, so that the system does not have to learn it by trial and error when the mobilization machinery warms up.

The idea of keeping the understanding of mobilization on ice comes easily to intellectuals, who believe that usable knowledge can be stored on paper or computer disks. It is easier said than done, especially for practitioners who are often convinced that one can only learn things by doing them. Skepticism is reinforced by the failure of past attempts at planning and preparation for mobilization to prevent mistakes in phasing and coordination.

Planning for Coordination: Practice

The stories in chapter 1 imply that there was no mobilization readiness in the United States before the world wars, that the government and military just scrambled, stumbled, and learned when the time came to mobilize again. This was more or less true before the First World War, but not the Second. It was even less true in mobilizing for the last world war of the twentieth century, the cold war.

Neither war plans nor mobilization plans were developed before the wars with Spain in 1898 or Germany in 1917. Despite two years of growing conflict between Washington and Madrid a century ago, there was not even an organization within the War Department directed to undertake mobilization planning. When the United States entered World War I in April 1917, army general staff officers were scattered around the world; there were only nineteen of them to prepare plans and handle routine staff work. Only fragmentary plans existed because of President Woodrow Wilson's opposition to preparation for war; the first plan in 1915 was for a *defensive* war against a German attack on the Atlantic coast. The Navy Consulting Board did some mobilization preparation of sorts in 1916, inventorying industrial facilities for the services. In August of that year legislation created the Council of National Defense and the National Defense Advisory Commission to advise the president on industrial mobilization, but they did not begin functioning until the following March, just before war was declared. As Ronald Schaffer writes, "There was no machinery for determining accurately what the Allies, the armed services, and Allied and American civilians would need; no satisfactory method of estimating what American industry could produce; no adequate procedure for apportioning food, fuel, raw materials and finished products; no effective mechanism for coordinating the country's transportation systems; and no agency to regulate prices."[17] Effective planning did not get into gear until July 1917, three months into the war.[18]

World War I was too short to learn fully the lessons that would prove relevant twenty years later, but much that was important was recognized quite well.[19] The World War I experience led the government to attempt significant organizational preparation and planning for future mobilization during the two decades between the world wars. In contrast to earlier periods, this one produced rather detailed plans for proper phasing.[20] The National Defense Act of 1920 established the Industrial Planning Branch in the army, which reported to the assistant secretary of war and was mandated to make mobilization plans; a series of such documents was produced beginning in 1930. The Army and Navy Munitions Board was formed in 1922 to plan for procurement, and in 1924 the Army Industrial College was set up to train officers in matters of industrial mobilization and supply.[21] What happened in this interwar effort helps explain why the mobilization mess in World War II was less than it could have been and as great as it was. What went wrong?

First, the task was inherently so difficult that it would have been hard to accomplish even if the administrative plans had been perfect and everything done as the planners intended. Accurately anticipating and providing for complex combinations and sequences of economic, technical, and social resources for uncertain contingencies is impossible, for all the same reasons that believers in the market reject planned economies. Plans were frequently reviewed and updated, but the data on which they were based were not always reliable.[22] When the time for mobilization came, many of the industrial mobilization plan's estimates for needed raw materials were also completely unrealistic: for example, they called for less than half the aluminum actually required. In August 1941 staff in the Office of Production Management reported of navy figures, "Most of the estimates we have received represent guess work."[23]

Second, the planning apparatus was not first-rate or unhampered, and much of what the planners mandated was not implemented by higher authorities. Most notably, the peacetime standing army fell far below the level envisioned in the 1920 National Defense Act, which made it impossible to maintain the structure required for efficient expansibility. The act stipulated a ceiling of 280,000 men on active duty and envisioned 425,000 in the National Guard. "Such a force was regarded by military planners as the minimum needed for initial defense and for providing a balanced nucleus from which Army expansion would be evenly and rapidly made in the event of war." Subsequent appropriations, however, slashed the number planned by more than half. By 1923 the number on active duty was below 120,000. The National Guard "stabilized at around 190,000 men in the early 1930s."[24]

More generally, preparations were compromised by organizational problems, civil-military relations, and national politics, none of which subordinated other concerns to the imperative of mobilization planning. For one thing, the services did not collaborate much on planning. The National Defense Act had not even mentioned the navy, which normally maintained more structural readiness in peacetime and was not expected to have to change its sources of supply or expand as radically as the army upon mobilization. The legislation had been silent, however, in large part for political reasons. The sponsors were convinced that passage required vague wording and innocuous presentation. When army planning cut into the navy's supply sources, consultation was established through the Army and Navy Munitions Board in 1922.[25]

While recognizing the importance of mobilization planning in principle, the military establishment did not give it a high priority in practice. The Army and Navy Munitions Board did not meet for *thirteen years* before World War II. In the navy, for example, the assistant secretary who had responsibility for planning was more interested in the department's civilian personnel problems. The small planning staff constituted by the Office of the Chief of Naval Operations and the Bureau of Supplies and Accounts was not regarded as very important, and the leaders of the service—who were primarily interested in planning combat operations—paid little attention to it. "The chief defect in the Navy's portion of the industrial mobilization planning was not so much with the contents of the plan as with the fact that the planners were buried far down in the administrative hierarchy of the Department."[26]

The services also did not attempt to integrate their focus on military requirements with a realistic estimate of the capacities of civilian industry or the conflicting demands upon it. Nor did civilian agencies participate in drawing up the plans. Had civilian requirements and national industrial capacity been assessed concomitantly, "these additional data would have indicated how much of a 'bank account' was available for war use."[27]

Another problem was the military propensity to develop formulaic plans premised on a clear decision point at which peacetime would give way to mobilization. It was assumed that there would be a declared M-Day to trigger the plan, which would then proceed like clockwork. This is an understandable simplifying assumption, typical in military analysis.[28] Perhaps it was even necessary for intelligible planning, and it did make careful balance and phasing feasible in principle. In particular, it provided for synchronizing the mobilization of manpower and materiel.[29]

Such an assumption makes sense for technocrats but not for politicians, and politicians are the ones who hold the power of decision. Today as much as in the first half of the century, such an assumption is an unrealistic basis for planning. As long as an evolving crisis stays short of shooting, the consensus for how serious an external threat is, and how much has to be done about it how soon, develops gradually.

It does not burst out at a single moment. The decision for mobilization is also a decision to regiment society and the economy. Until the unambiguous shock of an outright attack, a forthright decision to move rapidly to a war footing is a matter of utmost controversy. Political leaders have a natural interest in either avoiding such a decision or downplaying and disguising it by incremental steps.

At no point in the slide toward conflict from the time of the invasion of Manchuria through the Munich crisis, the fall of France, and Pearl Harbor did the president ever declare M-Day. Instead, the United States edged gradually toward mobilization. Increases in naval construction began early, in 1934, in response to Japan's withdrawal from the League of Nations and the naval arms limitation agreements of 1922 and 1930, and defense expenditures increased significantly each year thereafter. Franklin D. Roosevelt's message to Congress on January 28, 1938, marked another crucial step in rearmament. And the beginning of war in Europe in 1939 "helped to convert rearmament . . . into mobilization."[30]

Mobilization plans drawn up in the 1930s were controversial within professional circles, but the final one produced in 1939 gained more consensus. Professional agreement was not matched in the political arena. The plan was never implemented because of opposition from both the right (conservatives feared an authoritarian government and economic controls) and the left (labor feared the suspension of national and state labor laws). Pacifists and isolationists objected to such plans in principle, and public opinion in general was suspicious of any action that seemed to lead toward war.[31]

There was opposition in Congress to suspending legislation that stood in the way of parts of the plan and to the plan's provision for a war resources administration, a superagency to direct industry's war effort.[32] The delegation of such power to a single administrative czar would also have obstructed presidential control of mobilization strategy, and Roosevelt too resisted such a shift. FDR was no more anxious to delegate power (or dispense with what he saw as benefits of administrative competition) on war policy than he was on domestic issues. But despite the peacetime planning and the two-year mobilization run-up before Pearl Harbor, production bottlenecks worsened in mid-1942. Not until 1943, when the destructiveness of interagency conflict had become impossible to ignore, did he move to centralize the effort under the Office of War Mobilization.[33]

Part of the problem might have been avoided if the plan had been packaged and promoted by politicians rather than technocrats, for example, if it had been sold as a "defense plan" rather than slapped with the labels of "war planning" or "transition" to war. Ferdinand Eberstadt, in particular, believed that the 1939 plan was quite adequate in terms of administrative organization and that it "might have saved time, money, and lives" if it had been implemented expeditiously, rather than in the halting incremental manner that it was. Instead of leaving the development of the plan to the Army and Navy Munitions Board, more civilian involvement might have averted some of the political obstacles to setting it in motion.[34]

The other side of the coin was that the origins of the mobilization plan in the recesses of the professional military worked against adoption of the product after war broke out and released all the political brakes. Eminent civilian executives and economists who poured in to administer the buildup had their own ideas about the best way to do things, had scant respect for the military officers who had generated plans over the course of twenty years, and paid little attention to the existing plan.[35] This problem is virtually inevitable whenever the priority of a function changes radically in a short time. As long as finely tuned preparedness for mobilization is not recognized as being among the highest priorities in defense policy in peacetime—in practice as well as in rhetoric—the function is likely to be attended by middle-level bureaucrats and military officers whose careers have been stalled. When crisis catapults mobilization to the highest priority, elites on the fast track take charge and start over.

All the problems noted so far do not mean that the interwar planning was wasted. Much of the utility of the plans did not depend on a formal invocation of M-Day or a formal adoption of the industrial mobilization plan. The period before Pearl Harbor was put to good use in many ways to push mobilization far ahead of where it had been in 1917. Legislative authorization in 1938 for "educational orders" gave the services a head start in breaking in special technical requirements for manufacturers of war materiel, and in practical terms, the fall of France triggered a fair amount of what M-Day was supposed to start. Between the summer of 1940 and December 1941 tremendous progress was made in the construction of capital and command facilities.[36] The fact remains, nevertheless, that the process was less efficient or timely than hindsight indicates it could have and should have been.

Politics continued to compromise economic and technical criteria after Pearl Harbor. President Roosevelt's State of the Union message in January 1942 trumpeted the need to raise production drastically, and he directed specific goals involving major items—numbers of planes, tanks, guns, and merchant ships—rather than dollar totals. "The goals had no anchor either in feasibility or in need; they flew in the face of both the production authorities' notions of what could be produced and the military chiefs' claim to the right to determine what should be produced."[37] The army embraced the president's program, but only as an addition to the more balanced program for production of ancillary items that the service was planning. When this happened, civilian "officials threw up their hands in horror" and told the president that he had to choose between his own stated goals for high-profile items and the balanced program favored by the services. Everyone agreed in principle on the need for balance, but disagreed about what it required. Owing to "the lack of a firm policy and of effective machinery to decide among the competing claimants," priorities were not clearly determined. Of all the war expenditures planned as of February 1942, *more than half* were in the "top-priority" category.[38]

The significance of these failings should not be exaggerated. Not only did the United States and its allies win World War II despite them, but the U.S. record of efficiency in mobilization was superior to that of the Axis enemies. The latter chose armament in "width" rather than "depth," which made them better prepared for ambitious operations at the outset of war, but unprepared for a long war of attrition. This decision was rational to the extent that their inferior war potential made quick blitzkrieg victories their only hope. As a result, though, German production did not peak until four years after the war began, and the military authorities in Tokyo never achieved control of Japanese economic planning.[39] In war, performance in comparison with the enemy's performance is the most important verdict, irrespective of efficiency, since it determines victory or defeat. Performance in comparison with a standard of efficiency remains an essential concern, however, because it suggests how victory might be achieved at a lower cost in lives as well as dollars.

Mobilization within Mobilization: Cold War Planning

Avoidable problems occurred again after 1945. For example, the War Assets Administration unloaded machine tools at 15 percent of cost, flooding the market, and thirty-four machine tool companies closed as a result. By 1951 this industry's capacity was a third of what it had been when World War II began. When the Korean War broke out, substantial stockpiles of ammunition from World War II existed but were drawn down before the reactivation of government-owned manufacturing facilities could expand production sufficiently to prevent shortages.[40] The army estimated that if $10 million had been allocated "for maintenance during each of the five years preceding Korea it would have been able to save between $200 and $300 million in subsequent rehabilitation costs."[41]

Nevertheless, mobilization readiness was taken more seriously after World War II than after World War I. For one thing, the base created during World War II never completely withered away before containment was decisively militarized in 1950. Much more legislation was passed to provide the basis for mobilization preparations.[42] Organization to prepare for mobilization on the scale of a World War III was also at a higher political and administrative level than in the period after 1918. The National Security Resources Board (NSRB)—which was later superseded by the Office of Defense Mobilization (ODM), which in turn was replaced by the Office of Emergency Preparedness (OEP)—was officially deemed to be of such importance that it was constituted in the Executive Office of the President. Most significantly, until the latter part of the cold war the organization's head was one of the statutory members of the National Security Council (the only others being the president, vice president, secretary of state, secretary of defense, and assistant to the president for national security affairs). By late 1953, ODM had a staff of almost 300 people.[43]

The recognition that preparedness for mobilization was important did not mean that authority flowed to those responsible for it. The chairman and staff of the NSRB, with the support of a number of elder statesmen, argued that to carry out their function under the terms of the National Security Act they needed not only to advise and plan but to maintain a skeleton organization for implementing the plans in an emergency. The Bureau of the Budget disagreed. The president sided with the bureau and indicated that he would not cede authority to the NSRB to undertake executive functions that would bind any agency.[44] Just as Roosevelt had been unwilling to constitute the War Resources Administration as envisioned in the 1939 industrial mobilization plan,

Harry Truman had no intention of delegating power any sooner than necessary.

As the cold war progressed, *actual* mobilization undercut potential mobilization. When a high level of forces in being became a permanent peacetime condition, it competed with investment in preparations for all-out mobilization. First, the Eisenhower administration trimmed expenditures from the Truman program for mobilization requirements and slowed the acquisition of reserve stocks. This was intended to "keep production lines in operation and thus ready for acceleration in case of need," and because "in an age of rapid change, large stocks of equipment were subject to obsolescence."[45]

Secretary of Defense Charles Wilson (who had been head of ODM under Truman) sought further economies by cutting the projected size of stockpiles and concentrating production lines that the Truman administration had dispersed in order to reduce vulnerability to nuclear attack. Late in the second year of the Eisenhower administration, Wilson reversed that decision. The Joint Chiefs of Staff, however, argued in 1954 that "any increased expenditures for the mobilization base should be in addition to those needed to support the active forces." By 1957 ODM reduced stockpile objectives from a five-year emergency to three.[46] After 1950 a big defense industry kept functioning, ongoing production kept lines intact, and the overall level of actual mobilization was heightened in the 1960s by the flexible response buildup and the Vietnam War. This made it easy to assume that an accelerated emergency mobilization could take off from the cold war base more easily than the precipitous buildup after 1939 had been able to proceed from the emaciated base of the interwar period. Serious efforts to nurture mobilization readiness languished.

By the late 1970s, however, the assumption that actual peacetime mobilization at cold war levels provided the necessary base for all-out mobilization had become harder to sustain. "The many people who still think the United States could quickly resume the rate of industrial military production that was present at the end of World War II neglect the increased complexity of today's military equipment," wrote Jacques Gansler at that time. "The production process is more difficult, the skill levels required are higher, the material lead times longer, the part tolerances much tighter, and the designs far more complex."[47] Studies for the National Security Council and Defense Science Board in 1976 suggested major deficiencies. For example, raw materials stock-piles included items unlikely to be needed, while they lacked items deemed crucial. These were gaps that would cost billions of dollars to fill. Vested interests linked to the existing stockpiles stood in the way of legislative change in the program, and even if change were to be accomplished, other obstacles meant that it would have taken years to get the situation in line with the recommendations. The Defense Science Board study concluded that administrative arrangements in industry to maintain surge capability were gravely flawed since they did not take into account the interdependencies among separate programs or the bottlenecks: because preparation of the relevant forms was "charged to company overhead," personnel had little reason to put an effort into them.[48]

During the Reagan administration mobilization drew more attention.[49] Under Secretary of Defense Fred Iklé took a special interest in the problem, and the Mobilization Concepts Development Center was established as a think tank to deal with the question at the National Defense University. For all the studies produced, however, it is not clear how much the actual capacity to mobilize for large-scale conventional war improved. Toward the end of the first Reagan term, an air force report bemoaned the problem that military contractors would have trouble gearing up for wartime production even with a long warning period. Despite the administration's formal attention to the industrial base, the study found the government lacking in plans for rapid expansion or steady acceleration of defense production. Schedules for turning out C-5 transport planes or AH-64 Apache attack helicopters, for example, could not be speeded up because of "inadequate space, milling and machining equipment and chemical processing facilities . . . insufficient skilled labor, material handling equipment, inspection gauges and data processing."[50]

By the end of Reagan's second term, mobilization planning was characterized "by an absence of clear lines of responsibility and a complex management structure." Although plans were regularly tested by war games and simulations, such exercises revealed problems in decentralization: "One postgame report stated that there 'was no central data base' and that military planners 'paid little attention to the resource and economic implications of military operations . . . [and] that there was no single agency in charge of managing mobilization.'"[51]

All along, the good and bad news about mobilization were sides of the same coin. High levels of actual mobilization in peacetime put the country in a much better position than in 1940, 1917, 1898, or at any other time in history to ratchet up readiness quickly. At the same time, it diverted attention and resources from maximizing readiness for the conversion of economic to military power on a grand scale. Maintaining moderate mobilization, rather than optimizing readiness for all-out mobilization, was where the action was during the cold war. Earlier chapters discussed how structural and operational readiness competed with each other for resources during the cold war. Both of them together, however, worked against the diversion of resources into channels that would maximize *potential* power.

In the aftermath of the cold war, this tension is still present and will persist in the future. The need to place more emphasis on mobilization readiness is recognized, but the pressures on the standing forces are even more acute. Moreover, the future requirements of mobilization readiness are not entirely clear. The next major move to mobilize will occur a half century or more after the last. Economic, technological, and political conditions in the United States will all be quite different from what they were in 1950.

The Next Mobilization

Soon after the Berlin Wall opened, the shift from an emphasis on current readiness to mobilization and reconstitution gathered steam.[52] Despite the preceding remarks about the inadequate preparations for war in the past, there is no reason to believe that the United States would not be more successful in mobilization planning now than in previous eras. Mobilization readiness improved significantly in the twentieth century. It was better after World War I than before it, and still better after World War II. This time, Americans have a legacy of long peacetime mobilization that has created a reservoir of experience, skill, sensitivity, and vested interests in the problem that never existed before the major wars of the past. There are two main challenges: to identify the economic, technical, and military differences between conversion problems in the past and those in the future; and to deal with the administrative and political constraints that naturally affect mobilization planning under any circumstances.

Conversion in a Postindustrial Era

Mobilizations for World War II and the cold war, so close in time that they almost count as one, took place in a world where industrial mass production and the deployment of millions of troops were the prime determinants of conventional military power. In 1940 the United States also had the advantage of a quickly exploitable idle production capacity and unemployment due to the depression. These conditions do not apply as the United States moves into the twenty-first century. Technological substitution and increased ratios of support to combat forces, trends that have long characterized military development, continued throughout the cold war. By the post-Vietnam period the implications of postindustrial developments were becoming more apparent. The shift in importance for the economy as a whole of information, service, and education as compared with manufacturing—the comparative significance of hardware and software—is more and more reflected in the evolving nature of military power. Military systems have grown tremendously complex, and the cutting edge in capability no longer comes from manufacturing tens of thousands of tanks and aircraft, or equipping and training millions of infantrymen and sailors.

This development has implications not just for industrial production but also for military organization and manpower allocation. As forces become more complex, it becomes harder to maintain a fully diversified force structure with a constant level of resources, let alone a declining one. Since cadres need to be trained and maintained for a growing number of technical specialties, less "seed corn" can be kept on the shelf for each one of those specialties. As technology lengthens training cycles, the prospective rate of unit expansion in a future mobilization declines.[53]

In the past, the main problem was that manpower mobilization via conscription proved premature because equipment production always lagged behind. In the World War II effort as a whole, nevertheless, manpower proved the ultimate bottleneck because of uncertainties about how finite numbers should be allocated among the various services or in war-supporting labor, among mines, factories, and agriculture.[54] In the future, manpower recruitment will probably still be less crucial for military forces per se, but no less crucial for mobilization in general. The difference is that cannon fodder will become militarily less important, and technically trained human capital more important.

In a world of nuclear weapons and precise conventional ordnance it is hard to envision any buildup that would put more than 20 million American men and women in uniform (the analogue, in terms of proportion of population, to the size of the armed forces in World War II). Highly trained specialists and experienced command organizations to produce, use, and coordinate interdependent systems of high-tech weaponry, on the other hand, will be more important. There has been a secular trend away from pyramidal personnel structures; modern forces require a larger proportion of technicians and managers.[55] This trend will not only continue but should be accentuated in a military force more oriented to preparation for expansion.

Industrial consequences remain the most crucial manifestations of these economic and technical trends. Technological sophistication has increased both the unit effectiveness and cost of individual weapons, and skills in collaborative invention, design, engineering, and crafts-manship constitute a larger part of the base of military power. As Thomas McNaugher notes, research and development "has grown steadily more expensive, while production runs, especially for military aircraft, have lost whatever resemblance they once had to mass production and have instead acquired the character of customizing operations."[56]

Technical complexity increases lead times in fielding weapons, the trained personnel to support them, and the military organizations to integrate and use them. This simply continues the historic trend.[57] It took almost two years to reach peak production and combat force deployment in World War I and more than three years to do so in World War II. Thirty years into the cold war, with the mobilization base already functioning at half-throttle, Jacques Gansler estimated that it would take the aircraft industry three years "to reach a production level of any significant military value," and the shipbuilding industry longer.[58] Once the defense industrial base has finished winding down much further, opening up more lacunae in the system for expanding production of weapons that are dependent on numerous components and support establishments, the time lags are bound to be longer, and the probability of imbalance in phasing of mobilization is likely to be higher.

After the post–cold war demobilization, however, surge capacity for serial production will not be the main issue for mobilization readiness. Conversion to a war economy in the next generation will take a long time. It can be made shorter and more efficient by putting more emphasis on mobilization readiness, but it will be a long time nonetheless. Before planners worry about whether the United States can mass-produce military items, they need to ensure that the infrastructure for developing new weapon systems and integrating them with related technologies and organizations for support and maintenance remains in place. Quick expansion of military muscle should be a secondary concern for mobilization readiness in the future. Primary concern should shift to keeping the skeleton on which to develop the muscle.

This means that the first strategic priority is to preserve capacity to retool and organize quickly to turn out weapons never yet deployed in quantity; not to preserve a whole production organization as it was known in a period of permanent mobilization, but the nucleus from which a functioning production system can be reconstituted when resources are infused. This means focusing on preserving (in both industry and the military) pools of skills and teams for designing, engineering, crafting, testing, and experimenting with new weapons on the cutting edge. Prototype development and experimental units should take precedence over serial production and conventional combat units.

To some observers, this is a truism. To others (especially in defense industrial firms), it is a naive and impractical notion because design teams cannot be funded and kept together without profits from production. If R&D without production is to be possible, novel forms of subsidy will probably be necessary. Moving in this direction involves many choices that depart radically from business as usual in the cold war. The need for change is obvious in principle but likely to prove difficult in practice for reasons of both corporate and political habit. Consider the questions of R&D and supply sources.

To move toward a defense policy based more on mobilization readiness than structural readiness inevitably means putting more emphasis on research and less on production. Proposals to fund R&D alone, however, have met fierce resistance by aerospace executives on the grounds that the processes have proved too mutually supportive to separate. The chief executive officer of the Loral Corporation, for example, criticized as a myth the proposition that a viable defense industrial base can be preserved with research and development only.

This works nicely in theory but falls apart in practice because it underestimates the interdependence between production and engineering. R&D not translated into production is pure science, lacking the vitality of application. Defense capability requires production technology and experienced technicians. Engineering creativity does not end with the beginning of production; emphasis on value engineering—to make the product smaller, with more power, less costly—continues throughout its manufacture.[59]

Perhaps this observation is true.[60] Even if so, it is no help, since it will not override the tide of world politics and prevent the contraction of defense budgets below the cold war baseline. The only way to continue the process as described would be to develop many fewer weapons and spread the much smaller procurement budgets in the same old proportions between development and production. Whatever particular firms might wish for, that is no alternative.

One alternative is to subsidize technological mobilization readiness explicitly, to overcome the built-in obstacles to focusing on R&D that have characterized U.S. defense procurement. The cold war pattern forced firms to invest in R&D in order to compete for contracts and then to recoup the investment in receipts from long production runs. Firms could thus have no interest in innovations unless they were put into production. Similarly, firms' vast overhead costs in facilities were recovered by spreading them over manufacturing contracts.[61]

There are various possibilities along a continuum from pure research to all-out serial production: from design with no production, to prototype production with soft tooling, to limited production with hard tooling.[62] Different decisions along such a continuum can make sense at different times and for different technologies and purposes, but on average the best post–cold war solution is likely to be a compromise that maintains smaller teams for long periods—drawing out the research, development, testing, and engineering cycle—developing a few prototypes for experimentation and doctrinal feedback. In any case, if the government wants to continue technical development and maintain basic facilities while not fielding new weapons in numbers typical in past decades, it will have to *pay* firms *some* sort of separate mobilization retainer. If such a system is to be effective, the costs are not likely to be small.

In effect, this solution would recognize more explicitly that if the government is the only customer for military products, defense industries cannot operate like normal firms in a free market, that this was true in the cold war and simply more true afterward, and that the solution is to nationalize more of the function and operate more like an "arsenal" system. In past eras much U.S. military procurement was in this mode (and it persisted in the nuclear weapons complex during the cold war). The modern French defense industry is another example.[63] As the post–cold war shakeout is completed, leaving fewer firms with hope or interest in securing military business, direct acceptance of the arsenal model could become both more feasible politically and more necessary strategically.

Dependence on foreign suppliers for military items may pose similar choices. The globalization of trade that has increased interdependence in the civilian economy has not left the military economy immune.[64] As the military economy contracts in the United States, marginal domestic suppliers will disappear if they are left to the mercy of the market. In the current situation, many Americans might accept growing economic dependence in the spirit of free trade and celebration of cooperative security, especially since most of the foreign supply sources will be in currently allied countries. For that reason it is not worrisome strategically (domestic political resistance from failing industries aside) to rely on such sources for current development and production. Collaboration with foreign partners may become inevitable (as America's European allies were forced to recognize decades ago) if the absence of a Soviet-like threat precludes the sacrifices necessary to afford independent facilities.

The reasons for indifference to military dependence, however, are integrally linked to the reason that the United States has been *demo*bilizing: the outbreak of peace among the great powers. That logic does not apply to hedging against whatever future change in world politics would warrant remobilization. Such change presumes new cleavages and alignments that cannot yet be known and that could turn benign dependence into strategic vulnerability. Put this strategic uncertainty together with domestic pressure to Buy American, and a consensus could emerge to preserve the industrial elements necessary for remobilization within the boundaries of the United States.

It is by no means inevitable that policies will move this way. In fact, the Clinton administration's early initiatives for reform aimed in the other direction, toward integrating weapons acquisition with the civilian market. By streamlining procedures, encouraging the flow of research money between defense and commercial sectors, and discouraging excessive "mil specs"—that is, unique technical requirements for new systems that preclude buying commercial products without special modification—Secretary of Defense Les Aspin and then Deputy Secretary William Perry hoped to make Pentagon procurement more efficient and better able to exploit technologies from civilian industry that it will no longer have the resources to develop on its own. As Aspin wrote, the reforms were intended "to allow the Defense Department to run itself more like a business: buying products in the most competitive and sensible way, reducing massive paperwork requirements, and whenever possible, making purchases off the shelf."[65]

The goal of simplification has been promoted by almost all previous "blue ribbon" commissions that have addressed procurement problems and has never been implemented in a major way. One formidable barrier is the military bureaucracy's deeply ingrained "penchant for defining what it wants in ways that have no commercial equivalents."[66] Even if there is more progress this time, however, reforms of this sort are primarily relevant to procurement for continuing structural readiness: technologies fielded for existing forces. Despite budget cuts, by historic standards there is still an ample standing force to keep supplied and modernized in the 1990s. If reductions continue, however, the relative importance of providing for structural readiness and for mobilization readiness will shift. It is not clear that particular problems of mobilization readiness, which involves preparing for production more than actual production, can be solved by integrating military and commercial markets.

Explicit subsidies of R&D, industrial overhead, and uncompetitive domestic producers may ultimately be, in some form and combination, the only alternative to the collapse of the infrastructure needed to restore military power in a future conversion. The latter possibility is not out of the question, but it would put the United States in a situation potentially worse than those faced before the mid-twentieth century, since the complexity of a modern military economy is greater than that in the middle of the industrial era. To avoid that alternative by instituting some system of direct subsidy would cost money that Americans were not accustomed to spending, at least consciously, during the cold war. They would also be required to do so when aggregate defense budgets are far smaller. It means, in effect, that *Americans will have to spend money in order to save money.* Doing this between cross-pressures to maximize either unreadiness or structural readiness as opposed to mobilization readiness—that is, to either maximize the peace dividend or to preserve standing forces rather than preserve mobilization readiness—will be tricky.

Prescribing the specifics of industrial policy for mobilization readiness is beyond the scope of this book. The point of this summary discussion is to suggest the range of problems policymakers face. Chapters 4 and 5 showed that despite more than three decades of experience with building and maintaining large defenses in peacetime, readiness policy could spur extraordinary legislative-executive conflict and administrative-analytical confusion up to the last decade of the cold war. Future remobilization will pose bigger political challenges.

Politics of Planning Preparedness

The goal of mobilization readiness is not to have all of the conversion machinery in mothballs; technical obstacles would make that impractical even if there were no political pitfalls. Too many economic and technological complexities are constantly evolving, in addition to shifting vested interests, doctrinal concepts, and strategic priorities. A more realistic aim is to have plans that are not chiseled in stone but that put the mobilization system ahead of a tabula rasa—plans that preserve institutional memory and provide a basis for rapid revision of plans—and that put staffs in place who have an informed notion of how to coordinate and balance the initial phases of buildup when political decisions are made to undertake conversion. Previous experience shows how much more easily this is said than done.

The technical complexities reinforce the inherent political obstacles, since there is no solid consensus among the experts to override the pulling and hauling of the policy marketplace. There is also a natural tension between the logic of democratic pluralism and the diffusion of power, on one hand, and the logic of planning and central control, on the other. Democracy works against final decisions on resource allocation. From day to day, claimants rise and fall in status, change their priorities, and find and lose channels of influence, so the division of the budgetary pie is constantly being renegotiated. Centralized planning, on the other hand, requires authority to make reliable commitments long in advance of the time that they would be implemented.

In the political process immediate controversies take precedence over long-range problems.

Realistic preparation must anticipate threats to its own efficacy. Most of all, the organization of the effort must avoid the common technocratic orientation that downplays the prospect of constraints on implementing apparently "rational" plans. The technocratic impulse is to assess the policy issue analytically in terms of economic and technical criteria and relegate political concerns to an "all else being equal" assumption. If that happens, mobilization planning will prove no more effective than in the interwar period. Organization of the planning apparatus must take into account the possible reaction of parochial interests to its initiatives, as well as the balance of power among government agencies and services involved in the process.

The first step is to avoid relying on any singular plan. In an analysis at the time of the last major mobilization, William Yandell Elliott cast the choice between the "blueprint" approach and the "problem and method planning" approach. The former was used between World Wars I and II, but it presumed conditions that turned out not to exist when the time for mobilization came. This does not mean that the effort proved useless, just that it was less adaptive than it could have been.[67] The second approach, akin to what the effort should aim for in the future, was identified by the NSRB in 1949:

> Planning for war does not require that all wartime decisions or determinations be made in advance. With respect to controversial areas, at least, the approach should be rather to identify the critical problems, to suggest alternative solutions, and to indicate the merits and limitations of each alternative. Pushing for specific decisions in advance of need unnecessarily promotes controversy and may lead to undesirable compromise in the planning product. In any case, there is no certainty that wartime executives will accept peacetime decisions, or that present executives will not subsequently change their views. . . . [P]lanning should provide the basis for resolving issues rather than attempt to provide the final answers in advance.[68]

More than half the battle is developing some coherent idea of what the variables and their interdependencies are, which lead times are longest and most affect balance and phasing, and what bottlenecks will emerge if certain priorities take precedence. This sort of forecasting is difficult, but modern computers improve the options if good data are made available.

To give teeth to the planning effort, economic, administrative, and political resources have to be invested in it. Mobilization planning staff work has been done all along for most of the past century, but its chances of affecting the process when remobilization occurs vary directly with its profile in peacetime policymaking. The details of readiness issues became too politicized in the 1980s, but may become insufficiently politicized as post–cold war demobilization is completed. Mobilization readiness will become a decaying pretense unless it is evaluated and debated periodically in Congress and is given genuine rather than pro forma prominence in executive branch councils.

The problem is that, like logistics, the importance of mobilization readiness is recognized in principle but most high officials' eyes glaze over when the subject is actually discussed in any detail. If this unfortunate but natural tendency is to be overcome, the position of the planning apparatus in the bureaucracy is crucial. The function should not be housed in parts of the organizational wiring diagram that can be easily ignored by busy policymakers; this means that the planning unit needs some authority to require its concurrence on certain categories of policy and budgetary initiative. Nothing can force high-level decisionmakers to pay attention to a bureau if they do not want to unless they need that bureau's approval to move. Another main objective should be to ensure that the civilian and military staffs involved do not work independently of each other. Left to their own devices, military organizations will take the technocratic approach. They will refuse to pile complications onto their task by factoring political uncertainties (for example, the virtual impossibility that there will ever be a specific M-day in a peacetime buildup) into their studies. If past experience is a guide, they will also tend to focus on options that will optimize mobilization without constraint, rather than programs for a situation in which domestic commitment to conversion is hesitant and controversial. Military planners will need to have their feet held to the fire of political realism by civilian economists, but most especially by domestic policy officials and political appointees.[69]

If mobilization readiness is to have a higher priority after the cold war, organization needs to change. Forming the Mobilization Concepts Development Center in the 1980s was sensible, but locating it at the

National Defense University made it a peripheral rather than central player in defense policy. This was a reasonable arrangement in the cold war, when actual structural readiness made potential mobilization readiness less important. The clearest way to recognize the importance of preparing for mobilization would be to restore the units responsible for planning and monitoring to the high positions in the government structure that they lost in the latter part of the cold war. Formal position alone, however, will not be enough to make a difference.

The Federal Emergency Management Agency (FEMA), the unit most responsible for mobilization as of the end of the cold war, inherited the functions of the NSRB, ODM, and OEP but did not inherit their status as an agency within the Executive Office of the President, let alone a seat on the National Security Council. Such positions in themselves would not guarantee more influence for FEMA. The Emergency Mobilization Preparedness Board (EMPB) is linked to the National Security Council, since it is chaired by the assistant to the president for national security affairs, but there is no evidence that the board or its function ever garnered much attention of the Kissingers, Brzezinskis, Scowcrofts, or Lakes in that harried office. The EMPB is also composed of senior officials from other government agencies, who are preoccupied with other duties.

FEMA could be restored to the Executive Office and the National Security Council without ensuring a marked change in the status of mobilization planning, but something like that restoration is probably a prerequisite for change. Resurrecting some functions of the early cold war mobilization agencies could also be useful. For example, the NSRB did substantial staff work and cooperated with the Civil Service Commission on developing an "executive reserve" for use in emergencies.[70] More significant was the "observer system" used to keep the NSRB chairman apprised of relevant information. NSRB staff sat on major interagency committees and in meetings between agencies and industries. There were big limitations on the effectiveness of the observer system, but just by existing the system underwrote the status of mobilization planning and made it harder for the involved agencies to brush off the question of planning.[71] Dusting off practices such as these may be worthwhile, and it might also help to reestablish an agency focused on military mobilization. FEMA became primarily wrapped up in planning for natural disasters such as floods; that shift, and the downgrading of the agency's position in the National Security

Council system, reflected the atrophy of concern with mobilization in the second half of the cold war. Reactivating the Office of Defense Mobilization and putting it back in the Executive Office and the National Security Council would be the way to start a serious emphasis on mobilization readiness.

A serious apparatus for mobilization planning would link many agencies, including domestic ones such as the Treasury, Commerce, and Labor departments, the Council of Economic Advisers, and the Office of Science and Technology Policy. All the coordination in the world, however, will be pro forma unless the Department of Defense takes the leading role. That department will carry more clout in mobilization policy than any committee. The administrative change that would have the greatest impact, therefore, would be to institutionalize a higher profile for mobilization planning in the Pentagon. This would mean high rank (four stars, or under secretary) for a mobilization planning czar.

Inflating the portfolio risks feeding traditional pathologies of bureaucratic sprawl and turf fights. In an age of military contraction common sense implies that the boxes in the wiring diagram should be consolidated rather than multiplied, and the Clinton administration already established a new high-level focal point within OSD for readiness issues: an under secretary for personnel and readiness. In principle, this office could subsume the mobilization planning portfolio suggested here, integrate all the concerns about operational, structural, and mobilization readiness discussed in this book, and force the relevant trade-offs into high relief. In practice, however, the logical tie between current readiness and long-term readiness emphasized here is not generally recognized in the defense community. Mobilization planning and current readiness are most often thought of as opposites rather than as parts of the same problem, so a combination of the responsibilities would strike many as organizationally nonsensical. Moreover, much of what would be of concern to a mobilization planning czar lies in the current purview of the under secretary of defense for acquisition and technology, who oversees a vast empire compared with that administered by the under secretary for personnel and readiness.[72]

One way to keep the mobilization profile high without the messy juggling of the jobs of these two under secretaries would be to boost the portfolio yet higher. There is a precedent for creating a second deputy secretary of defense with responsibility for a major cluster of issues. This was done in 1976 when President Gerald Ford made Robert Ellsworth deputy secretary for intelligence. This really would be going too far, however, to deal with mobilization readiness, as important as it is. In any case, there is no consensus for such a high priority and no natural constituency for sustaining a second deputy secretary. (It is no accident that the last experiment lapsed within barely a year, as soon as Ford left office.)

An awkward but less impractical solution might be to vest the mobilization planning responsibility in an OSD troika of the two under secretaries and an assistant to the secretary of defense for mobilization readiness (ATSD/MR), comparable to the free-floating ATSDs that have occasionally existed for issues such as atomic energy, intelligence oversight, or NATO affairs. The under secretaries would have the rank to make mobilization planning serious business, and the ATSD would have the concentrated attention and access to the secretary to keep mobilization planning from getting lost in the shuffle of the under secretaries' other responsibilities. A parallel vesting of interest within the military could be accomplished by establishing another joint staff directorate (a new J-9) for mobilization planning, although this too would proliferate units instead of consolidating them. If the goal of simple organization takes precedence, however, and the aim is to house the mobilization portfolio under one main official, that authority should be the under secretary for personnel and readiness.

One of the main tests of whether mobilization readiness becomes as high a priority in practice as in principle will be how the military career system develops, institutionalizes, and rewards assignments of officers to mobilization planning jobs. During the cold war, the principal routes to professional success were through the operational command of combat units, or administration of crucial projects. Unless the career system shifts to give a higher payoff to assignments that nurture the dormant basis for building military power, rather than just ones that actually build and exercise it, the enterprise will not prosper. The Goldwater-Nichols reform of defense organization in the 1980s succeeded, where analysts' exhortations had not, in making joint assignments (those involved in integrating activities across separate services, as opposed to those strictly within one's own service) attractive by making them a prerequisite for individual career advancement. Since the United States is no longer fighting a cold war, it is time to do the same for mobilization assignments.

Beyond Planning

A credible effort to maintain data, do studies, and identify options for economic conversion is a big challenge, but it is not extraordinarily expensive. Even on a scale that would be lavish by academic standards, the money needed to staff research units and data processing is small change in the defense budget. Although the organization and procedures for instituting such an effort would be controversial, it should not be unusually difficult to secure the resources to support it if the president and secretary of defense want it.

Optimal preparation for mobilization would raise questions about investments that would be much more substantial, such as subsidies for R&D or the maintenance of production teams or skeletal organizations, as discussed previously. This poses rougher political questions, since competition for dwindling defense expenditures is fierce in some quarters and insufficient in others. (Firms that give up on defense business because of its unprofitability may have to be induced in various ways to keep a finger in the pie.) Resources invested in improving mobilization readiness are resources not spent on something else, and subsidies given to one firm or function are dollars not given to others. Distributive decisions are occasions for conflict, corruption, and distortion of the objective.

Since the payoffs from investments in mobilization readiness are also less tangible than for structural readiness—they will not yield things as visible as a wing of F-117s, or a submarine, or a brigade of tanks—it will be harder to prove clearly in the political arena which investments are wisest. Since future requirements are impossible to prove, no distributive decision can be guaranteed an analytical consensus, so none will be beyond political appeal. This makes preparation for mobilization a potential pork barrel, and one that could quickly create new vested interests that would then become obstacles to adaptation as technologies, strategies, and circumstances change.

There is an imbalance in the political strengths of constituencies or vested interests that need to be nurtured for mobilization readiness (such as research and development or cadre organizations within the military) and those that have been made prominent by the cold war tradition of structural readiness (production or fully mobilized standing units). Mobilization readiness implies emphasizing support tail over combat teeth, and doing so has never been popular among civilian managers or legislators, who mistakenly tend to see it as evidence of inefficiency and flab.

To change the balance of power among old constituencies and new ones, executives and legislators have to believe that mobilization readiness is important and that efficiency over the long term is worth additional investments—at the expense of structural readiness and vested interests associated with it—in the short term. There is no guarantee that this will happen. Any group with a conflicting interest will cloak its claims in the mantle of mobilization, just as everyone who wanted something in the 1980s claimed it was for "readiness."

Putting Readiness Together

The main problems of readiness until the middle of the twentieth century were different from those during the cold war. Rapid wartime mobilization of huge forces from scratch, with a small base of peacetime organization on which to build, posed more fundamental challenges than maximizing the operational efficiency of large existing forces. The two sets of problems, however, are similar. They both involve trade-offs between potential and actual power, which in turn depend on predictions about how quickly combat might erupt and how powerful the enemy forces engaged might be.

In contrast to either of the two previous traditions in U.S. military history, *both* of these sets of problems will figure in the post–cold war world. As the base of standing forces and defense infrastructure decline—and especially if the combined persistence of amity among the great powers and domestic budgetary pressures push the decline further than planned in the early 1990s—readiness to remobilize will become more important than at any time since 1950. But unless the United States abandons superpower status and embraces strategic isolation, it will continue to maintain some appreciable amount of capability for rapid intervention. Thus the questions about where to put marginal defense resources—into mobilization, structural, or operational readiness—will remain as relevant as ever.

Balancing the Stages of Readiness

This book began with a simple definition meant to encompass the many facets of readiness. The concept was defined as the degree to which actual military capability matches potential capability. As subsequent discussion showed, military potential exists in different forms, at different stages of the conversion process (see table 2-2). When there is no readiness, ultimate or *latent* potential is inherent in the economic, technological, and population bases of a society. Converting latent potential into effective military force requires years of mobilization and coordinated development. *Incipient* potential exists when the process for conversion is well planned in advance, with procedures and building blocks for mobilization in place: a situation of mobilization readiness. When mobilization then occurs, resources are converted into *organized* military potential: structures and units (mass) that are not yet optimized for combat performance (efficiency). These semiready units have actual capability, but less than they can have after being fleshed out and tuned to perfection. The capability that they embody is an aspect of readiness because large military organizations cannot be formed from scratch on short notice, while existing formations *can* be pumped up to full efficiency within such time. In the final stage, operational readiness, the potential in the structure is realized.

The ideal for combining security and economy is to maintain the above sequence of conversion: to develop military readiness in a linear fashion, refining potential and bringing it closer to actual capability in stages, optimizing capability shortly before the turning point of a crisis. The technical complexity of a modern military force and strategic uncertainty about when and where a war will start make the linear ideal hard to achieve. Three main problems stand out.

One was illustrated in chapter 1 and earlier in the present chapter: an imbalance in the process of rapid mobilization from peacetime unreadiness to war footing causes delay and waste in fielding forces. Instead of a smooth progression from low capability to high, the process has more often been fitful. In the past, inadequately coordinated crash programs—in the mobilization of industry and manpower, expansion of force structure and its molding into viable combat formations, and deployment of units and their supporting supply networks—jostled each other until the jumble was eventually shaken out. In the U.S. preparation for World War I, the shakeout was never achieved before the armistice; in World War II, it happened by late 1943, more than three years after mobilization began in earnest.

The other two main problems were peculiar to the high peacetime mobilization of the cold war. One was the tension between incentives to allocate resources to structural or operational readiness, whether to maximize potential for the next month or the next day. At the margin, those who focused on the danger of fighting the Soviet Union with forces too small to hold the line placed priority on numbers of organized units and modernized weapon systems, even though fielding them took resources from measures to optimize their immediate efficiency. Those who focused on the danger of having to fight on short notice placed priority on personnel and equipment fills, maintenance, and training to keep existing forces in fighting trim.

The former put the readiness for what question—the enemy's combat potential—ahead of the readiness for when question. They were willing, consciously or not, to gamble that enough time would be available to spin up the provisioning and proficiency of the larger force before it had to be thrown into battle. Those who favored emphasizing operational readiness, at a cost to the size of the total force, had the reverse priority. The inevitable trade-off was rarely acknowledged by anyone on either side of the issue, and this reluctance to face the choice confused the understanding of readiness. The tension interfered with the linear development of readiness when it led to booms and busts in spending for procurement and creation of new units and major weapons platforms, or for spare parts, exercises, and other measures to firm up existing units.

The third problem was the cyclical or "wave" phenomenon peculiar to crises, when the incentives seem highest to realize all the potential capability in a force and hold it in actual availability for combat. Unless the linear development of readiness peaks just when war starts or the crisis ends peacefully, it reverses.[73] This leaves the force less ready for war than it was before the crisis, unless fresh replacement units are available to rotate into position. Keeping extra units purely for rotation, however, carries the price of redundant structural readiness. There are two ways to avoid the wave problem: either predict accurately when the adversary will attack (or retreat) or start the battle oneself. When the United States takes the strategic initiative in combat, as in the war against Iraq, it can keep readiness linear by deciding when to fight and thus when to bring the generation of capability to a head. Deciding when to bring things to a head is harder when U.S. forces in prolonged crises are supposed to stay poised to react to the other side's initiatives.

At first glance the cyclical wave problem might seem to have gone away with the end of the cold war. When war with another superpower was the constant benchmark for the adequacy of U.S. forces, the drain on forces that rotation could cause in a prolonged crisis compromised structural readiness for the most demanding contingency. If that contingency is gone, so is the danger posed by a breaking readiness wave in a deployment for a third world crisis. At second glance, however, it is obvious that the slack in structural readiness will eventually go away as forces are reduced in post–cold war demobilization, so the old tension will reemerge.

Assessment and Policy

Technical and political decisions are interdependent at all stages of the process of converting potential into actual capability. The judgment about when it is necessary to mobilize a large standing military force— as in 1939–40, 1950, or sometime in the future—is a matter of high politics. It depends on fundamental judgments about the international balance of power, emerging adversaries, and strategic options. Those questions are constantly on the table for discussion and are ultimately the most important ones for defense policy. They are not questions for technical specialists or military professionals to answer. Where political and technical processes interact, however, progress depends on a clearer recognition of the competition between different aspects of readiness and the integration of absolute and relative standards for assessment.

The standard concept of readiness among professional analysts in the cold war—operational readiness alone—provides no basis on which to link resource allocation decisions with strategic decisions. The standard concept is not explicitly linked to any judgment about how much organized military potential is needed, given the strength of a specific adversary; it says nothing about how much actual capability is needed for the near future, as opposed to right away, if the latter comes at a cost to the former. The fact that the standard usage of the term "readiness" among technical specialists bore no direct relation to the question "how much is enough" is precisely why managers testifying in the political arena played fast and loose with the concept once it became entangled in the debate about the overall defense effort in the Carter and Reagan administrations.

The reference point for operational readiness is inward-looking: the gap between the combat potential of existing units (however many or few there happen to be) and their actual capability. Since this is independent of how much organized potential there is, the size of that gap does not in itself say anything about whether or when it should be closed. The answer depends on whether the risk that war will break out immediately is greater than the risk that existing forces might lose even if operating at full potential. If the latter risk is greater, it constitutes an argument for shifting marginal resources to structural readiness (to increase potential capability for the near future) and for accepting the higher risk that there might not be enough time to spin the force up to full efficiency.

Because basic estimates about evolving threats are matters of high politics and specific cases, it is hopeless to prescribe in advance or in the abstract when to begin climbing the readiness stairway, or how fast to do so. Clarifications in peacetime preparations, however, can help. One example is in the systems for rating unit readiness, the source of so much of the confusion noted in chapters 4 and 5. The most useful clarifications would avoid crossed signals about priorities on structural and operational readiness by linking the absolute and relative standards of performance, that is, the estimates of how close units come to their inherent potential, as compared to how well their potential stacks up against that of the enemy. In the past, reporting conventions have addressed only readiness of what, not for what.[74] The latter question was debated in other venues.

Addressing the questions simultaneously is naturally easier to do intellectually than bureaucratically but is hardly impossible. It would amount to instituting triple ratings, which together would bring "of what," "for what," and "for when" into simultaneous focus. One rating would be similar to the various conventions of recent years that measure units against the absolute standard of 100 percent of their ideal status in personnel, equipment, training, and maintenance. Which details of previous rating conventions are used is not crucial. They are less likely to be a contentious issue than they have been in the past if they are complemented by other ratings geared to estimating the aggregate capability of a force to succeed in a combat contingency;

the successive shifts from FORSTAT to UNITREP to SORTS noted in chapter 5 reflect the inadequacy of singular standards to capture the separate dimensions of the problem.

Two other complementary standards would be used in order to focus attention on the meaning of readiness as capability in variance with time. The second standard would estimate the actual capability of units against a putative adversary if committed to combat immediately; the third would estimate the time needed to reach full operational readiness once peacetime resource restraints are lifted. These two estimates would be more controversial than the first, but controversy would force policymakers to confront choices obscured in the past.

This combination of estimates would also focus attention on other imbalances that interfere with the synchronization of readiness. An example is the deployability of ground force units matched against the availability of transport. If the number of crack divisions exceeds the capacity of air and sealift to move them to the scene of action, their operational readiness turns out to be wasted. In terms of economic efficiency, the units would do better to stay less ready in peacetime, while planning to use the time in a crisis during which they must wait for transportation to get themselves up to operational snuff. Or if it is vital that they be able to deploy sooner, then more lift must be procured to do so (which may have to come at some cost to the number of combat units). A readiness rating system that declares an armored division C-1 when it would be unable to close with the enemy for weeks or months may be technically correct, but it is strategically meaningless at best and deceptive at worst.

The problem is far from hypothetical. Imbalance of this sort was typical in the past, as William Kaufmann noted when the post-detente buildup was getting under way:

> The strategic reserve is now badly out of balance with the capacity of the mobility forces to deploy it worldwide. The only theater to which forces could be moved rapidly . . . is central Europe. And even there the best that could be done now by way of reinforcement is no more than six divisions in two weeks or so, even if all heavy airlift capacity were committed. . . . [F]our Army divisions would be stranded in the continental United States. . . . [C]entral Europe would receive fewer divisions than the planners consider essential,

and the occurrence of a second and simultaneous contingency (outside of Korea) would find those four divisions in the continental
United States partly ready for it but unable to move.[75]

The following year the commandant of the Marine Corps testified, "I
have more fight than you can ferry."[76] A few years after that, Army
Chief of Staff Edward Meyer opposed full funding of operational readiness for army units because of the lift deficiency.[77] After the Reagan
buildup had peaked, and two years before the Berlin Wall fell, administration plans still did not envision satisfying total requirements until
near the end of the century. Meanwhile, the budget of the Military
Airlift Command was being cut 20 percent and exercises in joint training with the Army were being trimmed.[78] Yet critics frequently complained about deficiencies in army C-ratings without demanding more
air or sealift. That sort of concern with unit readiness divorced from
concern with the timing of overall engagement was strategically sense-
less, yet typical.

The end of the cold war temporarily makes some of these anomalies
beside the point, since the number of ground forces has fallen more
quickly than the number of ships and planes that could move them.
Demobilization is affecting everything, however, and the political and
organizational constituencies for combat forces have always been more
potent than those for transportation assets, so imbalances may easily
reemerge. The point should simply be to force the decisions about
buying combat readiness to conform with the other decisions that
govern the utility of military power. Integrating all these concerns in
readiness reporting systems may be more than the system can handle,
but unless there is progress in that direction, it is not clear that normal
readiness ratings are any more useful than they are deceptive.

Balanced Readiness after the Cold War

Economic efficiency and military effectiveness can be combined in
readiness only if the point at which optimal combat capability will be
needed is known, and the process of conversion of potential into actual
capability is planned well enough and begun soon enough to allow
the linear development of readiness. Those conditions are necessary
to avoid wasting resources in breathless attempts to catch up or in
premature peaking of capability. This formulation is an ideal type, of
course, and all the preceding discussions of inefficiencies and imbal-

ances only show degrees of imperfection common in most human endeavors. As with unrealistic economic models based on the assumption of perfect markets and information, however, fixing on the standard of efficiency in theory is useful even if it cannot be attained in practice.

The central issue at present is how the problem of integrating readiness choices in the post–cold war world differs from what it was in the past half century, when the baseline of peacetime structural readiness was high. The situation in years to come is not likely to be the same as it was under either of the two American military traditions surveyed. It is highly improbable that U.S. defense policy will revert all the way to the pre-1939 peacetime norm. The United States has gotten too accustomed to being the principal world power to go all the way back to the days when it was a secondary participant in the clash of major state interests. At the same time, without either a superpower military threat like the one it faced in the Soviet Union or a transnational ideological threat like fascism or communism, spending between 5 and 10 percent of the gross national product on military forces in peacetime (as the United States did in the past half century) will be insupportable.

What is most likely is that the United States will keep much more structural readiness than in most of its peacetime history, but not enough to avoid having to shift more concern to mobilization readiness. *The mistake that should be avoided is to assume that if the priority on structural readiness declines in relation to mobilization readiness, the priority on operational readiness should decline even further.* That assumption would be common sense, appearing consistent with the linear model in which the stages of readiness are sequential, but it misses one main point: mobilization readiness depends in some critical respects on elements of operational readiness more than on the size of standing forces.[79]

High structural readiness limits the efficiency of existing forces. This is not necessarily a problem in a large standing force, since the overall size leaves room for ample islands of efficiency. As defense resources shrink, all the components cannot shrink proportionally, across the board, because some elements of overhead are inelastic. If there was one school for widget repair in the cold war military, there would still have to be one in the shrunken force of the future, or the military might lose the ability to repair widgets forever. Much of the overhead in the U.S. military is funded through the O&M budget, which means that the accounts supporting current operational readiness are also supporting the base that must be preserved for future remobilization.[80]

As forces are scaled back in the direction of a skeletal structure and a professional cadre that can serve as a base for expansion, the smaller corps becomes the keeper of the flame. Personnel have to remain highly proficient in order to ensure the preservation of the minimum necessary pool of skills. The march of technology makes it progressively harder to maintain the variety and intensity of expertise and training in a small force. As the number and complexity of specialized skills and technical gadgets that must be integrated in a force structure grows, so does the overhead. Either the personnel and equipment for learning and practicing various skills must grow too (an improbable solution for a declining defense budget) or a smaller corps of people and machines must be more versatile and well-tuned. Thus, paradoxically, less readiness can require more readiness. As with all of the aspects of the problem explored here, the point is that saying anything useful requires specifying what kind of readiness is meant. Speaking of readiness in general—without specifying for when, for what, or of what—will leave debate about defense policy as confused and inconclusive as it has been all too often in the past.

Appendix

Linear and Cyclical Images

*F*IGURE A-1 illustrates the trade-off between time and capability discussed in chapter 2 in terms of four alternative mixes of readiness. Recall the formulations in chapter 2: net readiness is speed times effectiveness; effectiveness is mass times efficiency. The vertical axis represents effectiveness in terms of units of potential capability; the horizontal axis represents mobilization or conversion time. Assume that existing units can raise their operational readiness by 10 percent of potential in each increment of mobilization time until they reach 100 percent.[1]

Force A has 100 units and maximizes operational readiness by keeping all of those units at peak efficiency all the time; there is no gap between its actual and potential capability in peacetime, but it has fewer units than the other three alternative forces, which, in various proportions, trade peacetime efficiency for mass. Force A would be composed entirely of active service units, fully manned, with as much equipment, training, and supplies as the units could possibly absorb.

Force B has 150 potential units; the extra 50 units of structural readiness are bought by a peacetime status of 50 percent operational readiness. When the structure surges into high gear upon mobilization, the force does not reach its full potential until T6. If Force B enters combat at T1 or T2, it will be weaker than Force A, because its effectiveness (mass times efficiency) will be less than 100 units. If it does not have to fight until after T2, it will be stronger than Force A, which would still have only 100 units while the spinup in Force B's operational readiness would bring it to the equivalent of 105 by T3, and ultimately to 150 by T6. Force B would be composed of mostly active units and some reserves.

Force C has 200 units, double the potential of A and one-third more

FIGURE A-1. *Peacetime Readiness as a Stairway*

Potential units

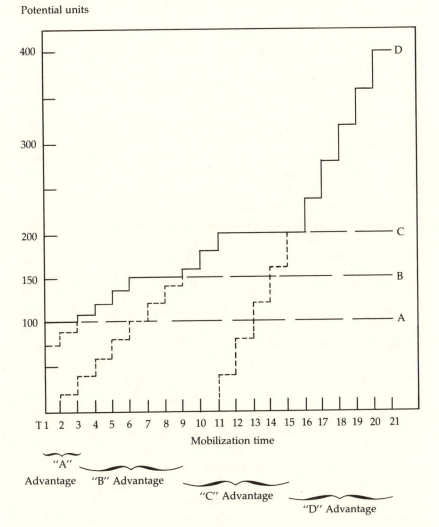

than B, but it does not reach that potential until T11 and does not match A's capability until T6 or B's until T9. Force C would consist mostly of reserve units.

Force D has by far the largest potential capability, 400 units, but that potential comes from not letting operational *or* structural readiness consume resources in peacetime. Force D would be raised from scratch, by the sequence of recruitment, organization, outfitting, basic training, and advanced training that begins only at T1. The longer lead time to create the basic structure means that *no* deployable capability exists, even at minimal levels of operational readiness, until long after Forces A or B could be fighting at peak efficiency, and only a handful of units from Force D could be available even after Force C has reached its full potential capability of 200 units.

In reality, great powers rely on a combination of these sorts of forces, some maximizing operational readiness (like Force A), some maximizing structural readiness (like Force C), some compromising between the two (like Force B), and some maximizing potential capability by eliminating any actual capability in peacetime (like Force D). The relative emphasis on these different choices depends on the total amount of resources allocated to defense in peacetime, and the match between the requirements of readiness for when and for what. In principle, countries should not have any units as fully ready as Force A unless they might have to enter combat (or deter attack by threatening to do so) before T3. If they have to be able to fight that early, their Force A should have no more units than necessary to handle the force the adversary could field at that time. *For any fight beginning after T3, Force A's efficiency is a waste*, a peacetime drain on its wartime mass. Conversely, if handling a prospective threat would require more than 200 units, then it is necessary to be confident that combat on that scale would not begin until T15 or later. Otherwise, better alliances or higher defense spending would be necessary in order to advance the date by which that many units could be available, by providing more structural readiness in peacetime.

Constant readiness on the model of Force A makes sense as a hedge against surprise attack, and negligible peacetime readiness on the model of Force D makes sense to the extent that a state can have confidence in detecting and acting on the evidence of a developing threat without delay. In a prolonged crisis, however, structural and operational readiness become complements rather than alternatives.

FIGURE A-2. *Readiness Waves in Prolonged Crisis*

Units

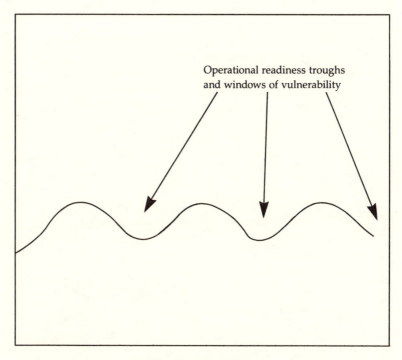

Operational readiness troughs
and windows of vulnerability

Duration of crisis deployment

Figure A-2 illustrates the cyclical problem of falling readiness as forces on high alert wear down. If a country's military force operates on a war footing in crisis without relief, it faces the "use it or lose it" problem.

That problem can be mitigated by reducing the pace of operations and postponing burnout, at the price of lower readiness for immediate combat, or duplicating the force of whatever size is necessary to achieve the combat mission, and rotating the two forces so that they alternate in readiness and recovery. The latter alternative is suggested in figure A-3.

FIGURE A-3. *Redundancy and Rotation*

Units

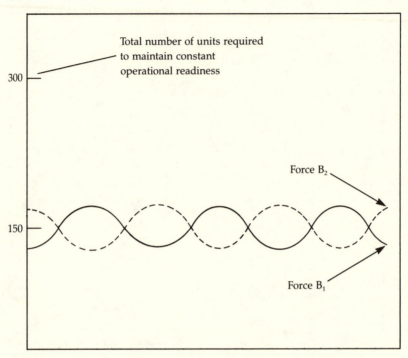

Duration of crisis deployment

Notes

Chapter One

1. The perceived urgency was reflected in additional initiatives: a high-level Senior Readiness Oversight Council, a Readiness Task Force of eight retired generals and admirals under the Defense Science Board, and a midlevel Readiness Working Group. See Secretary of Defense Les Aspin, *Report on the Bottom-Up Review* (Department of Defense, October 1993), p. 79.

2. *Trends in Selected Indicators of Military Readiness, 1980 through 1993* (Congressional Budget Office, March 1994), pp. 11–19; Bradley Graham, "Debate Erupts over Military Retirees' Pay," *Washington Post*, June 22, 1994, p. A19; and John G. Roos, "Redefining Readiness," *Armed Forces Journal International* (October 1994), pp. 34–40. The new Readiness Task Force reported that "the readiness of today's forces is acceptable," but that without more attention to the problem by the administration and Congress, "the armed forces could slip back into a 'hollow' status." *Defense Science Board Task Force on Readiness: Final Report* (June 1994), p. i. On the readiness scare at the midpoint of the Clinton administration, see Douglas Jehl, "Clinton to Ask Billions More in Spending for the Military," *New York Times*, December 2, 1994, p. A1; and Eric Schmitt, "G.O.P. Military Overseer Assails Troop Readiness," *New York Times*, November 17, 1994, p. A22.

3. See Francis Fukuyama, "The End of History?"; and John Mueller, "The Obsolescence of Major War," in Richard K. Betts, ed., *Conflict after the Cold War: Arguments on Causes of War and Peace* (Macmillan, 1994).

4. If the quick interventions of Turkey in Cyprus and the Soviet Union in Hungary are counted, the wars among Serbia, Croatia, and Bosnia are not the first. In four decades of cold war, however, the North Atlantic Treaty Organization never deployed military forces in combat. It took the end of the cold war and the outbreak of a hot war in Bosnia to make this happen, when NATO aircraft attacked Bosnian Serb forces in 1994.

5. John Shy, "First Battles in Retrospect," in Charles E. Heller and William A. Stofft, eds., *America's First Battles: 1776–1865* (University Press of Kansas, 1986), p. 329. The losses were Long Island, Queenston, Bull Run, Kasserine, and Osan/Naktong; the four costly victories were San Juan, Cantigny, Buna,

and Ia Drang. If Bataan was counted as the first battle in the Pacific war rather than Buna, the record would be even worse.

6. Frederic Louis Huidekoper, *The Military Unpreparedness of the United States: A History of American Land Forces from Colonial Times until June 1, 1915* (Macmillan, 1915), pp. 269–72.

7. James A. Huston, *The Sinews of War: Army Logistics 1775–1953* (U.S. Army, Office of the Chief of Military History, 1966), p. 277.

8. Maurice Matloff and others, *American Military History*, partly rev. ed. (U.S. Army, Office of the Chief of Military History, 1973), pp. 322–23. On the outbreak of war, the regular army consisted of 2,143 officers and 26,040 enlisted men. General Staff data quoted in Huidekoper, *The Military Unpreparedness of the United States*, p. 153.

9. Ronald Schaffer, *America in the Great War: Rise of the War and Welfare State* (Oxford University Press, 1991), p. 32; and Marvin A. Kreidberg and Merton G. Henry, *History of Mobilization in the United States Army, 1775–1945*, Department of the Army Pamphlet 20-212 (Department of the Army, June 1955), p. 317.

10. Schaffer, *America in the Great War*, pp. 33–34.

11. "Plans for Industrial Mobilization, 1920–1939," Study of Experience in Industrial Mobilization for World War II RP 28, II (Army Industrial College, Department of Research, November 1945), p. 7; Huston, *Sinews of War*, p. 328; and House Committee on Armed Services, Defense Industrial Base Panel, *Report: The Ailing Defense Industrial Base: Unready for Crisis*, 96 Cong. 2 sess. (GPO, 1980), p. 7.

12. Allen R. Millett, "Cantigny, 28–31 May 1918," in Heller and Stofft, eds., *America's First Battles*, pp. 150–51, 154; and William Addleman Ganoe, *The History of the United States Army*, rev. ed. (Ashton, Md.: Lundberg, 1964), pp. 473, 488.

13. *United States Army in the World War, 1917–1919: Organization of the American Expeditionary Forces* (Department of the Army, Historical Division, 1948), pp. 3, 7; and Matloff and others, *American Military History*, p. 373.

14. Conversations with Hitler reported by Generaloberst Franz Halder, MS B-809, p. 3–5, in Donald S. Detwiler, ed., *World War II German Military Studies: A Collection of 213 Special Reports on the Second World War Prepared by Former Officers of the Wehrmacht for the United States Army*, vol. 20 (Garland, 1979).

15. Calculated from data in *Selected Manpower Statistics* (Office of the Secretary of Defense, Directorate for Information Operations, April 1970), p. 19.

16. Bureau of the Budget, War Records Section, *The United States at War: Development and Administration of the War Program by the Federal Government* (GPO, 1946), p. 29.

17. Huston, *Sinews of War*, p. 657. The inadequacy of military-industrial coordination in World War II was also reflected in the fact that the draft took 48 percent of unskilled industrial workers, only to have groups of them furloughed later, for up to four months at a time, to keep certain industries going. "The Selective Service system is designed exclusively to procure manpower for military purposes. It is a blank check upon the total manpower of the

country, and as such cannot be lightly challenged on account of the secret nature of strategic requirements." "Manpower in Industrial Mobilization," RP 28 VIII-D (Industrial College of the Armed Forces, Department of Research, June 1946), pp. 1, 16.

18. *Industrial Mobilization for War: History of the War Production Board and Predecessor Agencies, 1940–1945*, vol. 1: *Program and Administration* (Bureau of Demobilization/Civilian Production Administration, 1947), p. 14.

19. Mark Skinner Watson, *Chief of Staff: Prewar Plans and Preparations* (U.S. Army, Historical Division, 1950), pp. 172–77; and Huston, *Sinews of War*, p. 657.

20. Richard M. Leighton and Robert W. Coakley, *Global Logistics and Strategy: 1940–1943* (Department of the Army, Office of the Chief of Military History, 1955), pp. 71–72.

21. Russell F. Weigley, *History of the United States Army*, enlarged ed. (Indiana University Press, 1984), pp. 435–36 (emphasis added). "17 of the divisions at home were rated as technically ready for combat. But these divisions lacked the supporting units and the training necessary to weld them into corps and armies." Matloff and others, *American Military History*, p. 435.

22. An average of 305 hours before assignment to the fleet, as opposed to 700. Russell F. Weigley, *The American Way of War: A History of United States Military Strategy and Policy* (Macmillan, 1973), p. 248.

23. Watson, *Chief of Staff*, pp. 185–87.

24. Kreidberg and Henry, *History of Military Mobilization*, p. 650.

25. Leighton and Coakley, *Global Logistics and Strategy, 1940–1943*, p. 202.

26. Robert W. Coakley and Richard M. Leighton, *Global Logistics and Strategy: 1943–1945* (U.S. Army, Office of the Chief of Military History, 1968), p. 418.

27. Coakley and Leighton, *Global Logistics and Strategy: 1943–1945*, p. 4.

28. Kreidberg and Henry, *History of Military Mobilization*, p. 678.

29. In the early 1930s army leaders protested the inconsistency of having a policy commitment to defend the islands and insufficient resources to do so. Commanders in Manila opposed War Plan Orange, arguing that "the Philippine Islands have become a military liability of a constantly increasing gravity," and recommended withdrawal to an Alaska-Oahu-Panama line. The navy disagreed. Watson, *Chief of Staff*, pp. 414–15.

30. Watson, *Chief of Staff*, pp. 414, 208.

31. Walter D. Edmonds, *They Fought with What They Had: The Story of the Army Air Forces in the Southwest Pacific, 1942* (Little, Brown, 1951), pp. xii, xiii, xvi, 32, 36. Edmonds drew on 141 interviews and Army Air Corps group and squadron diaries. See also Lewis H. Brereton, *The Brereton Diaries: The War in the Air in the Pacific, Middle East, and Europe, 3 October 1941–8 May 1945* (Morrow, 1946), pp. 65–67; and Michael S. Sherry, *The Rise of American Air Power: The Creation of Armageddon* (Yale University Press, 1987), p. 107.

32. William H. Bartsch, *Doomed at the Start: American Pursuit Pilots in the Philippines, 1941–1942* (Texas A&M University Press, 1992), pp. 25, 28, 30–36, 43, 44, 63, 430, and *passim*. The significance of the terrible lack of training,

maintenance, and coordination is highlighted by the far superior performance of the U.S. Flying Tigers in China, who flew the same P-40 aircraft against similar opposition. Bartsch, *Doomed at the Start*, p. 429.

33. Edmonds, *They Fought with What They Had*, pp. 44–45, 102, 185–86.

34. Louis Morton, *The Fall of the Philippines* (Department of the Army, Office of the Chief of Military History, 1953), pp. 8–9, 21–50, 63–67; Morton, "The Decision to Withdraw to Bataan (1941)," in Kent Roberts Greenfield, ed., *Command Decisions* (Harcourt, Brace, 1959), pp. 111–14, 118, 121; and Edmonds, *They Fought with What They Had*, p. 65. See also Edward S. Miller, *War Plan Orange: The U.S. Strategy to Defeat Japan* (Naval Institute Press, 1991), pp. 55–61.

35. Louis Morton, *Strategy and Command: The First Two Years* (Department of the Army, Office of the Chief of Military History, 1962), pp. 181–83.

36. Scott D. Sagan, "From Deterrence to Coercion to War: The Road to Pearl Harbor," in Alexander L. George and William E. Simons, eds., *The Limits of Coercive Diplomacy*, 2d ed. (Westview Press, 1994), p. 78.

37. Donald Knox, *Death March: The Survivors of Bataan* (Harcourt, Brace, Jovanovich, 1981), p. xi.

38. *Selected Manpower Statistics*, p. 53.

39. Louis-François Duchêne, "The Not So Hidden Hand," in Laurence Martin, ed., *Strategic Thought in the Nuclear Age* (London: Heinemann, 1979), p. 63. Duchêne cites a total of 66.7 million fatalities, which would make the point even more starkly than the prevalent 50 million figure.

40. On the distinction between the original guaranty pact and the later character of U.S. commitment, see Robert E. Osgood, *NATO: The Entangling Alliance* (University of Chicago Press, 1962), p. 25.

41. Roy K. Flint, "Task Force Smith and the 24th Division: Delay and Withdrawal, 5–19 July 1950," in Heller and Stofft, eds., *America's First Battles*, p. 266.

42. Roy E. Appleman, *South to the Naktong, North to the Yalu (June–November 1950)* (Department of the Army, Office of the Chief of Military History, 1961), pp. 68–75; T. R. Fehrenbach, *This Kind of War: A Study in Unpreparedness* (Macmillan, 1963), p. 102; and J. Lawton Collins, *War in Peacetime: The History and Lessons of Korea* (Houghton Mifflin, 1969), p. 50.

43. Flint, "Task Force Smith," pp. 269–70, 273, 298; Appleman, *South to the Naktong*, p. 62; Weigley, *History of the United States Army*, p. 507; quotations from Collins, *War in Peacetime*, pp. 66–67.

44. Appleman, *South to the Naktong*, pp. 61, 71; David Rees, *Korea: The Limited War* (St. Martin's Press, 1964), p. 36; Fehrenbach, *This Kind of War*, p. 104; Matloff and others, *American Military History*, p. 549; and Flint, "Task Force Smith," pp. 271–74.

45. Richard Halloran, "Experts Testify Again and Again U.S. Is Not Ready for War," *New York Times*, March 24, 1987, p. A16.

46. The following is drawn from Arthur W. Connor, Jr., "The Armor Debacle in Korea, 1950: Implications for Today," *Parameters: U.S. Army War College Quarterly*, vol. 22 (Summer 1992), pp. 66–76.

47. Connor, "The Armor Debacle in Korea, 1950," p. 70 (emphasis added).

48. Interview with William M. Rodgers in Clay Blair, *The Forgotten War: America in Korea 1950–1953* (Times Books, 1987), p. 213, quoted in Connor, "The Armor Debacle in Korea, 1950," p. 73.

49. Quoted in Samuel P. Huntington, *The Common Defense: Strategic Programs in National Politics* (Columbia University Press, 1961), p. 57.

50. Michael S. Sherry, *Preparing for the Next War: American Plans for Postwar Defense, 1941–45* (Yale University Press, 1977), chap. 2, esp. pp. 36–39; and Huntington, *Common Defense*, p. 59.

51. Colonel Wilfred L. Ebel, USAR, "Upgrading Reserve Readiness in the Eighties," *Defense Management Journal*, vol. 17 (3d Quarter 1981), p. 34.

52. "Robert Kennedy in His Own Words," *Newsweek*, May 9, 1988, p. 41.

53. The forces of many other countries participated in the coalition against Iraq, but this was more significant politically than militarily. The preponderance of power was controlled and applied by the United States.

54. One tragedy was that a significant portion of U.S. casualties resulted from "friendly fire," mistaken attacks by U.S. forces. Efforts have been undertaken to develop ways to reduce friendly fire accidents, but the main reason that the number of such casualties seemed large in this case was that the total number of casualties, including those inflicted by the enemy, was so low. If U.S. forces had been enjoined from being quick on the draw in the fog of war, they would have killed fewer of their own, but it is also conceivable that Iraqi gunners might have had more chances to fire, causing other U.S. casualties. This possibility is suggested by the story that the one U.S. plane downed by an Iraqi fighter during the war was hit after a U.S. AWACS aircraft had refused authorization to attack the Iraqi plane. This was allegedly because it lacked adequate radar confirmation and rules of engagement forbade shooting in such a situation, in order to avoid friendly fire accidents. Mark Crispin Miller, "Death of a Fighter Pilot," *New York Times*, September 15, 1992, p. A27.

55. Anthony H. Cordesman, *After the Storm* (Westview Press, 1993), p. 444.

56. Connor, "The Armor Debacle," p. 74.

57. Craig R. Whitney, "B-52 Crews in England Tell of High-Altitude Strikes on Iraqi Targets," *New York Times*, March 8, 1991, p. A9; *Conduct of the Persian Gulf War: Final Report to Congress, Pursuant to Title V of the Persian Gulf Conflict Supplemental Authorization and Personnel Benefits Act of 1991 (Public Law 102-25)* (Department of Defense, April 1992), p. 109; and *Army Focus* (Department of the Army, June 1991), p. 27.

58. Mark Crispin Miller, "Operation Desert Sham," *New York Times*, June 24, 1992, p. A21; and Theodore A. Postol, "Lessons of the Gulf War Experience with Patriot," *International Security*, vol. 16 (Winter 1991/92). See the rebuttal by the Raytheon Corporation, and Postol's reply, in *International Security*, vol. 17 (Summer 1992).

59. The quotations are from, respectively, Joint Chiefs of Staff, *Department of Defense Dictionary of Military Terms* (Arco, 1988), p. 221; Walter Kross, *Military Reform: The High-Tech Debate in Tactical Air Forces* (National Defense University Press, 1985), p. 57; *Report of the Secretary of Defense Frank C. Carlucci to the*

Congress on the FY 1990/FY 1991 Biennial Budget and FY 1990–94 Defense Programs (Department of Defense, January 1989), p. 129; *Review of Readiness Considerations in the Development of the Defense Budget*, Hearings before the House Armed Services Committee, Readiness Panel of the Procurement and Military Nuclear Systems Subcommittee, 96 Cong. 2 sess. (GPO, 1980), p. 36; Lawrence J. Korb, "Did Readiness Get Its Fair Share of the Defense Buildup in the First Reagan Administration?" in William P. Snyder and James Brown, eds., *Defense Policy in the Reagan Administration* (National Defense University Press, 1988), p. 403; U.S. Congress, Office of Technology Assessment, *American Military Power: Future Needs, Future Choices*, Background Paper OTA-BP-ISC-80 (GPO, October 1991), p. 11; and Colonel Stuart L. Perkins, *Global Demands, Limited Forces: US Army Deployment* (National Defense University Press, 1984), p. 42.

60. Les Aspin, *Report of the Secretary of Defense to the President and Congress: January 1994* (Department of Defense, January 1994), p. 28. Around the same time he also admitted, despite many years of wrestling with the question in the House Armed Services Committee, "The first problem in addressing the issue of readiness is that there is no simple way to define what readiness is." Aspin, *Report on the Bottom-Up Review*, p. 77.

61. *Department of Defense Authorization for Appropriations for Fiscal Year 1982*, Hearings before the Senate Armed Services Committee, 97 Cong. 1 sess. (GPO, 1981), pt. 5, p. 2811.

62. Ghulam Dastagir Wardak, comp., and Graham Hall Turbiville, Jr., ed., *The Voroshilov Lectures: Materials from the Soviet General Staff Academy*, vol. 1: *Issues of Soviet Military Strategy* (National Defense University Press, 1989), p. 177. See also the definitions by the Soviet Ministry of Defense quoted in John J. Yurechko, "The Soviet Combat Readiness System," *Journal of Soviet Military Studies*, vol. 1 (June 1988), p. 231.

63. *Department of Defense Authorization for Appropriations for Fiscal Year 1985*, Hearings before the Senate Armed Services Committee, 98 Cong. 2 sess., (GPO, 1984), pt. 4, p. 1832; quotation from *Department of Defense Authorization for Appropriations for Fiscal Year 1982*, Hearings before the Senate Armed Services Committee, 97 Cong. 1 sess. (GPO, 1981), pt. 5, pp. 2786–87.

64. Both notions are consistent with conventional definitions in the language at large: "equipped or supplied with what is *needed* for some action or event," or "fairly quick efficiency." *Webster's Third New International Dictionary* (Merriam-Webster, 1986), pp. 1890 (emphasis added), 1889.

65. The gap can also occur, hypothetically, because potential power was converted too soon, wound up being wasted in peacetime, and waned before war. Italy in the interwar period may be an example of that sort. See Alan S. Milward, *War, Economy, and Society: 1939–1945* (University of California Press, 1977), pp. 36–37. Demand can also exceed supply in peacetime, if a crisis occurs when a country lacks sufficient power to deter its adversary and must concede the stakes in dispute for fear of a war it cannot win.

66. Except to the degree that the country is committed to death before dishonor. It is hard to argue, however, that in terms of national welfare Poland wound up better off fighting in 1939 than Czechoslovakia did by not fighting.

After the war, "surveying Prague from the President's palace, Benes could say: 'Is it not beautiful? The only central-European city not destroyed. And all my doing.'" A. J. P. Taylor, *The Origins of the Second World War* (Atheneum, 1962), p. 185.

67. See Herbert Butterfield, *History and Human Relations* (London: Collins, 1951), pp. 19–20; John H. Herz, *Political Realism and Political Idealism* (University of Chicago Press, 1951), p. 4; Arnold Wolfers, *Discord and Collaboration: Essays on International Politics* (Johns Hopkins Press, 1962), p. 84; and Robert Jervis, "Cooperation under the Security Dilemma," *World Politics*, vol. 30 (January 1978).

68. See, for example, Jack Snyder, *The Ideology of the Offensive* (Cornell University Press, 1984); and Stephen Van Evera, "The Cult of the Offensive and the Origins of the First World War," *International Security*, vol. 12 (Spring 1988).

69. For a skeptical view, see Charles Fairbanks, "Arms Races," *The National Interest*, no. 1 (Fall 1985).

70. See Charles Perrow, *Normal Accidents* (Basic Books, 1984), chap. 3, esp. pp. 72, 87–88; and Robert Jervis's forthcoming book on systems.

71. See Richard K. Betts, *Surprise Attack: Lessons for Defense Planning* (Brookings, 1982), chaps. 1–6, 10.

Chapter Two

1. "To have a corps of, say, 60,000 men ready for overseas duty would require setting apart that considerable number of officers and men in an isolated group. . . . [T]hey would not be available as a training force to be broken up and scattered among recruit-training units." Equipment would also be diverted from training. Mark Skinner Watson, *Chief of Staff: Prewar Plans and Preparations* (Historical Division, U.S. Army, 1950), p. 188; see also p. 197.

2. Lewis Sorley, *Thunderbolt: General Creighton Abrams and the Army of His Times* (Simon and Schuster, 1992), p. 183. The impact of Vietnam on readiness in NATO and elsewhere only got worse after 1965.

3. John B. Abell, "Resources for Readiness: The Tactical Fighter Case," *Defense Management Journal*, vol. 18 (2d Quarter 1981), p. 16.

4. Lieutenant Colonel David Evans, quoted in Richard Halloran, "Report Disputes Pentagon on Readiness," *New York Times*, December 24, 1984, p. 10.

5. *Department of Defense Authorization for Appropriations for Fiscal Year 1982*, Hearings before the Senate Armed Services Committee, 97 Cong. 1 sess. (Government Printing Office, 1981), pt. 5, p. 2372.

6. Molly Moore, "Many B1s Grounded for Repairs," *Washington Post*, October 24, 1988, p. A1.

7. For this reason, as well as solicitude for individual soldiers' chances of survival, U.S. recruits are required by law to have twelve weeks of training before they may be deployed abroad. *Department of Defense Appropriations for 1988*, Hearings before the House Appropriations Committee, Subcommittee on the Department of Defense, 100 Cong. 1 sess. (GPO, 1987), p. 537. During

the cold war, troops deployed for combat always had a much longer training period, usually three times the legal minimum.

8. The Americans were not even effective in the first battle against the Germans at Kasserine Pass, but they did prevail in the North African campaign as a whole.

9. Needless to say, this heuristic characterization is not meant to be literally mathematical.

10. See Franklin C. Spinney, *Defense Facts of Life: The Plans/Reality Mismatch*, edited and with commentary by James Clay Thompson (Westview Press, 1983), pp. 30–33, 53.

11. See *Department of Defense Authorization for 1982*, Hearings, pt. 5, p. 2788. The Israeli system, in particular, subordinates economy to duplication and minimization of backlogs in order to maintain constant readiness. See Gerald M. Steinberg, "Israel's Advantage," *Military Logistics Forum* (March 1986), p. 52.

12. *Department of Defense Authorization for Appropriations for Fiscal Year 1983*, Hearings before the Senate Armed Services Committee, 97 Cong. 2 sess. (GPO, 1982), pt. 2, p. 749.

13. Molly Moore, "Army Ditched Usable Vehicles at Low Prices," *Washington Post*, January 10, 1988, p. A11.

14. Gaylord Shaw, "Navy Thefts Spark Fear for National Security," *Los Angeles Times*, July 17, 1985, p. 1. Other reasons contributed to overpricing, such as excessive detail in requirements that forced manufacturers to retool for small production runs.

15. Fred Hiatt, "Military Parts Said Scrapped," *Washington Post*, July 26, 1984, p. A13.

16. Fred Hiatt, "Airmen Say C5A Parts Are Vastly Overpriced," *Washington Post*, September 20, 1984, p. A8.

17. For example, a junior officer recalled that "the supply facility people made a regular practice of throwing away any turn-ins. Otherwise it became excess at their level." Christopher Bassford, *The Spit-Shine Syndrome: Organizational Irrationality in the American Field Army* (New York: Greenwood Press, 1988), p. 76.

18. Analysis similar to what follows was first developed in Richard K. Betts, "Conventional Forces: What Price Readiness," *Survival*, vol. 25 (January/February 1983), p. 25.

19. To illustrate more concretely, in 1984 it cost approximately $2,000 per hour to fly the F-14 and more than $2.8 million to train the pilot. The average U.S. pilot was flying twenty hours each month, but some on carriers off Lebanon in 1983 were flying fifty. (Rick Atkinson and Fred Hiatt, "Noisy Medley," *Washington Post*, July 22, 1984, p. A20.) By the time Operation Desert Shield began in August 1990 the per hour cost for flying each F-15E was estimated at $4,000. (Rick Atkinson, "Costs of Confrontation: Who Pays? How Much?" *Washington Post*, August 15, 1990, p. A12.) The overall cost of operational readiness is highly sensitive to the operating rates for the aircraft and

the number of pilot "flying career equivalents," as it were, for each plane over the course of its life.

20. Similarly, when Senator Gordon Humphrey queried, "Why is it in Europe, where we need to be presumably more fully manned than in the United States," that the authorized manning levels of army units were limited to 90 percent of wartime requirements? General Frederick Kroesen answered, "If the Army is given a certain amount of funds and a certain end-strength limitation on people it can have, it might rather have 100 units at 90 percent than 90 units at 100 percent, because having those 100 units . . . gives us then the structure . . . that would be filled with Individual Ready Reservists or draftees or whomever could be provided upon the outbreak of war or upon mobilization." *Department of Defense Authorization for Appropriations for Fiscal Year 1982*, Hearings, p. 2557.

21. But even with a lower rate of accidents, the force with the smaller size and higher readiness might not gain in comparative size over the life span of the two forces. In the cold war, the typical accident rate for U.S. planes and helicopters was 160–190 a year. Jacques S. Gansler, *Affording Defense* (MIT Press, 1989), p. 60 (citing *Washington Post*, March 18, 1985). Extra flying time generates disproportionately higher increases in safety. For example, an increase of less than a fourth in flight hours yielded a reduction of almost a third in the rate of "flight mishaps." *Department of Defense Authorization for Appropriations for Fiscal Year 1986*, Hearings before the Senate Armed Services Committee, 99 Cong. 1 sess. (GPO, 1985), pt. 6, p. 3332. It is unlikely, however, that the returns would not diminish as the gap in flying time increased. If the low-readiness force of 500 planes flew at half the rate of the high-readiness force of 375, and its accident rate remained less than double that of the smaller force, the size advantage of the larger force would grow over time. Accident rates correlate most closely with the number of take-offs and landings, not total flying time. Readiness increases that involve more flights probably produce more crashes than those that involve longer flights.

22. *Soviet Readiness for War: Assessing One of the Major Sources of East-West Instability*, Report to the House Armed Services Committee, Defense Policy Panel, 100 Cong. 2 sess. (GPO, 1988), p. 4.

23. Martin Binkin and William W. Kaufmann, *U.S. Army Guard and Reserve: Rhetoric, Realities, Risks* (Brookings, 1989), pp. 17–19, 28–32.

24. The uncertain trade-off between mass and efficiency in determining effectiveness further complicates the issue. In some respects, mass or quantity of forces is likely to prove more vital than efficiency or quality. See Michael I. Handel, "Numbers Do Count: The Question of Quality versus Quantity," in Samuel P. Huntington, ed., *The Strategic Imperative: New Policies for American Security* (Ballinger, 1982). In others—most clearly, air-to-air combat—the heightened efficiency that emerges from intense training can override large imbalances in mass, or can compensate for marginal limitations of technical quality in weapons. See Jack N. Merritt and Pierre M. Sprey, "Negative Marginal Returns in Weapons Acquisition," in Richard G. Head and Ervin J.

Rokke, eds., *American Defense Policy*, 3d ed. (Johns Hopkins University Press, 1973), pp. 492–93.

25. Max Hastings, *The Korean War* (Simon and Schuster, 1987), p. 18.

26. *Department of Defense Authorization for Appropriations for Fiscal Year 1986*, Hearings, pt. 6, p. 3047.

27. See Central Intelligence Agency, *National Basic Intelligence Factbook* (January 1978), p. 103, and (January 1979), p. 97. Later official data showed less extreme figures after the late 1970s, although in both 1983 and 1984 Israel's central government expenditures were 99 percent of its GNP. *World Military Expenditures and Arms Transfers, 1988* (U.S. Arms Control and Disarmament Agency, June 1989), p. 47.

28. Edward N. Luttwak and Daniel Horowitz, *The Israeli Army, 1948–1973* (Abt Books, 1983), pp. 334–35.

29. For example, a force could not be constituted completely from scratch in the fifth decade because some amount of mobilization readiness would have to be maintained, or the pool of skills and technologies necessary as a base for expansion would disappear; over fifty years, technical modernization would change the costs, number, operating expenses, and life cycle of the aircraft involved in the calculation; and it is politically unrealistic to assume that all the money not spent on constant military readiness would be "banked" and available for producing military power in the fifth decade, rather than consumed.

30. "The larger the proportion of total resources which a nation devotes to domestic investment in peacetime, the greater will tend to be the contribution to the war effort which a lowering of investment can make. . . . First, well-maintained and new capital resources reduce the need for new capital formation and can be under-maintained for a longer period of time before production and labor productivity commence to suffer. Secondly, gross domestic capital investment is more easily reduced than private consumption. In the experience of virtually all nations, investment cuts are more readily acceptable than consumption cuts." Klaus E. Knorr, *The War Potential of Nations* (Princeton University Press, 1956), p. 260.

31. For the different choices Japanese planners debated before World War II see Michael A. Barnhart, *Japan Prepares for Total War: The Search for Economic Security, 1919–1941* (Cornell University Press, 1987), pp. 37–38, 95–96, 107.

32. The seldom-recognized idea that reducing near-term military readiness helps long-term readiness, and not just civilian consumption or investment, is similar to the point Thomas F. Homer-Dixon makes in regard to common beliefs about the competition between economy and environment: "Gauging the actual economic cost of land degradation is not easy. Current national income accounts do not incorporate measures of resource depletion: 'A nation could exhaust its mineral reserves, cut down its forests, erode its soils, pollute its aquifers, and hunt its wildlife to extinction—all without affecting measured income.' The inadequacy of measures of economic productivity reinforces the perception that there is a policy trade-off between economic growth and en-

vironmental protection; this perception, in turn, encourages societies to generate present income at the expense of their potential for future income." Thomas F. Homer-Dixon, "Environmental Changes as Causes of Acute Conflict," in Richard K. Betts, ed., *Conflict after the Cold War* (Macmillan, 1994), p. 434 (quoting Robert Repetto, "Wasting Assets," *Technology Review*, January 1990, p. 40).

33. For the same reason, the fact that equipment for the U.S. Army was procured too slowly when mobilization accelerated after 1939 does not mean that it would have been better to procure in large quantities much earlier. Late in 1936 the Army General Staff pressed to shift funding for research and development to the procurement of developed equipment, but then reversed and put more emphasis on R&D after seeing the results of the war in Spain. Watson, *Chief of Staff*, pp. 42–44. If 1940 was too late and 1936 too soon, the problem in estimating the right time is evident.

34. Until the work of John Ferris, cited below, the definitive history of the adoption, operation, and cancellation of the ten-year rule was N. H. Gibbs, *Grand Strategy*, vol. 1: *Rearmament Policy* (London: Her Majesty's Stationery Office, 1976), especially pp. 3–6, 35–87. See also F. A. Johnson, *Defence by Committee* (Oxford University Press, 1960), pp. 198–200; and the exchanges in *RUSI: The Journal of the Royal United Services Institute for Defence Studies*: Peter Silverman, "The Ten Year Rule" (March 1971); Ken Booth, "The Ten Year Rule—An Unfinished Debate" (September 1971); and Stephen Roskill, "The Ten Year Rule—The Historical Facts" (March 1972).

35. Stephen Roskill, *Naval Policy between the Wars*, vol. 11: *The Period of Reluctant Rearmament, 1930–1939* (Naval Institute Press, 1976), p. 74; Winston Churchill, *The Second World War*, vol. 1: *The Gathering Storm* (Houghton-Mifflin, 1948), p. 50. Churchill quoted in Gibbs, *Grand Strategy*, vol. 1, p. 57.

36. Many date the death of the rule from March 1932, when an advisory body to the cabinet registered no objection to a proposal to cancel it. Although there was confusion as to whether the assumption continued to stand, it was not officially canceled until the cabinet meeting of November 15, 1933. Roskill, "The Ten Year Rule—The Historical Facts," p. 70.

37. Wesley K. Wark, *The Ultimate Enemy: British Intelligence and Nazi Germany, 1933–1939* (Cornell University Press, 1985), pp. 19–31. The military had been unhappy about the rule earlier, but mainly because of events outside Europe. After the Japanese invaded Manchuria in 1931, the services recommended canceling the rule *and* giving priority to commitments in the Far East. Brian Bond, *British Military Policy between the Two World Wars* (Oxford: Clarendon Press, 1980), pp. 94, 96.

38. Thomas L. McNaugher, *New Weapons, Old Politics: America's Military Procurement Muddle* (Brookings, 1989), p. 19, citing Irving B. Holley.

39. John Robert Ferris, *Men, Money, and Diplomacy: The Evolution of British Strategic Policy, 1919–1926* (Cornell University Press, 1989), pp. xii, 15–17.

40. Ferris, *Men, Money, and Diplomacy*, pp. 26–29. As to Churchill's responsibility for the rolling rule, "Churchill and Lloyd George had used the warning

period to govern strategic preparations because they expected subsequent governments to respond appropriately: they had not accounted for the nature of Baldwin and MacDonald," p. 181.

41. Ferris, *Men, Money, and Diplomacy*, pp. 179–81 (emphasis added).

42. *Tactical* warning is the most immediate level of warning, and is triggered by evidence that the enemy has actually commenced an attack; *strategic* warning is the prior indication that the enemy is preparing its forces to launch an attack; and *political* warning comes with the earlier evidence of threat, and the determination that the political conflict of interest is reaching the point that the enemy could decide to resort to war.

43. Wark, *The Ultimate Enemy*, pp. 38–39, 68–76; see also Williamson Murray, *The Change in the European Balance of Power, 1938–1939: The Path to Ruin* (Princeton University Press, 1984).

44. "We can see how much time we had. Up till 1934 at least, German rearmament could have been prevented without the loss of a single life." Churchill, *Gathering Storm*, p. 51.

45. Indeed, it had been adopted principally for domestic reasons: revolution in Ireland and the threat of labor unrest at home. Lloyd George considered reduced government spending imperative because, in 1919, "the Government could take some risks in defence but none in social and economic affairs." Gibbs, *Grand Strategy*, vol. 1, p. 5. The rule "originated in confused circumstances without the full participation of the Service Ministers or their professional advisers." Bond, *British Military Policy between the Two World Wars*, p. 25.

46. G. C. Peden, "A Matter of Timing: The Economic Background to British Foreign Policy," *History*, vol. 69, no. 225 (1984), pp. 16–17.

47. See the somewhat breathless account of peacetime nonalert in Fred Kaplan, *The Wizards of Armageddon* (Simon and Schuster, 1983), pp. 148–51. This was mainly because the Soviets had not yet deployed ballistic missiles, and U.S. intelligence monitoring could guarantee strategic warning of Soviet preparation of bombers for attack. By 1960 about a third of SAC was on alert; by the 1980s, about two-thirds of all long-range nuclear forces (including ballistic missiles) were on alert. Desmond Ball, "The Development of the SIOP, 1960–1983," in Desmond Ball and Jeffrey Richelson, eds., *Strategic Nuclear Targeting* (Cornell University Press, 1986), p. 57.

48. In its first two years, SAC was in sad shape, mainly because of personnel shortages and training problems. By 1948 the growth of East-West tension prompted the air force to make combat readiness a priority for the command. Herman S. Wolk, "George C. Kenney: The Great Innovator," in John L. Frisbee, ed., *Makers of the United States Air Force* (Office of Air Force History, 1987), pp. 146–48.

49. David Alan Rosenberg, "The Origins of Overkill," *International Security*, no. 4 (Spring 1983), p. 20.

50. *Department of Defense Authorization for Appropriations for Fiscal Year 1982*, Hearings, pt. 5, p. 2514. Such tests included operational readiness inspections, combat evaluation visits, and maintenance standardization evaluation teams. The managerial challenges and ethos of constant crisis in SAC were captured

in the 1962 film *A Gathering of Eagles* (written by Robert Pirosh, directed by Delbert Mann) better than in any published source.

51. *Department of Defense Authorization for Appropriations for 1982*, Hearings, p. 2419. This is not to say that commanders were ever satisfied. In the same testimony, General Ellis complained that SAC was undermanned and had insufficient flying time (pp. 2420, 2426). The fact remains that no other sizable military units anywhere in the world could have unleashed their capacity as fast and as thoroughly as U.S. nuclear forces could.

52. Donald R. Cotter, "Peacetime Operations: Safety and Security," in Ashton B. Carter, John D. Steinbruner, and Charles A. Zraket, eds., *Managing Nuclear Operations* (Brookings, 1987), pp. 24–25. In reality, the number of boats deployed unarmed for training, or in transit to firing areas, probably made the numbers lower.

53. This change did not eliminate readiness for Looking Glass altogether. The planes were shifted to ground alert, and thereafter made periodic rather than continuous flights. Michael R. Gordon, "U.S. Plans to Ground Air Fleet That Can Direct Nuclear War," *New York Times*, December 15, 1989, p. A1; Patrick E. Tyler, "Doomsday Flight Lands after 29 Years in Sky," *Washington Post*, July 28, 1990, pp. A1, A10; Eric Schmitt, "U.S. Curtails 24-Hour Duty of Its Flying Command Post," *New York Times*, July 28, 1990, p. 6.

54. Indeed, in SAC's case maintaining the standard for nuclear readiness required robbing it from conventional missions. Shortly after the conventional Strategic Projection Force was organized within SAC, primarily for Persian Gulf contingencies, General Ellis testified that the organization could not fully support the new unit's operations. *Department of Defense Authorization for Appropriations for 1982*, Hearings, pt. 5, p. 2499.

Chapter Three

1. *Department of Defense Authorization for Appropriations for Fiscal Year 1982*, Hearings before the Senate Armed Services Committee, 97 Cong. 1 sess. (Government Printing Office, 1981), pp. 2789, 2799, 2800; Colonel Harry L. Gregory, Jr., USAF, "Air Force Logistics Strategy for the 1990s," *Air Force Journal of Logistics*, vol. 7 (Spring 1983), pp. 7–8; Surveys and Investigations Staff, "A Report to the Committee on Appropriations, U.S. House of Representatives, on the Readiness of the U.S. Military," vol. 3, in *Department of Defense Appropriations for 1985*, Hearings before the House Appropriations Committee, Subcommittee on the Department of Defense, 98 Cong. 2d sess. (GPO, 1984), pt. 1, p. 927; and Lieutenant Colonel Phil Brown, "Logistics and Spares: Bridging the MAC Airlift Capability," *Airlift*, vol. 7 (Spring 1985), p. 9. There are tricky complexities in estimating spare parts lead times; see Report to the Secretary of Defense, *The Services Should Improve Their Processes for Determining Requirements for Supplies and Spare Parts*, PLRD-82-12 (General Accounting Office, November 30, 1981). Of course, war emergency can sweep away some of the reasons for sluggishness. When preparations began for the war with Iraq, the

flow of spares speeded up significantly (Michael R. Gordon, "A Base with No Name," *New York Times*, August 22, 1990, p. A12). Shortly before launching the U.S. attack, President Bush issued an executive order on "National Security Industrial Responsiveness" that gave the military "priority for the national production of energy, telecommunications, and other material in case of war." It required "private companies to give government contracts first priority." Ann Devroy, "U.S. Gives Priority to Army," *International Herald Tribune*, January 10, 1991, p. 1.

2. Lieutenant General Kelly H. Burke, USAF (Ret.), "The USAF of 1984: Can It Fight? Can It Win?" *Armed Forces Journal International* (October 1984), p. 129.

3. In the same way, the previous decrease in repair funding in 1971 did not show up in reduced mission capability data until 1973. *Review of Readiness Considerations in the Development of the Defense Budget*, Hearings before the House Armed Services Committee, Readiness Panel of the Procurement and Military Nuclear Systems Subcommittee, 96 Cong. 2 sess. (GPO, 1980), p. 102.

4. Franklin C. Spinney, *Defense Facts of Life: The Plans/Reality Mismatch*, edited and with a commentary by James Clay Thompson (Westview Press, 1983), p. 31.

5. Peter deLeon, *The Peacetime Evaluation of the Pilot Skill Factor in Air-to-Air Combat*, R-2070-PR (Rand Corporation, January 1977), pp. 35–36; and "Air Force Weighs Letting Pilots Fly Longer," *New York Times*, December 18, 1987, p. A20. See also Martin Binkin, *Support Costs in the Defense Budget: The Submerged One Third* (Brookings, 1972), p. 19; and Congressional Budget Office, *Alternative Compensation Plans for Improving Retention of Air Force Pilots* (August 1989), pp. 7–10.

6. See Jacques S. Gansler, *The Defense Industry* (MIT Press, 1980), p. 66 and chapter 5. For an example of the entanglement of mobilization base and readiness problems, see *Shipbuilding, Ship Maintenance, and Claims*, Hearings before the House Budget Committee, 95 Cong. 1 sess. (GPO, 1977), p. 77.

7. W. Stanford Smith, "Reserve Readiness: Proving the Total Force Policy a Success," in Bennie J. Wilson III, ed., *The Guard and the Reserve in the Total Force: The First Decade, 1973–1983* (National Defense University Press, 1985), p. 120.

8. *Department of Defense Authorization for Appropriations for Fiscal Year 1985*, Hearings before the Senate Armed Services Committee, 98 Cong. 2 sess. (1984), pt. 4, p. 2154.

9. Lieutenant Colonel David Evans (Ret.), "The B1: A Flying Edsel for America's Defense?" *Washington Post*, January 4, 1987, p. C1.

10. Quoted in John T. Correll, "AFLC Prepares for War," *Air Force*, vol. 66, (September 1983), p. 48.

11. Elmo Zumwalt and Worth Bagley, "GAO Misses the Mark with Report on Navy Readiness," *Washington Times*, January 4, 1984, p. 1C.

12. George C. Wilson, "Budget Shoals Stranding Reagan's 600-Ship Navy," *Washington Post*, February 8, 1988, p. A5; and Bill Keller, "The Navy's Brash Leader," *New York Times Magazine*, December 15, 1985, p. 69.

13. "SLEPing Rejuvenates Navy Carriers," *Armed Forces Journal International* (July 1988), p. 58.

14. Lieutenant Colonel Charles Lindbergh, "USAFE Operational Readiness," *Air Force Engineering and Services Quarterly*, vol. 18 (November 1977), pp. 20–22.

15. Units operating their vehicles for 850 miles were estimated likely to report readiness conditions of C_1 or C_2, while those operating at 750 miles would be more likely to range from C_2 to C_3. *Department of Defense Appropriations for 1988*, Hearings before the House Appropriations Committee, Subcommittee on the Department of Defense, 100 Cong. 1 sess. (GPO, 1987), pt. 4, pp. 245–46.

16. House Appropriations Committee Surveys and Investigations Staff Report, vol. 1, p. 690.

17. Rolf Clark, "Readiness as a Residual of Resource Allocation Decisions," *Defense Management Journal*, vol. 17 (First Quarter 1981), pp. 21–22; Douglas B. Feaver and Carlos Sanchez, "11 Men Escaped USS Iowa's Turret after Explosion," *Washington Post*, April 21, 1989, pp. A1, A8; Stephen Engelberg, "Navy's Operations to be Suspended," *New York Times*, November 15, 1989, p. A1; Timothy Egan, "Quiet Falls on Bases as Navy Asks Itself What's Gone Wrong," *New York Times*, November 16, 1989, p. A1; and Michael R. Gordon, "Drill Mistaken for Actual Attack Led to U.S. Firing on Turkish Ships," *New York Times*, November 28, 1992, pp. 1, 6. Safety in training is in part a vicious circle. The *Iowa* explosion was also blamed on insufficient training of the gun crew. George C. Wilson, "Navy Activities Halted to Reexamine Safety," *Washington Post*, November 15, 1989, pp. A1, A9. An analogy would be strenuous physical exercise that improves a person's fitness in general but makes the person more vulnerable to cardiac arrest during the exercise. Intense military operations improve safety for the future but are themselves dangerous. High operational rates for nuclear-powered ships improve safety and professionalism as increased experience raises expertise. In nuclear forces in general, though, there is some tension between readiness and safety and reliability. Desmond Ball, *Can Nuclear War Be Controlled?* Adelphi Paper 169 (London: International Institute for Strategic Studies, Autumn 1981), p. 8. See also Scott D. Sagan, *The Limits of Safety* (Princeton University Press, 1993).

18. Quoted in Joseph F. Bouchard, *Command in Crisis: Four Case Studies* (Columbia University Press, 1991), p. 76.

19. *Department of Defense Authorization for Appropriations for Fiscal Year 1982*, Hearings, pt. 5, p. 2327.

20. Brigadier General Robert H. Scales, Jr., and others, *Certain Victory: The U.S. Army in the Gulf War* (Office of the Chief of Staff, U.S. Army, 1993), pp. 150–51; Michael R. Gordon, "Army Limits Night Maneuvers in Effort to Prevent Accidents in Gulf," *New York Times*, October 10, 1990, p. A11; and "Gulf Notes," *International Herald Tribune*, January 14, 1991, p. 4.

21. *Department of Defense Authorization for Appropriations for Fiscal Year 1982*, Hearings, p. 2327.

22. Confidential interviews, June 7, 1984.

23. *Department of Defense Authorization for Appropriations for Fiscal Year 1984,* Hearings before the Senate Armed Services Committee, 98 Cong. 1 sess. (GPO, 1983), pt. 7, p. 3622.

24. "The Navy's Budget Crunch," *Newsweek,* October 26, 1987, p. 7; and Molly Moore, "Pentagon Sets Gulf Costs at $200 Million," *Washington Post,* September 5, 1987, p. A29.

25. Bouchard, *Command in Crisis,* pp. 54–55.

26. Secretary of Defense Les Aspin, *Report on the Bottom-Up Review* (Department of Defense, October 1993), pp. 78, 80; Eric Schmitt, "Military's Growing Role in Relief Missions Prompts Concerns," *New York Times,* July 31, 1994, p. 3; Perry quoted in Eric Schmitt, "Pentagon Worries about Cost of Aid Missions," *New York Times,* August 5, 1994, p. A6.

27. Roberta Wohlstetter, *Pearl Harbor: Warning and Decision* (Stanford University Press, 1962), pp. 22, 42, 48.

28. Walter D. Edmonds, *They Fought with What They Had: The Story of the Army Air Forces in the Southwest Pacific, 1941–1942* (Little, Brown, 1951), pp. 81–82.

29. Scott D. Sagan, "Notes on Alert Sustainability in a Prolonged Crisis," unpublished paper prepared for the Department of Defense Summer Seminar on National Strategy, Naval War College, August 1986, p. 3. DEFCON-2 involved a 550 percent increase in airborne alert of the B-52 force.

30. House Appropriations Committee Surveys and Investigations Staff Report, vol. 2, p. 854 (emphasis added).

31. R. W. Apple, Jr., "2 U.S. Ships Badly Damaged by Iraqi Mines in Persian Gulf," *New York Times,* February 19, 1991, p. A7. Similarly, a few weeks before U.S. troops entered Haiti in 1994, invasion preparations raised this problem: "'At some time soon, we won't be as ready, and we'll have to gear up training again,' said a senior Pentagon general. 'It's getting close to that now. We'd have to go back into a honing phase.'" Eric Schmitt, "U.S. Puts Off Any Decision on Haiti Issue," *New York Times,* August 29, 1994, p. A7.

32. For a theoretical discussion of different ways in which duplication or overlap can be designed to avert organizational failure under stress, see Allan W. Lerner, "There Is More Than One Way to Be Redundant: A Comparison of Alternatives for the Design and Use of Redundancy in Organizations," *Administration and Society,* vol. 18 (November 1986).

33. "Antiquated Rules of Engagement," *Aviation Week and Space Technology* (June 1, 1987), p. 11.

34. Thomas H. Etzold, *Defense or Delusion? America's Military in the 1980s* (Harper and Row, 1982), p. 119. When the plan was instituted, the army had sixteen active divisions; this later rose to eighteen, but with no increase in manpower because several of the total were new light divisions.

35. Martin Binkin and William W. Kaufmann, *U.S. Army Guard and Reserve: Rhetoric, Realities, Risks* (Brookings, 1989), p. 85; Congressional Budget Office, *The Army of the Nineties: How Much Will It Cost?* (December 1986), p. 12.

36. Secretary of Defense Caspar Weinberger, *Annual Report to the Congress, Fiscal Year 1983* (Department of Defense, February 1982), p. III-34; Secretary of Defense Harold Brown, interview transcribed in *Selected Statements 80-6* (Department of Defense, November 1, 1980), p. 49; *Soviet Military Power: An Assessment of the Threat, 1988* (Department of Defense, April 1988), p. 89; and Molly Moore, "Soviet Naval Cutbacks Reported," *Washington Post*, February 23, 1989, p. A12. See also *Department of Defense Authorization for Appropriations for Fiscal Year 1983*, Hearings before the Senate Armed Services Committee, 97 Cong. 2 sess. (GPO, 1982), pt. 2, p. 1147; Michael MccGwire, "Maritime Strategy and the Super-Powers," in *Power at Sea*, Part II: *Super-powers and Navies*, Adelphi Paper 123 (London: International Institute for Strategic Studies, Spring 1976), p. 23; Christopher Donnelly, *Red Banner: The Soviet Military System in Peace and War* (Jane's, 1988), pp. 153–54; and *Department of Defense Authorization for Appropriations for Fiscal Year 1984*, Hearings, pt. 8, pp. 3672–73. On submarine alert rates see Scott D. Sagan, *Moving Targets* (Princeton University Press, 1989), p. 168.

37. House Appropriations Committee Surveys and Investigations Staff Report, vol. 2, p. 809.

38. Preparing even a small attack is more complicated than most policymakers realize. Because of the problems in coordinating rapid shifts in political authorities' instructions to strike with the planning of specific targets, tactics, and weapon loads fitted to the instructions within the time stipulated at higher levels, awful foul-ups occurred in both the Tonkin Gulf raids of August 1964 against North Vietnam and the December 1983 strike against Syrian antiaircraft installations in Lebanon. See Captain R. N. Livingston, USN (Ret.), "The First Day of the War," *U.S. Naval Institute Proceedings*, vol. 115 (July 1989), p. 74; Bernard E. Trainor, "'83 Airstrike on Lebanon: Ill-Fated Mission," *New York Times*, August 6, 1989, p. 11; and George C. Wilson, *Supercarrier* (Macmillan, 1986), chaps. 10–11.

39. For armor units, in contrast, the grace period "may be as long as 12 hours," so if a tank can be repaired at the eleventh hour, it is ready enough. William C. Wall, Jr., and Lieutenant Colonel Raymond R. Ross II, "Reporting Missile Readiness," *Army Logistician*, vol. 11 (July/August 1979), p. 29.

40. *Development and Use of Training Simulators*, Hearings before the Senate Armed Services Committee, Subcommittee on Tactical Warfare, 98 Cong. 2 sess. (GPO, 1984), pp. 3–4; and Alan J. Marcus and Commander Lawrence E. Curran, USN, "The Use of Flight Simulators in Measuring and Improving Training Effectiveness," Professional Paper 432 (Center for Naval Analyses, January 1985).

41. Major General Thomas Darling, USAF, in *Department of Defense Authorization for Appropriations for Fiscal Years 1988 and 1989*, Hearings before the Senate Armed Services Committee, 100 Cong. 1 sess. (GPO, 1987), pt. 2, p. 445.

42. Testimony to a House Budget Committee task force, quoted in Grant Willis, "Analysts Challenge Pace of Training Operations," *Navy Times*, July 4, 1988, p. 36.

43. Report to the Congress by the Comptroller General of the United States, *The Readiness of U.S. Air Forces in Europe—Selected Aspects and Issues*, LCD-78-430A (General Accounting Office, February 1979), pp. i–ii, 18.

44. GAO, *Readiness of U.S. Air Forces in Europe*, pp. viii, 11, 19.

45. *Department of Defense Appropriations for 1981*, Hearings before the House Appropriations Committee, Subcommittee on the Department of Defense, 96 Cong. 2 sess. (GPO, 1980), p. 538.

46. *Department of Defense Appropriations for Fiscal Year 1986*, Hearings before the Senate Armed Services Committee, 99 Cong. 1 sess. (GPO, 1985), pt. 6, p. 3021; *Department of Defense Authorization for Appropriations for Fiscal Year 1985*, Hearings, pt. 2, p. 1001, and pt. 5, p. 2142; Fred Hiatt, "Budget Not Helping Response Capability," *Washington Post*, March 5, 1984, p. A17; and House Appropriations Committee Surveys and Investigations Staff Report, vol. 3, p. 925.

47. Some of the parts taken from war reserves were "not consumed, but simply moved through the use/repair/stockage cycle. The only real loss in parts [was] the 5–7% of these parts deemed irreparable. The loss to these stocks in 1984 was 1.2% of total parts funded. This was more than offset by the 21% 1984 increase in War Reserve Stocks' funding." *Department of Defense Authorization for Appropriations for Fiscal Year 1985*, Hearings, p. 2153.

48. House Appropriations Committee Surveys and Investigations Staff Report, vol. 3, p. 904.

49. An army inspector reported, for example: "Due to a policy of being able to use these [Theater War Reserve] stocks provided they are returned/replaced within 90 days, most had been used and were unserviceable. Fact is the majority of all lines were less than 20% serviceable." Colonel Jack L. Winkler, Memorandum for the Deputy Chief of Staff for Logistics, "Trip Report, HQ USAREUR 2nd, 3rd and 21st SUPCOM; 200 TAMMC. 7th ASG; DARCOM Forward; and ARC-13 through 23 October 1982," October 26, 1982, p. 1.

50. Mark Skinner Watson, *Chief of Staff: Prewar Plans and Preparations* (Historical Division, U.S. Army, 1950), pp. 214–31; William Addleman Ganoe, *History of the U.S. Army*, rev. ed. (Ashton, Md.: Lundberg, 1964), p. 525; and Forrest C. Pogue, *George C. Marshall: Ordeal and Hope, 1939–1942* (Viking, 1966), p. 154. As one of the representatives who voted against the bill noted, many confused that vote with a renewal of authorization for any draft at all, which made it seem that a negative vote would have disbanded the Army altogether. Thomas H. Eliot, "Did We Almost Lose the Army?" *New York Times*, August 12, 1991, p. A15.

Chapter Four

1. See Michael Rich, I. K. Cohen, and R. A. Pyles, *Recent Progress in Assessing the Readiness and Sustainability of Combat Forces*, R-3475-AF (Rand Corporation, October 1987), p. 9. For recent attempts to grapple with the problem,

see S. Craig Moore and others, *Measuring Military Readiness and Sustainability*, R-3842-DAG (Rand Corporation, 1991).

2. For example, proficiency of Tactical Air Command crews grew after 1980, not just because of more flying hours but also because of better combat training, "newer and safer aircraft with improved capabilities, reduced maintenance requirements, and increased spares inventory. Data concerning the relative impact each factor has on pilot proficiency are not available. Thus, the air force cannot identify the most cost-effective mix of flying hours and these factors." *Aircrew Training: Tactical Air Command and Strategic Air Command Flying Hour Programs*, Briefing Report to the Chairman, Subcommittee on Defense, Committee on Appropriations, House of Representatives, GAO/NSIAD-86-192BR (General Accounting Office, September 1986), p. 8.

3. Robert Shishko and Robert M. Paulson, *Resource Readiness of Armored Units*, N-1299-MRAL (Rand Corporation, November 1979), p. 5.

4. U.S. Department of Defense, *Improvements in U.S. Warfighting Capability FY 1980–84* (Government Printing Office, May 1984), p. 68. Throughout this chapter there are references to standards and rating systems that change frequently. Examples are drawn primarily from the 1980s, when the political debate over readiness was most pronounced. Some details therefore may be out of date. Also, particular instances of anomalies in measurement that are noted cannot be assumed to be typical or pervasive. The point of this chapter is to survey the frequency and variety of problems that complexity evokes rather than to inventory precise data about current practices or dysfunctions. The latter are technical tasks beyond the scope of this study.

5. On how reporting systems may exaggerate unreadiness by failing to disaggregate missions for which a machine is capable, see Major J. R. McNeece, "How Down—or Up—Is That Airplane?" *U.S. Naval Institute Proceedings*, vol. 109 (February 1983), pp. 103–09. As congressional investigators concluded, *"The very nearly perfect nature of the C-1 rating may make it virtually unattainable with today's complex, electronically oriented ships and planes."* House Appropriations Committee Surveys and Investigations Staff, "A Report to the Committee on Appropriations, U.S. House of Representatives, on the Readiness of the U.S. Military," vol, 2, March 1983, in *Department of Defense Appropriations for 1985*, Hearings before the House Committee on Appropriations, Subcommittee on the Department of Defense, 98 Cong. 2 sess. (GPO, 1984), pt. 1, p. 820.

6. House Appropriations Committee Surveys and Investigations Staff Report, p. 828.

7. Report to the Congress by the Comptroller General of the United States, *The Readiness of U.S. Air Forces in Europe—Selected Aspects and Issues*, LCD-78-430A (General Accounting Office, February 1979), pp. 17–18.

8. The example of Army Regulation 200-1 in this table represents the standards in the early 1980s, which were slightly relaxed from those in the late 1970s. For the latter, see table 1 in Shishko and Paulson, *Resource Readiness of Armored Units*, p. 4. The entire C-rating system was changed in the late 1980s, although actual criteria remained similar; see chapter 5 and table 5-1.

9. Melvin R. Laird with Lawrence J. Korb, *The Problem of Military Readiness* (Washington, D.C.: American Enterprise Institute, 1980), p. 17.

10. Theoretically, for some types of forces—ones that depend on tightly integrated components—the low rating could be legitimate. If ten cars with forty tires have a total of ten flat tires, but each car has one of the flats, none of them is ready.

11. Robert C. Toth, "Pentagon Disputes Report on Readiness Figures," *Los Angeles Times*, March 7, 1984, p. 17.

12. Government Accounting Office, *Readiness of First Line U.S. Combat Armored Units*, LCD-76-452 (July 23, 1976), p. 44.

13. Report to the Honorable Sam Nunn, Ranking Minority Member, Committee on Armed Services, United States Senate, *Measures of Military Capability: A Discussion of Their Merits, Limitations, and Interrelationships*, GAO/NSIAD-85-75 (General Accounting Office, June 1985), pp. 31–32.

14. Secretary of Defense Les Aspin, *Report on the Bottom-Up Review* (Department of Defense, October 1993), p. 78; *Defense Science Board Task Force Report on Readiness: Final Report* (June 1994), pp. ii, 22–25.

15. Shishko and Paulson, *Resource Readiness of Armored Units*, p. 7. On differences between operational, fleet, and composite readiness, see also "Strategic Concepts of the U.S. Navy NWP1 (Rev. A)" (Department of the Navy, Office of the Chief of Naval Operations, May 1978), pp. II-2-1, II-2-2.

16. Shishko and Paulson, *Resource Readiness of Armored Units*, p. 5.

17. GAO, *Measures of Military Capability*, p. 32.

18. Toth, "Pentagon Disputes Report on Readiness Figures," p. 17. Quotation from House Appropriations Committee Surveys and Investigations Staff Report, vol. 1, p. 668. See also Jean Lawrence and Candace Port, "(Be)rating the C-Ratings," *Military Logistics Forum* (July–August 1984), p. 14. Two years later the GAO noted, "Since Army units measure their equipment combat readiness ratings against new equipment requirements, the Army has difficulty accurately measuring . . . when it cannot provide the necessary equipment. Units in the other services do not measure against the new requirements until the equipment is available. . . . To compensate, the Army allows commanders to substitute other equipment for new requirements." Report to the Chairman, Committee on Armed Services, House of Representatives, *Measuring Military Capability: Progress, Problems, and Future Direction*, GAO/NSIAD-86-72 (General Accounting Office, February 1986), p. 15.

19. *Department of Defense Authorization for Appropriations for Fiscal Year 1982*, Hearings before the Senate Armed Services Committee, 97 Cong. 1 sess. (GPO, 1981), pt. 5, pp. 2563–64, 2603. See also "Army Reassesses Combat Readiness," *New York Times*, July 24, 1981, p. A9. The assessment was further complicated by the fact that the 106 percent figure was based on an authorized level of 90 percent of wartime requirements. When Senator Gordon Humphrey suggested that the 106 percent figure thus might not represent real overstrength, General Frederick Kroesen explained that the extra NCOs had been used for housekeeping details, for which soldiers were subsequently borrowed

from units. After the reduction, combat service support units remained overstrength, but combat arms units did not. *Department of Defense Authorization for 1982*, Hearings, p, 2564.

20. GAO, *Measuring Military Capability*, p. 15. See also GAO, *Readiness of First Line U.S. Combat Armored Units in Europe*, pp. 23–24.

21. GAO, *Readiness of U.S. Air Forces in Europe*, pp. 20–21.

22. Michael R. Gordon, "Defense Focus," *National Journal*, August 17, 1985, p. 1919; GAO, *Measures of Military Capability*, pp. 31, 46–47; and *Measuring Military Capability*, p. 12. The navy's reported reason for its deviation was that "units should not have to degrade themselves in both the training and personnel ratings if for budgetary reasons aircrews at the wartime levels cannot be provided." *Measuring Military Capability*, p. 12. This sounds peculiar, as if the purpose of the ratings were to grade officers' efforts rather than estimate the capacity for combat. Such differences in standards also suggest care in evaluating publicity such as reports in 1984 that naval readiness had increased more than 100 percent over the period that army and air force readiness had declined. According to a House Government Operations subcommittee report, planes removed from squadrons to depot maintenance were not included in the navy statistics. (See Toth, "Pentagon Disputes Report," p. 17; and Fred Hiatt, "Naval Air Readiness Reported Overstated," *Washington Post*, April 10, 1984, p. A9.) As Les Aspin, then chairman of the House Armed Services Committee, put it, "In other words if 10 percent of your squadron's planes couldn't be operated because of minor problems, you had a 90 percent mission capable rate. But if 10 percent of your planes were total duds, you were 100 percent mission capable." Aspin, "Ready or Not," *New Republic*, October 29, 1984, p. 22.

23. *Department of Defense Authorization for Appropriations for Fiscal Year 1985*, Hearings before the Senate Armed Services Committee, 98 Cong. 2 sess. (GOP, 1984), pt. 4, p. 1860.

24. Department of Defense, *Improvements in U.S. Warfighting Capability*, p. 82.

25. Quoted in "Gen. Vessey vs. Gen. Rogers on Readiness," *Defense Week*, March 12, 1984, p. 14.

26. Congressional Budget Office, *Options for Improving Munitions Sustainability: A Summary* (December 1989), pp. 2–3.

27. Richard Halloran, "Report Says Navy Lacks Capacity to Deploy Combat-Ready Carriers," *New York Times*, December 9, 1983, p. A24. More recently, Congressional Budget Office analysts still concluded "that the readiness indicators used within DoD are not well suited to identifying trends in readiness over time." *Trends in Selected Indicators of Military Readiness, 1980 through 1993* (Congressional Budget Office, March 1994), p. xi.

28. Richard Halloran, "Lacking Parts, Armed Forces Cannibalize Costly Warplanes," *New York Times*, July 16, 1987, pp. A1, A23; Franklin C. Spinney, *Defense Facts of Life: The Plans/Reality Mismatch*, edited and with a commentary by James Clay Thompson (Westview Press, 1983), p. 35; and U.S. General

Accounting Office, Report to the Chairman, Committee on Armed Services, House of Representatives, *Strategic Bombers: B-1B Parts Problems Continue to Impede Operations*, GAO/NSIAD-88-190 (July 1988), pp. 10–11, 14–31.

29. Purchase decisions were made when parts were unreliable, but improvements subsequently increased reliability, while other orders were placed for parts that subsequently had to be redesigned and modified. GAO, *Strategic Bombers*, p. 36.

30. House Appropriations Committee Surveys and Investigations Staff Report, vol. 3, p. 926.

31. *Authorization for Appropriations for Fiscal Year 1985*, Hearings before the Senate Armed Services Committee Hearings, part 4, p. 2151.

32. *Department of Defense Authorization for Appropriations for Fiscal Years 1988 and 1989*, Hearings before the Senate Armed Services Committee, 100 Cong. 1 sess. (GPO, 1987), pt. 2, p. 630.

33. Michael R. Gordon, "Business as Usual," *National Journal*, May 12, 1984, p. 938.

34. GAO, *Aircrew Training*, p. 8.

35. Lieutenant General Kelly H. Burke, "The USAF of 1984: Can It Fight? Can It Win?" *Armed Forces Journal International* (October 1984), p. 129.

36. Walter Borges, "General Defends Troop Readiness," *Dallas Morning News*, March 10, 1984, p. 45.

37. *Department of Defense Authorization for 1985*, Hearings, pp. 1858–60.

38. *Department of Defense Authorization for 1985*, p. 1841.

39. One exception was that the total air force mission capable rate grew by 24 percent from 1980 to 1986, during the same time that the number of aircraft deployed increased. *Department of Defense Authorization for 1988 and 1989*, Hearings, p. 497.

40. Harold Brown guidance memo and Thomas Ross public statement quoted in Benjamin F. Schemmer, "Pentagon, White House, and Congress Concerned over Tactical Aircraft Complexity and Readiness," *Armed Forces Journal International* (May 1980), pp. 28–34.

41. Lawrence J. Korb, Memorandum for the Secretary of Defense, "Readiness," Revised Copy (prepared by Charles Groover), February 17, 1984, pp. 2–4; Richard Halloran, "Combat Readiness Disputed in Memo," *New York Times*, August 2, 1984, p. A18; Gordon, "Defense Focus," p. 1919; and Toth, "Pentagon Disputes Report," p. 17.

42. Lieutenant Commander Thomas S. Tollefsen, USN, "Reports or Readiness: A Dilemma," *Naval War College Review*, vol. 26 (May–June 1974), pp. 74–81; Thomas H. Etzold, *Defense or Delusion?* (Harper and Row, 1982), p. 112; and Vice Admiral T. J. Kilcline, USN (Ret.), "The Paperwork Blizzard: Let's Unburden the Fleet!" *Wings of Gold*, vol. 11 (Spring 1986), pp. 32–33, 53.

43. Report to the Chairman, Committee on Government Operations, House of Representatives, by the Comptroller General of the United States, *The Air Force Can Improve Its Maintenance Systems*, GAO/GGD-83-20 (General Accounting Office, January 1983), pp. ii, 11–14, 16–17, 20 (emphasis added).

On the principle of the drunkard's search, see Abraham Kaplan, *The Conduct of Inquiry* (Chandler, 1964), pp. 11, 17–18.

44. Stanley A. Horowitz, "Quantifying Seapower Readiness," *Defense Management Journal*, vol. 18 (2d Quarter 1981), p. 4. See the discussion in Spinney, *Defense Facts of Life*, pp. 28–29.

45. Laird with Korb, *Problem of Military Readiness*, p. 21 (citing John Fialka).

46. GAO, *Measuring Military Capability*, p. 14; and Tom Burgess, "Analyst Sees Decline in Readiness Unless Spare Parts Are Bought," *Army Times*, January 21, 1985, p. 39. Congressman Les Aspin reported an example of the incentives at work: "I inspected the weekly reports of several units in Germany. Every time a new company commander was named, the readiness rating of that company plummeted as the new commander looked for every defect he could find. In succeeding months, the unit's readiness rating would progressively climb higher—due, of course, to the skill and leadership qualities of the new company commander." Aspin, "Ready or Not," p. 22.

47. GAO, *Measuring Military Capability*, p. 14; House Appropriations Committee Surveys and Investigations Staff Report, vol. 1, p. 693 (emphasis in original).

48. "Statement of Frank C. Conahan, Director, National Security and International Affairs Division, before the Subcommittee on Legislation and National Security, Committee on Government Operations, House of Representatives, on Readiness of Navy Tactical Air Forces" (typescript), U.S. General Accounting Office, November 2, 1983, pp. 2–3.

49. Representative Les Aspin and Representative William Dickinson, *Defense for a New Era: Lessons of the Persian Gulf War* (GPO, March 1992), p. 58 (emphasis added).

50. Captain John L. Byron, USN, "The Surface Navy Is Not Ready," *U.S. Naval Institute Proceedings*, vol. 113 (December 1987), p. 36. For criticisms of this article, see "The Surface Forces *Are* Ready." *U.S. Naval Institute Proceedings*, vol. 114 (May 1988), pp. 78–93.

51. Lewis Sorley, "Professional Evaluation and Combat Readiness," *Military Review*, vol. 59 (October 1979), pp. 41–53.

52. Lieutenant Colonel Monroe T. Smith, "Reporting Inaccuracies—A Rose by Another Name," *Air University Review*, vol. 25 (January–February 1974), pp. 83–88. See also Richard K. Betts, *Soldiers, Statesmen, and Cold War Crises*, 2d ed. (Columbia University Press, 1991), chap. 10; and Barry D. Watts, "Unreported History and Unit Effectiveness," *Journal of Strategic Studies*, vol. 12 (March 1989).

53. Smith, "Reporting Inaccuracies," p. 86.

54. See the intriguing chapter, "Falsification of Reporting," in Joseph S. Berliner, *Factory and Manager in the USSR* (Harvard University Press, 1957), pp. 160–80.

55. "The true function of the AGI [Annual General Inspection] is to see how well the unit draws itself together to pull off a collective con job. A successful unit approaches this administrative challenge as the moral equiv-

alent of war." Christopher Bassford, *The Spit-Shine Syndrome: Organizational Irrationality in the American Field Army* (Greenwood Press, 1988), p. 74; see also pp. 60–61, 76. Another army officer told me that as a platoon leader, he had equipment that was *never* used in training, in order to keep it always ready for the AGI.

56. See Etzold, *Defense or Delusion?* p. 113. He quotes a navy captain: "The inspectors are usually people who aren't terribly good at being naval officers. If they were better than they are . . . they would be commanding ships or squadrons, or working closer to the seats of power. These inspectors know they have been sidetracked, and they are usually bitter about it, determined to prove that they are better professionals than those whose units and equipment they inspect" (p. 113).

57. On Nifty Nugget, see Richard K. Betts, *Surprise Attack* (Brookings, 1982), pp. 185–86. On Coronet Warrior, see Jeffrey P. Rhodes, "Eagles 17, Bean Counters 4," *Air Force*, vol. 71 (April 1988), p. 74.

58. GAO, *Measures of Military Capability*, pp. 15–17. The fact that GAO had to supply the latter report to Senator Nunn, to explain the report that Congress had mandated, was a symptom of the problem.

59. *Department of Defense Authorization for Appropriations for Fiscal Year 1985*, Hearings, p. 1834.

60. That is, the real increase in terms of the original categorization was 28 percent rather than 35 percent. Stephen Alexis Cain, "Defense Budget: Assault on Readiness," *Military Forum*, vol. 14 (May 1988), p. 24.

61. Paul Taibl, with the assistance of Stephen Alexis Cain and Steven Kosiak, "Averting a Return to Hollow Forces: Readiness and the Operations and Maintenance Budget" (Washington, D.C.: Defense Budget Project, June 1993), p. 9.

62. *Department of Defense Appropriations Bill, 1988*, House Appropriations Committee Report, 100 Cong. 1 sess. (GPO, 1987), p. 47.

63. David K. Shipler, "Honduras Buildup: Variety of Means," *New York Times*, July 14, 1986, p. A3.

64. See *Defense Department Authorization and Oversight Hearings on H.R. 1872, Department of Defense Authorization of Appropriations for Fiscal Year 1986 and Oversight of Previously Authorized Programs*, Hearings before the House Armed Services Committee, 99 Cong. 1 sess. (GPO, 1985), pt. 5, title 3, pp. 66–69.

65. Lieutenant Colonel Charles E. Lindbergh, "USAFE Operational Readiness," *Air Force Engineering & Services Quarterly*, vol. 18 (November 1977), pp. 20–22; Congressional Budget Office, *Operation and Support Costs for the Department of Defense* (July 1988), p. 34; and *Department of Defense Appropriations for 1988*, Hearings, p. 282.

66. Lieutenant Colonel Faris R. Kirkland, USA (Ret.) and Pearl Katz, "Combat Readiness and the Army Family," *Military Review*, vol. 69 (April 1989), pp. 64–74.

67. George C. Wilson, "Fewer Weapons and Troops to Fire Them," *Washington Post*, April 25, 1988, p. A4.

68. *Department of Defense Authorization for 1986*, Hearings, pp. 3327–28; and *Department of Defense Authorization for 1985*, Hearings, pt. 6, p. 2019.

69. *Department of Defense Authorization for 1988 and 1989*, Hearings, pp. 452, 497; Congressional Budget Office, *Operation and Support Costs for the Department of Defense*, p. 38; and Frank C. Carlucci, Secretary of Defense, *Annual Report to the Congress: Fiscal Year 1990* (Department of Defense, January 1989), p. 143.

70. "Staffing is growing at a slower rate than structure, largely because Congress denied most of the end-strength increase we requested in FY 84. . . . Most of this manpower shortfall is found in the Navy, where structure is increasing at a faster rate than the Navy can fill it." *Department of Defense Authorization for 1985*, Hearings, pt. 4, pp. 1838–40.

71. Richard Halloran, "Navy Says Shortage of Sailors May Take Ships Out of Fleet," *New York Times*, April 13, 1987, p. A14; Peter Grier, "Budget Priority Is Readiness, Not New Weapons," *Christian Science Monitor*, February 19, 1988, p. 3; "Army to Reduce Officer Corps," *New York Times*, February 27, 1988, p. 12; Richard Halloran, "Budget Reductions Force Marines to Seek 3,100 Fewer Good Men," *New York Times*, January 20, 1988, p. A20; and Molly Moore, "Although Strapped, Corps to Toughen 'Boots,'" *Washington Post*, January 20, 1988, p. A21.

72. *Department of Defense Authorization for 1986*, Hearings, pt. 6, pp. 3018–19; *Department of Defense Appropriations for Fiscal Year 1988*, Hearings, pt. 1, p. 11; General John A. Wickham, Jr., *Collected Works of the Thirtieth Chief of Staff, United States Army*, n.d. [1987], p. 320; *Department of Defense Authorization for 1986*, Hearings, pt. 6, p. 3092; *The Posture of the United States Army for Fiscal Year 1987* (Department of the Army, n.d.), pp. 44–46; *Report of the Secretary of Defense Frank C. Carlucci to the Congress on the FY 1990/FY 1991 Biennial Budget and FY 1990–94 Defense Programs* (Department of Defense, January 1989), pp. 129, 159; and House Armed Services Committee, *Defense Department Authorization and Oversight Hearings on H.R. 4428 . . . for Fiscal Year 1987*, title 3, p. 861; Department of Defense, *Improvements in U.S. Warfighting Capability*, pp. 74–76. The army enhanced the emphasis on training in less quantifiable ways, for example, through more intensive use of military history in curricula at Leavenworth and Carlisle to sensitize commanders from brigade to corps level about operational mistakes. See Richard Halloran, "Trying to Make a First Punch Count," *New York Times*, March 13, 1988, p. 22.

73. Michael R. Gordon, "Ready . . . or Not?" *Military Logistics Forum* (September–October 1984), p. 40; *Department of Defense Authorization for 1986*, Hearings, p. 3012. By fiscal 1988 the navy's stocks of torpedoes and missiles were up 150 percent over 1980, but air force shortfalls in funding for spare parts were becoming more severe. Carlucci, *Annual Report 1990*, pp. 146, 160.

74. Ambassador Robert W. Komer, "Ready for What?" *Armed Forces Journal International* (December 1984), p. 128.

75. House Appropriations Committee Surveys and Investigations Staff Report, vol. 1, p. 706.

76. Department of Defense, *Improvements in U.S. Warfighting Capability*, pp. 84–87. A year later army data showed a slightly lower total figure for 1984 for that service, and a higher figure for munitions deployed overseas. House Armed Services Committee, *Defense Department Authorization and Oversight Hearings on H.R. 4428. Department of Defense Authorization Appropriations for Fiscal Year 1987*, 99 Cong. 2 sess. (GPO, 1986), title 3, p. 889; and Wickham, *Collected Works*, p. 138.

77. *Department of Defense Authorization for 1988 and 1989*, Hearings, pp. 376, 467–69, 679–80; George C. Wilson,"General Sees Army Short of Supplies," *Washington Post*, June 17, 1987, p. A28.

78. Congressional Budget Office, *Options for Improving Munitions Sustainability*, p. 4.

79. Congressional Budget Office, *Operation and Support Costs*, p. 1–2; see also p. 5.

80. Joshua M. Epstein, *The 1987 Defense Budget* (Brookings, 1986), p. 10.

Chapter Five

1. Right-wing critics attacked not just Jimmy Carter but his two Republican predecessors, as well, for underfunding defense. Remember that Ronald Reagan's first nearly successful presidential campaign was in the 1976 primaries against Gerald Ford.

2. Juan M. Vasquez, "U.S. Report Calls Many Units of Strategic Forces Not Ready," *New York Times*, May 18, 1972, p. 1; and *Congressional Record—Senate*, June 13, 1977, p. S 9523.

3. Richard Halloran, "Debate on Army's Readiness," *New York Times*, October 18, 1980, p. 7; Richard Halloran, "Navy Reports 6 Out of 13 Carriers Combat-Ready," *New York Times*, September 29, 1980, p. A16; Charles W. Corddry, "Army Leaders Say Cuts Would Result in Unpreparedness," *Baltimore Sun*, August 27, 1980, p. 1; George C. Wilson, "Shortages of Parts Hamstring Warplanes," *Washington Post*, March 17, 1980, p. A1, and Wilson, "Plane Readiness Report Stirs Dispute," *Washington Post*, March 18, 1980, p. A2; Stewart Lytle, "Lack of Ammunition Called Threat to U.S. Ability to Wage Long War," *Pittsburgh Press*, July 25, 1980; John Stevenson, "Check Found 50% of F14s Unprepared," *Norfolk Virginian-Pilot*, July 20, 1980, p. 1; and Jack Taylor, "Shortages Cripple U.S. Military's Readiness," *Daily Oklahoman*, August 31, 1980, p. 1, and Taylor, "U.S. Forces Not Ready for Prolonged War," *Daily Oklahoman*, September 7, 1980, p. 1. See also "6 of 10 Divisions in U.S. Are Not Ready but That's Not Unusual, Pentagon Says," *Washington Post*, September 10, 1980, p. A12; and John J. Fialka, "Brown's Claim of Military Preparedness Doesn't Ring True with Army Officials," *Washington Star*, October 17, 1980, p. 5.

4. Melvin R. Laird with Lawrence J. Korb, *The Problem of Military Readiness* (American Enterprise Institute, 1980), pp. 21–24 and *passim*.

5. "Excerpts from Secretary Brown's Address on the Nation's Military

Readiness," and Richard Halloran, "Brown Declares Nation's Forces Well Prepared," *New York Times*, October 10, 1980, pp. A1, A20; and "Brown Says Forces Ready for Battle," *Philadelphia Inquirer*, October 10, 1980, p. 24. Richard Allen, Reagan's chief campaign adviser on foreign policy, called a news conference to accuse Brown, on the basis of press reports of a memo leaked from a two-star general in the Pentagon that asserted, the secretary "has decided not to forward our readiness report synopsis to Congress. He has expressed concern that our current readiness reporting formats only emphasize the negative aspects . . . [and] has asked that we reexamine our readiness reporting system to develop a report format which places greater emphasis on the positive factors." Brown's spokesman announced that the secretary had never talked to the general, the information was incorrect, and no decision to withhold anything from Congress had been made. Warren Weaver, Jr., "Readiness Cover-Up Denied by Pentagon," *New York Times*, October 12, 1980, p. 19; and memo by Major General James H. Johnson quoted in Michael Getler, "A Combat Readiness Dispute," *Washington Post*, October 11, 1980, pp. A1, A6.

6. "Statement of the Honorable Robert B. Pirie, Assistant Secretary of Defense for Manpower, Reserve Affairs and Logistics before House Budget Committee," September 30, 1980 (mimeo), p. 4.

7. Richard Halloran, "Pentagon Orders Services to Shift Stress to Upkeep," *New York Times*, May 17, 1980, p. 8.

8. *Review of Readiness Considerations in the Development of the Defense Budget*, Hearings before the House Armed Services Committee, Readiness Panel of the Procurement and Military Nuclear Systems Subcommittee, 96 Cong. 2 sess. (Government Printing Office, 1980), pp. 65–66.

9. *Democratic Fact Book: Issues for 1982* (Democrats for the 80s, June 1982), pp. 318, 325.

10. "U.S. Reportedly Lags in Combat Readiness," *Chicago Tribune*, October 11, 1982, p. 6; Michael R. Gordon, "Pentagon May Face 'Readiness Crunch' If Weapons Buying Continues Apace," *National Journal*, January 22, 1983, pp. 157–61; and John Lehman, "The Navy Is Ready," *Washington Post*, December 23, 1983, p. A15.

11. Lawrence J. Korb, Assistant Secretary of Defense for Manpower, Installations and Logistics, Memorandum for the Secretary of Defense, "Readiness," Revised Copy (prepared by Charles Groover), February 17, 1984, pp. 6–7. See also Michael R. Gordon, "Weinberger's War Readiness Claims Spark Controversy within the Pentagon," *National Journal*, June 9, 1984, p. 1120. Korb spoke publicly as well about some of these problems.

12. Surveys and Investigations Staff, "A Report to the Committee on Appropriations, U.S. House of Representatives, on the Readiness of the U.S. Military" (March 1983), three volumes, with Addendum, in *Department of Defense Appropriations for 1985*, Hearings before the House Appropriations Committee, Subcommittee on the Department of Defense, 98 Cong. 2 sess. (GPO, 1984), pt. 1; Richard Halloran, "U.S. Forces May Lack Resources to Carry On a War, Officers Say," *New York Times*, May 14, 1984, p. A1; Halloran,

"18-Month Survey Finds U.S. Forces Lacking Readiness," *New York Times*, July 22, 1984, pp. 1, 14; Fred Hiatt, "Military Priorities Hit by Critics of Readiness," *Washington Post*, July 30, 1984, pp. A1, A23; and Les Aspin, "Ready or Not," *New Republic*, October 29, 1984, p. 22. In the spirit of full disclosure I should acknowledge that I was involved in flogging the readiness issue as a member of the Mondale campaign staff.

13. Quoted in Carl Levin, "Golden Arms, Leaden Readiness," *New York Times*, September 5, 1984. For examples of the controversial publicity comparable to that in 1980, see also "U.S. Military Shortages Assailed," *Philadelphia Inquirer*, July 23, 1984, p. 6; Brad Knickerbocker, " 'Readiness'—A Key Word in 1984 Defense Debate," *Christian Science Monitor*, July 24, 1984, p. 1; "Reagan Officials Dispute Military Readiness Report," *USA Today*, July 24, 1984, p. 3; Clark R. Mollenhoff, "DoD Rebuts House Report on Military," *Washington Times*, July 24, 1984, p. 4; Robert S. Greenberger, "Weinberger Charges Reports of Declines in Combat Readiness Prompted by Politics," *Wall Street Journal*, July 24, 1984, p. 62; "U.S. More Ready for War—Weinberger," *Chicago Tribune*, July 25, 1984, p. 2; "Dismal Picture of Defense," *Los Angeles Times*, July 24, 1984; "Republicans on the Defensive," *Boston Globe*, July 26, 1984; and Brad Knickerbocker, "Democrats Seize Offensive on Defense," *Christian Science Monitor*, July 26, 1984, p. 1.

14. *Improvements in U.S. Warfighting Capability FY 1980–84* (Department of Defense, May 1984), pp. 5–8 and *passim*.

15. Fred Hiatt, "Weinberger Hits Critical Reports as 'Dangerous,'" *Washington Post*, July 24, 1984, pp. A1, A6.

16. *Department of Defense Authorization for Appropriations for Fiscal Year 1985*, Hearings before Senate Armed Services Committee, 98 Cong. 2 sess. (GPO, 1984), pt. 2, pp. 557, 563–64; see also pp. 566–67.

17. Quoted in Major Ricky Lynn Waddell, *The Army and Peacetime Low Intensity Conflict, 1961–1993: The Process of Peripheral and Fundamental Military Change*, Ph.D. dissertation, Columbia University, 1993, p. 275.

18. *Department of Defense Authorization for 1985*, Senate Armed Services Committee Hearings, pt. 4, p. 1848.

19. For example, in the following year see testimony in *Department of Defense Authorization for Appropriations for Fiscal Year 1986*, Hearings before the Senate Armed Services Committee, 99 Cong. 1 sess. (GPO, 1985), pt. 6, pp. 2991–93, and pt. 8, pp. 4729–44.

20. Quoted in E. J. Dionne, Jr., "Dukakis on Foreign Policy: Two Instincts in Competition," *New York Times*, May 9, 1988, p. A17.

21. *Trends in Selected Indicators of Military Readiness, 1980 through 1993* (Congressional Budget Office, March 1994), p. 2.

22. Korb memo, February 17, 1984, p. 5. Jack Dorsey, "How Much of a Toll Will Cuts Take on Readiness?" in *The Almanac of Seapower 1987* (Navy League of the United States, 1987), p. 5, notes that "since 1983, the Navy has received only between 50 and 80 percent of the increases in personnel end strength it needs."

23. In fiscal 1982 the army requested 100 percent of requirements for spares

and received 98 percent; in fiscal 1983, 100 and 96 percent, respectively; in fiscal 1984, 96 and 92 percent. In the same period, the differences between requests and appropriations for munitions were comparable. *Department of Defense Authorization for 1985*, Senate Armed Services Committee Hearings, pt. 4, pp. 1865, 1850, 1868.

24. Adam Yarmolinsky, "Balance Our Forces or Risk Security," *New York Times*, July 24, 1986, p. A25.

25. *Department of Defense Authorization for Appropriations for Fiscal Years 1988 and 1989*, Hearings before the Senate Armed Services Committee, 100 Cong. 1 sess. (GPO, 1987), pt. 2, pp. 640–43.

26. Quoted in George C. Wilson, "Carlucci: New Budget Is Bid for National Consensus," *Washington Post*, February 23, 1988, p. A21.

27. See "Congressional Interplay," *Armed Forces Journal International* (October 1984), p. 129.

28. Samuel P. Huntington, "Defense Organization and Military Strategy," *The Public Interest*, no. 75 (Spring 1984), p. 32; Samuel P. Huntington, "The Defense Policy of the Reagan Administration, 1981–1982," in Fred Greenstein, ed., *The Reagan Presidency: An Early Assessment* (Johns Hopkins University Press, 1983), pp. 98–99; and "Korb Says Services Fail to Show Loyalty to Sec Def," *Army Times*, August 29, 1983, p. 3.

29. Lieutenant Colonel John M. Vann, "The Forgotten Forces," *Military Review*, vol. 67 (August 1987), pp. 4–5.

30. Vann, "Forgotten Forces," pp. 5–8. Keeping war plans from OSD may be motivated as much by military interests in preserving operational autonomy as by fear of leaks outside the government.

31. Vann, "Forgotten Forces," pp. 8–9.

32. "Congress Forces Reserve Affairs Post on Pentagon," *Defense Week*, July 25, 1983; John P. White and others, "Report of the Working Group on Defense Planning and Resource Allocation," in Barry M. Blechman and William J. Lynn, eds., *Toward a More Effective Defense: Report of the Defense Organization Project* (Ballinger, 1985), pp. 77–79; Barry M. Blechman, "Giving Readiness Clout," and comments in "A 'Readiness' Undersecretary and Budget," both in *Military Logistics Forum* (June 1985).

33. Rowan Scarborough, "Getting the Troops over There New Unit's Mission," *Defense Week*, December 7, 1987, p. 3. On Nifty Nugget, see Richard K. Betts, *Surprise Attack* (Brookings, 1982), pp. 185–88.

34. Franklin C. Spinney, *Defense Facts of Life: The Plans/Reality Mismatch*, edited and with commentary by James Clay Thompson (Westview Press, 1983), p. 117.

35. Congressional Budget Office, *Operation and Support Costs for the Department of Defense* (July 1988), p. 3 (citing Rolf Clark).

36. See data on ship overhaul backlogs, aircraft mission capable rates, operating tempos, the casualty reporting system, Force Status Reporting System, Board of Inspection and Survey, and Propulsion Examining Board in *Shipbuilding, Ship Maintenance, and Claims*, Hearings before the House Budget Committee, 95 Cong. 1 sess. (GPO, 1977), p. 118; *Department of Defense Au-*

thorization for 1982, Hearings, pt. 4, p. 1876 ; and Stanley A. Horowitz, "Quantifying Seapower Readiness," *Defense Management Journal*, vol. 18 (2d Quarter 1981), p. 5.

37. Points in this and the following two paragraphs are based on data in Congressional Budget Office, *Defense Spending and the Economy* (February 1983), table I; and Lawrence J. Korb and Stephen Daggett, "The Defense Budget and Strategic Planning on a New Plateau," in Daggett and others, *The Military Budget on a New Plateau: Strategic Choices for the 1990s* (Committee for National Security, 1988), pp. 113–14.

38. Quoted in Dorsey, "How Much of a Toll Will Cuts Take on Readiness?" pp. 13.

39. *Defense Department Authorization and Oversight Hearings on H.R. 1872, Department of Defense Authorization of Appropriations for Fiscal Year 1986 and Oversight of Previously Authorized Programs*, Hearings before the House Committee on Armed Services, 99 Cong. 1 sess. (GPO, 1985), pt. 5, titles 3 and 4, pp. 2–3.

40. See Joshua M. Epstein, *The 1987 Defense Budget* (Brookings, 1986), pp. 4–9. Spinney characterized a modernization plan that creates a bow wave on the assumption of indefinitely increasing funds as "an optimistic, high-risk plan that relies on a historically discredited assumption." Spinney, *Defense Facts of Life*, p. 138.

41. Epstein, *1987 Defense Budget*, p. 5. "[I]n a new fiscal year total outlays will be the sum of all outlays resulting from budget authority granted in previous years, plus the first-year outlay from the new fiscal year's budget authority. The prior-year backlog, therefore, is simply the year's total outlays net of the first-year outlays from the new budget authority. . . . [B]ecause of the investment decisions taken during the first six years of the [Reagan] administration, the backlog now represents nearly 40 percent of total outlays—a 50 percent increase over its 1981 value of about 26 percent, inherited from the Carter administration." Joshua M. Epstein, *The 1988 Defense Budget* (Brookings, 1987), p. 11. By fiscal 1991, defense budget authority had fallen 9.5 percent in real terms from the preceding year but outlays were down only 5.7 percent because of the "large balances of prior-year budget authority still on the books." William W. Kaufmann and John D. Steinbruner, *Decisions for Defense: Prospects for a New Order* (Brookings, 1991), p. 23.

42. Epstein, *1987 Defense Budget*, p. 7.

43. Eric Schmitt, "Aspin Tells Pentagon to Find Billions More in Budget Trims," *New York Times*, June 10, 1993, p. A22; John G. Roos, "Redefining Readiness," *Armed Forces Journal International* (October 1994), p. 34.

44. *Department of Defense Appropriations for 1988*, Hearings before the House Appropriations Committee, 100 Cong. 1 sess. (GPO, 1987), p. 330.

45. James Kitfield, "Defense Budget: Assault on Readiness," *Military Forum*, vol. 14 (May 1988), p. 27; John H. Cushman, Jr., "Air Force Is Facing Critical Gap in Combat Readiness," *New York Times*, April 6, 1988, p. A16.

46. Major Kent N. Gourdin, "Can the CRAF Survive Another Year Like 1986?" *Defense Transportation Journal* (June 1987), p. 39.

47. William W. Kaufmann, *The 1985 Defense Budget* (Brookings, 1984), pp. 38–39.

48. Les Aspin, "The Mayaguez Stumper, or: How to Figure What's Enough for Military Readiness," press release, House of Representatives, April 1984, pp. 1–6. The lag problem is illustrated by the fact that, according to the General Accounting Office, between 1980 and 1983 appropriations for navy aircraft procurement went up at eight times the rate for O&M—83.6 percent versus 10.4 percent (Richard Halloran, "Report Says Navy Lacks Capacity to Deploy Combat-Ready Carriers," *New York Times*, December 9, 1983, p. A24)—yet by 1984 the navy had registered huge increases in reported readiness in general and aircraft mission capable rates in particular (see Department of Defense, *Improvements in U.S. Warfighting Capability*, p. 70; and chapter 4 in this book).

49. George C. Wilson, "600–Ship Navy Is Sailing toward Rough Fiscal Seas," *Washington Post*, March 16, 1987, pp. A1, A6.

50. Major General Gene E. Townsend, "Air Force Maintenance—Issues and Challenges for the Eighties," *Air Force* (January 1980), p. 57. See the case discussed in *Department of Defense Authorization for 1985*, Senate Armed Services Committee Hearings, pt. 4, p. 2154.

51. Briefing Report to the Chairman, Subcommittee on Defense, Committee on Appropriations, House of Representatives, *Aircrew Training: Tactical Air Command and Strategic Air Command Flying Hour Programs*, GAO-NSIAD-86-192BR (General Accounting Office, September 1986), p. 5.

52. Major General Thomas L. Craig, cited in Congressional Budget Office, *Operation and Support Costs* (July 1988), p. 40. Similarly, in mid-decade, questions from members of Congress indicated that much administration testimony on alleged improvements in readiness was not backed by UNITREP statistics. *Department of Defense Appropriations for 1986*, Hearings before the House Appropriations Committee, Subcommittee on the Department of Defense, 99 Cong. 1 sess. (GPO, 1985), pt. 8, pp. 212, 217.

53. "Excerpts from Secretary Brown's Address on the Nation's Military Readiness," *New York Times*, October 10, 1980, p. A20.

54. Testimony of Charles Groover and General David Jones, in *Department of Defense Authorization for Appropriations for Fiscal Year 1981*, Hearings before the Senate Armed Services Committee, 96 Cong. 2 sess. (GPO, 1980), pt. 1, p. 71, and pt. 4, p. 1975. Army Major General William R. Ward also noted in 1988 that the C-5 designation obscured the residual readiness of units relegated to that artificial "transitional category." *Department of Defense Appropriations for 1989*, Hearings before the House Appropriations Committee, Subcommittee on the Department of Defense, 100 Cong. 2 sess. (GPO, 1988), pt. 4, p. 526.

55. Laird with Korb, *The Problem of Military Readiness*, p. 24.

56. Hiatt, "Naval Air Readiness Reported Overstated," p. A9; Ward testimony in *Department of Defense Appropriations for 1989*, Hearings, pt. 4, p. 526 (emphasis added).

57. *Department of Defense Appropriations for 1980*, Hearings before the House Appropriations Committee, Subcommittee on the Department of Defense, 96 Cong. 1 sess. (GPO, 1979), pt. 5, p. 708.

58. "Statement of the Honorable Robert B. Pirie," p. 2; "Brown Says Forces Ready for Battle," p. 24.

59. *Department of Defense Authorization for 1985*, Senate Armed Services Committee Hearings, pt. 4, pp. 1847, 1858–60, 2031, 2153–54; quotation on p. 2150.

60. Quoted in *Department of Defense Authorization for 1985*, pt. 4, p. 2153.

61. Interview, "Korb: First, The Good News," *Military Logistics Forum* (September–October 1984), p. 67. A year later Air Force testimony again cited the tightening of criteria for C-1 and C-2 status and noted that because sustainability measurements had been revised to focus on the most critical spares, "it became harder to get a higher C-rating. We were trying to put the focus of the managers on this particular problem. And of course, when you do that sometimes you don't look as good." *Department of Defense Authorization for 1986*, Hearings, p. 3328.

62. See Captain David R. Mynatt, USAR, "Reserve Force Readiness Snapshot," *Translog* (March 1984), p. 2.

63. *Department of Defense Authorization for 1985*, Senate Armed Services Committee Hearings, pt. 2, p. 557; see also p. 578. On the same theme, see Brigadier General Robert F. Durkin, "Air Force Readiness—1984," *Security Affairs* (January 1985), pp. 4, 7.

64. "Address at the Civilian Aides Conference," June 26, 1984, in *Selected Works of the Thirtieth Chief of Staff, United States Army, John A. Wickham, Jr. General, United States Army Chief of Staff June 1983–June 1987*, n.p., n.d., p. 57. Subsequent revision of rating practice assigned units in the process of turnover between old and new weapons to C-5 status (scheduled unreadiness for re-equipment or reorganization) instead of C-4 (not ready for combat). This made the service look more managerially competent, but did not reflect any increase in deployable combat capability over the previous rating practice.

65. *The Posture of the United States Army for Fiscal Year 1987*, p. 8.

66. *Department of Defense Authorization Fiscal Year 1985*, Senate Armed Services Committee Hearings, pt. 2, p. 1148.

67. Thomas L. McNaugher, "Readiness: Money Isn't Everything," *Military Logistics Forum*, vol. 1 (May 1985), p. 38.

68. *Department of Defense Authorization Fiscal Years 1988 and 1989*, Hearings, pt. 2, p. 365.

69. Quoted in House Appropriations Committee Surveys and Investigations Staff Report, vol. 3, p. 948.

70. *Department of Defense Authorization for 1982*, Hearings, pt. 5, pp. 2515, 2749.

71. *Department of Defense Authorization Fiscal Year 1985*, Senate Armed Services Committee Hearings, pt. 4, pp. 1896–97, 1921–25; *Department of Defense Appropriations for 1985*, House Appropriations Committee Hearings, pt. 1, pp. 660–61; quotations in *Department of Defense Authorization Fiscal Year 1982*, Hearings, pp. 2734, 2771.

72. *Department of Defense Appropriations for 1979*, Hearings before the House

Appropriations Committee, Subcommittee on the Department of Defense, 95 Cong. 2 sess. (GPO, 1978), pt. 2, p. 814.

73. *Department of Defense Authorization for Appropriations for Fiscal Year 1985*, Senate Armed Services Committee Hearings, pt. 2, p. 988.

74. *Department of Defense Appropriations Fiscal Year 1980*, Hearings before the Senate Appropriations Committee, 96 Cong. 1 sess. (GPO, 1979), pt. 1, pp. 842–43.

75. *Reserve Component Programs Fiscal Year 1987: Annual Report of the Reserve Forces Policy Board* (Office of the Secretary of Defense, February 1988), pp. 160–61.

76. Melissa Healy, "New Measure of Readiness," *Defense Week*, March 15, 1985, pp. 1, 3; House Appropriations Committee Surveys and Investigations Staff Report, vol. 1, pp. 686–88; and *Defense Department Authorization and Oversight Hearings on H.R. 4428, Department of Defense Authorization for Appropriations for Fiscal Year 1987 and Oversight of Previously Authorized Programs*, Hearings before the House Armed Services Committee, 99 Cong. 2 sess. (GPO, 1986), title 3, pp. 843–52.

77. *Hearings on H.R. 4428*, pp. 843–52 (emphasis added).

78. *Department of Defense Authorization for Appropriations for Fiscal Year 1981*, Hearings before the Senate Armed Services Committee, 96 Cong. 2 sess. (GPO, 1980), pt. 1, pp. 288–90.

Chapter Six

1. Albert Z. Conner and Robert G. Poirier, "Soviet Force Mobilization Potential: Lessons of the Past and Implications for the Future," *Journal of Soviet Military Studies*, vol. 1 (June 1988), p. 218.

2. U.S. forces were more evenly distributed among land, sea, and air, but suffered much fewer losses. The main reason for the cap on American combat formations was the overwhelming drain imposed by logistics and support requirements. Organizations for those purposes, such as the Merchant Marine, supplied the USSR as well as American forces. See Russell F. Weigley, *History of the United States Army*, enlarged ed. (Indiana University Press, 1984), pp. 435–40; and Klaus E. Knorr, *The War Potential of Nations* (Princeton University Press, 1956), p. 53. The U.S. strategic bombing campaign also siphoned a tremendous amount of combat capacity from ground forces.

3. Based on data in *The Military Balance 1988–1989* (London: International Institute for Strategic Studies, Autumn 1988), pp. 18–20, 23, 33–34. Other sources cite varying figures, but the rough magnitudes are what dominated policymakers' impressions.

4. For another survey of weaknesses in old Soviet operational readiness, see Joshua M. Epstein, "On Conventional Deterrence in Europe: Questions of Soviet Confidence," *Orbis*, vol. 26 (Spring 1982), pp. 71–88.

5. Thorough net assessments would have compared all NATO and Warsaw

Pact forces with each other, and potential enemies in other regions (for example, North Korea, Iran, Libya, or Cuba) against U.S. and local allies' forces. This chapter concentrates on the United States and Soviet Union in order to keep the illustration manageably focused, rather than provide some final answer.

6. Herbert Goldhamer, *The Soviet Soldier: Soviet Military Management at the Troop Level* (Crane, Russak, 1975), p. 326. Another example was cited by Major B. Khudoleyev. Although civilian labor functions reduced combat training time significantly in some units, numbers indicating a mastery of subjects were entered in the training records "completely contrary to reality." *Krasnaya Zvezda*, January 5, 1986, translated as "Diversion of Draftees to Economic Work Lowers Training Results," Foreign Broadcast Information Service, *USSR Report: Military Affairs*, April 23, 1986, pp. 43–45.

7. *Department of Defense Authorization for Appropriations for Fiscal Year 1981*, Hearings before the Senate Armed Services Committee, 96 Cong. 2 sess. (GPO, 1980), pt. 4, p. 2006.

8. *Allocation of Resources in the Soviet Union and China—1981*, Hearings before the Joint Economic Committee, Subcommittee on International Trade, Finance, and Security Economics, 97 Cong. 1 sess. (GPO, 1980), pt. 7, p. 199.

9. *Soviet Military Power: An Assessment of the Threat, 1988* (U.S. Department of Defense, April 1988), p. 92.

10. Joshua M. Epstein, *Measuring Military Power: The Soviet Air Threat to Europe* (Princeton University Press, 1984), pp. 27–28, 30, 139–40.

11. Epstein, *Measuring Military Power*, p. 25n.

12. For example, Christopher Bassford, *The Spit-Shine Syndrome: Organizational Irrationality in the American Field Army* (Greenwood Press, 1988).

13. F. W. von Mellenthin and R. H. S. Stolfi with E. Sobik, *NATO under Attack: Why the Western Alliance Can Fight Outnumbered and Win in Central Europe without Nuclear Weapons* (Duke University Press, 1984), chaps. 3–5. See also Major General F. W. von Mellenthin, *Panzer Battles: A Study of the Employment of Armor in the Second World War*, trans. H. Betzler, ed. L. F. C. Turner (University of Oklahoma Press, 1956), pp. 295–98; and Lieutenant Colonel David M. Glantz, "Soviet Offensive Ground Doctrine since 1945," *Air University Review*, vol. 34 (March–April 1983), p. 38.

14. Earl F. Ziemke, *Stalingrad to Berlin: The German Defeat in the East* (U.S. Army Center of Military History, 1966), p. 25.

15. Epstein, *Measuring Military Power*, pp. 117–22.

16. John Shy, "First Battles in Retrospect," in Charles E. Heller and William A. Stofft, eds., *America's First Battles: 1776–1965* (University Press of Kansas, 1986), pp. 330–31. Americans have also been surprised before when enemies considered backward in prewar estimates turned out to be highly effective in battle. The North Koreans in June 1950 are a prime example. See Roy K. Flint, "Task Force Smith," in Heller and Stofft, *America's First Battles*.

17. Surveys and Investigations Staff, "Addendum to a Report to the Committee on Appropriations, U.S. House of Representatives, on the Readiness of the U.S. Military," September 1983, in *Department of Defense Appropriations*

for 1985, Hearings before the House Committee on Appropriations, Subcommittee on the Department of Defense, 98 Cong. 2 sess. (GPO, 1984), pt. 1, p. 981.

18. Richard Halloran, "Military Recruiting Hurt by Tight Labor Market," *New York Times*, August 1, 1989, p. A16; George C. Wilson, "Army's Recruiting Falters as Manpower Pool Shrinks," *Washington Post*, February 14, 1989, p. A5; George C. Wilson, "Military Faces Shortage of Qualified Volunteers," *Washington Post*, July 29, 1989, p. A5. Overall, the shift from the draft to the AVF did not affect the quality of recruits, as far as their scores on the armed forces qualification test were concerned. Almost exactly the same percentages scored above 50 in 1964–72 (56.5 percent) and 1974–83 (56.6). Mark J. Eitelberg and others, *Screening for Service: Aptitude and Education Criteria for Military Entry* (Office of the Assistant Secretary of Defense/Manpower, Installations, and Logistics, September 1984), p. 47.

19. Of 26.8 million men who were eligible for the draft during the years of direct U.S. intervention in Vietnam, almost 16 million never served in the military at all. Of those from high-income families, only 24 percent served in the military, and only 9 percent in Vietnam. Lawrence M. Baskir and William A. Strauss, *Chance and Circumstance: The Draft, the War, and the Vietnam Generation* (Knopf, 1978), pp. 5, 9; and James Fallows, "What Did You Do in the Class War, Daddy?" *Washington Monthly* (October 1975). On general systems of conscription, see Eliot A. Cohen, *Citizens and Soldiers: The Dilemmas of Military Service* (Cornell University Press, 1985), chapters 3–4, 7–8.

20. Viktor Suvorov (pseud.), *Inside the Soviet Army* (Macmillan, 1982), pp. 218–19; Ellen Jones, *Red Army and Society: A Sociology of the Soviet Military* (Allen and Unwin, 1985), pp. 58–60; and Michael Dobbs, "Soviet Union Ends Military Draft for Students," *Washington Post*, March 31, 1989, pp. A1, A28; "Soviet Top Command Appears to Reject Radical Restructuring of Soviet Military," Radio Free Europe/Radio Liberty, *Soviet/East European Report*, vol. 6 (May 10, 1989), p. 1; and Michael Dobbs, "Soviet General Faces Challenge," *Washington Post*, March 24, 1989, pp. A1, A18.

21. Goldhamer, *Soviet Soldier*, p. 325.

22. Viktor Suvorov (pseud.), *The Liberators* (W. W. Norton, 1981), p. 140.

23. Colonel Lloyd N. Cosby and others, *Net Assessment of US and Soviet Tank Crew Training*, Report prepared for OSD/NA (U.S. Army Training and Doctrine Command, September 1977; declassified April 1987), pp. 2/11–12, 2/24, 6/20.

24. "Such interference hits tank crews extremely hard. Unlike an infantry squad which . . . could continue to function with the loss of a man, tank crew training becomes difficult when one man is missing, and virtually impossible when two are gone." Cosby and others, *Net Assessment of US and Soviet Tank Crew Training*, pp. 2/14, 2/20. The study does not indicate the sources for the data on training time, which contradict anecdotal literature.

25. Senator Carl Levin, *Beyond the Bean Count: Realistically Assessing the Conventional Military Balance in Europe*, January 20, 1988, pp. 24–25; *Soviet Military Power 1986* (Department of Defense, March 1986), p. 98; *U.S. Defense Policy*, 3d ed. (Congressional Quarterly, 1983), p. 163; Epstein, *Measuring Mil-*

itary Power, p. 108; Robert P. Berman, *Soviet Air Power in Transition* (Brookings, 1978), p. 57; and Steven Zaloga, "The U.S.-Soviet Training Gap," *Armed Forces Journal International* (May 1991), p. 18. Yazov stated, "Our tankmen shoot two times with combat shells during their service." "Dmitry Yazov and the Art of Defense" (Interview), *Moscow News*, Weekly No. 29, 1989, p. 11.

26. Goldhamer, *Soviet Soldier*, pp. 47–48, 52–53, 61–66; Cosby and others, *Net Assessment of US and Soviet Tank Crew Training*, p. 6/6; Ronald R. Nelson and Peter Schweizer, "A New Soviet Military? The Next Generation," *Orbis*, vol. 33 (Spring 1989), p. 203; Jones, *Red Army and Society*, pp. 63–70; and Christopher Donnelly, *Red Banner: The Soviet Military System in War and Peace* (London: Jane's Information Group, 1988), pp. 175. According to Donnelly, by 1986 one Soviet publication cited a membership figure of 107 million for DOSAAF (pp. 175, 196n.).

27. Goldhamer, *Soviet Soldier*, p. 64. By the same token, the fact that most American teenagers entering the military already knew how to drive a motor vehicle gave the U.S. Army a comparable advantage over the Soviet force.

28. See S. Enders Wimbush and Alex Alexiev, *Soviet Central Asian Soldiers in Afghanistan*, N-1634-NA (Rand Corporation, January 1981), pp. 10–12; and Alexander Alexiev, *Inside the Soviet Army in Afghanistan*, R-3627-A (Rand Corporation, May 1988), pp. 14–15. The quotation is from Donnelly, *Red Banner*, pp. 176–77, 179.

29. Field Manual 30–40, *Handbook on Soviet Ground Forces* (Headquarters, U.S. Department of the Army, June 30, 1975), pp. 3/17–19.

30. Mark L. Urban, *Soviet Land Power* (New York: Hippocrene Books, 1985), p. 59; *Soviet Military Power 1986*, p. 98; Cosby and others, *Net Assessment of US and Soviet Tank Crew Training*, pp. 2/9, 2/13, 2/18, 5/15–16. Donnelly (*Red Banner*, p. 177) says that Soviet conscripts learned a second skill in the latter part of their tour. Emphasis on cross-training can also retard the readiness of a force in development. This occurred with the Strategic Air Command during its formation in the late 1940s. Harry R. Borowski, *A Hollow Threat: Strategic Airpower and Containment before Korea* (Greenwood Press, 1982), pp. 145–48.

31. Supplement A to a Report to the Chairmen, Committees on Armed Services, U.S. Senate and House of Representatives, *NATO-Warsaw Pact: U.S. and Soviet Perspectives of the Conventional Force Balance*, GAO/NSIAD-89-23A (General Accounting Office, December 1988), p. 48.

32. Bassford, *Spit-Shine Syndrome*, p. 67, discussing practices in units in Korea. Quotation from Andrew Cockburn, *The Threat: Inside the Soviet Military Machine* (Random House, 1983), p. 164.

33. Personal communication, U.S. military officer; *U.S. Defense Policy*, 3d ed. pp. 162–63; Lieutenant Steven W. Smith, USN, "Combat Readiness: Naval Air vs. Air Force," *U.S. Naval Institute Proceedings*, vol. 108 (February 1982), pp. 41–45. By Smith's account, tactical training for carrier pilots as of the early 1980s emphasized World War III antiship and nuclear strikes: "Conventional interdiction missions are few and far between and usually result in a Southeast Asia-type Alpha strike . . . an outdated tactic left over from Vietnam where

we had mastery of the air and where the only ground threats were antiaircraft artillery and SA-2 missiles" (p. 44).

34. Daniel J. Corbet, "Combat Sustainability Analysis of NATO Center Region Tacair in Support of the U.S. Planning, Programming, Policy and Budgeting Process," in Reiner K. Huber, ed., *Systems Analysis and Modeling in Defense: Development, Trends, and Issues* (Plenum Press, 1984), p. 868.

35. Top Gun is the nickname for the Navy Fighter Weapons School. Before it was initiated in 1972, losses against North Vietnamese planes ran at a ratio of one to two; after the program began, it plummeted to one to thirteen. At the time the air force had no such program, and its air-to-air loss ratio remained closer to the navy's old one. Jim Robbins, "America's Red Army," *New York Times Magazine*, April 17, 1988, p. 44.

36. *Soviet Military Power 1986*, p. 98.

37. Levin, *Beyond the Bean Count*, p. 25; Berman, *Soviet Air Power in Transition*, p. 57; and *Soviet Military Power 1986*, p. 98. The army study claimed, however, that Soviet armor crews practiced combined arms teamwork with motorized rifle and engineer units more than their U.S. counterparts did. Cosby and others, *Net Assessment of US and Soviet Tank Crew Training*, p. 2/21.

38. Goldhamer, *Soviet Soldier*, p. 322.

39. Sergei Zamascikov, "Insiders' Views of the Soviet Army," *Problems of Communism*, vol. 37 (May–August 1988), pp. 110–16. See also Cockburn, *The Threat, passim*; and Bill Keller, "Restlessness in Soviet Ranks: Order of the Day Is Disorder," *New York Times*, April 21, 1989, pp. A1, A10.

40. Epstein, *Measuring Military Power*, p. 97; James C. Bussert, "Soviet Military Maintenance Looks to ATE for Solutions," *Defense Electronics*, vol. 15 (March 1983), pp. 104–05.

41. Epstein, *Measuring Military Power*, pp. 23, 70. For arguments that Soviet reliance on base dispersal and war reserves made base-level and intermediate-level maintenance relatively unimportant for them, see Richard D. Ward, "Readiness, Soviet Style," *Air Force*, vol. 72 (March 1988), p. 54.

42. Major Kenneth L. Privatsky, "Comparing U.S. and Soviet Maintenance Practices," *Army Logistician* (September–October 1986), pp. 7–8; Mark Evans, "Battlefield Recovery and Repair: The Soviet Approach," *International Defense Review*, vol. 22 (1989), p. 1027.

43. Privatsky, "Comparing U.S. and Soviet Maintenance Practices," p. 9.

44. Christopher N. Donnelly, "The Development of Soviet Military Doctrine," *International Defense Review*, vol. 14 (1981), p. 1595; General Accounting Office, Supplement A, *NATO-Warsaw Pact*, p. 47; *Handbook on Soviet Ground Forces*, pp. 6-111, 6-113.

45. The quotation is from Bussert, "Soviet Maintenance Looks to ATE," p. 105. See also Bussert, p. 107; Donnelly, "The Development of Soviet Military Doctrine," p. 159; and Epstein, *Measuring Military Power*, p. 71.

46. Admiral Thomas B. Hayward, in *Department of Defense Authorization for Appropriations for Fiscal Year 1983*, Hearings before the Senate Armed Services Committee, 97 Cong. 2 sess. (GPO, 1982), pt. 2, p. 1147.

47. Cockburn, *The Threat*, p. 161.

48. "Soviet equipment is returned for overhaul at the peak of its reliability. The Soviets have determined how many hours each weapon can be expected to last in war. By subtracting that number from total hours of reliable life in an aircraft, they determine the time at which an overhaul must be performed. This takes place even if the aircraft happens to be working extremely well." Ward, "Readiness, Soviet Style," p. 52.

49. Cockburn, *The Threat*, p. 121; Cosby and others, *Net Assessment of US and Soviet Tank Crew Training*, pp. 2/22, 7/31; and Bussert, "Soviet Maintenance Looks to ATE," pp. 105–06.

50. Donnelly, *Red Banner*, p. 155. MiG-23 and -27 engines can run only about 150 hours before major overhaul, while the U.S. F-4's could go over 1,000. According to Donnelly (p. 155), "This gives the US engine a more useful peacetime life when used continually. . . . However, the US engine is considerably more complex, with six times more working parts than its Soviet equivalent, and is therefore *much* more expensive to manufacture. The question must then be asked: What is the life expectancy *in war* of those comparable aircraft? . . . 150 hours is a more realistic figure than 1,000."

51. The same trade-off is reflected in training restrictions against complex and risky aerial maneuvering. Epstein, *Measuring Military Power*, p. 105. The notion that lopsided attrition in the Gulf War proves the disproportionate payoff from weapon quality ignores the large effect of operational factors apart from the weapons themselves—especially attacks on Iraqi command and communications systems—in producing the uneven result.

52. For emphasis on the NATO advantages see Barry R. Posen, "Measuring the European Conventional Balance: Coping with Complexity in Threat Assessment," *International Security*, vol. 9 (Winter 1984–85), pp. 51–54. Some analysts argued that Soviet forces all along had far greater logistical capacity than usually estimated, because it was organized differently and not understood by those who judged it according to U.S. patterns of organization. C. N. Donnelly, "Rear Support for the Soviet Ground Forces," *International Defense Review*, vol. 12 (1979), pp. 344–50; Graham Turbiville, "Soviet Logistics Support for Ground Operations," *RUSI: Journal of the Royal United Services Institute*, vol. 120, (September 1975), pp. 63–69; Harriett Fast Scott and William F. Scott, *The Armed Forces of the USSR*, 3d ed. (Westview Press, 1984), pp. 245–46, 252. While noting that requirements clearly increased after World War II, Donnelly quotes a passage from Fitzroy McLean's *Eastern Approaches*, which he says still reflected Soviet plans, including provisions for local forage, three decades later: in 1945, south of Belgrade, McLean encountered "a continuous stream of Red Army trucks, tanks and guns flowing northwards into battle. One thing in particular struck us now, as it had struck us from the first, namely, that every Soviet truck we saw contained one of two things: petrol or ammunition. Of rations, blankets, spare boots or clothing there was no trace. The presumption was that such articles, if they were required at all, were provided at the expense of the enemy or the local population. Almost every man we saw was a fighting soldier. What they carried with them were materials of war in

the narrowest sense. We were witnessing a return to the administrative methods of Attila and Ghengis Khan, and the results seemed to deserve careful attention. For there could be no doubt that here lay one reason for the amazing speed of the Red Army's advance across Europe." "Rear Support for the Soviet Ground Forces," p. 344.

53. Berman, *Soviet Air Power in Transition*, pp. 56–57.

54. John Erickson, "The Soviets: More Isn't Always Better," *Military Logistics Forum* (September–October, 1984), pp. 59–60.

55. *Soviet Military Power 1984* (Department of Defense, April 1984), pp. 79–80; *Soviet Military Power 1987* (Department of Defense, March 1987), pp. 100–02; *Soviet Military Power 1988* 55 685 851 (Department of Defense, April 1988), p. 91; John G. Roos and Francis Tusa, "Former Warsaw Pact Sites Surprise Some in NATO Intelligence Community," *Armed Forces Journal International* (August 1991), p. 32; and Captain George T. Norris, "Bite the Bullet: Looking at Red CSS," *Field Artillery Journal* (March–April 1986), p. 25.

56. Graham H. Turbiville, Jr., "Soviet Logistics Support Concepts Change," *Army Logistician* (March–April 1987), p. 2; and *Soviet Military Power 1988*, p. 91.

57. Brown speech in U.S. Department of Defense, *Selected Statements* 80–6, November 1, 1980, pp. 53–54. In 1987, the only two divisions not ready were the two light infantry divisions that were still being formed. *Department of Defense Appropriations for Fiscal Year 1989*, Hearings before the Senate Appropriations Committee, 100 Cong. 2 sess. (GPO, 1988), pt. 1, p. 387.

58. Unclassified data about Soviet readiness vary in different accounts (almost none of which indicate a source) and over time. The following paragraphs are based on *The Military Balance 1987–1988* (London: International Institute for Strategic Studies, Autumn, 1987), p. 34; *The Military Balance 1988–1989*, pp. 34, 39; David C. Isby, *Weapons and Tactics of the Soviet Army*, 3d ed. (London: Jane's, 1988), pp. 36–41; *Soviet Military Power 1986*, p. 98; *Soviet Military Power 1987*, p. 96; *Soviet Military Power 1988*, p. 89; Suvorov, *Inside the Soviet Army*, pp. 138–39; Barry R. Posen, "Is NATO Decisively Outnumbered?" *International Security*, vol. 12 (Spring 1988), p. 194; and Jeffrey Record, *Sizing Up the Soviet Army* (Brookings, 1975), pp. 22–23.

59. U.S. data from AR 220–1, Appendix D: "Rating Criteria," June 1981, p. D-1. The category I–III designations for Soviet divisions were American conventions and do not correspond exactly with the Soviet Union's own breakdown. "The Soviets themselves apparently grade forces as 'ready' (*razvertavie*), 'semi-ready' (*polurazvertavie*), 'cadre' (*kadrirovanaya*) or 'training' (*uchebnaya*). There may be further distinctions within each category. Training divisions retain full operational capability." Isby, *Weapons and Tactics of the Soviet Army*, p. 38. Divisions that the United States ranked as category I, for example, varied widely in strength, with higher levels of manning for those in Eastern Europe, but more modern equipment for those in the Soviet Union. "Even when manning is high or even overstrength, this seems to mean a unit has a special training role and may actually be unusually short of combat ready manpower." Anthony H. Cordesman, "The NATO Central Region and the

Balance of Uncertainty," *Armed Forces Journal International* (July 1983), p. 36. It is also more common outside the United States to refer to category A, B, and C, rather than to use roman numerals; the lettered designations are technically more accurate (see Suvorov, *Inside the Soviet Army*, p. 138), but because the numbers were in common usage in the United States, they are used in this book.

60. John M. Collins, *US-Soviet Military Balance: Concepts and Capabilities, 1960–1980* (McGraw-Hill, 1980), pp. 309–10.

61. Suvorov, *Inside the Soviet Army*, p. 138, cites a low range of 5–10 percent manning; Isby, *Weapons and Tactics of the Soviet Army*, p. 38, says 10–33 percent and 33–50 percent of required equipment; and *The Military Balance 1989–1990* (London: Brassey's, Autumn 1989), p. 34, says 20–50 percent of manpower and "possibly complete" equipment.

62. *Military Balance 1988–1989*, p. 34; *Soviet Military Power 1988*, p. 89.

63. Donnelly, *Red Banner*, p. 157; Suvorov, *Inside the Soviet Army*, pp. 141–45.

64. Posen, "Is NATO Decisively Outnumbered?" p. 194; *Soviet Military Power 1988*, p. 89; *Soviet Military Power 1987*, p. 96; *Soviet Military Power: Prospects for Change, 1989* (Department of Defense, September 1989), p. 64; and *Soviet Military Power 1986*, p. 98. David M. Shilling said that "about 70% of the divisions in the Soviet Union normally considered to threaten NATO's Central Region are in the not-ready status." "Europe's Conventional Defense: Solid Progress but Challenges Remain," *Survival*, vol. 30 (March–April 1988), p. 127.

65. Michael Getler, "Study Insists NATO Can Defend Itself," *Washington Post*, June 7, 1973, reprinted in *U.S. Forces in NATO*, Hearings before the House Foreign Affairs Committee, Subcommittee on Europe, 93 Cong. 1 sess. (GPO, 1973), pp. 405–09.

66. *Soviet Military Power 1988*, p. 89.

67. *Soviet Readiness for War: Assessing One of the Major Sources of East-West Instability*, Report to the House Armed Services Committee, Defense Policy Panel, 100 Cong. 2 sess. (GPO, 1988), p. 2. See also Goldhamer, *Soviet Soldier*, p. 91.

68. *Handbook on Soviet Ground Forces*, pp. 4–9; *Military Balance 1987–1988*, p. 34; and Isby, *Weapons and Tactics of the Soviet Army*, p. 38.

69. Less than sixty days (*Military Balance 1988–1989*, p. 34); 14–90 days (William Kaufmann, *A Reasonable Defense* [Brookings, 1986], p. 64); 130 days (Cordesman, "The NATO Central Region and the Balance of Uncertainty"); and 90–120 days (Isby, *Weapons and Tactics of the Soviet Army*, p. 38). Mobilization base divisions, according to Isby (p. 38), would take six months or more to deploy.

70. Ghulam Dastagir Wardak, compiler, Graham H. Turbiville, ed., *The Voroshilov Lectures: Materials from the Soviet General Staff Academy*, vol. 1: *Issues of Soviet Military Strategy* (National Defense University Press, 1989), pp. 190–200. See also John J. Yurechko, "The Soviet Combat Readiness System," *Journal of Soviet Military Studies*, vol. 1 (June 1988), pp. 235–38.

71. Rather than assume any minimum threshold much beyond the time required for assembly, therefore, some analysts assumed that all Soviet divisions could be counted as available for a prospective war, with their presumed effectiveness degraded to the degree that training time falls short of the optimum. James A. Thomson, *An Unfavorable Situation: NATO and the Conventional Balance*, N-2842-FF/RC (Rand Corporation, November 1988), pp. 14–15. Notional estimates of the range of time required, depending on the tactical purpose and degree of effectiveness desired, can be found in Paul K. Davis, *Toward a Conceptual Framework for Operational Arms Control in Europe's Central Region*, R-3704-USDP (Rand Corporation, November 1988), pp. 54–57.

72. See Richard K. Betts, *Surprise Attack* (Brookings, 1982), pp. 8–9.

73. Isby, *Weapons and Tactics of the Soviet Army*, p. 41. He also notes that "some of the divisions that invaded Afghanistan in 1979 may have been Category III units mobilised in 60 days. The additional resources available when only a few divisions are mobilised at a time may have allowed a quicker mobilisation. It has been estimated that composite divisions could be put into the field 60 days after mobilisation by merging two Category III divisions into one" (p. 38). According to Marshall Lee Miller, the withdrawal from Afghanistan of the divisions that were apparently category III "may have been normal demobilization, but the Western consensus is that the reservists proved ineffective and unreliable." Marshall Lee Miller, "A Numbers Game: How Many Russian Soldiers Does It Take to Make a Horde?" *Armed Forces Journal International* (May 1986), p. 30.

74. Lieutenant General Saad el Shazly, *The Crossing of the Suez* (San Francisco: American Mideast Research, 1980), pp. 202, 205, 207–08, 211.

75. C. N. Donnelly and M. J. Orr, "Soviet Logistics Flexibility," *International Defense Review*, vol. 19 (1986), p. 948. See also R. Tasha Wallis and I. C. Oelrich, "Fuelling the Blitzkrieg," *International Defense Review*, vol. 19 (1986), p. 949; Graham H. Turbiville, Jr., "Sustaining Theater Strategic Operations," *Journal of Soviet Military Studies*, vol. 1 (April 1988); Turbiville, "Soviet Logistic Support for Ground Operations," p. 65; Norris, "Bite the Bullet," p. 25; and Levin, *Beyond the Bean Count*, p. 28.

76. Bussert, "Soviet Maintenance Looks to ATE," p. 105.

77. "Typically those who have planned and conducted air interdiction operations have been too optimistic. . . . the natural result of overestimates of enemy supply needs (perhaps conditioned by the very high consumption rates of U.S. units), together with underestimates of the flexibility and adaptability of transportation systems under attack." Edmund Dews and Felix Kozaczka, *Air Interdiction: Lessons from Past Campaigns*, N-1743-PA&E (Rand Corporation, September 1981), p. vii.

78. Epstein, *Measuring Military Power*, pp. 94–95 (quoting Andris Trapans, *Organizational Maintenance in the Soviet Air Force*, RM-4382-PR [Rand Corporation, January 1965]).

79. *German Tank Maintenance in World War II*, CMH Pub. 104-7 (U.S. Army Center of Military History, 1988), pp. 4, 17, 21–26. This study was originally prepared in 1954 for the U.S. European Command by a group of former

German generals, General Staff officers, and armor maintenance specialists.

80. This is demonstrated at length in Betts, *Surprise Attack*, chaps. 2–6.
Ariel Levite, *Intelligence and Strategic Surprises* (Columbia University Press,
1987), attempts to challenge the historical basis for the high probability of
surprise, but without success; see Richard K. Betts, "Surprise, Scholasticism,
and Strategy," *International Studies Quarterly*, vol. 33 (September 1989), p. 329.
In previous analyses I conceded, for the sake of argument, that modern American intelligence collection capabilities would not fail to promptly detect evidence of Soviet preparations for war. Leaving that argument uncontested
served to focus attention on the powerful political reasons why governments
rarely choose to react quickly with full military counterpreparations. In fact,
the adequacy of intelligence collection, processing, and dissemination need
not be conceded, despite the unprecedented technical richness of monitoring
resources. Consider, for example, how something as obtrusive as the Soviet
brigade in Cuba remained undetected for nearly two decades after the 1962
missile crisis. For elaboration on intelligence collection and processing problems in NATO see Paul B. Stares, *Command Performance* (Brookings, 1991).

81. James Kitfield and Frank Elliott, "The Defense Transportation Dilemma," *Military Forum* (September 1988), p. 22; House Appropriations Committee Surveys and Investigations Staff Report, p. 690; Shilling, "Europe's
Conventional Defense," p. 127. The mobility study produced a goal of 66
million ton-miles per day of airlift, compared to an existing capability in 1988
of 48 million, if all Military Airlift Command and Civil Reserve Air Fleet assets
were combined. Many experts, however, said that a realistic requirement was
closer to 100 or 125 million ton-miles, but was set arbitrarily at 66 because
"the actual requirement was so high that officials felt it would prove useless
even as a target." Some analyses of sealift estimated requirements for general
war at 2,300 ships to support military operations and Western European pop-
ulations and economies, but U.S. and NATO ships available amounted to about
930. Kitfield and Elliott, "The Defense Transportation Dilemma," p. 22.

82. Calculated from data in Directorate for Information, Operations, and
Reports (DIOR), *Department of Defense Selected Manpower Statistics, Fiscal Year
1987* (Office of the Secretary of Defense, n.d.), pp. 67–68; and DIOR, *Department of Defense Military Manpower Statistics, Quarter Ending June 30, 1988* (Office
of the Secretary of Defense, n.d.), p. 5.

83. Lewis Sorley, *Thunderbolt: General Creighton Abrams and the Army of His
Times* (Simon and Schuster, 1992), pp. 363–64. Army Chief of Staff Creighton
Abrams "did not trumpet the rationale behind the total army; instead, he
allowed the belief to spread that manpower and budgetary considerations
impelled the change, although these were in fact secondary." Colonel Harry
G. Summers, Jr., "A Bankrupt Military Strategy," *Atlantic Monthly*, vol. 263
(June 1989), p. 37.

84. Samuel J. Newland, "The National Guard: Whose Guard Anyway?"
Parameters: The Journal of the Army War College, vol. 18 (June 1988), p. 40.

85. In planning for the abortive system of universal military training, some leaders of the professional military in the mid-1940s had also sought unsuccessfully to abolish the guard and streamline the reserves under federal control. Martha Derthick, *The National Guard in Politics* (Harvard University Press, 1965), pp. 60–68; Michael S. Sherry, *Preparing for the Next War: American Plans for Postwar Defense, 1941–45* (Yale University Press, 1977), pp. 36, 59. See also, George C. Wilson, "House Panel Considers Defense Bill That Hints Strongly of Pork," *Washington Post*, March 29, 1988, p. A3; Eric Schmitt, "Focus of Clash on Military Budget Is How to Reduce Reserve Forces," *New York Times*, May 26, 1991, p. 28; Eric Schmitt, "Pentagon Seeking 140,000 Reduction in Reserve Forces," *New York Times*, March 27, 1992, pp. A1, A14.

86. Martin Binkin and William W. Kaufmann, *U.S. Army Guard and Reserve: Rhetoric, Realities, Risks* (Brookings, 1989), p. 58.

87. "Although Britain, France, and Belgium had a potential superiority of about ten divisions on the western front, more than twenty French reserve divisions were absent from the opening battles. By August 23 only four French reserve divisions—as opposed to seventeen on the German side—had seen action in the field. . . . As a consequence, the Germans were able to match French forces in Lorraine and the Ardennes while outnumbering the French and British by 24 divisions to 17-1/2 divisions in the north. On the far left, the British were outflanked and outnumbered by about two to one." Jack Snyder, *The Ideology of the Offensive: Military Decision Making and the Disasters of 1914* (Cornell University Press, 1984), p. 99; see also pp. 101–02 on reasons for the erroneous estimates.

88. Martin Binkin, *U.S. Reserve Forces: The Problem of the Weekend Warrior* (Brookings, 1974), p. 40; Binkin and Kaufmann, *U.S. Army Guard and Reserve*, pp. 1, 14, 28, emphasis added.

89. Charles Joseph Gross, *Prelude to the Total Force: The Air National Guard, 1943–1969* (Office of Air Force History, 1985), pp. 70–72, 132, 137, 144, 156, 159–65.

90. Major General W. Stanford Smith (Ret.), "Reserve Readiness in a Changing Environment," *Defense Management Journal*, vol. 17 (3d Quarter 1981), pp. 22, 25–26; Karl H. Lowe, "US Mobilization for Reinforcing Europe," in Jeffrey Simon, ed., *NATO-Warsaw Pact Force Mobilization* (National Defense University Press, 1988), p. 102; Congressional Budget Office, *Structuring U.S. Forces after the Cold War: Costs and Effects of Increased Reliance on the Reserves* (September 1992), p. 20.

91. Congressional Budget Office, *Improving the Readiness of the Army Reserve and National Guard: A Framework for Debate* (February 1978), p. 18.

92. *United States Military Posture for FY 1989* (Joint Staff, n.d.), p. 72; *Department of Defense Appropriations for Fiscal Year 1989*, Hearings before the Senate Appropriations Committee, 100 Cong. 2 sess., 1988, Part 1, p. 383.

93. Binkin and Kaufmann, *U.S. Army Guard and Reserve*, pp. 1, 14, 28 (emphasis added); Bernard E. Trainor, "Pentagon Worried by Use of Reserves," *New York Times*, July 16, 1989, pp. 1, 22. See also Wilfred L. Ebel, "Toward

Total-Force Mobilization Readiness," in Bennie J. Wilson III, ed., *The Guard and Reserve in the Total Force: The First Decade, 1973–1983* (National Defense University Press, 1985), p. 260.

94. Report to the Chairman, Committee on Armed Services, House of Representatives, *Measuring Military Capability: Progress, Problems, and Future Direction*, GAO/NSIAD-86-72 (U.S. General Accounting Office, February 1986), p. 13.

95. Congressional Budget Office, *Improving the Army Reserves* (November 1985), p. 18.

96. *Department of Defense Authorization for Appropriations for Fiscal Year 1986*, Hearings before the Senate Armed Services Committee, 99 Cong. 1 sess. (GPO, 1985), pt. 5, p. 2741; Congressional Budget Office, *Improving the Army Reserves*, pp. 18–19; Richard Halloran, "Reserve Officers Warn Forces Are Unprepared," *New York Times*, March 3, 1987, p. A19; *Reserve Component Programs Fiscal Year 1987: Report of the Reserve Forces Policy Board* (Office of the Secretary of Defense, February 1988), p. 163.

97. *Department of Defense Authorization for Appropriations for Fiscal Year 1984*, Hearings before the Senate Armed Services Committee, 98 Cong. 1 sess., 1983, pt. 6, p. 3529; *Department of Defense Appropriations for 1989*, Hearings before the House Appropriations Committee, Subcommittee on the Department of Defense, 100 Cong. 2 sess., 1988, pt. 4, p. 306; Roy A. Werner, "Resources and Requirements," in Kenneth Rush and others, *Strengthening Deterrence* (Ballinger, n.d.), p. 237; Major Thomas B. Sharratt, "The Reserves—Full Partners at Last, but How Ready?" *Army*, vol. 29 (June 1979), p. 40; *United States Military Posture for FY 1983* (Organization of the Joint Chiefs of Staff, n.d.), p. 52. See also *Status of the Guard and Reserves*, Hearings before the Senate Armed Services Committee, Subcommittee on Preparedness, 97 Cong. 1 sess, 1981, pp. 5–7.

98. Sharratt, "The Reserves," pp. 41–42.

99. Martin Binkin and William W. Kaufmann, "U.S. Army Reserves: Rhetoric, Realities, and Risks," (Brookings, December 1987), pp. 5–14.

100. *Department of Defense Appropriations for 1989*, Hearings, pt. 1, p. 529: 72.5 percent of the sample reported for duty and most of the rest were excused; only 1.5 percent were unexcused no-shows. "94 Percent of Reservists Are Reached in a National Drill," *New York Times*, November 23, 1987, p. A20.

101. Colonel Irving Heymont, "Can Reserve Units Be Ready on Time?" *Army*, vol. 28 (March 1978), p. 24; Senate Armed Services Committee, *Status of the Guard and Reserves*, p. 84; Binkin and Kaufmann, *U.S. Army Guard and Reserve*, pp. 70, 72.

102. *Department of Defense Authorization for 1984*, Hearings, pt. 6, p. 3535; Smith, "Reserve Readiness in a Changing Environment," pp. 22, 25–26; Binkin and Kaufmann, *U.S. Army Guard and Reserve*, p. 75.

103. Binkin and Kaufmann, *U.S. Army Guard and Reserve*, p. 15.

104. House Appropriations Committee Surveys and Investigations Staff Report, vol. 1, p. 717. The number in the IRR for those reasons, however, was still a small portion of the total—about 14 percent for the army, according to

Bennie J. Wilson III and James R. Engelage, "Pretrained Individual Manpower: Albatross or Phoenix?" in Wilson, ed., *The Guard and Reserve in the Total Force*, p. 126. In 1987 the services experimented with a requirement for IRR personnel to serve one day of active duty during the year, in order to evaluate skill degradation and remind the members of their legal obligation; reported results were good. *Department of Defense Appropriations for 1989*, Hearings, pt. 1, p. 539.

105. Congressional Budget Office, *Structuring U.S. Forces after the Cold War*, p. 36.

106. Army Reserve equipment levels fell to 59 percent of requirements, while National Guard levels rose to 77 percent. Senate Armed Services Committee, *Status of the Guard and Reserves*, p. 101; Trainor, "Army Is Criticized on Use of Reserves," p. 18.

107. Congressional Budget Office, *Improving the Army Reserves*, p. 42n.

108. Government Accounting Office, Supplement A, *NATO-Warsaw Pact*, p. 20.

109. Report to the Chairmen, Committees on Armed Services, U.S. Senate and House of Representatives, *NATO-Warsaw Pact: Assessment of the Conventional Force Balance*, GAO/NSIAD-89-23 (General Accounting Office, December 1988), p. 8; General Accounting Office, Supplement A, *NATO-Warsaw Pact*, p. 16; *Department of Defense Appropriations for 1979*, Hearings before the House Appropriations Committee, Subcommittee on the Department of Defense, 95 Cong. 2 sess. (GPO, 1978), pt. 2, p. 814. The army also wanted more recruits with less experience in order to keep a balance in the mix of junior and senior personnel. Congressional Budget Office, *Improving the Army Reserves*, p. 13.

110. Congressional Budget Office, *Improving the Army Reserves*, pp. 5, 12, 21; Captain Jeffrey A. Jacobs, "RC Reform," *Military Review*, vol. 69 (September 1989), p. 98; Congressional Budget Office, *Improving the Readiness of the Army Reserve and National Guard*, p. 20; and Binkin and Kaufmann, *U.S. Army Guard and Reserve*, pp. 77–78, 80–83.

111. Vernon A. Guidry, Jr., "Training the Reserves," *Military Logistics Forum* (March 1987), p. 53.

112. Report to the Assistant Secretary of the Navy for Manpower and Reserve Affairs, *Observations on Naval Reserve Training for Selected Reserve Reinforcing and Sustaining Units*, GAO/NSIAD-84-35 (General Accounting Office, January 1984), p. 1; Binkin and Kaufmann, "U.S. Army Reserves," pp. 5–24; Office of the Secretary of Defense, *Reserve Component Programs Fiscal Year 1987*, p. 166; Les Aspin, *Report of the Secretary of Defense to the President and the Congress: January 1994* (Department of Defense, January 1994), p. 114; General Accounting Office, Report to the Chairman, Subcommittee on Military Personnel and Compensation, Committee on Armed Services, *Army Training: Management Initiatives Needed to Enhance Reservists' Training*, GAO/INSIAD-98-140 (June 1989), p. 4.

113. General Accounting Office, *Army Training*, p. 33. As the chairman of an Army Science Board panel put it, an Idaho tank mechanic "is not going to be able to repair an M1 tank turret, because he is going to school on the M60A3, and he's going back to his unit and practicing on the M48. He's never

going to see an M1 before he goes to war." Peter Weddle, quoted in Guidry, "Training the Reserves," p. 54. An inspector some years ago discussed the problem in an even worse form in practice. "Current readiness reporting is such that maintenance units can report a high state of readiness . . . and actually have no capability to support specific areas of combat power equipment (tanks) or particular models (M1). . . . Maintenance unit hard skill MOS's such as 41C Fire Control Instrument Repair, 45K Tank Turret Repair, and 45L Artillery Repair, of units not supporting tanks and artillery are not sustaining their MOS skills. Most maintenance unit sustainment training done in the RC [Reserve Component] is accomplished on wheeled vehicle and engineer equipment. System of providing two week annual training missions for RC maintenance units usually results in wheeled [vs. tracked] vehicle work. Very little tank turret and/or artillery experience is gained. . . . Cross training has become a universally accepted excuse for the absence of opportunities to train on tank and artillery tasks . . . although a maintenance unit reports a high degree of readiness, unless the unit is currently supporting combat power equipment it will not have the tools, test items, manuals, repair parts, or personnel currently skilled in combat power equipment repair tasks to actually accomplish a wartime support mission. The number of maintenance units providing peacetime support to combat power equipment is a small percentage of the total of maintenance units." Colonel Jack L. Winkler, Memorandum for the Deputy Chief of Staff for Logistics, "Report of the Initial Investigation of a Logistical Assessment of the Readiness to Mobilize (ALARM)," January 21, 1983, p. 2.

114. Guidry, "Training the Reserves," p. 54; Congressional Budget Office, *Improving Army Reserves*, p. 44.

115. *Department of Defense Appropriations for 1986*, Hearings before the House Appropriations Committee, Subcommittee on the Department of Defense, 99 Cong. 1 sess. (GPO, 1985), pt. 8, p. 57. The quotation is from General Accounting Office, *Army Training*, p. 5.

116. Wallace Earl Walker, "Comparing Army Reserve Forces: A Tale of Multiple Ironies, Conflicting Realities, and More Certain Prospects," *Armed Forces and Society*, vol. 18 (Spring 1992), pp. 311–14.

117. Captain Jeffrey A. Jacobs, U.S. Army Reserve, "Today's National Guard: Time to Federalize," *Armed Forces Journal International* (April 1990), pp. 56, 58.

118. See table 3.3 in General Accounting Office, *Army Training*, p. 30.

119. Graham H. Turbiville, Jr., "Soviet Military Planning and the Role of Reserves," *National Guard* (July 1981), pp. 8–11.

120. Defense Intelligence Agency testimony in *Allocation of Resources in the Soviet Union and China—1981*, Hearings before the Joint Economic Committee, Subcommittee on International Trade, Finance, and Security Economics, 97 Cong. 1 sess. (GPO, 1980), pt. 7, p. 199.

121. Suvorov, *The Liberators*, pp. 139–40; and House Armed Services Committee, *Soviet Readiness for War*, p. 9.

122. *Soviet Military Power 1987*, p. 97; *Military Balance 1988–1989*, p. 33;

Turbiville, "Soviet Military Planning and the Role of the Reserves," p. 9; Scott and Scott, *Armed Forces of the USSR*, p. 341; and John J. Yurechko, "Soviet Reinforcement and Mobilization Issues," in Jeffrey Simon, ed., *NATO-Warsaw Pact Force Mobilization* (National Defense University Press, 1988), pp. 80–82. On reservists discharged within five years, *Soviet Military Power* says 9 million, the International Institute for Strategic Studies says 6,217,000; on the number discharged from service each year, Turbiville says 1.7 million, Scott and Scott say 1.6. Not all Soviet reservists fulfilled the complete two-year tour of conscript service, but those with less than a year of active duty were not to be called in the initial mobilization. Colonel Irving Heymont, USA (Ret.) and Colonel Melvin H. Rosen, USA (Ret.), "5 Foreign Army Reserve Systems," *Military Review*, vol. 53 (March 1973), p. 89.

123. See "Some Theses for the Report of the Foreign and Defense Policy Council," Foreign Broadcast Information Service, *Central Eurasia*, FBIS-USR-92-115, September 8, 1992, p. 63.

Chapter Seven

1. "In the Iraqi Air Force, generals had been executed if they lost a certain number of planes. Consequently, they had made sure the planes weren't flown much, leaving Iraq with mostly inexperienced and untrained pilots." Bob Woodward, *The Commanders* (Simon and Schuster, 1991), p. 286. The most essential U.S. superiority, especially for the ground war, was the combination of high levels of training with tactical doctrine that emphasized initiative, in the German tradition of *Auftragstaktik*. For an organizational and sociological analysis of the approaches to flexibility and initiative in military doctrines, see Dan Horowitz, "Flexible Responsiveness and Military Strategy: The Case of the Israeli Army," *Policy Sciences*, vol. 1 (Summer 1970), especially pp. 198, 201–02.

2. Modernity in organization and coordination proved a crucial part of the American edge. Speaking of the war's vindication of high technology, Les Aspin said, "we know how to orchestrate its use in a way that makes the sum bigger than the parts. In fact, the synergism of our sophisticated systems may be the biggest story about technology. Individually our weapons systems were better than the Soviet-made Iraqi equipment on the order of 20 to 30 percent. . . . That would explain a victory but it would not explain a complete rout.

"What did explain the complete rout, in my view, was the compounding of technologies." Rep. Les Aspin, "Desert One to Desert Storm: Making Ready for Victory," Speech before the Center for Strategic and International Studies/Press Release, House Committee on Armed Services, June 20, 1991, p. 5.

3. U.S. military officials were reported to have characterized the 82d in the first month of the buildup as a "speed bump."

4. One vital support to structural readiness developed for Middle East contingencies was the logistical infrastructure in Saudi Arabia, much of it

developed with the cooperation of the U.S. Army Corps of Engineers. See Jeffrey Record, *Hollow Victory: A Contrary View of the Gulf War* (Brassey's, 1993), pp. 73–75. For other background, see Thomas L. McNaugher, *Arms and Oil* (Brookings, 1984); Michael Gordon and Bernard E. Trainor, *The Generals' War* (Little, Brown, 1995); Norman Friedman, *Desert Victory: The War for Kuwait* (Naval Institute Press, 1991); James Blackwell, *Thunder in the Desert: The Strategy and Tactics of the Persian Gulf War* (Bantam, 1991); and Rick Atkinson, *Crusade: The Untold Story of the Persian Gulf War* (Houghton Mifflin, 1993).

5. Lawrence Freedman and Efraim Karsh, *The Gulf Conflict, 1990–1991: Diplomacy and War in the New World Order* (Princeton University Press, 1993), p. 299. The one important qualification, discussed below, is that once the huge U.S. force was deployed it almost *had* to be used before the summer.

6. General John J. Yeosock, quoted in Michael R. Gordon with Eric Schmitt, "Radios and Mine Sweepers: Problems in the Gulf," *New York Times*, March 28, 1991, p. A19. See also William J. Taylor, Jr., and James Blackwell, "The Ground War in the Gulf," *Survival*, vol. 33 (May–June 1991), p. 232.

7. "Darts and Laurels," *Armed Forces Journal International* (March 1991), p. 55. See also U.S. Department of Defense, *Conduct of the Persian Gulf War: Final Report to Congress, Pursuant to Title V of the Persian Gulf Conflict Supplemental Authorization and Personnel Benefits Act of 1991 (Public Law 10225)* (Department of Defense, April 1992), pp. 106–07, Appendix D, pp. 14–15, and Appendix F, pp. 61–69; Taylor and Blackwell, "Ground War in the Gulf," p. 232; and Colonel Wilson R. Rutherford III and Major William L. Brame, "Brute Force Logistics," *Military Review*, vol. 73 (March 1993), p. 61.

8. Lieutenant Colonel Ky L. Thompson (USMC-Ret.), "Sealift Testimony Irks Some on Hill," *Armed Forces Journal International* (April 1991), p. 12; Gordon with Schmitt, "Radios and Minesweepers," p. A19.

9. Department of Defense, *Conduct of the Persian Gulf War*, Appendix E, p. 30.

10. Thomas A. Keaney and Eliot A. Cohen, *Gulf War Air Power Survey Summary Report* (U.S. Air Force GWAPS, 1993), p. 207.

11. Representatives Les Aspin and William Dickinson, *Defense for a New Era: Lessons of the Persian Gulf War* (Government Printing Office, March 1992), p. 57.

12. Eric Schmitt, "Forces Not Ready for January War, U.S. General Says," *New York Times*, December 20, 1990, pp. A1, A20; and Thomas L. Friedman, "U.S. Says General's Remark Is Hurting Its Gulf Strategy," *New York Times*, December 20, 1990, p. A20.

13. George C. Wilson, "Pentagon Fears Shortage of Materiel," *Washington Post*, November 23, 1990, pp. A1, A38.

14. Department of Defense, *Conduct of the Persian Gulf War*, Appendix F, pp. 75–76.

15. Eric Schmitt with Philip Shenon, "Medical Teams in Gulf Disagree over Readiness," *New York Times*, January 6, 1991, pp. 1, 6. See also *Preparedness for the Persian Gulf*, Hearings before the U.S. Senate Committee on Appropriations, 102 Cong. 1 sess. (GPO, 1991); and Brigadier General Robert H. Scales,

Jr., and others, *Certain Victory: The US Army in the Gulf War* (Office of the Chief of Staff, U.S. Army, 1993), pp. 80–81.

16. Department of Defense, *Conduct of the Persian Gulf War*, app. G, pp. 28–29, and app. Q, p. 11; Department of Defense, *Conduct of the Persian Gulf Conflict: An Interim Report to Congress* (n.p., July 1991), p. 18-2; and Philip Shenon, "Troops Who'll Counter Gas Attack: Ready or Not?" *New York Times*, December 13, 1990, p. A20.

17. Lieutenant General William G. Pagonis with Jeffrey L. Cruikshank, *Moving Mountains: Lessons in Leadership and Logistics from the Gulf War* (Harvard Business School Press, 1992), p. 101; and Department of Defense, *Conduct of the Persian Gulf War*, app. H, pp. 11, 18, 22. The 22d Support Command, however, was not a reserve unit itself, but was Pagonis's own creation, and bypassed the TAACOM, a National Guard unit supposed to latch into CENTCOM.

18. Department of Defense, *Conduct of the Persian Gulf War*, app. H, p. 14; Aspin and Dickinson, *Defense for a New Era*, p. 50; and Cheney quoted in Eric Schmitt, "Combat Reserves May Get Called Up," *New York Times*, September 29, 1990, p. 4. The advisory body charged with assessing readiness policy at the beginning of the Clinton administration recommended that the president's authority to call up reserves be doubled to a 180-day mobilization with a 180-day extension. *Defense Science Board Task Force Report on Readiness: Final Report* (June 1994), p. 34.

19. Congressional Budget Office, *Structuring U.S. Forces after the Cold War: Costs and Effects of Increased Reliance on the Reserves* (September 1992), p. 16.

20. See Eric Schmitt, "U.S. Weighs Doubling Reservists' Tours in Gulf," *New York Times*, December 15, 1990, p. 9.

21. Aspin and Dickinson, *Defense for a New Era*, p. 51; Andrew Rosenthal, "Buildup in Gulf Seen as Signal on Use of Force," and Michael R. Gordon, "Pressure on Iraq," both in *New York Times*, November 10, 1990, pp. 1, 6; and Eric Schmitt, "Pentagon Will Call Up Combat Reserve Units," *New York Times*, November 5, 1990, p. A10. The problem of sustaining carrier deployments reflected the navy's interest in a maximal role, not an overall military requirement. Navy planes flew less than a fifth of the total sorties during the war. Benjamin F. Schemmer, "Six Navy Carriers Launch Only 17% of Attack Missions in Desert Storm," *Armed Forces Journal International* (January 1992), pp. 12–13.

22. Department of Defense, *Conduct of the Persian Gulf War*, app. H, p. 15.

23. Department of Defense, *Conduct of the Persian Gulf War*, app. H, p. 14. See also Lieutenant Colonel Richard L. Stouder, "Roundout Brigades: Ready or Not?" *Military Review*, vol. 73 (June 1993), p. 39; John G. Roos and Benjamin F. Schemmer, "Desert Storm Bares 'Roundout' Flaw but Validates Army Modernization Goals," *Armed Forces Journal International* (April 1991), p. 14; Seth Mydans, "Limbo of Mojave Tests Mettle for Hell of War," *New York Times*, February 17, 1991, p. 20; and Peter Applebome, "Guardsmen Return from War They Didn't Fight," *New York Times*, March 27, 1991, p. A14. For a discussion of deficiencies revealed in the roundout brigades' training after call-

up, see Congressional Budget Office, *Structuring U.S. Forces after the Cold War*, pp. 16–17.

24. See James C. Hyde, "Congress Skeptical that DOD Lives Up to Total Force Policy," *Armed Forces Journal International* (May 1991), p. 8; Schmitt, "Pentagon Will Call Up Combat Reserve Units;" and Schmitt, "Combat Reserves May Get Called Up."

25. Hyde, "Congress Skeptical That DOD Lives Up to Total Force Policy," p. 8.

26. Marine Corps combat reserves proved more usable in Desert Storm because they were organized in companies and battalions rather than brigades and did not have as many of the demanding staff requirements for high-level coordination that crippled the army roundout brigades. See Congressional Budget Office, *Structuring U.S. Forces after the Cold War*, p. 18.

27. The second would resemble the Soviet system of the cold war. It would amount, however, to a decision to use family men and women called out of civilian life as cannon fodder, which is politically unimaginable.

28. Secretary of Defense Les Aspin, *Report of the Bottom-Up Review* (Department of Defense, October 1993), pp. 93–95; and Aspin, *Report of the Secretary of Defense to the President and Congress: January 1994* (Department of Defense, January 1994), pp. 231–32.

29. See Stouder, "Roundout Brigades," pp. 46–49.

30. In addition to the ideas for ground force reserves discussed in the next section, options such as "nested ships" for the navy, or "teamed and stored planes" for the air force may be relevant. See Congressional Budget Office, *Structuring U.S. Forces after the Cold War*, pp. 28–30. See also Eric Schmitt, "Pentagon Sees a Greater Role for Reservists," *New York Times*, September 3, 1993, pp. A1, A16.

31. In the past the Germans took advantage of consecutive four-week training for reservists by requiring it only once every three years, allowing enough flexibility to accommodate individuals' schedules. Colonel Irving Heymont, USA (Ret.) and Colonel Melvin H. Rosen, USA (Ret.), "5 Foreign Army Reserve Systems," *Military Review*, vol. 53 (March 1973), p. 91. It is doubtful, however, that the complicated skills increasingly required in a modern force could be maintained with such long periods of time off.

32. Congressional Budget Office, *Improving Army Reserves* (November 1985), p. 21. In the early 1980s the army developed the "RDF-A" concept, whereby reserve units associated with the Rapid Deployment Joint Task Force would get preferential treatment in supplies and training. By the mid-1980s political pressures to equalize treatment of units had killed the plan. Despite past evidence that Congress balks at unequal treatment, however, the Clinton administration once again planned to discriminate in favor of early-deploying units in the distribution of resources. Aspin, *Report of the Secretary of Defense*, pp. 234–35.

33. Wallace Earl Walker, "Comparing Army Reserve Forces," *Armed Forces and Society*, vol. 18 (Spring 1992), pp. 316–17.

34. For example, the proposals for centralizing reforms in Brigadier General

Raymond E. Bell, "Army Reserve Components: Breaking the Mold," *Armed Forces Journal International* (January 1993), p. 31, would make good political grist if promoted by the Joint Chiefs of Staff in public.

35. For almost half of World War II, for example, information security kept naval logistic planners in the dark about strategic plans. Only late in 1943 did the chief of Naval Operations' Director of the Logistics Plans Division get "access to the 'Top-Secret' dispatch board of the Commander in Chief." Duncan S. Ballantine, *U.S Naval Logistics in the Second World War* (Princeton University Press, 1949), p. 289.

36. Perry McCoy Smith, *The Air Force Plans for Peace, 1943–1945* (Johns Hopkins Press, 1970), pp. 51–53.

37. Klaus E. Knorr, *The War Potential of Nations* (Princeton University Press, 1956), p. 25.

38. Robert W. Coakley and Richard M. Leighton, *Global Logistics and Strategy: 1943–1945* (U.S. Army, Office of the Chief of Military History, 1968), pp. 797–98.

39. Coakley and Leighton, *Global Logistics and Strategy: 1943–1945*, p. 797.

40. Harry B. Yoshpe, *Plans for Industrial Mobilization: 1920–1939*, RP No. 28 (Army Industrial College, Department of Research, November 1945), pp. 3, 79.

41. Robert H. Connery, *The Navy and the Industrial Mobilization in World War II* (Princeton University Press, 1951), pp. 296–97.

42. R. Elberton Smith, *The Army and Economic Mobilization* (Department of the Army, Office of the Chief of Military History, 1959), p. 520.

43. Smith, *The Army and Economic Mobilization*, pp. 519–20, 524; and Richard M. Leighton and Robert W. Coakley, *Global Logistics and Strategy: 1940–1943* (Department of the Army, Office of the Chief of Military History, 1955), p. 201.

44. Quoted in Coakley and Leighton, *Global Logistics and Strategy: 1943–1945*, p. 796.

45. Coakley and Leighton, *Global Logistics and Strategy: 1943–1945*, pp. 109–10, 798–99.

46. See Richard K. Betts, "Conventional Deterrence: Predictive Uncertainty and Policy Confidence," *World Politics*, vol. 37 (January 1985), pp. 163–70. An attacker can more easily risk leaving much of his territory lightly defended in order to concentrate forces in the sector where the attack is launched. In contrast, the side that waits to be struck faces more pressure to deploy enough forces to defend all the sectors of the front. Thus parity of forces in a theater as a whole can translate into substantial superiority for the attacker at the point of engagement, unless the defender reacts instantaneously to perfect intelligence on the attacker's movements.

47. See U.S. Mission to the United Nations, "The Clinton Administration's Policy on Reforming Multilateral Peace Operations," Press Release, May 6, 1994, pp. 4–5; Eric Schmitt, "Pentagon Worries about Cost of Aid Missions," *New York Times*, August 5, 1994, p. A6; and Schmitt, "Military's Growing Role in Relief Missions Prompts Concerns," *New York Times*, July 31, 1994, p. 3.

48. The Clinton administration's initial study of military requirements

skirted this question: "Fortunately, the military capabilities needed for these [peace] operations are largely those maintained for other purposes—major regional conflicts and overseas presence. Thus, although specialized training and equipment may often be needed, the forces required will, for the most part, be selected elements of those general purpose forces maintained for other, larger military operations." Aspin, *Report on the Bottom-Up Review*, p. 9.

49. Points in this paragraph were suggested by Barry Posen and Bernard Trainor.

50. Elaine Sciolino, "New U.S. Peacekeeping Policy De-emphasizes Role of the U.N.," *New York Times*, May 6, 1994, p. A7.

51. Aspin, *Report of the Secretary of Defense*, pp. 29, 32.

52. In neither case were the attackers warned that the United States would defend the victims; indeed, signals from Secretary of State Dean Acheson's "perimeter speech" and Ambassador April Glaspie's hands-off stance could easily have been read the other way.

53. Patrick E. Tyler, "Pentagon Imagines New Enemies to Fight in Post-Cold-War Era," *New York Times*, February 17, 1992, pp. A1, A8; Patrick E. Tyler, "U.S. Strategy Plan Calls for Insuring No Rivals Develop," *New York Times*, March 8, 1992, pp. 1, 14; Patrick E. Tyler, "Pentagon Drops Goal of Blocking New Superpowers," *New York Times*, May 24, 1992, pp. 1, 14; and Barton Gellman, "On Second Thought, We Don't Want to Rule the World," *Washington Post National Weekly Edition*, June 1–7, 1992, p. 31.

54. Patrick E. Tyler, "War in 1990s: New Doubts," *New York Times*, February 18, 1992, pp. A1, A12; Michael R. Gordon, "Cuts Force Review of War Strategies," *New York Times*, May 30, 1993, p. 16; Eric Schmitt, "Pentagon Is Ready with a Plan for a Leaner, Versatile Military," *New York Times*, June 12, 1993, pp. 1, 11.

55. Aspin, *Report on the Bottom-Up Review*, pp. 13–31.

56. Michael R. Gordon, "Pentagon Seeking to Cut Military but Equip It for 2 Regional Wars," *New York Times*, September 2, 1993, pp. A1, A18.

57. Quoted in Eric Schmitt, "Senators Challenge Pentagon's War Scenarios," *New York Times*, February 21, 1992.

58. The principle of economy of force is stated in Napoleon's maxim: "The art of war consists in always having more forces than the adversary, even with an army weaker than his own, on the point where one is attacking or being attacked." Quoted in Marshal Ferdinand Foch, *The Principles of War*, trans. Hilaire Belloc (New York: Henry Holt, 1920), p. 48.

59. Complications in alliance politics and opportunities in the Pacific modified the plan. See Samuel Eliot Morison, *Strategy and Compromise* (Atlantic/Little, Brown, 1958), pp. 75–82.

60. Aspin, *Report on the Bottom-Up Review*, p. 19.

61. See Richard K. Betts, *Surprise Attack* (Brookings, 1982), pp. 8–9, 179–84.

62. Between April and August official statements by Secretary of Defense Dick Cheney and Joint Chiefs of Staff Chairman Colin Powell spoke of several

months, then up to a year, and finally up to two years. Michael R. Gordon, "Cheney Proposes Sharp Reduction in New Warplanes," *New York Times*, April 27, 1990, p. A12; R. Jeffrey Smith, "Powell Says Defense Needs Massive Review," *Washington Post*, May 7, 1990, p. A8; and Michael R. Gordon, "Pentagon Drafts Strategy for Post–Cold War World," *New York Times*, August 2, 1990, p. A1.

63. See Richard K. Betts, "Wealth, Power, and Instability: The United States and East Asia after the Cold War," *International Security*, vol. 18 (Winter 1993/94). On the cosmic questions that govern basic assumptions about prospects for military conflict, see Richard K. Betts, ed., *Conflict after the Cold War: Arguments on Causes of War and Peace* (Macmillan, 1994).

Chapter Eight

1. In his 1994 State of the Union address President Clinton declared that there would be no further military budget cuts. If that policy holds, the problems discussed in this chapter may not rise to the top of the defense agenda. Given other pressing desires for tax cuts, domestic programs and deficit reduction, however, it is unlikely that further erosion will not occur if no major new international threat becomes evident.

2. See the epigraph at the beginning of the book.

3. Klaus E. Knorr, *On the Uses of Military Power in the Nuclear Age* (Princeton University Press, 1966), p. 19.

4. Marvin A. Kreidberg and Merton G. Henry, *History of Mobilization in the United States Army, 1775–1945*, Department of the Army Pamphlet no. 20-212 (Department of the Army, June 1955), p. 695 (emphasis in original).

5. Surging requires a substantial level of mobilized capacity to start with. As Ethan Kapstein notes, "the threat of a conflict may cause decision makers to order that defense production facilities operate on a three-shift, around-the-clock basis; mobilization, in contrast, would require the conversion of civilian production to military purposes." Ethan B. Kapstein, *The Political Economy of National Security: A Global Perspective* (McGraw-Hill, 1992), p. 68.

6. "Mobilization base" was defined by Defense Mobilization Order no. 23 early in the cold war as "that capacity available to permit rapid expansion of production, sufficient to meet military, war-supporting, essential civilian, and export requirements in event of a full-scale war. It includes such elements as essential services, food, raw materials, facilities, production equipment, organization, and manpower." Quoted in Henry H. Fowler, "The Mobilization Base Concept," *Federal Bar Journal*, vol. 13 (April–June 1953), pp. 144–45. "Reconstitution" was defined by the Office of the Secretary of Defense in 1991 as ensuring "the capability to expand the existing force posture by maintaining and investing in the necessary 'long lead elements.'" Quoted in John R. Brinkerhoff, "Reconstitution: A Critical Pillar of the New National Security Strategy," *Strategic Review* 19, no. 4 (Fall 1991), p. 10. See also Dick Cheney, *Report of the Secretary of Defense to the President and Congress, January 1993* (Government

Printing Office, n.d.), p. 6; *1992 Joint Military Net Assessment* (Directorate for Force Structure, Resources, and Assessment, The Joint Staff, August 1992), chap. 10.

7. James R. Schlesinger, *The Political Economy of National Security* (Praeger, 1960), pp. 74, 76. In World War I, economic centralization was not enforced immediately, so "government offices bid against each other on prices, facilities, and delivery. The results were sharp price rises, congestion, and chaos in industrial production." Legislative Reference Service, *Mobilization Planning and the National Security (1950–1960): Problems and Issues*, S. Doc. 204 (GPO, 1950), p. 153.

8. Klaus E. Knorr, *The War Potential of Nations* (Princeton University Press, 1956), p. 133.

9. For example, "between April 1917 and June 1918, we spent $4 billion for 50,000 pieces of artillery and the ammunition for these guns. Only 143 pieces of artillery actually reached American forces in time to be used. Although 23,405 tanks were ordered . . . none of these tanks was received for training, much less for use in Europe." Roderick L. Vawter, *Industrial Mobilization: The Relevant History*, rev. ed. (National Defense University Press, 1983), p. 5.

10. Knorr, *War Potential of Nations*, p. 111.

11. Henry E. Eccles, *Military Concepts and Philosophy* (Rutgers University Press, 1965), pp. 83, 85 (emphasis deleted). "If and when damaging reverberations are set up by the resonance of the system, the overall operational effectiveness can be restored only by drastically *reducing* the apparent performance of the particular subsystem where the attempt to optimize one without regard for the side effect on the other systems has set up reverberations." Eccles, "How Logistics Systems Behave," *Logistics Spectrum* (Summer 1982), p. 32 (emphasis added).

12. Schlesinger, *Political Economy of National Security*, p. 93.

13. As R. Elberton Smith wrote of the World War II conversion, "throughout the life of the priorities system it was apparent that most compliance problems resulted from the novelty and complexity of the regulations, their frequent internal inconsistency or seeming lack of relevance to the job at hand, the task of educating and disseminating information to all concerned, and the very nature of production under wartime conditions. It was difficult to expect industry to comply with regulations which were often not known by contracting officers and field representatives of civilian agencies. These in turn were continually hampered by inadequate staff and facilities, personnel turnover, and the incessant pressure to reach quick decisions and turn out work at top speed. . . . dependable contract objectives and production schedules were nonexistent. A prime CPFF contract with an initial ceiling value of $20 million might be raised by a stream of amendments to ten times its original figure. Neither the contractor nor the military countersigning officer could tell what the production objective would be. . . . The countersigning officer might be a Reserve officer suddenly recalled to active duty from a banking firm, an automobile dealership, or a college faculty to find himself confronted with the task of approving scores of complex purchase orders and rating extensions

daily." R. Elberton Smith, *The Army and Economic Mobilization* (Department of the Army, Office of the Chief of Military History, 1959), p. 548. "New administrative bodies, moreover, cannot be fully efficient, since they will not have had time to implant in their personnel an awareness of how the parts of an organization are supposed to function . . . and since it also takes time to set up routines that permit similar situations to be quickly identified as such and 'routine' choices made with relative dispatch and economy of effort." Knorr, *War Potential of Nations*, p. 154.

14. Knorr, *War Potential of Nations*, p. 154.

15. Richard M. Leighton and Robert W. Coakley, *Global Logistics and Strategy: 1940–1943* (Department of the Army, Office of the Chief of Military History, 1955), p. 329. This is an example of the sort of problem that might be ameliorated in a future mobilization, since the information revolution and computers have vastly improved ability to deliver specific items at specific times.

16. Knorr, *War Potential of Nations*, p. 66.

17. Ronald Schaffer, *America in the Great War* (Oxford University Press, 1991), p. 31.

18. Paul A. C. Koistinen, "The 'Industrial-Military Complex' in Historical Perspective: World War I," *Business History Review*, vol. 41 (Winter 1967), pp. 381, 383, 391; Kreidberg and Henry, *History of Mobilization*, pp. 150, 152, 235–236, 374.

19. The economy did not become completely "tight" by the end of fighting in 1918, and the full extent of economic controls that would be necessary the next time was not fully evident. Vital lessons about bottlenecks in industrial conversion and training, though, were applied before Pearl Harbor. Luther Gulick, *Administrative Reflections from World War II* (University of Alabama Press, 1948), pp. 43–44.

20. See "Plans for Industrial Mobilization, 1920–1939," Study of Experience in Industrial Mobilization in World War II RP no. 28, II (Army Industrial College, Department of Research, November 1945), pp. 63–66.

21. Timothy D. Gill, *Industrial Preparedness* (National Defense University Press, 1984), p. 5.

22. Also, production schedules had to assume many provisos about "availability of buildings, equipment, personnel, and raw materials." Army Industrial College, "Plans for Industrial Mobilization," p. 27.

23. Bureau of the Budget, War Records Section, *The United States at War: Development and Administration of the War Program by the Federal Government* (GPO, 1946), p. 81.

24. Smith, *The Army and Economic Mobilization*, p. 121.

25. Smith, *The Army and Economic Mobilization*, p. 42; Army Industrial College, "Plans for Industrial Mobilization," pp. 13–14.

26. Robert H. Connery, *The Navy and the Industrial Mobilization in World War II* (Princeton University Press, 1951), pp. 31, 53.

27. Connery, *The Navy and the Industrial Mobilization*, p. 35.

28. During the cold war, official estimates of the military balance in Europe in the event of war were almost always based on projected reinforcement

schedules and buildups that would follow smartly from M-Day. The notion that in a developing crisis unprecedented enough to make war between nuclear superpowers a possibility, the fifteen NATO governments either individually or in concert would make the political decisions to begin mobilization at the same time, rate, and scale as assumed in musty plans developed by Defense Ministry bureaucrats and professional military leaders was fanciful.

29. Smith, *The Army and Economic Mobilization*, p. 82.

30. Kreidberg and Henry, *History of Military Mobilization*, pp. 542, 548. From 1935 through 1939 U.S. defense expenditures grew by annual percentages of 11.2, 43.3, 10.4, 10.6, and 22.1; in 1940 the increase was 38.6 percent, and in 1941, 298.8. See table 5.2 in Arthur A. Stein, "Domestic Constraints, Extended Deterrence, and the Incoherence of Grand Strategy: The United States, 1938–1950," in Richard Rosecrance and Arthur A. Stein, eds., *The Domestic Bases of Grand Strategy* (Cornell University Press, 1993), p. 108.

31. Connery, *The Navy and the Industrial Mobilization*, pp. 49–52. "By 1938 M Day had been widely publicized as the date marking the adoption of a complete 'military dictatorship,' and 'iron-heeled Fascism,' whose basic purpose was to 'save capitalism' and the opportunities for war and postwar profits. M Day would bring . . . the denial of the right of workers to strike, to quit their jobs, to choose their occupations, and demand higher wages." Smith, *The Army and Economic Mobilization*, p. 83. See also Bureau of Demobilization, Civilian Production Administration, *Industrial Mobilization for War: History of the War Production Board and Predecessor Agencies, 1940–1945*, vol. 1: *Program and Administration* (Government Printing Office, 1947), p. 6.

32. Gill, *Industrial Preparedness*, p. 6. In July 1939 Roosevelt set up a less ambitious War Resources Board (WRB), which reviewed and approved the industrial mobilization plan. The board itself, however, was criticized politically for being unrepresentative (in addition to chairman E. R. Stettinius, Jr., it consisted of business leaders and the presidents of MIT and the Brookings Institution), and the president was especially skittish about isolationist opinion after the reception of his "quarantine" speech in Chicago. When the 1939 war scare abated, Roosevelt put the brakes on the WRB, and after its report was submitted in November he never used it again. Legislative Reference Service, *Mobilization Planning and the National Security*, pp. 158–60; Paul A. C. Koistinen, "The 'Industrial-Military Complex' in Historical Perspective: The InterWar Years," *Journal of American History*, vol. 56 (March 1970), p. 838. There was foot-dragging on the business end of the political spectrum as well. "Until there were enough contracts to convert all major firms from private to public use and enough *immediate* demand to justify expanding production capacity . . . industrialists serving within and advising the mobilization agencies resisted forthright preparation for war." Paul A. C. Koistinen, "Mobilizing the World War II Economy: Labor and the Industrial-Military Alliance," *Pacific Historical Review*, vol. 42 (November 1973), p. 447. See also Herman Miles Somers, *Presidential Agency: The Office of War Mobilization and Reconversion* (Harvard University Press, 1950), pp. 5–20, 41.

33. Bureau of the Budget, *The United States at War*, pp. 23, 117; John W.

Eley, "Management Structures for Industrial Mobilization in the 1980s: Lessons from World War II," in Hardy L. Merritt and Luther F. Carter, eds., *Mobilization and the National Defense* (National Defense University Press, 1985), p. 29.

34. Connery, *The Navy and the Industrial Mobilization*, pp. 52, 443–44.

35. Army Industrial College, "Plans for Industrial Mobilization," p. 80.

36. Smith, *The Army and Economic Mobilization*, pp. 83, 85, 437; Army Industrial College, "Plans for Industrial Mobilization, pp. 30–31.

37. Leighton and Coakley, *Global Logistics and Strategy: 1940–1943*, p. 198.

38. Leighton and Coakley, *Global Logistics and Strategy: 1940–1943*, p. 199. "A 'balanced program,' in the eyes of each contending claimant for high priority ratings, tended to be the one which placed its own claims at the head of the list and balanced the remainder of the program around its own as the independent variable." Smith, *The Army and Economic Mobilization*, p. 524.

39. Alan S. Milward, *War, Economy, and Society, 1939–1945* (University of California Press, 1977), chap. 2; T. A. Bisson, *Japan's War Economy* (Macmillan, for the Institute of Pacific Relations, 1945); Bureau of the Budget, *The United States at War*, pp. 505–18; Knorr, *War Potential of Nations*, pp. 57–58, 125–26.

40. Vawter, *Industrial Mobilization*, p. 8; Gill, *Industrial Preparedness*, p. 11.

41. Robert L. Finley, "The Need for Maintenance of Facilities for Defense," *Federal Bar Journal*, vol. 13 (April–June 1953), p. 173.

42. Laws passed then that are still relevant include the Strategic and Critical Materials Stockpiling Act of 1946, National Security Act of 1947, Armed Forces Procurement Act of 1947, and National Industrial Reserve Act of 1948. Enabling legislation allowed the Munitions Board to prepare the Industrial Mobilization Plan of 1947, "which was really a detailed plan for a plan." Vawter, *Industrial Mobilization*, pp. 8–9.

43. See Harry B. Yoshpe and Stanley L. Falk, *Organization for National Security* (Industrial College of the Armed Forces, 1963), pp. 136–45.

44. *The U.S. National Security Resources Board, 1947–1953: A Case Study in Peacetime Mobilization Planning* (Executive Office of the President, April 1953), pp. 20–23.

45. Robert J. Watson, *History of the Joint Chiefs of Staff*, vol. 5: *The Joint Chiefs of Staff and National Policy, 1953–1954* (Historical Division, Joint Chiefs of Staff, declassified 1986), p. 151.

46. Huston, *Sinews of War*, pp. 657–58; Yoshpe and Falk, *Organization for National Security*, p. 145; Watson, *Joint Chiefs of Staff and National Policy, 1953–1954*, pp. 151, 158. Joint Chiefs of Staff quoted in Watson, p. 157.

47. Jacques S. Gansler, *The Defense Industry* (MIT Press, 1980), p. 109.

48. Gansler, *The Defense Industry*, p. 112. See also Kapstein, *Political Economy of National Security*, p. 71.

49. See Lawrence J. Korb, "A New Look at United States Defense Industrial Preparedness," *Defense Management Journal*, vol. 17 (3d Quarter 1981).

50. Richard Halloran, "Air Force Finds Industry Limited in Ability to Supply Arms for War," *New York Times*, July 9, 1984, p. A17.

51. Kapstein, *Political Economy of National Security*, pp. 72–73, quoting NMIG Special Working Group, "Evaluation of War Mobilization Board Play in Global War Game 88," August 1988 (mimeo).

52. See, for example, Under Secretary of Defense Paul Wolfowitz's speech a week after the event. "Wolfowitz: Mobilization to be Emphasized as U.S. Forces Are Cut," *Aerospace Daily*, November 27, 1989, p. 317.

53. In 1940 the army planned to use a *ninety-day* training cycle to provide the necessary geometric increase in units. Mark Skinner Watson, *Chief of Staff: Prewar Plans and Preparations* (Historical Division, U.S. Army, 1950), p. 186. None but the most primitive military skills could now be imparted in such a brief time. See also Knorr, *War Potential of Nations*, p. 21.

54. Gulick, *Administrative Reflections from World War II*, pp. 24–25, 49–52.

55. This trend was often criticized because it was mistaken for bloat. Edward N. Luttwak, for example, railed against the fact that the U.S. military had become top-heavy in rank during the cold war: *The Pentagon and the Art of War: The Question of Military Reform* (Simon and Schuster, 1984), pp. 157–65. Some unnecessary rank inflation doubtless occurred, but the general trend in the military was not evidently different from occupational structure in the civilian economy. See the discussion of why the middle part of the military grade structure expanded more rapidly, in Kurt Lang, "Technology and Career Management in the Military Establishment," in Morris Janowitz, ed., *The New Military: Changing Patterns of Organization* (Norton, 1964), pp. 67–68.

56. Thomas L. McNaugher, *New Weapons, Old Politics: America's Military Procurement Muddle* (Brookings, 1989), p. 155.

57. See Knorr, *War Potential of Nations*, p. 27.

58. Gansler, *The Defense Industry*, p. 121.

59. Bernard L. Schwartz, *The Future of the U.S. Defense Industrial Base*, FPI Policy Brief (Foreign Policy Institute, Paul H. Nitze School of Advanced International Studies, Johns Hopkins University, 1992), p. 4.

60. The Office of Technology Assessment suggests that an industrial strategy that relies on pure research may become less unrealistic: "No prototype would be built. Instead, designers would develop components and use computer-aided design techniques to test concepts and develop technical data packages that could subsequently be produced when needed. While this type of 'research strategy' is many years from being a practical reality, manufacturing technology is moving in that direction. Computer-aided design, computer simulation of operational environments, a design philosophy emphasizing high reliability and ease of maintenance, and automated flexible manufacturing would all make this . . . a more practical alternative." U.S. Congress, Office of Technology Assessment, *Redesigning Defense: Planning the Transition to the Future U.S. Defense Industrial Base*, OTA-ISC-500 (GPO, July 1991), pp. 89–91.

61. See McNaugher, *New Weapons, Old Politics*, chap. 6; Gansler, *The Defense Industry*, p. 103; Ethan B. Kapstein, *Reconstitution: Force Structure and Industrial Strategy*, Conference Report (U.S. Army War College Strategic Studies Institute, June 1992), p. 2.

62. See Office of Technology Assessment, *Redesigning Defense*, pp. 89–91.

63. Office of Technology Assessment, *Redesigning Defense*, p. 87.

64. See Theodore H. Moran, "International Economics and National Security," *Foreign Affairs*, vol. 69 (Winter 1990–91), pp. 80–82; Robert C. Fabrie, "Structural Change in the U.S. Industrial Base," in Merritt and Carter, eds., *Mobilization and the National Defense*, pp. 100–04.

65. Memorandum from the Secretary of Defense, "RE: Acquisition Reform," November 16, 1993, p. 1. See also *Report of the Defense Science Board Task Force on Defense Acquisition Reform* (Office of the Under Secretary of Defense for Acquisition, July 1993); Les Aspin, *Report of the Secretary of Defense to the President and the Congress: January 1994* (Department of Defense, January 1994), pp. 104–10; and Thomas L. McNaugher, "Break a Few Rules," *International Defense Review*, vol. 2 (1992), p. 24.

66. McNaugher, "Break a Few Rules," p. 25. See also Stephen C. LeSueur, "DoD Acquisition Reform Plan Stalls," *Defense News*, October 25–31, 1993, pp. 1, 28, and Mike Mills, "Giving Contractors a Break," *Congressional Quarterly Weekly Report*, October 30, 1993, p. 2947.

67. One advantage of "blueprint" planning that compiles detailed answers for specific questions is that, if done thoroughly, it provides an inventory of options that have been explored, and evidence about which alternatives are most reasonable. Legislative Reference Service, *Mobilization Planning and the National Security*, p. 55 (Elliott was the author of the report); see also pp. 53–54.

68. National Security Resources Board Document 116, quoted in Legislative Reference Service, *Mobilization Planning and the National Security*, p. 55.

69. The typical military tendency to develop strategic analyses in a political and economic vacuum was exemplified during the cold war in the annual exercises known as the Joint Strategic Objectives Plan (JSOP) and Joint Strategic Capabilities Plan (JSCAP). These ostensibly identified threats and contingencies and estimated the U.S. forces that would be needed to handle them with high confidence of success in the event of war. The estimates uniformly generated force requirements astronomically higher than any that could be built within the defense budgets that peacetime political leaders would authorize. As a result, these annual planning exercises consumed staff resources but were utterly irrelevant to policy.

70. *U.S. National Security Resources Board*, p. 141.

71. In interagency meetings observers could not represent the position of NSRB on matters where policy had not been established, and their participation in discussion was supposed to be restricted to ascertaining matters of fact. Participation in industry advisory committees was even more circumscribed. *U.S. National Security Resources Board*, pp. 150–51.

72. As of early 1994, eleven major officials (including the Director of Defense Research and Engineering) reported to the under secretary for acquisition and technology, while only two (the assistant secretaries for reserve affairs and for health affairs) reported to the new under secretary for personnel and readiness. Initially, the plan for the new readiness portfolio had been to make it an assistant secretary position.

73. If the crisis ends peacefully by the time the readiness wave breaks, the linear model holds, since the force achieves the objective of deterrence or coercion.

74. C-ratings "do not refer to any particular oplan [operations plan]. A unit that may be ready to perform its mission under one plan may be unprepared to perform its mission under another." Robert Shishko and Robert M. Paulson, *Relating Resources to the Readiness and Sustainability of Combined Arms Units,* R-2769-MRAL (Rand Corporation, December 1981), p. 5. See also Robert Shishko and Robert M. Paulson, *Resource Readiness of Armored Units,* N-1299-MRAL (Rand Corporation, November 1979), p. 7.

75. William W. Kaufmann, *Planning Conventional Forces 1950–1980* (Brookings, 1982), p. 17.

76. *Department of Defense Authorization for Appropriations for Fiscal Year 1982,* Hearings before the Senate Armed Services Committee, Subcomittee on the Department of Defense, 97 Cong. 1 sess. (GPO, 1981), pt. 5, p. 2374.

77. Surveys and Investigations Staff, "A Report to the Committee on Appropriations, U.S. House of Representatives, on the Readiness of the U.S. Military," Addendum, September 1983, in *Department of Defense Appropriations for 1985,* Hearings before the House Appropriations Committee, 98 Cong. 2 sess. (GPO, 1984), p. 974.

78. *Department of Defense Authorization for Appropriations for Fiscal Years 1988 and 1989,* Hearings before the Senate Armed Services Committee, 100 Cong. 1 sess. (GPO, 1987), pt. 2, p. 454; and Molly Moore, "Budget Cuts Curtail Military Airlift," *Washington Post,* April 9, 1988, p. A13.

79. In 1994 operational readiness is not in immediate danger of being shortchanged; if anything, it may be overemphasized. The fear of a hollow force now risks overcompensating by keeping operational tempos high, wearing out personnel and equipment. (I owe this observation to Thomas Hawkins.) Increases in operations and maintenance accounts may stave off this result for awhile. The fiscal 1995 budget reduced troop strength and units by 7 percent, while increasing O&M and training expenditures by 5.6 percent. (Steven Pearlstein, "Clinton Puts His Stamp on a 'New Democrat' Budget," *Washington Post National Weekly Edition,* February 14–20, 1994, p. 31.) Diversion of money from modernization to personnel later in the year further eased the pressure on operational readiness. Underfunding of the five-year defense program, however, means that a crunch will come between structural and operational readiness, and the crunch will come all the sooner if the official commitment to keeping force structure to fight two simultaneous major regional conflicts is not abandoned.

80. See "Averting a Return to Hollow Forces: Readiness and the Operations and Maintenance Budget" (Defense Budget Project, June 1993), p. 15. The problem is obscured by the linear model of readiness, which implies improvement or degradation proportional to amounts of effort. The way in which incremental changes in resources may yield huge changes in readiness is illustrated by General Hamilton H. Howze's recollection of training in the 7th Cavalry of the interwar period: "A cavalry troop had only 90-odd men. . . .

so many men were required for special duty, post fatigue, KP, dental appointments and the like that only 15 or 20 would turn up for drill." Much training time was consumed by exercising horses. "When present-for-duty strength falls below 95 percent of table of organization strength, things at once go out of balance, for many jobs of a unit do not change whether the unit strength is 50 percent or 100 percent." Howze, "Shrink Army If We Must, But Don't Hollow It Out," *Army* (May 1990), p. 11.

Appendix

1. The vertical axis multiplies mass and efficiency for a composite total of equivalent units. That is, a force of 10 units in terms of actual structural readiness and potential operational readiness registers on the graph as 10 units if it is at 100 percent efficiency. If its peacetime status is 50 percent efficiency, rising by 10 percent of potential with each increment of mobilization time, it registers on the graph as 5 units at T1, 6 at T2, and so forth, until it counts as 10 at T6.

Index